## Praise for *Young Hawke*

David Day's biography of the young man who became Australian Labor's longest-serving – and perhaps most beloved – prime minister brings a fascinating new dimension to this complex and deeply flawed man.

While Hawke loved his religiously zealous parents intensely, the young man who grew from their sometimes-neglectful care emerges – inevitably, perhaps – as something of a rebel against their militant abstemiousness and anti-licentiousness. But the young Hawke is also so much more in this fascinating, elegantly written account.

Paul Daley, *The Guardian*

Like any good historian, Day is adept at debunking myths and making tough judgements. As Day's clear-eyed examination of Hawke's life makes plain, his so-called larrikinism camouflaged a multitude of less admirable traits that would have ended the political careers of just about anyone else. Somehow he managed to survive and became one of our best prime ministers. Therein lies the mystery of Robert James Lee Hawke.

Brett Evans, *Inside Story*

Day shows that [Bob Hawke's] rise to the top came on his own terms, built as much on his weaknesses – for women to whom he was not married, to the high life funded by rich friends, to the grog, to public adulation – as on his strengths.

Hawke, in truth, could only have risen in the Australia of the 1960s and 1970s, a country that had translated to the city pub and union office something of the rugged, hard-drinking masculine world of the bush frontier. It is among Day's achievements that we can better see how this career was of its time and place, even as it also had about it a touch of the miraculous.

Frank Bongiorno, *The Age*

Also by David Day

*Menzies and Churchill at War* (1986)

*The Great Betrayal: Britain, Australia and the Onset of the Pacific War, 1939–42* (1988)

*Reluctant Nation: Australia and the Allied Defeat of Japan, 1942–45* (1992)

*Smugglers and Sailors: The Customs History of Australia, 1788–1901* (1992)

*Contraband and Controversy: The Customs History of Australia from 1901* (1996)

*Claiming a Continent: A New History of Australia* (1996)

*Brave New World: Dr H.V. Evatt and Australian Foreign Policy*, ed. (1996)

*Australian Identities*, ed. (1998)

*John Curtin: A Life* (1999)

*Chifley* (2001)

*Celtic-Australian Identities*, ed. with Jonathan Wooding (2001)

*The Politics of War* (2003)

*Conquest: A New History of the Modern World* (2005)

*The Weather Watchers: 100 Years of the Bureau of Meteorology* (2007)

*Andrew Fisher: Prime Minister of Australia* (2008)

*Antarctica: A Biography* (2012)

*Flaws in the Ice: In Search of Douglas Mawson* (2013)

*Paul Keating: The Biography* (2015)

*Antarctica: What Everyone Needs to Know* (2019)

*Maurice Blackburn: Champion of the People* (2019)

*Young Hawke* (2024)

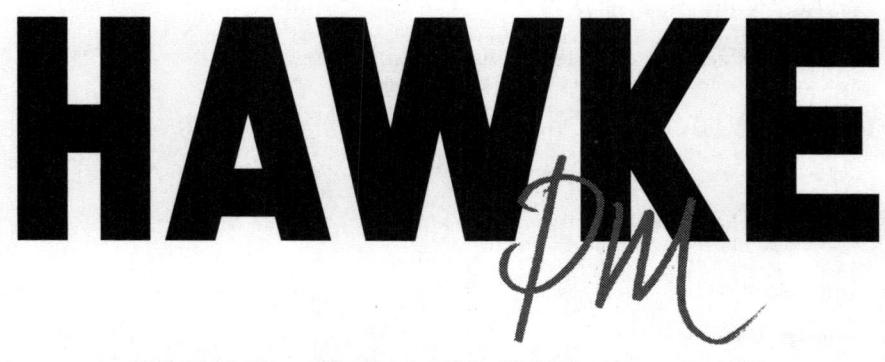

# HAWKE

## THE MAKING OF A LEGEND

## DAVID DAY

HarperCollins*Publishers*

Aboriginal and Torres Strait Islander readers are advised that this book includes names and images of people who have died.

**HarperCollins***Publishers*
Australia • Brazil • Canada • France • Germany • Holland • India
Italy • Japan • Mexico • New Zealand • Poland • Spain • Sweden
Switzerland • United Kingdom • United States of America

HarperCollins acknowledges the Traditional Custodians of the lands upon which we live and work, and pays respect to Elders past and present.

First published on Gadigal Country in Australia in 2025
by HarperCollins*Publishers* Australia Pty Limited
ABN 36 009 913 517
harpercollins.com.au

Copyright © David Day 2025

The right of David Day to be identified as the author of this work has been asserted by him in accordance with the *Copyright Act 1968*.

All rights reserved. Apart from any use as permitted under the *Copyright Act 1968*, no part may be reproduced, copied, scanned, stored in a retrieval system, recorded, or transmitted, in any form or by any means, without the prior written permission of the publisher. Without limiting the exclusive rights of any author, contributor, or the publisher of this publication, any unauthorised use of this publication to train generative artificial intelligence (AI) technologies is expressly prohibited. HarperCollins also exercises its rights under Article 4(3) of the Digital Single Market Directive 2019/790 and expressly reserves this publication from the text and data-mining exception.

HarperCollins*Publishers*
Macken House, 39/40 Mayor Street Upper
Dublin 1, D01 C9W8, Ireland

A catalogue record for this book is available from the National Library of Australia

ISBN 978 1 4607 6661 3 (hardback)
ISBN 978 1 4607 1794 3 (ebook)

Cover design by Design by Committee
Cover images by Adam Knott / Newspix
Author photograph by Emily Day
Index by Antipodes Indexing
Typeset in Minion Pro by Kirby Jones
Printed and bound in Australia by McPherson's Printing Group

*To Tsila*

# Abbreviations

| | |
|---|---|
| ABC | Australian Broadcasting Commission (or Corporation from 1983) |
| ACT | Australian Capital Territory |
| ACTU | Australian Council of Trade Unions |
| *ADB* | *Australian Dictionary of Biography* |
| ADFA | Australian Defence Force Academy |
| AFAP | Australian Federation of Air Pilots |
| ALP | Australian Labor Party |
| ANU | Australian National University |
| ANZUS | Australia, New Zealand and United States Security Treaty |
| APEC | Asia-Pacific Economic Cooperation |
| ASIO | Australian Security Intelligence Organisation |
| ASIS | Australian Secret Intelligence Service |
| BHP | Broken Hill Proprietary |
| BHPML | Bob Hawke Prime Ministerial Library |
| CIA | (US) Central Intelligence Agency |
| CHOGM | Commonwealth Heads of Government Meeting |
| CPI | consumer price index |
| DSD | Defence Signals Directorate |
| ERC | Expenditure Review Committee |
| GATT | General Agreement on Tariffs and Trade |
| GDP | Gross Domestic Product |
| GST | Goods and Services Tax |
| ILO | International Labour Organization |
| JCPML | John Curtin Prime Ministerial Library |
| ML | Mitchell Library |
| NBAC | Noel Butlin Archives Centre |
| NCA | National Crime Authority |

| | |
|---|---|
| NFSA | National Film and Sound Archive |
| NLA | National Library of Australia |
| NSW | New South Wales |
| OHI | oral history interview |
| OPH | Old Parliament House |
| OSW | Office for the Status of Women |
| RAAF | Royal Australian Air Force |
| RSL | Returned Services League of Australia |
| SBS | Special Broadcasting Service |
| TAA | Trans Australia Airlines |
| TNT | Thomas Nationwide Transport |
| UN | United Nations |
| UNSW | University of New South Wales |

# Contents

| | |
|---|---:|
| Abbreviations | vii |
| Introduction | 1 |

**Part One: Parliament**

| | |
|---|---:|
| Chapter One: 1979–1980 | 9 |
| Chapter Two: 1981–1982 | 31 |
| Chapter Three: 1982–1983 | 51 |
| Chapter Four: 1983 | 63 |
| Chapter Five: 1983 | 72 |

**Part Two: Power**

| | |
|---|---:|
| Chapter Six: 1983 | 87 |
| Chapter Seven: 1983 | 100 |
| Chapter Eight: 1983 | 105 |
| Chapter Nine: 1983 | 112 |
| Chapter Ten: 1984 | 120 |
| Chapter Eleven: 1984 | 131 |
| Chapter Twelve: 1984–1985 | 148 |
| Chapter Thirteen: 1986 | 161 |
| Chapter Fourteen: 1987 | 181 |
| Chapter Fifteen: 1988 | 207 |

| | |
|---|---|
| Chapter Sixteen: 1989 | 225 |
| Chapter Seventeen: 1989 | 242 |
| Chapter Eighteen: 1990 | 250 |
| Chapter Nineteen: 1990 | 261 |
| Chapter Twenty: January–June 1991 | 272 |
| Chapter Twenty-One: June–December 1991 | 284 |

**Part Three: Postscript**

| | |
|---|---|
| Chapter Twenty-Two: 1992–1994 | 297 |
| Chapter Twenty-Three: 1995 | 307 |
| Chapter Twenty-Four: 1996–2019 | 314 |
| | |
| Endnotes | 325 |
| Bibliography | 353 |
| Acknowledgements | 363 |
| Index | 365 |

# Introduction

By 1979, Bob Hawke had become the most popular political figure in the country. Which is when the fifty-year-old trade union leader finally decided to stand for federal parliament. Under pressure from his mother, he'd been talking about his political ambitions for decades and now would finally put himself to the test.

The pressure to measure up to his mother's hopes and expectations had been the bane of his young life. As was explored in *Young Hawke*, he had always been conscious that his mother had wanted him to be a girl. In the absence of a daughter, she had surrounded herself, and him, with young girls, whether from the Sunday school she supervised, the local primary school she volunteered at, or from the girl guide movement that she led, while young women were drawn upon to help with the housework and the child-minding.

That was the home environment into which Bob Hawke was born in December 1929. During his childhood in Bordertown in South Australia, where his father served as the Congregational minister, and later in Maitland on the Yorke Peninsula, he would be forced to compete with his favoured elder brother for the attention and approval of his parents. He also had to compete with his parents' time-consuming mission to recruit people to their church and the temperance movement.

His father had often left young Bob in the lurch, going off on excursions for work or pleasure while his mother often did likewise, leaving Bob in the care of others for days or weeks at a time. When his gifted elder brother won a scholarship to a private school in Adelaide, Bob lived a life that was akin to that of an only child. Even when the taller and more athletic Neil returned home on school holidays, he would often spend those weeks working and living on a nearby farm. After Neil's untimely death from amoebic meningitis, the family moved to Perth and shifted the expectations they had for Neil onto the slim shoulders of young Bob.

With the Second World War having just erupted, Bob was often left without the presence of either parent. While his father left home for a position as a padre in an army camp north-east of Perth, his mother threw herself into the work of the Woman's Christian Temperance Union, sometimes serving as the live-in matron of its shelter for young women. Which left Bob at home in the care of a female lodger.

Despite these periods of abandonment, his mother had big plans for her surviving son. Under her tutelage, he gained entry to the academically selective Perth Modern, where he struggled to measure up to his fellow students. It was there that he became the class clown in an attempt to win approval. After almost being expelled for repeated misbehaviour, it was only in the final term that he managed to do sufficiently well to gain admission to the University of Western Australia.

A serious motorbike accident at the end of his first year at university changed his life. As he looked up from his hospital bed, the doubts he harboured about the love of his worried parents were swept away. In their turn, they became obsessed with ensuring his success. Anxious to please them, Hawke improved his results, taught Sunday school with his mother and played as many sports as he could muster to impress his father.

Politics had also become part of his life when he became a founding member of the university's ALP Club. With his uncle Albert being the state Labor leader and a frequent visitor to the Hawke home, politics was part of the family's kitchen conversation. Practical political experience came when he was elected president of the university's student guild.

With the end of his degree in sight, he and his parents focused on him winning a Rhodes Scholarship to Oxford, only for him to be beaten by a fellow student from Perth Modern. Not to be outdone, he began another degree so that he could try again. This time, his application was much stronger, not least because he'd become friendly with the state governor, who would be chairing the selection committee. The scholarship was his.

The governor wasn't privy to the larrikin side of Hawke's nature. Despite his mother's devotion to the temperance cause, the Sunday School teacher had become a budding alcoholic with a libido that was given frequent expression on hastily-spread blankets in the sand dunes of Perth. As Oxford beckoned, he was faced with the pregnancy of his fiancé, Hazel Masterson, with the couple deciding on an abortion so he could keep his scholarship.

Although some of the world's greatest thinkers were at Oxford, Hawke didn't seek them out. His narcissist nature made him believe that he didn't have much to learn from them. Instead of doing the usual multi-discipline degree taken by Rhodes scholars, Hawke switched to a minor thesis on a topic – Australian industrial relations – that no-one in Oxford knew much about. Despite Hazel's presence, he was distracted by frequent dalliances, too much booze and too much cricket. He was lucky to return with an Oxford degree.

Brimming with confidence and newly married in Perth, Hawke believed that he could use his B.Litt. thesis as the basis for a PhD thesis at the Australian National University, which could allow him to pursue an academic career. But nothing came of it. He'd chosen a topic that couldn't be turned into a thesis. Moreover, he was fortunate not to be expelled after a drunken bout of boisterous behaviour saw him harassing female students and annoying a clutch of visiting bishops.

Blessed by good luck, Hawke was saved by the university not wanting to expel a Rhodes scholar and by a new opportunity opening up when the Australian Council of Trade Unions offered him a temporary position as its advocate at the arbitration commission, where he would present the trade union case for a wage increase. He'd found his calling. And he took to his position with a passion, gaining a reputation as a radical warrior fighting for the interests of workers.

Although his employment was meant to be temporary, Hawke quickly made a career of it. Instead of returning to academia, he remained as the ACTU advocate for more than a decade. The times suited him. Television had begun and Hawke boasted a natural charisma that was made for the small screen. Although he wasn't an elected official of the ACTU, he was often in the media and assiduously cultivated journalists over multiple beers in the pub where he also seduced a succession of women.

Such was his success at the arbitration commission and his media profile that he was elected in 1969 as the ACTU president. It was an extraordinary rise for someone who hadn't come from the ranks of the trade union movement. It was also a great leap of faith by the hundreds of delegates at the ACTU congress who chose him over the opposing candidate, a longtime official who was serving as ACTU secretary. Their faith wasn't misplaced. Over the following decade, Hawke would invest the presidency with an importance it had never enjoyed before and would never enjoy again.

Taking the West German and Israeli trade union movements as his examples, Hawke had a vision of the ACTU one day having similar political and economic heft. Not all of his initiatives were successful. Taking part-ownership of Bourke's discount store in Melbourne did help to end the pernicious system of retail price maintenance but union members didn't respond in sufficient numbers to ensure the store's financial survival.

Similar problems dogged his other schemes, whether it was holiday camps or discount petrol stations. More ambitious initiatives to offer insurance or mortgages collapsed before they could begin, while the ACTU Travel company had to be rescued and rebadged as Jetset Tours. Hawke simply couldn't compel the constituent unions to support the ACTU businesses. Nevertheless, he did give the ACTU much more political influence, while his own political influence increased when he also became president of the ALP.

All the time, and despite the public attention he received, Hawke was such a heavy drinker that he once had to go to hospital with alcohol poisoning. He also continued to poison his marriage with a succession of casual relationships, and several more serious and long-lasting ones. Home often became a battleground and divorce was discussed but never pursued. Both he and Hazel recognised that a divorce could destroy his hopes of ever becoming prime minister.

That ambition had been instilled in him by his ever-zealous mother. By the late 1970s, after the collapse of the Whitlam government, the weight of expectation had become overwhelming. Not only from his ageing mother. He was popularly regarded as the prime-minister-in-waiting. If only he would take the plunge and test his ability and popularity. Instead, he kept shrinking from the challenge, seemingly content to continue as the powerful ACTU president, playing the industrial peacemaker and media junkie.

He seemed perfect for those fearful and conflict-ridden times, whether it was a world riven by a dangerous divide between the nuclear superpowers or an Australia divided after the contentious dismissal of the Whitlam government. Hawke promised to bridge this divide, while his larrikin personality appealed to men and women alike as cultural changes and the rising tide of Australian nationalism swept away the conservative atmosphere that had previously prevailed.

By 1979, as his mother lay in a coma, the pressure on Hawke became more intense than ever. His close friend, the influential businessman Peter Abeles, offered to finance an independent party for Hawke to lead. But that wouldn't assure him of the prime ministership. Despite his supporters in the Labor Party pressing him to make the leap into politics, he continued to dither. It was a difficult decision. Embracing the challenge would require him to give up all the perks of his powerful position as president and face the possible risk of an historic failure.

It was only in the wake of his mother's death, and the opening up of a safe Labor seat, that Hawke finally announced his resignation as ACTU president. The course that he'd long talked about was now his to pursue.

# PART ONE
# Parliament

CHAPTER ONE

# 1979–1980

Bob Hawke had been president of the Australian Council of Trade Unions (ACTU) for four years longer than he'd originally intended. Now, in October 1979, he'd finally overcome his fear of failure and secured preselection for the safe Labor seat of Wills. The years of indecision had worked to his advantage, allowing time for the Labor Party to partially recover from the devastation of the Whitlam dismissal. It also allowed time for voters to realise that Malcolm Fraser was just as incapable as Whitlam of solving the country's economic woes. Once again, voters were looking favourably towards the Labor Party and its very able leader, Bill Hayden.

It was Hayden, as Whitlam's health minister, who'd ushered in the Medibank health system, the precursor of today's Medicare, before serving briefly as treasurer and earning a reputation as a responsible economic manager. Hayden was one of the few ministers who hadn't been tarnished by their time in the Whitlam government and whose best political years were still ahead of him. He was intent on doing the policy work that would make Labor electable again. And his efforts were paying off, with the party leading in the polls. Despite his aloofness and whining voice (caused by partial deafness), Hayden's standing in the polls was higher than Fraser's – at least in a head-to-head contest. When Hawke's name was added to the mix and people were asked to nominate their preferred prime minister, Hawke beat both Fraser and Hayden, as well as another Labor possibility, the recently elected New South Wales premier Neville Wran. Unlike Hayden, Hawke was even preferred as prime minister by some Liberal voters.[1]

Because Hawke was such a familiar figure on television, Australians felt an easy familiarity with him. He'd been relatively frank about his frailties, particularly his drinking and his womanising, and it hadn't caused him to lose public support. His confessions made him appear human, just like them, and he seemed to have the interests of working people at heart. That sense was reinforced when the first biography of Hawke was published in 1979, authored by the industrial relations journalist John Hurst. Written with Hawke's cooperation and drawing on a wide range of interviews, it focused on his time at the ACTU. Although it presented a positive portrait, Hurst included mention of Hawke's alcoholism and his fitful attempts to abstain.

Hurst also noted how women were attracted to Hawke, and that he could be chauvinistic and paternalistic in return. He described Hawke turning up at a charity luncheon where 320 women were waiting to hear him speak. Walking in, Hawke enthused that his female audience was 'a real smorgasbord'. When asked what he thought of women wearing the newly fashionable pants suits, he replied cheekily, 'I prefer pants-suits off a lady.'[2] While some women would at least have raised an eyebrow at such boorish comments, and feminists would have been appalled, Hawke's schoolyard humour still brought a laugh from many men and women, who liked him for his larrikinism and found his unvarnished way of speaking refreshing.

That wouldn't necessarily make him prime minister, of course. For that, he needed to display a more serious side, one that reflected his Oxford education, offered a vision to which people could relate, and showed him to be a man of ideas. He'd tried to do so with an inebriated address to the National Press Club three years before, and now had another opportunity when he was invited to present the annual Boyer Lectures on ABC Radio.

Hawke understood that this was a great honour. The series of five lectures couldn't be based on a half-formed idea and strung together the night before, as had been his speech at the National Press Club. This time, he shut himself away in the study of his Sandringham home during the latter part of August 1979 so that he could marshal his thoughts, free from the many distractions of his daily life. It wasn't a good time for him, between the Labor conference in Adelaide and the imminent ACTU Congress, where he was expected to announce his nomination for the seat of Wills. His mother was also nearing death, his private life was in turmoil, he was drinking heavily and he feared he was suffering from a brain tumour. Yet he was able to pull himself together sufficiently to write on a theme that had dominated his public life: 'The Resolution of Conflict'.

The broadcast of the lectures in October 1979 reinforced Hawke's reputation as a man of consensus and contrasted him to the divisive politics of Malcolm Fraser. At the ACTU, he'd resolved many industrial disputes that had seemed intractable; he'd played a similar role at the International Labour Organization (ILO), where the representatives of workers, employers and governments had to bridge deep differences to reach compromise agreements; and he'd tried with limited success in Moscow to reach agreement on the issues of the Russian Jews, known as 'refuseniks', who'd been refused visas to emigrate, and on the security of Israel from attack by its Russian-supported neighbours.

Hawke wrote his Boyer Lectures with the passion that he'd brought to the refusenik issue, believing that the 'survival of civilisation [was] in question'. On a national level, he argued that Australia was hampered in finding solutions to unemployment and inflation because of the division of powers between the federal and state governments; he proposed that the states and local councils be replaced by regional governments. He also suggested, in passing, that Australia would be improved by becoming a republic, albeit with a president performing a purely ceremonial role. Hawke reprised the argument from his earlier press club speech for a quarter of government ministers to be appointed by the prime minister from outside the parliament, and for a strengthened system of parliamentary committees with the power to question ministers, public servants and external experts.[3]

While Hawke's first two lectures were concerned with improving the governance of Australia, he then suggested ways that political and social divisions could be bridged, claiming that the country was 'more divided within itself, more uncertain of the future, more prone to internal conflict, than at any other period in its history'. A cursory examination of modern Australian history would have shown that claim to be nonsense. There were much deeper divisions and greater threats to democracy during World War I, the Depression of the 1930s and the Cold War years of the 1950s. Yet the recent ending of full employment and the dismissal of the Whitlam government had certainly exposed new rifts within Australian society, not least in the experience of the many young people who could not find work and were disparaged in the media as 'dole bludgers', and in the experience of women, who were moving into the workforce in great numbers while still being denied equal pay and opportunity. At the same time, as great improvements in productivity were being wrought by technological change, jobs in the manufacturing and service industries was being destroyed. Hawke wanted a 'national summit conference of major employer organisations, trade unions and other relevant bodies' that might reach an understanding on the country's economic problems. He suggested that this would create a 'greater degree of positive co-operation', from which solutions to those problems could be found. Although he called for a return to full employment, greater democracy in the workplace and the amalgamation of unions to reduce the incidence of demarcation disputes, he recognised that the pace of technological change could destroy more jobs than the number that had to be created to keep pace with the growing population. In such a situation, and drawing on the experience of his own children, he suggested that Australians should respect the rights of those who chose to live an alternative lifestyle, rather than compel them to search for jobs that had disappeared.[4]

The reaction to the lectures was mixed. The media focused on Hawke's call for the abolition of the states, dismissing it as impractical, and derided his suggestion that the unemployed be encouraged to become hippies. Political scientist Gordon Reid thought Hawke's idea of unelected ministers had 'some ominous fascist qualities'. Hawke had tried to display his understanding of international relations by mounting his familiar defence of Israel and highlighting the rise of Japan and China, predicting that Japan would become a nuclear power and be a big seller of armaments to China, neither of which have come to pass.[5] These forecasts seem to have been based on discussions he'd had with Soviet officials in Moscow, and perhaps with Israeli officials in Jerusalem, rather than on any wide reading or deep thinking.

In the minds of voters, Hawke hadn't disgraced himself in his lectures. However, the members of the caucus had also been listening, as had the powerbrokers of his party. And they hadn't been impressed by Hawke's suggestion of drawing a quarter of the ministry from outside the parliament, which implied that there was insufficient talent within the caucus and meant there would be fewer ministerial positions for ambitious MPs. But because it pandered to voters' eagerness to denigrate politicians, it wouldn't do him any harm in the polls – and it was the view in voter-land that mattered most to Hawke. After all, he'd always planned to be swept into the parliament, and thence into the prime ministership, on a wave of popular adulation.[6] And he was determined to be a long-term, successful prime minister.

Hawke was already preparing for that eventuality. Soon after he'd secured the party's nomination, he moved to establish what he called a confidential think tank of the country's leading thinkers, approaching forty-five of them by letter and phone call. He wanted them to provide confidential advice whenever he needed it on the most pressing issues facing Australia. The readiness with which most of them agreed to help him was a sign that they saw him as a likely future prime minister. There were coal mine owners and oil executives, economists and educationalists, constitutional lawyers and defence analysts, washing machine manufacturers and architects, foreign policy academics and retired diplomats. Most were pleased, and often eager, to be a source of advice for the 'coming man'. Former ambassador Mick Shann told him that the 'critical key to the future of this country is some sense of national purpose and unity', which Hawke happened to be intent on providing, while the former ambassador to Washington, Alan Renouf, told Hawke he was 'the great hope of the country and the sooner you get hold of the reins, the better'. Economist Dick Blandy responded at length, setting out a political and economic prescription for a future Labor government, including lower tariffs, greater links with Asia and less restrictive capital and labour markets.[7] They were the sort of ideas that Hawke was already absorbing from his time on the Reserve Bank board and from his prosecution of so many wage cases before the Arbitration Commission.

Creating a group of experts he could individually consult was a sign of Hawke's self-confidence and further evidence, if such were needed, of his ultimate ambition. If he couldn't appoint outside experts to a future Hawke cabinet, he would get their inputs by other means. Their advice would help him face off against Malcolm Fraser during a future election campaign, since he needed to be knowledgeable on more topics than he'd encountered over his previous twenty-two years at the ACTU. It would make him a man of more ideas than he'd displayed during the Boyer Lectures and help give confidence to the many doubters in the Labor caucus that he was capable of providing steady, strong and visionary leadership to the party and the nation.

Not all of the people he approached were willing to join a think tank to support someone who hadn't yet been elected to parliament. Some were public servants who felt conflicted about their responsibility to serve the current government. Other issues included defence and foreign affairs, about which he had only a glancing knowledge from his campaign on behalf of Israel and the refuseniks. In November 1979, he was sent defence material by analyst Major Peter Young, which Hawke added to the mass of information that he was already planning to read over the summer. When Hawke approached historian Geoffrey Blainey, who was chair of both the Australia Council and the Australia-China Council, Blainey wryly observed that an American-style think tank smacked too much of water torture. Nevertheless, he was happy to respond to any questions from Hawke and wished him good luck. Hawke wanted to become a 'compleat politician' so that he would be ready for what he hoped the future would hold.[8] For his part, Fraser was determined that Hawke's political career would end before it began.

As part of his campaign, Fraser tried to diminish the union leader's standing with the public before Hawke made his transition into the parliament. With Labor looking likely to win the next election, the best outcome for Fraser would be for Hawke to win a seat at a by-election prior to the 1980 federal election, so as to cause divisions in Labor ranks and destabilise Hayden's leadership. Failing that, Fraser would diminish Hawke's standing by pressing ahead with the industrial relations changes that were inciting strikes and other unrest among the public service unions that had recently affiliated with the ACTU. There were also prolonged work bans imposed by 25,000 telecommunications technicians in pursuit of a 20 per cent wage increase. Among other things, Fraser's new industrial relations law allowed the Arbitration Commission to seize the assets of unions and permitted public servants to be sacked. The government also moved to give itself more influence over the decisions of the previously independent Arbitration Commission, with commissioners such as the left-wing Jim Staples being too independent-minded for Fraser's liking.

Despite the incitement from the government, Hawke's reaction was muted. He was in no mood to lead a campaign to protest the laws, and continued to be a settler of industrial disputes rather than an instigator of them. The ACTU had been pressured by its state branches to support a 'national day of protest' in June, following the arrest of ten trade unionists for holding an illegal meeting of striking miners in the Pilbara, and Hawke wasn't about to hold another one after a stoppage to defend Medibank had failed. He believed that the country's economic problems required wage restraint by unions and would not be helped by an outbreak of militancy.[9] Anyway, his mind was elsewhere.

Although Hawke had been anointed as the Labor candidate for Wills, he had to wait a year for the next federal election before he could get into parliament – and it was possible that Hayden would win that election and become prime minister. If that occurred, Hayden could expect to remain as prime minister for at least a term, and maybe two or even three, which might see Hawke denied the prime ministership altogether, as other upcoming MPs staked their claims to the succession. There was one way he could avoid that eventuality. If Gordon Bryant could be persuaded to stand down as the member for Wills prior to the election, Hawke could take it in a by-election and then, as an MP, mount a challenge to Hayden before the federal election.

Hawke was coy about the idea when questioned by journalists. He denied that he'd been exploring the possibility, but did concede that 'some pretty convincing arguments can be mounted in favour of the suggestion'. Given his distaste for serving a long apprenticeship on the backbench, it was clearly Hawke's preferred option. But Bryant wasn't prepared to cooperate, and Hayden certainly wasn't going to encourage him to do so. Although Hayden told journalists that he was 'delighted' about Hawke's preselection, since it would mean that Hawke would be 'joining us at Canberra after the next election when we form the next Labor Government', he made clear that Hawke's ambition should be limited to becoming the industrial relations minister in a Hayden government.[10] That was as far as some thought he should go. And they would use their caucus numbers to deny him the advancement he craved. Hawke and his supporters were just as determined to shore up his numbers in the post-election caucus by denying preselection to candidates who were unlikely to vote for him as leader.

One of those candidates was the independent-minded Jean Melzer, who'd been a member of the Communist Party until 1957 and was now a member of Hawke's Centre Unity faction, although on the issue of uranium mining she was on the opposite side from Hawke and many of her factional colleagues. Melzer had been elected secretary of the Victorian branch of the ALP after the federal intervention in 1971. She had replaced Bill Hartley but did not wield the same political power after the secretary's position was downgraded in the branch hierarchy. In 1974, she had been placed in an unwinnable position on the Victorian Senate ticket, only to have it suddenly became winnable when Whitlam called a double-dissolution election, which meant that ten rather than five Senate seats were up for grabs in each state. That election saw Melzer – a single mother with six children – and two other women join the otherwise male-only Labor caucus.

In parliament, Melzer became a strong voice for women's rights and civil liberties while also remaining a leading opponent of uranium mining. In 1978, she was elected as the first female secretary of caucus, and the following year addressed an anti-uranium meeting outside the ACTU Congress, when Hawke suffered a humiliating defeat on the issue. As if that wasn't enough, she showed her independence from the Centre Unity faction by opposing its nominee for the seat of Melbourne Ports following the retirement of Frank Crean. Rather than supporting Crean's son and staunch Hawke supporter Simon, Melzer supported the candidature of the former state Labor leader Clyde Holding. Her vote tipped the balance in Holding's favour. According to Melzer, it was this that caused the faction to take its revenge by placing the former schoolteacher and right-wing apparatchik Robert Ray above her on the Senate ticket for the 1980 election.[11]

The dumping of a sitting female senator – one of the few women in the parliament – provoked a grassroots revolt in the branches and calls for Ray to switch places with Melzer. This was something that Hawke couldn't afford to have happen, since it would mean one less vote for him in any leadership ballot. Melzer's many supporters included the increasing number of Labor women who regarded her demotion as a retrograde step in their campaign for greater female representation. They circulated a petition calling for Melzer to be restored to a winnable position and threatened to publicise the name of any Labor official who refused to sign it. Hawke responded with an angry letter in support of Ray, blasting the petition as 'a perverse form of sexism' which suggested that 'a woman should have additional rights and special immunities'.[12]

The petition and a public meeting attracting some 500 party members failed to convince Ray to swap his position. The issue came to a head at the state conference, when delegates tried to pressure him to do so by voting overwhelmingly for the elevation of Melzer, while Hawke used the occasion to reprise his attacks on the Socialist Left, likening Hartley and his associates to an 'eating, spreading sore, or ulcer, a gangrene'. Many of the delegates had heard his bitter attacks before and weren't swayed by his vitriol. Unfortunately for Melzer, the conference had no power to force Ray to step aside. Ray had tried unsuccessfully to stand for parliament before and wasn't going to miss his chance now. As Hawke later observed, Ray was 'as hard and remorseless as anyone I have ever met in politics', citing 'the way he stared down for a year the orchestrated and venomous campaign' to give up his place to Melzer.[13]

Despite Melzer's demotion, she would remain in the Senate and be a powerful voice in the caucus until finally relinquishing her seat to Ray in June 1981. Her strong support among rank-and-file members of the party prompted Hawke and his supporters to mount a recruitment drive to encourage people to join their local branches in order to dilute the power and influence of the Socialist Left. Advertisements were run in newspapers, while Hawke did likewise in the Wills electorate, where the Socialist Left had a strong hold.

He also moved to build up his public profile in preparation for the time when he'd no longer be the ACTU president and have the services of its media adviser. As it happened, an industrial relations journalist, Barry Donovan, had recently established a media consultancy that worked for the state Labor Party and several powerful unions from the Labor Unity faction, including the Amalgamated Postal Workers' Union (led by George Slater), the Transport Workers' Union (led by Ivan Hodgson) and the Storemen and Packers' Union (led by Bill Landeryou). When Hawke made his run for parliament, Donovan was employed by these unions to support his political aspirations. Donovan hired a young ABC journalist, Alistair Young, to advise Hawke on his presentation at televised press conferences.[14]

Rather than suggesting how Hawke could modify his sometimes abrasive public persona, Donovan commissioned a survey on how Hawke was perceived by the public. It was a roundabout way of getting him to soften the hard edges of his personality, which some found off-putting. The survey indicated that he wasn't marked down for his colourful personality and was widely admired for resolving industrial disputes, but was seen by some as 'being brash and big-noting himself'. Hawke took the results seriously, and Donovan believed it had the desired result. Donovan then suggested that he put together a book about Hawke's achievements, tentatively titled *Fixing It*, which would focus on the positive role he'd played in the resolution of conflicts. However, the pressure of events caused the book to be abandoned.[15]

While Donovan would help to maintain the flow of favourable mentions in the media, the appointment of Blanche d'Alpuget as Hawke's official biographer was designed to provide voters with the first in-depth look at his life and personality. D'Alpuget had pressured Hawke's earlier biographer, John Hurst, not to describe his book as a biography, only to have Hurst's publisher dub it 'the definitive biography'. It was far from that. In a review in *The National Times*, D'Alpuget suggested that the 'biography' should have been subtitled 'Everything-You-Already-Know-About-Bob-Hawke-Plus-One-Million-Undigested-Facts'. Hurst was careful not to delve into Hawke's private life, presumably out of concern about Hawke's readiness to use Australia's strict defamation laws whenever he thought a lucrative case could be mounted.[16] A second biography, by Sydney-based journalist Robert Pullan, provided a 'portrait' of the 'the major events in [Hawke's] life, the ideas that move him and the passions of his heart'. Hawke refused to cooperate with Pullan and encouraged his friends and family to do likewise. Pullan worked away nonetheless, but Hawke need not have worried, since Pullan was acutely aware of the legal pitfalls facing biographers of living subjects.[17]

The defamation laws couldn't save Hawke from attacks by his political opponents when they were made under the protection of parliamentary privilege. And such attacks would surely come if Hawke ever became the Labor leader, when the exposure of his seedier activities and questionable associates could cruel his chances of winning the prime ministership. The appointment of an authorised biographer, Hawke reasoned, would allow him to expose himself within limits to the Australian public and ask for their understanding and approbation.

D'Alpuget was the perfect choice. She had started work as a journalist before becoming a respected writer of the well-received biography of Sir Richard Kirby, which was praised for its 'refreshing objectivity'. The research for that book had given her a keen insight into the workings of the arbitration system and Hawke's place in it. As early as 1975, she had been thinking of turning her attention to Hawke, but was dissuaded by her conservative publisher, Peter Ryan, who thought a biography of Hawke was premature. Initially accepting that advice, she had told Hawke the following year that she would like to write his biography in ten or twenty years' time.[18]

She'd reacquainted herself with Hawke – and become his sometime lover – when she'd interviewed him for the Kirby book, which he had launched at Canberra's Lakeside Hotel in November 1977, extolling Kirby's conciliatory approach to industrial relations. Hawke called for a similar 'togetherness' in Australian politics. After Hawke told her in April 1978 that Hurst was writing his biography, she pressured him to appoint her as his *official* biographer. Four months later, he promised to give her the go-ahead once he'd settled the question of when he was going to enter parliament. He thought she'd be able to begin the project in 1980.

D'Alpuget celebrated the news by going out to buy a pair of stiletto shoes 'of sublime discomfort' by French designer Charles Jourdan. She planned to write a popular biography to be published in early 1983. It was designed to appear just prior to that year's general election, by which time, she expected, Hawke would have become Labor leader. She wanted her book to give readers the feeling that 'they known [sic] Bob intimately, [in the same way] as people feel they know characters in a good novel'.[19] Which should boost his chances of becoming prime minister.

Apart from her Kirby biography, D'Alpuget was a prize-winning short-story writer and novelist who could bring a fiction writer's eye to her new subject. She couldn't begin immediately, as she'd secured a writer's fellowship to complete a novel that would be set in Malaysia. That work had to be finished before she could begin the Hawke research. Part of it would be based upon thirty hours of interviews with Hawke, which she'd been contracted to do by the National Library. Although her book would be the last of the three to be published, she was sure that it would be worth the wait. 'I will be researching in Geneva, Israel and Moscow so, obviously, mine will be the most fascinating tome,' she said in 1979. Because it was an authorised biography, she would be shielded from a defamation action, at least as far as Hawke was concerned, so her work could be expected to be more revealing than those of her rivals.[20]

While Hawke was intent on maintaining his public profile and popularity once he left the ACTU, some of his caucus colleagues were making preparations of their own to position themselves as Hayden's successor. The most ambitious of all was Paul Keating, who'd had his sights on the prime ministership for almost as long as Hawke. Not wanting to be third in line behind Hayden and Hawke, which he recognised could see him thwarted altogether, Keating encouraged Bob Carr – his former confederate in the Young Labor Movement and now a *Bulletin* journalist – to follow up a favourable profile that he'd written about Keating back in October 1979 with a piece that was critical of Hawke. The article became the magazine's lead story when it appeared on city newsstands on 9 January 1980. According to Carr, Keating 'twisted my arm' to write the 'really tough' article, which 'reflected material Keating was just pumping into me about Hawke'.[21]

The influential magazine splashed an unflattering photograph of an exhausted-looking ACTU leader across its front page, accompanied by a banner headline: 'Has Hawke blown his chance?' According to Carr's account, Hawke had left his run too late and couldn't hope to become leader in the face of the open opposition of Tom Uren's Left faction in caucus, which would deny him the numbers he needed. Carr predicted that Hayden's 'deputy Lionel Bowen or even Paul Keating would beat Hawke overwhelmingly' in the event of a contest for Hayden's position. Hawke's reputation, Carr said, had been undermined by his Boyer Lectures, which had not served their intended purpose of establishing his intellectual credentials to be a future prime minister. Carr also questioned Hawke's achievements at the ACTU, suggesting that they amounted to little more than settling some industrial disputes earlier and on better terms than might otherwise have been done, while he'd failed to bring the many independent unions under the authority of the poorly resourced ACTU, nor had he brought his many commercial schemes to a successful conclusion. The general opinion in caucus, wrote Carr, was 'that Hawke's intellectual stature is over-rated, his record as ACTU president is unimpressive and overall his run for political leadership is taking place too late'.[22]

Hawke was devastated by the article. It articulated his innermost fears about his achievements at the ACTU and his political prospects now that he'd turned his back on his former career. Worse, it portrayed him as a person of promise who'd become a pathetic failure, a figure who deserved to be ridiculed. He was so distraught that he drank himself senseless, ending up prostrate and unconscious at a friend's house in South Yarra.[23] Which rather confirmed the point of the article.

The article had coincided with several events that had shaken Hawke. For one thing, Cliff Dolan had publicly accepted the presidency of the ACTU, which signalled Hawke's retirement and the formal closing of that door behind him. Making a bid for parliament had also signalled an end to his many other influential positions: on the Australian Council for Union Training, the National Labor Consultative Council, the Australian Population and Immigration Council, the Australian Manufacturing Council and his lucrative position on the board of the Reserve Bank, which paid him $6350 a year.[24] Then there was his position on the board of the ILO, with the many first-class flights to Geneva, the home of a long-time lover, Helga Cammell, as well as to elsewhere in the world.

Financially, Hawke had done well during his twenty-two years working for the ACTU. At a time when most workers didn't receive superannuation, the ACTU had a very generous scheme that contributed seventeen per cent of Hawke's salary. By the time he reached the normal retirement age of sixty-five, he could expect to receive nearly $250,000. In the meantime, he would get nearly $32,000 as a termination payment.[25]

Hawke would always say that he had no interest in money, which was somewhat belied by the size and relative luxury of his Sandringham home and his close friendships with wealthy businessmen, with

Hawke revelling in their expansive mansions and enjoying their fancy cigars and fast cars. Yet Hawke allowed Hazel to manage the family's finances. He later told an interviewer that he 'had a sort of condition of marriage with [Hazel] that I would have nothing whatsoever to do with the financial side of the marriage', perhaps because she couldn't trust him to have sufficient funds on hand to pay the mortgage and household bills after spending time in pubs and restaurants and enjoying himself at the racetrack and casino. His expenses had to come from the money Hazel allowed him from his salary, or which he could otherwise procure, which meant that his drinking partners usually paid when it was his time to shout a round, and his rich friends were sometimes called upon to cover his gambling losses and other expenses of his fast life.[26]

Hawke had enjoyed the power, the celebrity and the public acclaim that came with being president of the ACTU and of the Labor Party. Now the power was going and the celebrity status was diminishing. He was a political candidate facing an uncertain path to the top. What if Carr had been correct about his moment having passed? He needed support and reassurance. But his personal assistant and constant lover Jean Sinclair had told him she was taking off on a six-month holiday with her husband, which left him moaning about being alone and being forced 'to look after myself'. His reaction was reminiscent of his childhood tantrums whenever his father Clem was away from home.

On top of this was the continuing saga of his marriage, about which nothing had been resolved. Matters were coming to a head. In just a few days, he was due to fly to Hawaii with Hazel, during which time he'd promised D'Alpuget that he would have 'decisive' discussions that would bring the marriage to an end. It wouldn't be easy. As he told D'Alpuget, 'he was being emotionally torn apart by feeling forced to rupture his relationship with the woman who, 'out of her loins, bore me four children'.[27] He wanted it all and didn't want to give up anything, but realised he had to do so if he was going to fulfil the destiny that he had repeatedly trumpeted.

When he'd sobered up after the shock of reading Carr's assessment of him, D'Alpuget reassured him that it wasn't as dire as he believed. Moreover, there was much to encourage him in the same issue of *The Bulletin*, which reported the results of its latest poll, in which

Malcolm Fraser received only a 37 per cent approval rating, and Bill Hayden did little better at just 43 per cent.[28]

These poor figures should have reassured Hawke that the times could still suit him. After the mayhem of Whitlam's final year and the subsequent divisive years of the Fraser government, the poll confirmed that Australians were yearning for a unifying and inspirational leader. This was a role for which Hawke had been rehearsing for the past forty years. He planned to do what his father had tried to do from his many church pulpits. For that, he would need to maintain at least the appearance of a happy and supportive marriage. And so, rather than agreeing to a divorce, the Hawkes' 'decisive' discussions ended in an uneasy modus vivendi. Hazel would continue to link her life to his as he headed for the Lodge. Rather than divorcing and selling their Sandringham home, Hazel's diary reveals, they discussed shifting to the Wills electorate to ward off the criticisms of him being an outsider, which was something he'd struggled to overcome during the Corio by-election.[29] In the event, they remained living in their Sandringham home. The outcome in the safe Labor seat wasn't going to hinge on their place of residence.

Hawke quickly put the *Bulletin* article behind him, resuming his roller-coaster life. Just one week later, a grinning, cigar-smoking Hawke was photographed by *Woman's Day* at a table in a swish South Yarra restaurant with his arm around the waist of former prime minister Harold Holt's daughter-in-law Fiona Holt. He was at a lunch 'hosted by 16 sassy Melbourne ladies', which would have raised eyebrows in the hairdressing salons of Sandringham.[30]

Back home, his arrangement with Hazel continued. The couple would probably have divorced by now had Hazel not been working at the Brotherhood of St Laurence, which provided her with an outside interest separate from Bob's, and with friends and colleagues who boosted her self-confidence. She also consulted a psychologist to help with her insomnia and to deal with her drinking. Her self-confidence was further increased when she was accepted at the age of fifty to do a diploma in welfare work at the Caulfield Institute of Technology, after being encouraged to do so by her boss and close friend Connie Benn.[31] As Hazel was beginning these studies, Hawke was continuing his addictions to women, booze and gambling, conscious that he would have to bring them under control if he was to achieve his political ambition. This pressure added to the tension during the occasional times that he was at home.

Although the Hawke children had left, they continued to have issues, which were left largely to Hazel to handle. That had long been a source of tension between them. In diary entries in March 1980, Hazel described how Hawke phoned her early one morning, only to hang up 'when we shouted about Susan'. Then came news from the Kimberley, where 21-year-old Stephen was working as the press liaison officer for the First Nations community at Noonkanbah, and had been arrested for organising Indigenous voters at the recent state election. Hazel heard this news on 24 March before heading off to the opera with a friend; when she got home, she found that Hawke had not returned. Early the next morning, after speaking by phone to Stephen and to a lawyer in Perth, she was disconcerted to hear noises from the garden, where she found 'Bob asleep on garden lounge under lilo. Roused him – some yelling!' After telling him to make phone calls to Perth, she went off to her classes. Later that day, she met with their close friend George Rockey, who was the business partner of Sir Peter Abeles and regarded by Hawke as a father figure. He was so close to Hawke that he would buy him his underpants and the two often gambled at casinos late into the night. Hawke had been devastated to learn that Rockey was terminally ill with pancreatic cancer, and was angry with Hazel for apparently burdening Rockey with their marital problems. When she told Hawke about it the following day, 'his manner was R[at] S[hit]', wrote Hazel, who 'left for school angry'.[32]

For decades, Hawke's heavy drinking had exacerbated his bad moods. Although he knew it was threatening his health and his reputation, his attempts to stop drinking never lasted long. It was difficult when he had such a reputation for overindulgence. When people pressured him to drink, he usually succumbed. He might have been drinking less overall by early 1980, but he was 'a more unpleasant drunk', wrote D'Alpuget. His health was suffering, he was struggling to sleep and he looked a decade older than his age. It was made worse by the news about Rockey. Hawke was so distraught that he would frequently visit his friend in Sydney and sometimes accompany him to Australia's only legal casino in Hobart to play blackjack, with the trips continuing until Rockey's demise in September 1981.[33]

Something had to give. With the election due by the end of 1980, Hawke couldn't continue drinking if he was to achieve his ambition. To the extent that his drinking had been an act of rebellion against his mother, that psychological impulse should have died with her. To the extent that drinking had become an integral part of his life as a trade union official, that stage of his life had also ended. For years Hawke had been urged to abstain, not least by Hazel, but he'd only tried to do so when he'd become set on entering politics. His first attempts didn't last long. When he finally stopped in May 1980, it was after a hectic round of activities interstate and just prior to leaving again for Geneva. According to his account, he did it of his own volition, making the decision while urinating one evening: 'I was having a leak and I said to myself, "Well, bugger it. You'd be better off not drinking. Why don't you give it up?"'[34] Which he did. Many thought it was going to be impossible for him.

Alcohol had been Hawke's crutch for nigh on thirty years, and now it was gone. He wasn't looking forward to 'life without grog', since he'd 'got close to a helluva lot of people through drinking'. But he was worn out by the events of the previous year and wary of what was to come once he began his parliamentary life. His heavy drinking, and the outrageous behaviour that went with it, had been tolerated in the union movement, but he knew it was unlikely to survive the close attention that he would attract in Canberra. There'd be 'a lot of people wanting to destroy me', Hawke recognised. Alcohol had helped to end the career of Liberal prime minister John Gorton, and Hawke was determined not to have that happen to him. Otherwise, all he'd worked for and all he aspired to do would be ruined.[35] Sober, and with his health on the mend, he would be able to face the voters at the election with renewed confidence. First, though, he was off to Europe for an extended visit to five of its capitals, beginning with a week in Geneva.

He was there for an appearance at the annual conference of the ILO, in his final visit as ACTU president, and presumably to meet with Helga Cammell, who would have been surprised to see him sober. Then he was off for a three-day stay at the swanky George V hotel on the Champs-Elysées in Paris, followed by three days in Vienna, where he taught an Australian diplomat and his wife 'the intricacies of gambling' at a casino in nearby Baden. After that, it was time to board a plane to Rome, where he spent three days at the luxurious Hotel de la Ville, with its stunning views of the city's historic sites. From this former eighteenth-century palazzo, favoured for centuries by aristocrats on their European tours, he used the Australian embassy to set up meetings with minor functionaries, although they couldn't arrange one with a trade union official before Hawke left for Athens, where he spent a further three days. Flying home by way of Singapore, he backtracked for a weekend in Malaysia, where he stayed at the sumptuous Genting Highlands Hotel near Kuala Lumpur, which had a casino that he doubtless patronised. Apart from being good at blackjack, Hawke remained a keen punter at Australian racecourses and continued to be part-owner of several racehorses, three of them with the Liberal MP James Killen, while another, Buoyant Bird, was co-owned with successful breeder Robin Levett and Hawke's long-time friend Col Cunningham. On Melbourne Cup Day in 1980, Hawke was there with Levett to watch Buoyant Bird storm home to win one of the day's races.[36]

Although no longer drinking, he continued to pursue a wild life.

Support for his lifestyle continued to come from some prominent members of the Jewish community, who were anxious to have the Labor Party abandon its 'even-handed' policy vis-à-vis Israel and the Palestinians. They were worried that Hayden would make the Middle East an issue in the upcoming election. As prime minister, Whitlam had been the originator of the 'even-handed' policy, and Hayden had continued the tradition by meeting with Yasser Arafat, the leader of the Palestinian Liberation Organisation, when he toured the Middle East in July 1980. That had caused so much dismay among supporters of Israel that the leader of the Executive Council of Australian Jewry, and close friend of Hawke's, Isi Leibler, had asked Hawke to arrange a meeting with Hayden at which the Labor leader could be pressured to confirm Labor's support for Israel and its right to exist within 'clear and defensible borders'. Whatever that might mean after the 1967 war had seen Israeli forces occupy the West Bank, the Gaza Strip and East Jerusalem. Wary of what was afoot, Hayden sidestepped Hawke's suggestions for a meeting.[37] Hawke would have to wait until he became Labor leader himself.

While the outcome in his electorate of Wills was never in doubt, the national outcome was less certain. Australia was still dogged by the unemployment and inflation that had swept across the developed world in the wake of the first oil price crisis of 1973, and again in 1979 after the Iranian revolution. The dismissal of the Whitlam government had made voters reluctant to trust Labor to manage the economy, even though Fraser had been unable during his five years in power to produce the promised recovery. The economy remained in a state of 'stagflation', where high unemployment was combined with high inflation. According to the economic textbooks, there was no easy fix. In a memorable comment, Fraser had told Australians that 'life wasn't meant to be easy'. And it certainly wasn't easy being prime minister during such times.

Bill Hayden believed he had a solution to Australia's malaise, if workers could be convinced to forgo, or at least moderate, their wage demands in return for lower taxes, a universal health system and various social welfare payments. He had convinced the ALP national conference in 1979 to support this notion of a 'social contract', but had much more trouble convincing the unions to give up the automatic cost-of-living increases each quarter that compensated workers in full for the effect of inflation. He went ahead anyway, holding a meeting with the ACTU in August 1980, during which the executive agreed to consult with a Hayden government on any wage claim being made. It was hardly the much-hyped 'social contract', but it would have to suffice as one of Labor's centrepieces for the coming election campaign.

Fraser had called the previous election a year early so that he would be facing off against the discredited Whitlam rather than having Hayden, or perhaps Hawke, as the Labor leader. With the next election due by December 1980, Fraser again called it early, albeit by only seven weeks, this time in the hope of avoiding an expected worsening of the inflation figures. He had the advantage of a 48-seat majority, which it would be difficult for Hayden to overturn in one election. Yet when Fraser announced that the election would be held on 18 October, the opinion polls had the two major parties fairly evenly matched.

They were not evenly matched in other ways. Although Hayden had a fully developed suite of policies to present to voters, the Labor Party's depleted bank balance left it poorly placed to advertise them. And while the austere figure of Malcolm Fraser wasn't popular with voters, the serious-minded Hayden struggled to take advantage of that. The former policeman was respected but lacked the animal magnetism of Hawke. To burnish his image and boost Labor's popularity, the party's election photographs saw Hayden buttressed by Hawke on one side and Neville Wran on the other. It was an implicit admission that Hayden needed shoring up. Together, the three were expected to add a couple of percentage points to the votes that Labor could otherwise have counted upon. But it was only Hawke who would be joining Hayden on the hustings, since Wran was recuperating from a series of throat operations.[38]

Within days of Fraser calling the election, and despite Hawke still officially being president of the ACTU, Hayden announced that he had appointed him in place of Mick Young as the shadow minister for industrial relations. It was an extraordinary move – Hawke wasn't even in parliament – and provided confirmation of Hayden's reliance on Hawke's personal popularity. Hayden's position was made worse when he had to withdraw from the campaign for several days with a sore throat, leaving Hawke to lead a series of meetings and media appearances across Hayden's home state of Queensland. Hawke even challenged Fraser to a debate, predicting that the prime minister would be 'done like a dinner'. Fraser refused to accept the challenge, instead warning darkly about Labor being under the influence of the Socialist Left. A Hayden government would be run by the trade unions, he said, and he duly ran a scare campaign about Labor introducing a wealth tax.[39]

The fearful talk was overdone. Industrial disputes had abated and Hawke, familiar as the industrial peacemaker, wasn't a bogeyman to most Australians, who were concerned instead about Fraser's failure to reduce the debilitating trifecta of unemployment, soaring inflation and high interest rates. These were the issues at which Hayden and Hawke kept hammering away, with Hayden proposing modest initiatives that were designed to restore Australians' living standards, which had been eroding for a decade.

On 30 September, Hawke finally retired as ACTU president, spending the day at the office and enjoying a farewell lunch with staff in the organisation's boardroom.[40] There would be no turning back on his path to parliament.

Although Labor enjoyed a lift in the polls, Hayden needed a swing of historic proportions to defeat Fraser, and it had to occur in the places where the party could win additional seats. In Queensland, Labor held only three of the nineteen seats. Yet the opinion polls looked so promising during the campaign that Hayden had to caution his candidates against 'gloating' in anticipation of victory. He instructed them to stick strictly to the party's 'family policies' of living standards, petrol prices, taxation and unemployment, and not be diverted by any distractions that Fraser might mount in the final weeks. The disciplined strategy worked so well, despite Fraser claiming that a Labor government would introduce a 'wealth tax', that Hayden felt assured of victory.[41] But what would that mean for Hawke?

Although he had his eyes on the prime ministership for himself, Hawke had campaigned strongly for a Hayden victory. Fuelled by nothing stronger than orange juice and mineral water, he had to hope that Hayden would get close to securing sufficient seats but ultimately fall short. That would make his own task easier at the subsequent election, once he became leader.

On 18 October, the day of the election, Hawke greeted voters at booths in Wills before heading to Canberra to be part of the Channel Nine election panel. He'd hardly spent any time canvassing for votes in his own electorate, and his decision was justified by the early returns, which showed him receiving a swing of more than 7 per cent. His predecessor, Gordon Bryant, had held the seat since 1955 and built up his two-party majority to 62 per cent. With Hawke's immense popularity, and despite the bitterness of the preselection battle, Hawke now secured an unassailable 70 per cent of the two-party vote. He could be confident that the seat would be his for as long as he wanted it.

As Hawke sat before the television cameras in Canberra on election night and watched the numbers going up on the Electoral Commission's giant board, his attention was elsewhere. The final opinion polls suggested that the voters were going to give Fraser a 'severe battering' and could make Hayden prime minister.[42] Hawke was conflicted. He wanted a Labor victory, since a Labor government could do so much to improve the lives of ordinary Australians, but he wanted it to be led by him. If the former police sergeant emerged triumphant, Hayden would be cemented into the prime ministership by a Labor caucus beholden to the leader who'd led them to such a momentous victory.

It was the most anxious election night of Hawke's career. At the age of fifty-one, he'd finally joined the political game, but it was the national outcome that would determine whether he'd made the right call. His eyes remained firmly fixed on the ultimate prize of the prime ministership.

CHAPTER TWO

# 1981–1982

The opinion polls had convinced Bill Hayden that he was set to win the 1980 federal election. And while the early results seemed to bear out his hopes, the final two-party preferred swing of 4.2 per cent wasn't enough. Indeed, Malcolm Fraser had seen enough of the figures to claim victory on election night without waiting for the bitterly disappointed Labor leader to concede defeat. When the final votes were tallied, Fraser had lost only thirteen seats, which left him with a comfortable majority of twenty-three. It was a different story in the Senate. If Labor could secure the support of the five senators from Don Chipp's Australian Democrats, along with the independent MP Brian Harradine – who was a former right-wing member of the ACTU Executive – it could block any contentious government legislation.

Despite Fraser's victory, it had been a poor night for the prime minister. This had been his third election as Liberal leader and his haughty persona had never been popular. 'Malcolm Fraser's days are numbered,' warned Hawke cheekily on election night. Despite pestering from journalists, he declined to say whether Hayden's days were also numbered.[1]

The size of the swing and the loss of the Liberal majority in the Senate were of little solace to Hayden. He didn't help his own position with the New South Wales Right by supporting a left-wing Tasmanian for the deputy Labor leadership in the Senate in preference to a right-wing senator from New South Wales whom he'd previously agreed to support. While Hayden claimed to have 'punched a hell of a hole in the Liberal Party majority', the party hardheads knew there could be no certainty that Hayden would get Labor over the line in 1983.[2]

That uncertainty was to Hawke's benefit, but he couldn't play his cards just yet. For the time being, the size of the swing made Hayden impregnable. Which was the impression he tried to give to Hawke when he sent him a congratulatory telegram on the Monday after the election, telling Hawke that he 'will add greatly to the vitality of the Federal Parliamentary Labor Party in the course of this parliament as it works for government in 1983', when Hayden expected to become prime minister.[3] Although Hawke had other ideas, he would have to prove himself as a parliamentary performer, and hope that Hayden wouldn't give Labor an unassailable lead in the polls before the next election and that his own personal poll results would hold up.

Hawke also had to watch his own back, since he wasn't the only Labor MP aspiring to become leader. Apart from Keating, who'd become president of the New South Wales branch, there was also Keating's New South Wales colleague Lionel Bowen, and the newly elected Western Australian Kim Beazley, whose father had once been touted as a successor to Ben Chifley. There were others besides, including a former Rhodes Scholar and politics professor from Adelaide, Dr Neal Blewett. But it was Hawke who had the highest public profile and the least time to waste. He wasn't in parliament to play the part of an Opposition MP, even if he was now the shadow minister for industrial relations, employment and youth affairs. Hawke couldn't wait for Hayden to make political mistakes. He had to prove those many detractors wrong who wondered whether he had the skill and the temperament for parliament, let alone to be the prime minister. Many of those detractors were in the Labor caucus, where most of his colleagues regarded him 'as arrogant, boastful, self-indulgent and a bad drunk'. He had a reputation for not taking his turn to pay for drinks and being reluctant to settle on losing bets at the races.[4] Of course, none of this would matter if he could guarantee them success in an election.

Twenty-five years before, Hawke had been living in Canberra and occasionally catching the bus to Parliament House, where he'd seen Billy Snedden sitting on the government benches behind Bob Menzies. Since then, Snedden had risen to become Liberal leader, only to be toppled before getting the chance to become prime minister. Now it was Sir Billy Snedden, wearing a flowing wig as Speaker of the House of Representatives, who presided when Governor-General Sir Zelman

Cowen presented the government's program on 25 November 1980. Once that formality was concluded, Hawke wasted no time in making his own mark, giving notice on his first day in parliament that he would move for the establishment of a joint committee to report on the dire unemployment situation. On his third day, he made a major speech defending the right of public servants to engage in industrial action.

In between, with Hazel and his father, Clem Hawke, looking on from the gallery, he gave his maiden speech, in which he thanked the trade union movement for giving him 'unique opportunities to develop whatever intrinsic talents I may possess'. He promised to do all he could over the next three years to ensure the election of a 'compassionate, competent government concerned with the welfare of all Australians'. Rather than using the speech to reminisce at length about his life and the roots of his political beliefs, as most MPs did, Hawke launched a defence of the more than 100,000 young Australians who were unemployed and the many more Australians living in poverty, and called on the government to stop widening the division between rich and poor. Hawke suggested that it would cost only $600 million to end poverty.[5] It wasn't a particularly revealing or inspirational speech and would do little to get the caucus behind him, but it did reveal his deeply held beliefs and set the tone for his time in parliament.

Having finally entered politics, Hawke had to come to grips with the challenges of his new life. Earlier that year, he'd been advised by one of his new colleagues, John Kerin, that he would learn quickly 'that you are on your own in Canberra and that alliances, allegiances and attitudes by one's peers/colleagues change rapidly'.[6] Rather than enjoying the almost untrammelled power he'd exercised as ACTU president, he was now a middle-ranking shadow minister subject to those shifting attitudes and allegiances, as well as to the discipline of the caucus and of Hayden as its leader. Conservative columnist David McNicoll had told Hawke he would be 'a whale among minnows' if he ran for parliament, but a bored-looking Hawke lounging on the green-leather front bench of the House of Representatives gave little sign of this greatness.[7] He was more like a fish out of water. Although he'd been a frequent visitor to Parliament House over the years, Hawke now had to find his way around the long corridors and several levels of the parliamentary rabbit warren, build relationships and alliances with his fellow MPs, and strengthen his links with the journalists of the press gallery, all the while trying to maintain the high public profile and popularity on which his future political success depended.

On a more mundane level, Hawke also had to find a place to live. Rather than staying at a hotel or sharing a house or flat with colleagues, he bought a two-bedroom flat of his own in a three-storey complex of thirty-seven units at 18 Currie Crescent, Kingston, which Hazel helped him to decorate. It was only two kilometres to the old Parliament House by way of Kurrajong House, where John Curtin and Ben Chifley had once stayed. Some MPs had to share an office in the overcrowded quarters of Parliament House, but Hawke had his own office. There, Jean Sinclair brought a sense of continuity and order to his parliamentary life and often entertained him in her flat at night. Hawke was endowed with funds from Peter Abeles and other leading members of the Jewish community that helped to supplement his parliamentary salary and enable him to enjoy a level of office support and travel, both interstate and overseas, that other Opposition MPs could not. Before Hawke stood as a Labor MP, Abeles had offered him $250,000 to start a party of his own, a proposal Hawke had rejected. The funds that were provided in lieu of that would help him to organise his eventual challenge for the leadership. He also enjoyed free use of a penthouse suite in Sydney's Boulevard Hotel, where he could meet privately with Labor powerbrokers and influential media owners.[8]

Although he was no longer the nation's union leader, Hawke continued to feature prominently in the media, whether he was commenting on industrial relations, launching a book, opening an art exhibition or being profiled in newspapers and magazines. Some of this was due to the work of his media consultant, Barry Donovan. Having Hawke appear at an event was a guarantee that it would attract an audience and be reported. Rumours of his drinking, which were unfounded, and womanising only added to his appeal. However, there were fears among his supporters that his popularity could be threatened if he divorced Hazel; at this time divorce remained a matter of some shame. Hawke told D'Alpuget that a divorce could shrink a Hawke-led Labor Party's vote by 3 percentage points at an election, which could cost him the prime ministership. That was too big a sacrifice. There was also the possibility that an acrimonious split could expose unsavoury aspects of his private behaviour. For years, Abeles and Rockey had counselled the couple against divorce, which Hazel had also effectively resisted by insisting she remain in Sandringham. Neither of them wanted to split their assets and give up the comforts of their home. Although Hazel had consulted a divorce lawyer, she'd made no move to initiate proceedings.[9] Their acrimonious relationship remained at a stand-off.

It was only when Hawke finally set his sights on the Lodge that Hazel decided she would accompany him there and see off the lovers who wanted to marry him. She'd suffered the humiliations of his public drunkenness and flagrant infidelity, and she'd borne the burden of the homemaking and child rearing. She told a close friend that 'she'd put up with years of Bob's shenanigans and she'd be buggered if she would miss out on moving into the Lodge as the First Lady'. Apart from the luxury of their Sandringham home, there were the perks that came with being Bob Hawke's wife, which she had grown to enjoy. She sometimes arrived at work in his chauffeured limousine and used her position to get good seats at the theatre.[10]

There were deeper reasons, though, for Hazel to stay married to him. As she explained in her memoir, they'd had 'such unforgettable years together when we were younger', and she wasn't 'going to walk away from my whole adult lifetime's thirty-three-year input to a partnership, marriage and family, only to carry with me the sense of failure that I knew would engulf me'. Once the children had left home and she began working at the Brotherhood of St Laurence, Hazel had grown in confidence and developed new interests and friendships of her own. Being middle-aged and in the public eye, she was encouraged by a friend to have plastic surgery to conceal some of the effects of ageing that had been exacerbated by her recent years of drinking and smoking. Aside from boosting her self-confidence, it was likely an attempt to rekindle Hawke's interest in her.[11] But his eyes would continue to roam.

While a sober Hawke established himself in Canberra, Hazel remained in Sandringham, working and studying for her diploma. Ever since the early years of their relationship, she had blamed Hawke's bad behaviour and angry outbursts on his alcohol use. If he gave up the grog, she hoped, he might revert to the person who'd first attracted her as a teenager. That would never happen. But his abstinence did improve his health and his moods, which made their relationship easier. When he was interviewed by Michael Parkinson in May 1981, the television celebrity couldn't help noticing the change in Hawke's appearance. Which Hawke was happy to acknowledge. 'I just feel enormously better,' he said, 'better than I've felt for as long as I can remember.'[12]

Much to the surprise of Hawke's friends and associates, he remained true to his commitment to quit drinking. Winston Churchill may have got away with heavy drinking as a wartime prime minister, but Hawke's idol was Churchill's Australian counterpart, John Curtin, who'd been an alcoholic before promising his supporters that he would give up the drink if they made him Labor leader, which the caucus duly did in 1935. Despite Curtin's commitment, there is evidence that he may have continued drinking surreptitiously after becoming leader. That was never publicly known at the time, and Hawke was certainly unaware that his political hero had occasional lapses – or that Curtin had to have a temperance campaigner accompany him to public functions as prime minister. As far as Hawke was concerned, Curtin provided an example of abstinence that was worthy of emulation.[13]

For a time, Hazel was the only one still abusing alcohol. She had much to be stressed about. Their three children were scattered across Australia, with Stephen working in the Kimberley, while Sue was in Sydney, where she was also politically active. Rosslyn was living a hippie-like existence in New South Wales. Although Hazel was getting great satisfaction from her job and her studies, she spent much of her time alone in Sandringham. She had been buoyed by Hawke's improved behaviour after he gave up the grog but remained uncertain about her own future. She sought solace in her garden and escaped from periods of extreme stress with yoga and transcendental meditation. Alone at night, she frequently found herself downing several glasses of wine with dinner, perhaps musing on what Blanche d'Alpuget might write in her biography.[14]

By the time D'Alpuget was able to begin her research, it was late 1979 and Hawke and Hazel were discussing divorce, with D'Alpuget hoping to become his wife. The situation couldn't have been more awkward when D'Alpuget sat down in her Canberra home on 29 February 1980 to type a letter to Hazel requesting an interview. She apologised for having previously, as Hawke's lover, written angry letters to Hazel. Now that she was Hawke's biographer, her overwhelming desire was to build on her growing reputation by writing an accurate biography. For that, she needed Hazel's cooperation, since no one knew Hawke better than his long-suffering wife.

Hazel's initial response was to rebuff D'Alpuget's request. It wasn't a good time. The letter arrived just as she was starting her diploma course, and Hazel was living partly at a friend's home to ensure she could study without the distractions her husband created when he was home in Sandringham. Cooperating with D'Alpuget would only cause her more emotional turmoil. Apart from bristling at the prospect of sitting down with her husband's lover and possible future wife, Hazel feared that the process would expose their family, and particularly the children, to unwanted scrutiny and publicity. Only when she was convinced that the book was crucial to Hawke's hopes of becoming prime minister did she relent. After all, she reasoned, it could put him in a position to address the issues of poverty and inequality, to which Hazel had been exposed through her work at the Brotherhood. Her cooperation might also give her a greater say on what was included in the book.[15]

Not that it could ever be a hagiography. There were so many witnesses to Hawke's bad behaviour that his political opponents, both Labor and Liberal, were sure to refer to his unsavoury exploits as a means of blocking his political ascendancy. Far better for the biography to partially lift the cover on his playboy lifestyle in the hope it could stop his opponents from throwing the covers aside completely. It might also drown out the whispered warnings in the caucus room about his fitness for high office.

With all the insights she'd gained since meeting Hawke more than a decade before, D'Alpuget would be able to provide a revealing portrait that would add to her standing as a writer and biographer and enhance her subject's political prospects. Hawke encouraged his friends and associates to cooperate, trusting that she would write a book that would attract a wide readership and deal sympathetically with his failings. D'Alpuget duly tracked down a horde of family, friends and colleagues, and consulted psychologists as well. She'd been critical of the recent biographies by Robert Pullan and John Hurst, and wanted to present a classy and positive image of her lover. She urged Donovan to do likewise with the book he was preparing. 'Bob's now been associated with two el cheapo books,' she wrote, '[and] it's really important, for his image, that he is not associated with a third. Dis is big bickie, as they say.'[16]

In mid-May 1980, her long-awaited interview with Hazel finally occurred, with Hawke arranging for D'Alpuget to stay at the Sandringham home of their family doctor, which was just ten minutes' walk from the Hawke home. There were obvious areas that neither woman wanted to explore, with D'Alpuget being anxious to at least partially allay Hazel's hostility towards her and to retain her cooperation. It seems that she was relatively successful in both aims, later thanking Hazel 'for going through what [was] for both of us I think – certainly for me – a difficult interview'. She acknowledged that, prior to the interview, she was 'very conscious of being in your eyes a species of leper', since 'you would have thought only the worst of me, aware as you are, more than any other person, of the most flagrant period of being mad, bad and dangerous to know in my life'.[17]

It was a measure of Hazel's commitment to Hawke's political ambition that she'd agreed to the interview. Some sensitive matters were traversed as background for the book, with D'Alpuget promising to keep them confidential. Having broken the ice, she asked that they meet again six weeks later, when she would next be in Melbourne. It's not clear whether Hazel agreed to this, because D'Alpuget made a further attempt in July to get her cooperation by sending a typescript copy of her forthcoming novel, *Turtle Beach*, which would be published to great acclaim in 1981, in the hope that Hazel might 'feel a bit more confident of my ability, and therefore a bit more enthusiastic about a book on Bob'. She hoped to convince Hazel to see her in September, although it seems that no such meeting took place.[18]

D'Alpuget pressed on with the writing, going to Geneva and Israel in late September 1981 to research Hawke's activities in those places, with Hawke paving the way with a letter to Israeli politician Shimon Peres and arranging for her to stay at the home of American diplomat Jim Shea.[19] Time was short, because the book was being done according to Hawke's political timetable as much as that of her publisher, Morry

Schwartz. It was important that the biography appear well before the election that was due in 1983. That meant it had to be in the hands of the publisher by mid-1982 and released later that year. It would give voters a more rounded view of Hawke and his background, while also neutralising the political dirt that the Liberals might throw his way if he became leader, or that investigative journalists might discover. First, though, the manuscript had to be checked by several readers and approved by both Hawke and Hazel.

The first part was ready in early January 1982 and sent separately to them both. D'Alpuget was anxious that Hazel approve her warts-and-all approach, even though much was left out that might have been included. She realised that the stories of his womanising would be the most sensitive things for Hazel, but explained that it 'would have been sheer foolishness ... to remain silent about Bob's womanising in view of the fact that it's been discussed on national television and in the Press'. She pointed out that the book would portray this as 'a thing of the past', which she assured Hazel was true and that Hawke was '"normal" now in that respect'. D'Alpuget asked again for Hazel's forgiveness for the 'silly and malevolent' letters that she'd sent her in the past, and pointed to her positive portrayal of Hazel. Apparently placated to some extent, Hazel went through the manuscript, marking up her changes, which were mostly concerned with her children.[20]

As for Hawke, D'Alpuget recalled how her psychological study left him 'quite traumatised' and unable to speak for some time after reading it. Of course, he'd read profiles of himself in newspapers and magazines, but this was an extended study of his childhood and his psychological underpinnings. As a narcissist, he was not given to much self-reflection. Nor did he have much self-awareness. It was therefore a shock for him to read the judgements of so many people, including his parents, closest friends and colleagues. Looking up from the pages, he finally described the experience as being akin to 'looking into a mirror with a thousand facets'.[21] The final judgement would be made by the voters.

For decades, Hawke had told everyone that there was an inevitability about his pathway to the Labor leadership, and many expected that he would quickly become leader once he entered parliament. 'I don't know why he tells people these things,' said Jean Sinclair, because it created expectations that he had little hope of fulfilling. Without a majority of caucus behind him, he just had to 'sit tight': Hayden would take some shifting. Sinclair had become convinced by November 1981 that a Labor victory was unlikely in 1983, and that Hawke's chance would only come once Hayden had suffered a second election loss.[22]

Hawke didn't want to wait for that to play out. He took heart from the toppling in September 1981 of unpopular Labor Opposition leaders in Victoria and Western Australia, where John Cain and Brian Burke had been installed, which Hawke regarded as a sign that 'the doctrine of inviolate tenure has been badly dented'. Hayden could be next, thought Hawke. He was further encouraged by talk in the media about unrest within caucus and by approaches he'd had from MPs within the Left faction, led by Tom Uren, who regarded Hawke as having a better chance of getting Labor into government. He was so encouraged that he became convinced he would have the numbers to win in the event of a spill motion being held for the leadership. Hawke was dreaming. The polls weren't sufficient in themselves. While most Australians would have endorsed him in a heartbeat, most MPs were still loyal to Hayden or retained misgivings about Hawke's personal failings and lack of parliamentary experience. It would require Hayden's position to be weakened and Hawke's parliamentary performance to be strengthened before MPs adopted the majority view of Australian voters. Yet Hawke continued to put his faith in the polls, assuming that his popularity would make the pressure for a spill motion overwhelming as the 1983 election loomed ever closer. In the view of Hawke and his close supporters, the crunch time would come by mid-1982, when Labor was due to hold its next federal conference.[23] It couldn't come soon enough.

Hawke didn't want to spend any more time than he had to on the Opposition benches. Moreover, if Hayden won the 1983 election, it could scupper Hawke's chance of ever becoming prime minister. His preference was for Hayden to be compelled to acknowledge Hawke's greater appeal in the electorate and to stand aside in his favour. He wanted to take possession of Hayden's office without leaving any blood on the carpet. Hayden might have lacked Hawke's overweening self-confidence, but he made clear that this wasn't going to happen. It would have seemed inconceivable to Hayden that caucus would turn on him after the swing he'd gained for Labor at the last election. He would also have been conscious that both Evatt and Calwell had been allowed three election losses and Whitlam two election losses before they'd been forced to resign as leader. But those leaders hadn't had to contend with such a dogged and popular challenger.

After spending more than a year in parliament, Hawke was no closer to his prize. It didn't help when he embarrassed the party and himself by putting on a mock Indian accent to tell a crude joke about Indian prime minister Indira Gandhi at Labor's national conference in 1981, not long before she was due to make an official visit to Australia. When the tasteless joke was reported in the media, Hawke's invitation to attend a reception for Mrs Gandhi was withdrawn by the organisers. Not that he would have been bothered. He'd been telling such juvenile, misogynist jokes ever since he'd been at Perth Modern and he wasn't about to stop.[24]

Meanwhile, he pressed on with his campaign to undermine Hayden among the caucus, the Canberra press gallery and Labor Party powerbrokers by pointing to a succession of polls in April and May 1981 that showed him to be the most popular political figure in the country. According to a briefing paper that was apparently circulated by Hawke, one of the polls said that Hawke 'had greater leadership qualities than Hayden, that he had a stronger personality, that he was better educated and a better speaker, and that he was more honest and straightforward'. The polls also showed that he was much preferred as leader by the minority Australian Democrat voters, whose preferences could determine the next election. Although Labor might 'just win' with Hayden as leader, the polls suggested 'the ALP would definitely win the next Federal election' with Hawke as leader.[25] It was a compelling argument for those who wanted a Labor government and were unsure whether Hayden could get them there. But their numbers weren't sufficient in caucus to topple the leader. Hawke would have to take a different tack. With time running out, he confronted Hayden directly.

Late at night on 18 February 1982, Hawke boldly walked into Hayden's office and sprawled across an armchair, from where he pointed to the latest polling figures and called on his bemused leader to resign for the good of the party. It was midway through the electoral cycle and Hawke was concerned that Fraser would call another early election, catching Labor with Hayden as leader, just as he'd done in 1978 to Whitlam. Hawke couldn't allow that to happen.

'His body language, his mood, were unmistakeable,' wrote a still smarting Hayden in his memoirs. 'This was his office!' Remaining behind his desk, Hayden told Hawke to 'go and get stuffed'. He then explained to his aspiring usurper how he 'lacked certain important leadership qualities' that made him unsuited to be Labor leader, let alone prime minister.[26]

Hawke had no immediate comeback. He would have to keep amassing the numbers in caucus and let the polling figures speak on his behalf as the election loomed closer.

Despite his bravado during their late-night set-to, Hayden was privately rattled. He would later tell Barry Jones that his favourite painting was Edvard Munch's *The Scream*, which 'tells you something', said Jones. Writing in his memoirs, Hayden confessed: 'My act was getting ragged – like that of a threadbare juggler, or a fortune-teller in baggy pants,' whereas Hawke 'had only to be there and wave the latest popularity poll ratings'. At the time, though, Hayden believed he could stare down the sentimental Hawke in a face-off.[27]

During their tense meeting, Hayden had assured Hawke that he would be able to translate Labor's present poll lead into an election victory. He had an opportunity to prove his confident assertion just a few weeks later, when a by-election was caused by the resignation of the former prime minister Billy McMahon from his New South Wales seat of Lowe. The 73-year-old McMahon had held on for a decade after losing government in 1972, only to resign in a final act of spite against Fraser. It was good news for Hayden, since McMahon's electorate required less than a 2 per cent swing for Labor to win. If Hayden could secure a sizeable swing, it would shore up his leadership until the coming federal election. He was helped by having a popular Labor candidate, Michael Maher, who had the enthusiastic support of the New South Wales Right machine. There was little Hawke could do but watch the voters of Lowe give Labor a thumping victory on 13 March, with a swing of 9 per cent. Hayden was exultant.[28] His path to the next election now seemed secure against a Hawke challenge.

Hayden was further buoyed just a few weeks later when the Victorian state election saw Labor's John Cain sweep to victory with a swing of nearly 5 per cent. The state had been a conservative bastion since the Labor split of 1955, but could now be counted upon to swing Labor's way at the federal election. Labor was on a roll. Yet Hayden could feel Hawke's hot breath coming closer, and betrayed his anxiety by excluding Hawke from his so-called kitchen cabinet, consisting of Labor's four parliamentary leaders and three other shadow ministers – Paul Keating, Ralph Willis and Mick Young. In an editorial on 4 May, *The Age* argued that it was a mistake for Hayden to overlook Hawke, given his role as the Opposition's industrial relations spokesman, his poll numbers exceeding Hayden's and him being one of Labor's best electoral assets. The paper thought that it would 'fuel suspicion that Mr Hayden is nervous about Mr Hawke and anxious to keep him down'.[29] Which of course he was.

Despite the electoral victories boosting Hayden's confidence, Hawke's strong suit remained the opinion poll numbers, especially the ALP's private polling, which revealed the deep reservations that voters had about Hayden. Rather than the public opinion polls, which showed Labor several points ahead of the Liberals, the qualitative interviews conducted by Labor's pollster Rod Cameron showed that Fraser was regarded as a much stronger leader than Hayden. It wasn't just the comparative strength of the party leaders that concerned Cameron. As he confided to Hayden on 18 May, voters saw him as 'honest and modest, but also as weak, wishy-washy, a whinger, and people often just cannot understand what you are saying'. This was poison for a politician, and Hayden refused to accept it. He cast doubt within caucus on Cameron's methods and pointed to the published opinion polls.[30]

But the damage was done, and the party polling undermined Hayden's confidence and fed his paranoia. Importantly for Hawke, it added to the fear within Labor ranks that, under Hayden, they might not win the next election. Increasingly, Hawke would be able to count on support from the party's powerbrokers: the Victorian state secretary, Bob Hogg; the New South Wales state secretary, Graham Richardson; and the federal secretary, Bob McMullan. Unlike many caucus members, who felt a debt of gratitude for Hayden's electoral performance in 1980, and who were conscious that Labor had never voted a leader out of office, the powerbrokers wanted victory above all things. After all, Labor's policies couldn't be implemented if the party didn't win government.

Although his political trajectory remained unclear, Hawke could be quietly confident on 24 May 1982, when he flew out of Australia for a meeting of the Socialist International in Helsinki. Accompanying him on the extended trip was Hazel, who'd been rushed to hospital in late March with appendicitis. She'd spent more than a week in hospital recovering from the appendectomy and surgery to correct gynaecological issues before being taken home by Susan, who'd flown from Sydney to care for her. Now she and Bob were off to Europe. There would be no more talk of divorce. Much to D'Alpuget's chagrin, Hawke would maintain the semblance of his marriage. Now that he was off the grog and behaving in a more civilised manner, he and Hazel would develop an accommodation that would allow them to present as a flawed but apparently loving couple. For her part, Hazel came to see their relationship as a 'partnership'. As she later explained to a journalist, 'My major role is to support my husband and to do my duties within the partnership.'[31]

Just how that partnership would work was tested during their trip. On their arrival in Helsinki, the pair walked around the city, with Hazel doing further exploration the following day while Hawke was presumably occupied at the conference. They were due to meet up that evening to attend a symphony concert, only to have Hawke go to dinner with former German chancellor Willy Brandt. Undaunted, Hazel sold his ticket to a Finn, 'who was good company'. She spent most of the next day alone before they hired a car to drive to a fishing village. She was 'feeling good', wrote Hazel, 'and Bob and I were more relaxed together'.[32]

Not that they spent much time together. Hazel went to Berlin and Paris, staying with acquaintances for several days in each city before rejoining Hawke in Geneva on 6 June. She wasn't impressed when he took her to a casino and flew off the next day for a meeting of Labor's National Executive in Tasmania. Rather than going home, she flew to New York, where she enjoyed Broadway shows, visited galleries, attended classical music concerts and shopped. She enjoyed her new-found independence and anonymity, 'in my denim skirt and comfy shoes, with my suitcase on a wheel'.[33]

Back in Canberra, Hawke was circling Hayden, sensing political blood and making sure that dubious Canberra journalists also noticed. The hapless Labor leader had responded to a commitment by the new Victorian premier, John Cain, to deny port facilities to nuclear-armed ships of the US Navy, with Hayden promising that, as prime minister, he would do likewise. He regarded it as an uncontroversial commitment after Fraser had promised that American B-52 bombers calling at Darwin would not be carrying nuclear bombs. However, ships were different. The US had always refused to indicate which of its ships might be nuclear-armed, which would mean that a Hayden government would have to deny entry to *all* American naval vessels, thereby putting the future of the ANZUS alliance at risk. Moreover, Hayden had gone further than Labor's policy allowed, which caused unease among his caucus colleagues and joy among his political opponents. Hayden was motivated by a long-held scepticism about the American alliance, particularly after the Central Intelligence Agency's (CIA's) alleged involvement in the undermining and sacking of the Whitlam government. He was also driven by a desperate desire to 'wrong-foot' Hawke, hoping that Hawke's staunch support for the Americans would put him offside with the Labor Left.[34]

Unfortunately for Hayden, he'd wrong-footed himself. This was political manna for Fraser, and suited the Americans, too, who'd never liked Hayden's push for a more independent foreign policy. Despite this, Hayden allowed the damaging issue to run for several weeks, during which time the visiting US deputy secretary of state, Walter Stoessel, called on Hayden to give him a stern dressing-down and then told journalists that Hayden's commitment threatened the ANZUS alliance. Hayden was forced into a humiliating backdown, which gave Hawke the confidence to prepare for a showdown.[35]

That confidence was strengthened when a poll by a market research company included panels of swinging voters who expressed sobering views of Hayden. The results showed Hayden scored just 5.3 out of 10 for 'strength', compared with 7.9 for Fraser and 8.4 for Hawke. On five other qualities – intelligence, competence, likeability, trustworthiness and concern about ordinary people – Hawke outranked both Hayden and Fraser, often by a lot. It was only when the swinging voters were asked which of the three politicians was the most stable that both

Hayden and Fraser slightly outranked Hawke. It angered Hawke when journalist Anne Summers misread the results, claiming in *The National Times* that *all* voters judged Hayden to be more stable than Hawke. In fact, the survey of all voters judged Hawke to be more stable than Hayden. He couldn't allow that claim to stand, taking Summers to task for fear that it would otherwise reinforce the doubts about him that were harboured by his opponents in caucus. To further boost his campaign, Hawke took a copy of the poll results to a meeting of Labor's National Executive. He presumably brought the meeting's attention to the perception by swinging voters of 'Hawke's powerful potential to unite Australians and eliminate the kind of acrimony in politics which they have now come to detest'. And so the debate continued, with commentator Phillip Adams describing Hawke as 'a natural leader in a country crying out for leadership' and warning that Labor's support would 'just fade, fade, fade away' without him. Thrashing around, Hayden implied that Hawke was 'a half-baked vaudevillian', and he would refuse to emulate him. He would 'just rely on what I am and what I've got'.[36] It wasn't enough.

Flying to Sydney, an ebullient Hawke sought assurances of support from the leaders of the New South Wales Right. He wanted to seize the moment and challenge Hayden at a time when caucus members were having renewed doubts about their leader's ability to guarantee victory. Hayden's deputy, Lionel Bowen, wasn't willing to give Hawke his vote, but did concede that Hayden had little hope of winning the next election. That was good enough for Hawke.[37] It reinforced the argument that he'd been making ever since he'd entered parliament, which was calculated to appeal to those party pragmatists who might be persuaded to abandon Haydon if they thought it was the only way to ensure a Labor government after more than seven years in opposition.

Hawke hoped that the party president, Neville Wran, would support him, but Wran was noncommittal. Wran, too, was being urged by Peter Abeles to set his sights on Canberra. The powerful New South Wales secretary, Graham Richardson, was more supportive of Hawke. He and Hawke had been close ever since a young Richardson had driven Hawke around Sydney and its surrounds during the 1972 election campaign. He believed Hawke was destined for the leadership, and that Hayden would have to be toppled before the election.[38]

However, in a meeting at the Boulevard Hotel on 25 June, Richardson counselled an excited Hawke against moving just yet. Although Hawke claimed to have the solid support of Victoria's Centre Unity faction, Richardson couldn't guarantee that the New South Wales Right would fall in behind Hawke. For that, Keating would be key. He was the New South Wales state president, had been in parliament for thirteen years and was still backing Hayden when the state Labor conference met at the end of June in Sydney Town Hall. Keating regarded Hawke as a 'show pony' and a Johnny-come-lately who hadn't proved himself in parliament. It was Keating who introduced Hayden to the delegates, describing him as 'a leader of courage and determination, a man of integrity and principle'. Keating was just as hungry as Hawke for the prime ministership, and calculated that he would be better placed to follow Hayden rather than wait in line for both Hayden and Hawke to run their separate political races.[39]

No matter, thought Hawke; he would bring the majority of caucus on board by mounting the challenge regardless. His chest-beating hunger for the leadership would be there for all to see, and caucus would realise that the consequent turmoil within the party could only be settled by appeasing Hawke. He was buoyed by a radio interview Clyde Cameron gave on 29 June. Cameron was no friend of Hawke's, but now called on the party to 'face facts' and acknowledge that Labor 'would romp home with Hawke as leader'. He wanted caucus to make Hawke leader before Fraser could catch the party 'with its pants down with a leader that can't win enough public support to take us to victory'. Hawke was also mindful of this. His plan was to mount a challenge in early August, after the party's national conference in early July and before the federal budget was brought down in mid-August, as he believed Fraser would want the budget out of the way before calling an election.[40]

Ironically, it was Hayden who gave further impetus to Hawke's campaign. He wanted to go into the election campaign with policies on uranium mining and capital gains tax that couldn't feed a fear campaign by Fraser. With Hayden's support, the previous party conference had defeated Hawke's attempt to allow uranium mining and instructed a future Labor government to tear up any export contracts, hoping that the policy would deter the establishment of new mines. It hadn't worked. The mines had been developed anyway.

Hayden now wanted to allow existing mines to go ahead. Hawke was agreeable, as were Richardson and Keating. But parts of the Left, who'd been supporting Hayden, were outraged. The emotional Tom Uren, a former prize fighter, was particularly passionate about the issue, having witnessed the results of the atomic bombs in Japan, and decided that he could no longer trust Hayden. In a phone call to Hawke, he confided that he would now back him for the leadership. Uren hadn't consulted his colleagues before making his commitment, and many of the Left didn't share his new-found enthusiasm for Hawke.[41]

Although the national conference, held at the Lakeside Hotel in Canberra, supported a triumphant Hayden on both uranium mining and the capital gains tax, it was clear that the political ground was shifting beneath his feet. With unfortunate timing, a *Bulletin* poll published on 7 July, in the middle of the conference, revealed a big jump in Fraser's popularity and a slump in Hayden's. A beaming Hawke basked under the television lights in the hotel foyer as journalists asked about the poll, while Hayden was warned by his press secretary, Alan Ramsey, that he was 'bleeding to death'.[42] If he was going to staunch the bleeding, Hayden would have to confront his challenger before Hawke's campaign gathered more momentum.

Hayden struck the very next day, crossing the conference hall to inform Hawke, who was about to make a speech on industrial relations, that he was calling a special caucus meeting for eight days hence to decide the leadership. Hayden told the media that he was determined to put an end to the 'deliberate campaign' that was 'doing serious damage to the morale and credibility of the party'. Hayden had to hope that his cocky challenger wouldn't have time to lock in sufficient votes.[43]

While Bill Landeryou and Hawke's other supporters in Victoria's Centre Unity faction hit the phones in Melbourne, Hawke flew to Sydney. Operating out of the familiar surrounds of the Boulevard Hotel, Hawke had an impossible task. The fear of Fraser calling an early election, coupled with the encouragement of Uren, had caused him to go too early against Hayden, who'd hunkered down in the Opposition leader's Sydney office. As Labor MPs tore open urgent telegrams from the caucus chairman, Dr Harry Jenkins, which notified them of a special meeting in the parliamentary party room on 16 July to resolve 'the gravely destabilising speculation which is damaging the morale and credibility of the party', Hawke scribbled down a list of his likely supporters within the caucus, and focused his phone calls on those waverers who might be swayed to join his side. His list showed him falling just short of a majority.[44] Hayden had caught him on the hop. Hawke would have been better placed if he'd been able to stick to his mid-August timetable, which might have allowed two more *Bulletin* polls to erode Hayden's support even further. He pressed on regardless, hopeful that his fellow MPs would realise that the best chance of securing a Labor government was by electing him as leader.

Keating would later say that he couldn't believe Hawke's stupidity in launching a challenge 'that he couldn't complete', describing it as an 'ill-conceived, ill-timed, ill-thought-through, ill-advised operation'. But the self-confident Hawke couldn't imagine the caucus continuing to support Hayden, which would mean further instability and the likelihood of Labor losing the next election. As he told the media, he wasn't standing on policy issues, since he didn't have any big differences with Hayden, but simply on his 'record as a communicator and persuader'.[45]

Hawke's victory would depend upon the Left voting as a bloc with Uren, and the New South Wales Right switching from Hayden to Hawke. The prospects didn't look good. The Left was divided, as was the New South Wales Right. Keating was conflicted. He had a sense of loyalty to Hayden and doubted Hawke's fitness to be prime minister. Moreover, his own interests would be best served by Hayden decisively defeating Hawke and going on to win the election. Keating's initial refusal to support Hawke caused the challenger to return to Melbourne, now disconsolate about his chances. *Age* journalist Michael Gawenda accompanied him to the airport, describing how Hawke 'sat low in his seat, his head on his chest, his overcoat collar drawn up around his ears', the windscreen wipers providing the only sound.[46]

Even if Hawke failed to win a majority, he needed to come close if he was going to have any hope of mounting a follow-up challenge prior to the election. Hayden had the harder task. Although he had the support of most of the media, he needed a decisive victory to secure his leadership from a second challenge.

It wasn't just Labor MPs or party members who were drawn into Hayden's campaign. In a desperate attempt to beef up the numbers, two powerful trade unionists made a public appeal for the Left faction to support Hayden. One was the leader of the manufacturing workers, Laurie Carmichael, and the other was John Halfpenny of the engineering union. Carmichael was a member of the Communist Party, while Halfpenny was a former member who'd just joined the ALP.

It was an ill-judged intervention. The Catholic Keating had begun his political life during the Labor split of the 1950s, when the Cold War caused a bitter schism between the communist and non-communist sections of the labour movement. As such, Carmichael's support for Hayden provoked a visceral reaction from Keating and the New South Wales Right, causing them to switch their support to Hawke. It may not have been Keating's preferred outcome, but it would help to preserve the relative unity of his power base.

After being a roadblock on Hawke's path to the prime ministership, Keating was now waving him on. At a meeting in Hawke's suite at the Boulevard Hotel, Keating gave in to pressure from his factional allies, conscious that his leadership of the faction and his chances of one day becoming prime minister would otherwise be imperilled. With Keating finally in the bag, Hawke believed he had it won.[47]

CHAPTER THREE

# 1982–1983

When caucus gathered at Parliament House on 16 July to decide the party leadership, Hayden moved straight to a vote. Doing so avoided the risk of a debate, which could have allowed the confident Hawke another chance to demonstrate his communication skills, and caused the self-doubting Hayden to display his often convoluted speaking style. It was best for Hayden to let Labor MPs dwell on the thought of dumping a leader who'd recently led them to the cusp of victory.

Hawke had claimed that the calling of the meeting was due to the constant media speculation, which had to be laid to rest, rather than to any campaign of destabilisation by him. It was the journalists who had been reacting to the polls and he had just been answering their questions, claimed Hawke. It was only Hayden's calling of the meeting that forced him to declare himself as a challenger. And he was only doing it so that the party would maximise its chances of winning the forthcoming election, assuring colleagues that there would be no blood-letting in their ranks if he became leader and that Hayden would be 'an extremely valuable member' of a Hawke-led government.[1]

Hawke called his father, Clem, on the morning of the vote to assure him that he had the numbers. However, when the votes were tallied, sufficient MPs had baulked at the thought of toppling their leader, or had harboured reservations about Hawke, to give Hayden a narrow victory, forty-two votes to thirty-seven. Some of Hawke's doubters may have been made uneasy by the stories in the Fairfax-owned *National Times* of Hawke's links with businessmen like Abeles and by questions about the free accommodation he'd long been receiving at the Boulevard Hotel.[2]

Despite those stories, and the questions they raised about Hawke's probity, he'd come close to toppling Hayden, whose winning majority needed to be bigger if he was to be safe from Hawke. 'He'll be back someday,' predicted Clem. One of Hayden's core supporters, the impish John Button, had told Hayden as much as they went into the meeting. Despite the celebratory champagne and victory cake in his office, Hayden later conceded that he 'was not far enough ahead of the pack to cause them to lose interest in their quarry'.[3]

Hawke also knew it. At a joint news conference, he went through the motions of expressing support for the victor, only for Hayden's face to fall as Hawke refused to say that his leadership aspirations were at an end. Later, Button had an encounter with Hawke in a toilet of the parliamentary offices in Sydney, where he implied that Hawke would receive his support if he mounted another challenge. Hawke was also urged on by Richardson, who rang Hawke in Melbourne while he was having a council of war with several supporters in the kitchen of his lawyer, party official Peter Redlich.[4] It wouldn't be as simple as Richardson imagined, but Hawke was very much seen as the coming man. Which is why another aspiring leader sought him out.

Several weeks after he'd lost his challenge against Hayden, a bright-eyed Tony Blair, who was still a year away from being elected as a backbencher to the British House of Commons, called on Hawke. It was a meeting of minds, as Blair sought to understand how democratic socialist parties could find a path to power in a Western world that was now dominated by the politics of Reagan and Thatcher. With the ALP seemingly on the cusp of being returned to power after an eight-year hiatus, Hawke was happy to preach his gospel of political pragmatism to the 29-year-old barrister, and to have him meet with several like-minded Labor officials. In an appreciative letter sent to Hawke after his return to London, Blair said he was 'particularly impressed' with the Victorian ALP secretary, the left-wing Bob Hogg, who 'encapsulated very well the pragmatic sense of the ALP at the present time'. He could only wish that the British party would 'appreciate that passing resolutions is not the same as taking and wielding power and that the people we want to represent are only helped by the latter'.[5] It would not be the last lesson that Blair learned from Hawke, who was achingly close to taking and wielding power in Australia, from which he was not going to be distracted.

It was during his campaign for the leadership that Hawke was told by his daughter Rosslyn the shocking news that she'd been raped three times by Bill Landeryou and feared she was pregnant. Rosslyn was twenty-one and had been working in Landeryou's Melbourne office after Hawke had asked the Labor powerbroker and staunch supporter to provide her with employment in the hope of distancing her from the Sydney drug culture into which she'd become immersed. It's not clear when Hawke first heard of this, but the sparse entries in Hazel's diary suggest that she might have been alerted on her return from New York at the end of June: she referred to the 'leadership momentum' and linked it to 'Roz problem re work'. She noted that Rosslyn had apparently talked to Hawke about an abortion.[6]

By 12 July, Rosslyn had taken leave from Landeryou's office to spend a week working on Hawke's 'leadership challenge', with Hazel noting a few days later that Rosslyn had had a period and was likely not pregnant. On 16 August, Hazel returned from Perth to a 'message re Roz – threat to Bob', with Rosslyn appearing 'confused'. A few days later, a doctor was arranged to see Rosslyn in the seaside resort of Lorne, where she'd gone to stay; she then drove alone to Sydney on 23 August. Hazel met her there a week later, taking Rosslyn to Katoomba for a few days, before they were joined in Sydney by Sue. After a dinner with her daughters on 8 September, Hazel noted that Rosslyn was 'quiet, sad'.[7]

The news of the alleged assault couldn't have come at a worse time for Hawke, who was dependent on Landeryou as one of his key numbers men. According to Rosslyn, her father told her: 'I can't have any controversies right now. I am sorry but I am challenging for the leadership of the Labor Party. You can't go to the police.' It could have upset everything. Landeryou would have been sure to deny the allegation and likely change from being a staunch supporter of Hawke to being an opponent. That could have tipped the balance against Hawke becoming Labor leader prior to the upcoming election, which could cruel his chances for all time. He'd always been close to Rosslyn and she succumbed to his pressure, later saying, 'I did so for him.'[8]

In convincing his daughter not to complain to the police, Hawke would have doubtless consoled himself that he was also protecting her, since any prosecution would have seen her sexual history and heroin use become the stuff of lurid headlines at a time when rapists were rarely convicted and when their victims usually suffered a second assault at the hands of defence counsel. Although she'd agreed to remain silent, Rosslyn's allegations cast a pall over the family and Hawke's campaign – which was only deepened by the publication of D'Alpuget's biography.

The book created a sensation. Although not appearing in bookshops until 5 October 1982, it was serialised beforehand for seven days in the Fairfax press, accompanied by a flurry of news stories, along with radio and television appearances by D'Alpuget. On 21 September, *The Bulletin* devoted more than three pages to the biography. Penned by Bob Carr, the review traversed Hawke's well-known strengths and weaknesses (although there was no mention of his womanising), and recounted Carr's occasional interactions with him.[9] Carr had been pushing Keating's claim to be the next Labor leader and he wasn't ready to switch sides.

While Carr was full of praise for D'Alpuget's 'very fine Australian biography, easily one of the best', he remained equivocal about Hawke as a possible prime minister. He noted that Hawke's supporters pointed to his popularity, his ability to build 'national unity and consensus' and his 'distinctive Australian quality', while his detractors claimed he was 'unstable and emotional', lacking in 'intellectual depth' and a 'bad administrator and hence [would be] a bad Prime Minister'.[10] While Carr's review failed to make a conclusive judgement about Hawke, many readers of the biography would finish the book with a feeling that they now knew and understood him. Whether or not they liked the figure D'Alpuget depicted, only time would tell.

There was a fevered nature to the media attention about a biography of a man who was widely seen as a soon-to-be prime minister. Much of the attention was focused on the accounts of his drinking and womanising, although D'Alpuget had been careful not to include anything that was 'likely to be misused by his enemies'. And when she was asked by the ABC's Geraldine Doogue about Hawke's 'screwing around', she assured the huge audience of ABC's *Nationwide* that 'he's got a lot of fidelity in the emotional sense' – which presumably meant that his philandering and love for other women didn't stop him from also loving Hazel.[11]

Hazel would have been hard-pressed to agree about her husband's fidelity, and the publication of the book tested their relationship anew. After spending time with Rosslyn in Sydney, she returned to Melbourne as the media interest in the biography was gathering momentum. She wrote in her diary how she met Bob for dinner and a film, during which she 'blasted him re Bl[anche] d'A[lpuget]'. The following day, she described how 'Bob thanked me for coping with [the] book but qualified it.'[12] Ironically, the public reception to D'Alpuget's book could determine whether their fractured marital relationship might be refashioned into a workable partnership based on Hawke becoming prime minister.

Hawke had taken a big risk by resigning from the ACTU presidency and going into parliament. Agreeing to a supposedly warts-and-all biography was arguably a bigger risk, which could have seen his political star crash and burn if the revelations of his antics and his friendships with millionaires prompted readers to take a negative view of the aspiring prime minister. The fact that the biography was written by an excellent writer who also happened to be his lover, and that it was vetted by him and Hazel, would have given him some confidence about its likely reception. Moreover, as a narcissist, he expected to be forgiven and embraced whatever he did. After all, his outrageous behaviour under the influence of alcohol had usually been excused by those who'd witnessed or been subject to it. He also would have been reassured by his long experience of revealing his foibles in the media, and even of weeping in parliament, without it affecting his poll ratings.

During the launch of the book at the Lakeside Hotel in Canberra on 5 October – with Hazel notably absent – Hawke and D'Alpuget talked about their reason for exposing so much of him, with Hawke conceding that 'the writing of the book, its publication and some of the reviews had hurt him and his wife and family, and he was sorry about that'. D'Alpuget said that she and Hawke had wanted Australians 'to make judgments, not guesses, about their political leaders'.[13]

Hawke had invited his parliamentary colleagues to the launch, along with about twenty of his closest friends, party officials and some of his former associates from the ACTU. They included Peter Abeles, Eddie Kornhauser, Isi Leibler and David Combe, the former national secretary of the Labor Party. Also on the short list of invited guests was Hawke's numbers man, Bill Landeryou, although it was only weeks since Ros had confided her account of being raped by him.[14]

The pair would have been encouraged when they opened *The Canberra Times* to read the page-two headline describing the book as a 'warts-and-all portrayal of a man who "could make a good PM"'. No prospective leader had ever been so exposed, Hawke would later remark, noting that now no one would 'be able really to worry me by attempting to rattle skeletons'. The headline drew readers to a timely review by former politician Jim Cairns, whose love life was almost as colourful as Hawke's. He lauded D'Alpuget as 'a biographer of extraordinary capacity' and dismissed the supposed 'warts' in the book as mere 'dimples' that would not prevent Hawke becoming 'a good and successful Prime Minister'. To Hawke and D'Alpuget's relief, most of the other reviews, news stories and interviews were of a similar ilk, and the relatively expensive book sold well in the lead-up to Christmas, as the leadership contest also gathered pace.[15]

The vote in July had left the caucus bitterly divided and provided an ideal opportunity for Fraser to catch Hayden off-guard with an early election, before Hawke had a chance to re-group and bring on another challenge. Fortunately for Hawke, Fraser was thwarted by the release in September of an interim royal commission report that exposed widespread tax evasion by wealthy shysters who'd been exploiting loopholes in the law. Fraser had wanted the royal commissioner, Frank Costigan, to concentrate his inquiry on the Federated Ship Painters and Dockers Union, which counted some of Australia's most notorious criminals among its members, as a way of discrediting the Labor Party. The interim report certainly found serious criminality, including murder, by union members, but the headlines were reserved for the so-called bottom-of-the-harbour schemes, in which union members were involved but that were set up to strip thousands of companies of their assets in order to avoid tax. The beneficiaries were wealthy company owners who were largely supporters of the Liberal Party. It seemed that the Fraser government had allowed such corruption to become endemic.[16]

Hayden sought to inoculate the Labor Party from the Costigan report by disaffiliating the Painters and Dockers, which would allow public attention to be focused on the Liberal links with prominent tax avoiders. The report was such an embarrassment for the government that an early election would not be feasible until the stink had subsided. With the Liberal Party organisation urging him to wait until 1983, when he might be able to go to the voters with a campaign based upon falling unemployment and inflation, Fraser had to hope that Hayden would remain Labor leader until then.[17] If Hawke looked like mounting another challenge, Fraser would have the option of pulling the election trigger before Hawke could complete his move. It was a high-risk game that all three politicians were playing.

As always with Hawke, luck continued to play a role. Hayden, in particular, needed everything to go his way to keep Hawke at bay. A by-election in the Victorian seat of Flinders on 4 December 1982 could have reinforced his position by again demonstrating his vote-winning ability and confirming that Labor really was on track to win the next federal election. The omens seemed promising. A state election in South Australia on 6 November, in which Hawke had campaigned, had seen the Liberal government of David Tonkin toppled by Labor's John Bannon with a swing of 5.9 per cent.[18] A swing of the same magnitude in Flinders would deliver the seat to Labor.

It wasn't in Hawke's interest for Hayden to have a thumping victory. Rather than throwing himself into the campaign, as he had in South Australia, Hawke went on ABC radio at the very beginning of the campaign to raise questions about Hayden's leadership. He was interviewed by Michael Schildberger, whose midday radio program often featured Hawke. Although Labor was ahead by a couple of percentage points in the opinion polls, Hawke suggested to Schildberger they should be much further ahead, and it wasn't sufficient to guarantee victory at the federal election, particularly when Hayden's personal approval rating remained dismal.[19]

Although Hawke had been singing this refrain for years, mostly privately but sometimes publicly, his comments sparked a frenzy of media speculation that threatened to cruel Labor's chances, not just in the by-election but also in the federal election. While Hawke's intervention might have had the desired effect of raising questions about Hayden in the minds of swinging voters, it caused outrage among many of his parliamentary colleagues, who'd taken Hawke at his word about not mounting another challenge. With Hayden now accusing him publicly of destabilising the party, Hawke was forced by his leading supporters, Gareth Evans and Clyde Holding, to write a conciliatory letter to caucus members in which he promised to stand by his commitment not to mount another challenge prior to the federal election. Moreover, he promised to work alongside Hayden 'to play a major role in ensuring a decisive victory for the party in the Flinders by-election'.[20] That way, if a decisive victory was achieved, he could claim to have been instrumental in achieving it. Of course, if victory wasn't achieved, it would be Hayden's fault.

The electorate of Flinders is a mix of urban and rural areas on the Mornington Peninsula. Although normally held by the conservatives, it was the site of a historic Labor victory when the incumbent member, Prime Minister Stanley Melbourne Bruce, was defeated in 1929 by the Labor candidate, leading trade unionist Jack Holloway. It was now up for grabs again after former treasurer Sir Phillip Lynch had been dumped as deputy Liberal leader by Fraser in favour of John Howard – only for Lynch, who was suffering from bowel cancer, to repay the compliment by resigning from parliament and forcing an unwelcome by-election for his seat. The outcome of the Flinders by-election could determine who the prime minister was going to be after the next election – Fraser, Hayden or Hawke.

With unemployment peaking and Fraser bedridden for weeks after a back operation, it was looking good for Hayden. The Liberals fielded a 32-year-old solicitor, Peter Reith, as their candidate, despite him not living in the electorate, while Labor put forward a local real estate agent, Rogan Ward, who'd served briefly as the mayor of Frankston, the major centre on the northern edge of the electorate. With the sniff of victory in its nostrils, Labor mounted a major effort to enlist support for its 39-year-old candidate, who was photographed alongside his attractive wife, Diana. However, for all his local links, the diminutive Ward wasn't the ideal candidate. Button later described him as 'an almost impossible candidate to sell', as he had 'the style and reputation of a used car salesman'. Ward had been selected prior to Lynch's resignation, when it was expected that he would be representing Labor at the federal election in a seat that he had little chance of winning. Lynch's resignation changed the party's calculations, since such contests usually attracted an average swing of

5.5 per cent against the government, which would be sufficient to give Labor the seat.²¹

With so much riding on the result, Hayden might have emulated Whitlam's unstinting effort in the Corio by-election of 1967. However, the besieged leader would be operating in Hawke's backyard, with bayside Frankston just 30 kilometres south of his Sandringham home. Rather than mounting a powerful campaign, Hayden turned up at the campaign launch on 14 November without a set speech. With Hawke and other Labor luminaries in the front row, Hayden gave a long-winded talk that left the gaggle of bemused journalists without a hook on which to hang their stories. When he returned for another attempt later in the campaign, the media were assured that, this time, he would be reading from notes.

The lack of carefully crafted speeches wasn't Hayden's only problem. He simply didn't put in the effort that was required to win a by-election that could make or break his leadership. Rather than basing himself in the electorate, as Whitlam had done in Corio, he flew in by helicopter for a factory-gate meeting and a business lunch in Frankston, then disappeared into the sky again. Hawke spent more time there. Along with parliamentary colleagues, but not Hayden, he headed to an oval in Rye on 21 November for a Sunday-morning cricket match between MPs and a team of local party members, led by Ward. Taking up the bat, Hawke wasn't troubled by Ward's bowling, scoring 25 not out, only to see the local team win by eight runs. After a barbecue, Hawke joined hundreds of party members in a massive doorknock of the electorate. At every appearance, Hawke was pestered by journalists about whether he was planning another leadership challenge. Each time, he waved them off with a denial. Few were fooled. It would all depend on the by-election result.²²

There was no joy for Hayden from the voters of Flinders, who effectively gave his leadership the thumbs-down. The final days of the campaign had been disastrous, as Hayden failed to reach agreement with the ACTU on a prices and incomes accord, while Rogan Ward was accused by *The Age* of sharp practice as a real estate agent and had his behaviour on the local council criticised by five former mayors. Despite national opinion polls showing a big swing to Labor, and predictions by both sides that the result would be tight, the swing to Labor was only 2.3 per cent, which meant Reith was elected comfortably.

Not surprisingly, the result sparked a flurry of leadership speculation, which Hayden tried to dispel by calling a meeting in Canberra of the party's leadership group, including Hawke, Button, Willis and Keating, to review the campaign. While Hawke said he was 'puzzled and disappointed' by the Flinders result, Hayden pointedly told journalists that the party didn't need to abandon its policies and turn to 'charismatic personalities at the top'. But the national opinion polls had also shown a Liberal resurgence. Again, Fraser could have seized the moment, but he was in no condition to fight a federal election. It would have to wait until the new year, after Fraser had left his Melbourne hospital, with the media predicting that a March election was the most likely.[23]

The brief delay took the pressure off Hawke, who could postpone another divisive challenge in the hope that the wavering MPs in caucus would see that he was their best chance of victory and elevation to the government benches. With polls showing that only a bare majority of Labor voters approved of Hayden as Opposition leader, and with psephologist Malcolm Mackerras predicting that 'Australia's next Labor Prime Minister will be Bob Hawke', Hawke had more reasons to hope that Hayden's supporters would convince him to step down. That would allow Hawke to avoid another challenge and be ushered unanimously into the Labor leadership. It was how he'd always expected to realise his life's destiny, with the acclamation of the Australian people at a federal election following in natural succession the acclamation of the caucus.[24] After all, he wanted as prime minister to bring Australians together. It wouldn't be a good beginning to have the party presenting a picture of disunity in the lead-up to the election.

Hawke knew that gaining the support of John Button would be crucial in convincing Hayden to step down. Button was one of the leading members of the Independents faction and prided himself on being principled but pragmatic. His loyalty to Hayden and his reservations about Hawke had kept him in the former's camp during the first challenge in July. After the Flinders by-election and more evidence from the opinion polls confirming Hawke's popularity, Button's pragmatism came to the fore. Anxious not to see blood on the caucus floor, Button began a quiet campaign to convince the reclusive Hayden to resign. Before heading to Fiji for a Christmas holiday, Button confided to members of the New South Wales Right that he would reconsider his support for Hayden while he was away. Anxious to maintain pressure on Hayden, Richardson told a journalist about Button's attitude, which produced the hoped-for headlines about Hayden losing crucial support.[25]

Realising that his opponents wanted to avoid a frontal attack, Hayden proved hard to convince that his leadership had to end for the good of the party and its millions of supporters. In letters and meetings, Button struggled to make any headway with him. In a meeting over lunch at a Brisbane restaurant on 6 January 1983, Button listened with incredulity as the embattled leader compared himself to Macbeth. Like Macbeth, said Hayden, he wouldn't ask for mercy if he lost the federal election. Such throwaway lines in which he foreshadowed losing the election helped to condemn him in the eyes of Button and a growing number of MPs. And even if Hayden won against the odds, Button had become doubtful whether he 'would be a good prime minister'.[26] Such doubts tipped the balance in Hawke's favour.

On 13 January, in an act of desperation, Hayden tried to avert the inevitable by dumping Ralph Willis as shadow treasurer and appointing Keating in his place, hoping that this would secure the support of the New South Wales Right. At first, Keating was reluctant, after having spent years mastering the minerals and energy portfolio and being averse to usurping Willis. But he couldn't afford to spurn such an important promotion. The move didn't have the desired effect for Hayden. It was too late: most of the faction were firmly and irrevocably in the Hawke camp. With Richardson as its backroom Svengali, the faction had for months been intent on undermining Hayden and replacing him with Hawke. Yet Hawke was still rattled by Hayden's appointment of Keating, fearing the last-ditch move might slow the momentum that was building against Hayden. When phoned by Keating, he shouted in exasperation: 'He's fucked us all. He's fucked you by giving you the job. He's fucked Ralph and he's fucked me.'[27]

But Hawke was far from done. Hayden had been planning to go to the election with a campaign based on the themes of 'Reconstruction and Recovery', in which a prices and incomes accord with the trade unions would be a central plank. Fraser had been trying to circumvent these plans by proposing a six-month wages freeze. Hayden had opposed this but the ACTU had expressed its support – only to then oppose it when Hayden changed his position and expressed support. Hayden's planned accord with the trade unions was blocked by Hawke, who used his influence with the new ACTU president, Cliff Dolan, to kill the proposal for so long as Hayden remained leader. Despite a desperate meeting with Dolan at Sydney's Trades Hall, Hayden was unable to reverse the decision by Hawke's acolytes. The knives were out. Hayden couldn't survive, let alone win the election, without the support of the union movement.[28]

Lying back in his skimpy bathers on his sun lounge beside the pool at his Sandringham home, a supremely confident Hawke prepared to meet Button and his colleague Michael Duffy on 16 January. Like a pope receiving a supplicant priest, Hawke was happy to give Button his benediction. Hayden hadn't yet signed his resignation letter, but he had acknowledged that he was a dead man walking by seeking assurances from Hawke that no retribution would be sought against his closest supporters. While Hawke lay back and rubbed suntan lotion over his body until 'he glistened like a turkey gobbler about to go into the oven', Button sought a similar assurance about Hayden, which Hawke willingly gave, declaring that 'there is not a vindictive bone in my body'. Button felt that some of his political opponents would have testified otherwise, but he 'couldn't help but admire Hawke's capacity to stand back, look at himself and like what he saw'.[29]

Although he was amused by Hawke's self-delusions, Button also liked what he saw: an election-winner who had a unique capacity to connect with the Australian people and no doubts about his own leadership abilities. Moreover, he had a palpable hunger for the prime ministership that couldn't be gainsaid. That was always an advantage in an election.

The only person now standing in Hawke's way was the wavering Hayden, who was miserable at the idea of losing the leadership on the cusp of an election. He told everyone that the poll was months away, perhaps hoping that Fraser would call a snap election before parliament resumed in February and the caucus had a chance to convene. That could see Hayden remain as leader for the election and frustrate Hawke's climb to the top. Hawke could not allow that to happen.

CHAPTER FOUR

# 1983

Labor's failure to win the Flinders by-election had doomed Bill Hayden's leadership. All that was needed was someone to play the part of Brutus while Hawke remained in the shadows.

John Button had been one of Hayden's most loyal supporters, and had felt a personal debt when Hayden and his wife had flown to Melbourne for the funeral of one of Button's sons, who'd died of a heroin overdose. In the end, his loyalty to the party leader was trumped by his loyalty to the party. For several months, he'd been under pressure from colleagues and party apparatchiks, who realised he would be key to convincing Hayden to accept his fate. Without a strong factional base in Victoria to secure his position on the Senate ticket, Button was vulnerable. He was warned by Richardson that he would be blamed by the party faithful for Labor's loss if he helped shore up Hayden's position. It was made clear to him that he would kill his political career and doom Labor's election chances if he didn't shift his support to Hawke.[1]

Having been a witness to Hawke's drunken behaviour for more than twenty years, Button had serious doubts about his suitability for becoming prime minister. On the other hand, he was increasingly doubtful about the depressive Hayden's ability to lead Labor to victory. On 28 January, he put those doubts in a letter to Hayden, bluntly telling him that 'you cannot win the next election', 'your performance as party leader has declined considerably' and you will lose the 'respect and affection' of your colleagues if you refuse to step down. Button reminded Hayden how he'd once declared that he wouldn't step down for 'a "bastard" like Bob Hawke', but pointed out that being 'a bastard (of one kind or another) has never been a disqualification for leadership of the party', and that they all had a bit of bastard in them.[2]

While Button wrestled with his conflicting loyalties to his leader and his party, Hawke remained confident that his opponents in caucus would put aside their reservations as the election loomed closer. Despite Labor's winning position in the opinion polls, Fraser had always enjoyed a strong lead over Hayden as preferred prime minister. It was a harsh truth, but a truth nonetheless, that Labor's lead was lower than it should have been because Hayden was leader. As Hawke never tired of saying, only he could ensure that Labor would win the election. Button's defection indicated that a majority of the caucus now agreed with him.

Yet Hayden remained desperate to hold on. On 1 February, when Button was in Brisbane for the funeral of former Labor prime minister Frank Forde, an exhausted Hayden tried to convince Button to change his mind. As they sat through the service, Hayden had more than an inkling that his own leadership might also be buried that day.

After the funeral, the meeting between the pair dragged on for more than two hours, with Button remaining adamant that Hayden had to step down. At first, Hayden refused to do so. He was demoralised and wallowing in self-pity when he made this half-hearted attempt to hold on, pointing in vain to the party's lead in the opinion polls. Button lunged in to deliver the coup de grâce, telling his morose leader that an opinion poll about to be published in *The Bulletin* would reveal a slump in the party's figures. In fact, when the poll was published, it would show Labor's vote up by 5 per cent, while 50 per cent of respondents (up by 6 per cent from November) thought Fraser would be the better prime minister, compared to just 33 per cent support (down by 5 per cent) for Hayden. Taking Button at his word about the poll, Hayden realised there was no coming back. Defeated and dejected, and with both men reduced to weeping, he turned his mind to the terms of his surrender, asking that he be given until the weekend to resign.[3] Events would prevent even that small concession being allowed him.

A desperate Malcolm Fraser had by now been discharged from hospital, and was looking for any sign that Hawke was about to swoop on Hayden. If Fraser was going to hold on to the prime ministership, he had to move before Hawke. When rumours reached him that

Hayden was going to resign within days, Fraser decided to strike first by asking the governor-general to call an early election, in the hope that this would lock Hayden in as his opponent. One of the people who reportedly called Fraser during these climactic days was Tom Uren, who wanted to head off Hawke's challenge.

Made confident by all this incoming intelligence, Fraser timed his move for the morning of Thursday, 3 February, when Labor's shadow cabinet was due to meet in Brisbane to finalise its plans for the opening of parliament the following week. Fraser was conscious that the Labor caucus would have to approve any change of leader, which could only be done when MPs returned to Canberra the following Monday.

On the surface, it was a brilliant plan, designed to unfold just as Hayden was chairing the shadow cabinet meeting in Brisbane's Commonwealth Government Offices. Once the political bombshell was detonated in Canberra, Fraser imagined, there would be confusion and consternation among the Labor leadership in Brisbane. Although he couldn't be certain how they would react, Fraser expected that his move would impel Hayden to fight the election as leader. Alternatively, it could cause Hawke to accelerate his plan to force Hayden out, which would create an unfortunate hiatus for Labor of several vital days before its caucus could anoint Hawke as leader. Fraser hoped this would allow the Liberals to seize the initiative in the election campaign, but also that Labor would be seen by voters as divided and in disarray.[4] Events did not unfold in the way he anticipated.

Labor had been on alert for any sign that Fraser was about to call an early election. Hayden had been involved in three straight election defeats since 1975, including one as leader, and he didn't want to lead Labor to another. As it became clear from media reports that an election was about to be called, he brought forward his planned resignation. Rather than waiting for the weekend, he resolved to pre-empt Fraser by announcing it to the shadow cabinet on the Thursday morning so that he couldn't be depicted as running from an electoral contest.

Hayden kept to that commitment even after receiving an early-morning phone call from journalist Laurie Oakes warning him that Fraser was intent on calling the election within hours. Had he reneged on his planned resignation, he would have remained as leader and might have won the ensuing election and become prime minister. But he recalled the advice of his mother to 'never hang around where you're not wanted'. If Hayden resigned at the shadow cabinet meeting, Hawke could be anointed immediately by the leadership group and then have the decision rubber-stamped by caucus the following Monday. This would avoid the possibility, long feared by Hawke, of rejection by caucus.[5] Once again, his luck was holding.

After meeting beforehand with Button to confirm his decision, Hayden began the shadow cabinet meeting as normal on the Thursday morning. Everyone around the table knew Hayden's leadership was under threat, but few knew it was his last day as leader. Even Keating was unaware until Hawke whispered to him, 'He's quitting today' – although Hawke couldn't be certain that Hayden would follow through with the promised resignation. He had to watch po-faced as Hayden worked his way down the prepared agenda, before using the mid-morning break to take the lift to his twelfth-storey office, where Hawke joined him along with Button and Lionel Bowen. The four men were going to hammer out the details of the handover. Many were already understood, having been agreed to by Hawke in his poolside meeting with Button. It was now time for them to be formally stated by Hayden and agreed in front of witnesses.[6]

After holding Hawke off for two years, Hayden was ready to retrieve what he could from the wreckage of his leadership. The final details agreed to that morning, which were set down in writing, were about ensuring jobs for his staff and confirming that Hayden, rather than a bitterly disappointed Bowen, would be the minister for foreign affairs in a Hawke government. Hayden only wanted the job for a year, envisaging that he would then be appointed as Australia's high commissioner in London. Bowen reluctantly agreed, not wanting his ministerial ambition to be an impediment to the expected Labor victory.

Hayden could have forced Hawke to have another leadership vote by the caucus, in which both would be candidates, but the result would have been fresh humiliation for Hayden, and the intervening days of uncertainty would have produced images of Labor disunity that might fatally harm the party's electoral prospects. Hayden had been preparing for the 1983 election in the hope that he would be leading Labor to victory. It had been he who'd led the effort to rewrite policies and reorganise branches to make the post-Whitlam Labor Party fit for office. Now he would have to watch on as Hawke reaped the benefit of that work and occupied the office that was meant to be his.

At the end of their discussions, Hawke and Hayden stayed behind in the leader's office for a few minutes to absorb the impact of what they had just agreed. For their different reasons, both men wept, before a composed Hayden returned downstairs to announce his resignation. When he delivered the news to the shadow cabinet, Hawke recalled, there was 'exuberance' among Hawke's supporters, while Hayden's 'anguish and disappointment were palpable'. Although he was sensitive to Hayden's hurt, Hawke naturally shared the excitement of his supporters. 'It seemed a moment of destiny,' he later wrote, 'as if the whole of my life had been lived in anticipation of, and preparation for, that day.'[7] Which, of course, it had.

Paul Keating, meanwhile, had banked on Hayden winning the 1983 election, after which he had hoped to succeed him as prime minister. Now he watched as Hawke stepped into the leading role, taking some solace in the thought that he might succeed Hawke instead. Or not. Keating would later talk of his 'mixed feelings' that day, as he balanced his own political ambitions with thoughts 'about Bill losing his great shot at history'.[8]

The exuberance in the conference room was not just about Hawke's victory. As the shadow cabinet was meeting, frantic phone calls revealed Fraser's desperate attempt to pre-empt Hawke by having Governor-General Sir Ninian Stephen announce an early double-dissolution election. After racing to Government House just before lunchtime, Fraser was informed by Stephen that he would have to fulfil his pre-existing luncheon engagement with the Polish ambassador before considering Fraser's request. The prime minister, who had been planning a press conference at 1 p.m. to announce the election, now had to return to Parliament House and await the governor-general's pleasure. It was an exquisite irony, wrote Hawke, that after Fraser's manoeuvring to oust Whitlam in 1975 with the tacit connivance of Governor-General Sir John Kerr, now it was his turn to be foiled by the hesitancy of a governor-general. For his part, Stephen must have been mindful of the reputational damage Kerr had suffered.[9]

When Fraser finally heard from Government House at 3.30 p.m., it was a request from Stephen for Fraser to justify the request for an early election by assuring him that the parliament would be otherwise unworkable. Although parliament was far from deadlocked, Fraser's office drew up a new note with just such an assurance and sent the departmental secretary scurrying off to Government House. Well before then, Hawke and Hayden had appeared in Brisbane before a crush of journalists, photographers and cameramen. As a triumphant Hawke spoke of leading a government intent on 'national reconciliation', a stony-faced Hayden sat alongside, suppressing the bitter emotions that bubbled beneath his fixed demeanour.[10]

Hayden said he'd decided to step down for the good of the party, to end the picture of disunity created by their rivalry, which might otherwise see voters return Fraser to office. That might have been the news headline had Hayden not added that Labor didn't have to install Hawke to be certain of victory. With a flash of bitterness, he said that even a 'drover's dog could lead the Labor Party to victory'.[11]

Although Hayden's comment annoyed Hawke intensely when it was run on that night's television news, it was drowned out by the events that Hawke's ascendancy had unleashed. It was drowned out too by the exultation among the many members of the public who welcomed the change of leadership. Journalist Paul Kelly was with Hawke in Brisbane and described 'a mass of people surrounding him and ... women crying. They just wanted to touch him and they were weeping in the street.'[12]

The cameras had been packed away and the journalists rushed from the press conference in Brisbane long before Fraser was finally advised by Government House that his request had been granted: the election would be held on Saturday, 5 March 1983. It was after 5 p.m. when Fraser fronted the media in Canberra, barely in time for that night's television news. It made no difference whether Hawke or Hayden was the Labor leader, said Fraser, but few were fooled by his bravado. Not even his wife, Tamie, who recalled how she now 'knew Labor would win, hands down'. And not the recently installed treasurer, John Howard, who heard the news of Hawke's leadership coup while he was driving with his family to their beachside holiday, and now wondered whether it spelled the end of his tenure at the Treasury.[13]

While others in the government camp shared Howard's doubts, Fraser presented a picture of unruffled sanguinity. He was still basking in a brief burst of economic sunshine and enjoying a sudden boost in his poll numbers. Although Fraser had given some fleeting thought to dropping his request for an election, he'd come too far and would have been lampooned if he was seen as chickening out because Hawke was now his opponent. As it was, the cartoonists made fun anyway of a prime minister who'd boasted of catching Labor with its pants down, only to find himself with his political pants around his ankles. Facing a fight with the former trade union leader, Fraser decided to make industrial relations the core of his four-week campaign. This was another serious error, as it made Hawke's embrace of 'reconciliation' even more appealing to voters. After years of Australians being set against one another and the government picking fights with the union movement, Hawke was able to promise voters something simple and alluring: peace.[14]

The publication of D'Alpuget's biography had helped to secure Hawke the leadership by laying out his life story for all the country to read, thereby neutralising accusations that might otherwise have been levelled against him. As Paul Kelly later observed, '[T]he book served Bob well because it revealed not all of his sins but a lot of his sins … and the entire purpose of the exercise of course was for him to seek absolution from the country. And I think they gave it to him.' With the election now having been called, the federal parliament was no longer sitting, which meant that government politicians couldn't claim parliamentary privilege when making accusations about his private life. Hawke might have been grateful to his biographer, but she was nowhere to be seen when he finally achieved the Labor leadership.

Neither was Hazel in Brisbane when Hawke was effectively anointed as Labor leader. She'd missed most of the discussions that had taken place at their Sandringham home, when Hawke's allies had gathered to talk about the next moves in their campaign to topple Hayden. The house had been unusually full that Christmas, as all three children and Ros's partner, Matt Dillon, gathered for the celebrations. Driven low by drugs, Ros had returned to live there and was out shopping with her mother and Hazel's close friend, Vera Wasowski, while the climactic events played out in Brisbane and Canberra. According to the memoir of the bemused Wasowski, 'Bob and Blanche have renewed their affair, and Hazel hears little of Bob's plans and progress: far less than Blanche.'[15]

Although Hazel knew that the decision could be made that day, it was only as she drove along Royal Avenue and saw the journalists and cameramen coming towards her car that she knew her life had taken a new turn. Talking to the journalists, Wasowski thought that Hazel 'wants to scream'. It would end the ordered existence she'd recently developed for herself. As Wasowski observed: 'Her marriage is held together (in a sense) by her loyalty to Bob's ambition, and now she has to spend the next so-many years smiling in public like a crazy person.' Hazel tried to track Hawke down to sort out what it would mean for her.[16]

For the last decade or so, Hazel had developed a life that had become increasingly separate from Hawke's. Her studies and her work had opened up a new world for her outside of the home and brought with it new friendships. As her relationship with Hawke deteriorated during the 1970s, she had often refused to accompany him to official events in his role as president of the ACTU and of the ALP. When she did go, it was usually grudgingly. Although she travelled with him on several overseas trips, these often involved her spending days by herself or taking off alone on long side trips. With Hawke away from home for days or weeks at a time, she also went with Wasowski and other friends to the theatre and concerts, and travelled alone to visit Stephen in the Pilbara and her daughters in Sydney. She'd baulked at the idea of going to cultural events alone, telling Wasowski that it would 'look pathetic [and] Bob would hate it'. So Wasowski often accompanied her. As she immersed herself in her studies, Hazel arranged to rent a studio at the house of a friend so she could be free of the interruptions and distractions and arguments that inevitably occurred in her own home. In the event, when Hawke gave up drinking, she found that she had less need of the studio. It was the garden of the Sandringham home that remained her sanctuary and in which she invested a lot of her time and creativity.[17]

Although Hazel had always encouraged Hawke to pursue his political ambitions, she'd become an increasingly distant observer of how events were playing out. 'The intricacies of the power struggle going on in the ALP largely passed me by,' she wrote of those final months before Hawke became leader. The emotional distance that had yawned between them as they discussed divorce, and as he dallied with the idea of marrying one or other of his lovers, inevitably increased the distance between Hazel and her husband's career. When Hawke took the Labor leadership, Hazel at first imagined that she would be able to continue her life in Sandringham. Having spent years qualifying as a social worker, she now wanted to pursue a career in Melbourne rather than move to Canberra as Hawke's chatelaine.[18] That illusion was shattered once the election campaign began.

The theme of Labor's election campaign was reconciliation, with Hawke putting himself forward as the healer of the nation, bridging divisions that had plagued Australia since the Whitlam years. It was after the fall of Whitlam, and the emotions it unleashed on both sides of politics, that Hawke had confidently predicted that the nation would need a leader who could bring them back together. After a decade of resolving industrial disputes, he intended to be that leader. With unemployment and inflation both hovering around 10 per cent, and with productivity among the lowest in the developed world, there was a widespread mood for change. However, the party's focus on recovery and reconstruction was not sufficient to address this mood, argued Hawke. He had told the party leadership on 20 January that Labor also had to present itself as the party of 'reconciliation' – that it had to address the country's 'desire for healing, for a sense of common purpose in the face of increasing social disintegration'.[19]

His heartfelt pitch was dismissed by party hardheads like Neville Wran, who thought Labor should do what it had always done at election time, which was to appeal to the 'hip-pocket nerve' of voters, a term first coined by Chifley. As Wran told a meeting of campaign workers in Sydney on 4 February, '[I]f the greedy bastards [the voters] wanted spiritualism, they'd join the fucking Hare Krishnas.' It must have seemed to Wran that Hawke was spruiking another of the half-baked ideas that he was prone to broach in his hastily written speeches, whether it was doing away with the states or appointing outsiders to the federal cabinet. In this case, though, Hawke had tapped into the zeitgeist.[20] Australians wanted a leader who could bring them together and lead them to a more hopeful future. Hawke still had to prove that he was such a leader.

CHAPTER FIVE

# 1983

Hawke's election campaign did not begin well. During more than twenty years in the labour movement, he had often tried to intimidate opponents with displays of anger, and would sometimes do likewise to deter searching questions from journalists. His quick resort to defamation actions also formed part of his armoury. That might have worked to his advantage as president of the ACTU, when he wanted to portray himself as the champion of the workers, but now that he was running for the prime ministership, he needed to project himself as a champion for all Australians. Campaigning on the theme of reconciliation, too, demanded that he win people over rather than bludgeon them into submission.

But old habits take time to change, as was clear immediately following Hawke's assumption of the ALP leadership. He sat down for an interview with the feisty ABC presenter Richard Carleton, who was determined to prod his subject into overreacting to an opening jibe about whether he was feeling 'a little bit embarrassed tonight at the blood that's on your hands'. This was sufficient for Hawke's temper to get the better of him, and he launched the sort of personal attack that he'd often made against opponents at an ACTU Congress. Hawke replied angrily that this was 'a ridiculous question, you know it was a ridiculous question', and he 'hoped the standard of your questioning improves'. With the prime ministership in sight, Hawke denied that he had any blood on his hands or that he had any part 'in the discussions' that forced Hayden's resignation.[1]

Carleton then asked how the electorate could be expected to believe he'd played no part in the plotting. Hawke blasted the 'stupidity' of this question, declaring that voters would trust his integrity over Carleton's. Leaning forward and almost shouting, Hawke reiterated his denial, claiming to have had 'no knowledge whatsoever' that Hayden was going to announce his resignation that morning. When Carleton rightly looked disbelieving, Hawke pointed to Carleton's 'silly quizzical face' and his 'reputation for impertinence'. Hawke hated having his veracity challenged even when, as in this instance, there were good grounds for doing so. In fact, as Graham Richardson later observed, Hawke 'had more blood on him than the entire stage at the end of *Hamlet*'. Richardson was deeply involved in the campaign against Hayden and had good reason to know that 'every blow that had rained down on Hayden for the previous six months had been reported to Hawke in advance'.[2]

Hawke's aggressive display would not have impressed those voters who had reservations about his behaviour as ACTU leader or who recalled such episodes as his drunken outburst at the ALP conference in Adelaide. Indeed, it was fortunate that Hawke was no longer on the grog, or his performance with Carleton might have killed his election campaign virtually before it began. Back in 1981, he'd conceded to interviewer Michael Parkinson that he had 'too short a temper at times'. Most people could probably sense that he was like a smoking volcano, always ready to erupt. But his temper would need to be held in check once he became prime minister. In this case, it caused a public backlash that was seized upon by the Liberal Party, which pivoted its campaign to portray Hawke as an admittedly likeable rogue but a man whose temperament made him unsuited to the prime ministership. Hawke's concerned advisers warned him to keep a tighter rein on his temper or face losing the election. He readily complied, thereafter becoming, according to Richardson, 'well mannered and calm to the point of tranquillity'. The lifelong prize mustn't be allowed to slip away now that it was within his grasp. His mother, who'd directed him in so many church plays, would have been proud of his transformation. It was so dramatic that Paul Kelly likened the toned-down Hawke to 'a benevolent prophet radiating peace'.[3]

Although many Australians had become inured to Hawke's bellicose behaviour, he couldn't afford to lose those 'swinging' voters who were liable to take offence. Some were planning to give their first preferences to Don Chipp's party, the Australian Democrats, and it was vital that they direct their second preferences to Labor so Hawke could secure the eleven additional seats he needed to form government.

While his new phalanx of minders had shaken their heads in dismay at the Carleton interview, it's doubtful that Hawke had any immediate regrets. He was used to being forgiven for his transgressions, and he was seeking to unseat an arrogant and aloof prime minister who was regularly depicted by cartoonists as an Easter Island monolith, and who now tried vainly to compete with Hawke by appearing 'the calm, confident elder statesman', wrote Bob Carr, who exuded 'charm and *bonhomie*' with interviewers. It didn't change Fraser's reception. He was greeted with indifference or even hostility wherever he appeared, whereas Hawke was mobbed like a rock star by adoring crowds. The 'magnetism of the Hawke personality', argued Carr, could prove crucial to the success of a Hawke government.[4] It would also prove crucial to Labor's success in the 1983 election.

For Hawke, the polls were looking propitious, just as he'd always predicted they would be. While Hayden had dragged Labor's approval rating down, Hawke had the opposite effect. A poll taken a few weeks before he toppled Hayden showed that 56 per cent of respondents favoured him as Labor leader, compared to 32 per cent for Hayden. Crucially, 67 per cent of Australian Democrats voters favoured Hawke, compared to 23 per cent for Hayden.

After Hawke assumed the leadership, Labor's poll results improved markedly. The *Bulletin* poll taken on the weekend after the election was called found that Labor's approval had improved by 4 per cent, giving the party a commanding lead of 52 per cent against the government's 41 per cent, with the Australian Democrats on 6 per cent. If those figures were replicated on election day, Labor would win in a landslide, since it would mean a swing of 6 per cent when only 1 per cent was required to take government.[5]

However, the same poll reported a 9 per cent slump in Hawke's personal approval to 53 per cent. This surprising result might have reflected a negative reaction to the Carleton interview and would have disappointed Hawke's supporters. No matter. Although his approval was now below the 60 per cent Whitlam scored at the beginning of his successful campaign in 1972, it remained far above Fraser's 39 per cent.[6]

Hawke had always relied on others to do his bidding, to shore up his weaknesses, to burnish his ego, to gather the numbers, to laugh at his long and risqué jokes, to do the administrative work, to let him win whatever game he was playing. Now that he was engaged in the climactic contest of his life, there was no shortage of advisers to guide him through the campaign. Neville Wran's political adviser, Peter Barron, was enlisted by Richardson to become Hawke's electoral guru, while Labor's national secretary, Bob McMullan, moved Hawke around on the political chessboard, and journalist Richard Farmer suggested the phrases and slogans that Hawke could deploy to attract the attention of the nightly news programs. The party's election slogan was decided the day after Hawke took over: 'Bob Hawke – Bringing Australia together'. It wrote itself, really. Fraser responded with a catchcry of his own invention: 'We're not waiting for the world'. Whatever that was meant to mean. On first hearing it, Richardson realised 'we had the chance not just to beat Fraser but to slaughter him'. From Fraser's initial misstep in calling the election, the Liberals always seemed to be off-balance. And it wouldn't get any better.[7]

The climate didn't help. A terrible drought was besetting much of eastern Australia during 1982, drying the forests and spreading despair among farmers. At a press conference in September 1982, the director of the Bureau of Meteorology had predicted that the spring rains were also likely to fail and called on Australians to start saving water. There was little water to save. Meteorologists were beginning to suspect a connection between cyclical changes in the surface temperature of the Pacific Ocean off the coast of South America and a reversal of wind patterns causing droughts or floods in Australia. The coming of warm waters presaged the disappearance of sardines for the fishermen of Chile and Peru, and were matched by the coming of cooler waters to the western Pacific and reduced rainfall for farmers across eastern Australia. This phenomenon would come to be known as El Niño.

While Hawke had lapped up the sunshine by his pool in Sandringham that summer, bushfires had begun to spark here and there, only to be beaten back by volunteer firefighters. Not for long. On 8 February, the day that caucus confirmed Hawke as leader, the calamitous conditions were brought forcefully to the attention of the citizens of Melbourne when a massive dust storm, 500 kilometres across, lifted the topsoil from the barren paddocks of north-western Victoria and sent it across the parched countryside towards the city, extinguishing the afternoon light and wreaking a trail of destruction.[8] As a wealthy grazier from Victoria's Western District, Malcolm Fraser should have been able to interpret this extraordinary event for his fellow citizens and calm their fears. But it required more than a farmer. The almost biblical proportions of the dust storm seemed to call for a messiah, and Hawke was at hand.

The natural calamities of bushfires, drought and dust storms added to the economic calamities of inflation and unemployment, which Fraser had been unable to solve during his more than seven years in office. Hawke offered solutions to these seemingly intractable economic problems, and much more besides. The day after the storm, Hawke appeared alongside his close political ally Gareth Evans, the shadow attorney-general, to announce Labor's planned changes to the machinery of government. These had been worked out by a group of senior Labor MPs and advisers under Hayden's direction over the previous two years and were designed to allay fears that a Labor government would replicate Whitlam's mismanagement of the relationship between ministerial offices and the public service, as well as between the Labor caucus, the cabinet and the prime minister. The following day, Hawke was back on the night-time news, sitting alongside his shadow treasurer, Paul Keating, and Ralph Willis, who'd worked under Hawke at the ACTU before entering parliament in 1972. Willis had briefly been shadow treasurer before being dumped by Hayden in favour of Keating just a few months before. Now he was at Sydney's swanky Wentworth Hotel with Keating to support Hawke in the release of Labor's economic policy, which promised to end Fraser's contractionary policies and introduce Keynesian-type stimulus measures to expand the economy. Once again, it was pitched as a contrast to Whitlam, who had focused on redistributing the fruits of the post-war economic boom, only to have it come to an abrupt end during his time in power. A Hawke government would focus instead on re-creating the boomtime conditions so that Australia's wealth could be redistributed, with bigger slices of the cake for all.[9]

The launch of the economic policy was a difficult occasion for the recently promoted Keating, who had no formal economic training.

According to Hawke's account, Keating 'was nervous and plainly out of his depth', giving 'perhaps the worst display I have ever seen him give'. Fortunately, Keating's performance didn't matter as much in the presidential-style election campaign, which was pitched as a contest between Hawke and Fraser. That was just as well, since Keating conceded to the Sydney radio interviewer John Laws that the centrepiece of Hawke's campaign – the much-vaunted 'accord' between the ALP and the trade union movement – might not end the constant wage-price spiral that had bedevilled the Whitlam and Fraser governments over the previous ten years.[10]

Hawke was campaigning in North Queensland at the time, and was blissfully unaware for some hours of Keating's misstep. It might have had more serious political consequences had not Fraser's deputy and political nemesis, Andrew Peacock, agreed with Keating that it was difficult to know for certain how such policies would pan out. Much to Fraser's chagrin, Hawke's fleeting embarrassment soon disappeared. That was fortunate, since the promised accord was essential to Hawke's credibility.[11]

It wasn't the only weapon in his electoral armoury. There were promises aplenty. Hawke had been working on the details with his close coterie of supporters, including Gareth Evans, who recalled visiting Hawke's Boulevard Hotel suite at about 1.30 a.m. one night in the lead-up to the campaign launch. He was met at the door by Hawke, who stood there 'stark naked' before asking Evans to take a seat while he went through the proffered paper, which he held in one hand, while 'with the other hand' he idly stroked his penis. 'Total narcissism, total[ly] consumed by his body, his glamour, his importance, [and] total indifference' to others, recalled Evans.[12] Fortunately, a majority of Australian voters loved Hawke as much as he loved himself.

Although Labor built its campaign around Hawke, the party didn't stake its electoral success wholly on a television-driven personality contest between Hawke and Fraser. The conventions of a campaign launch were followed, with Whitlam's speechwriter, the chain-smoking Graham Freudenberg, enlisted to write an inspirational screed that also offered a shopping list of promises for those voters who were used to weighing up the policies of the different parties and choosing the one that offered them the most. Fraser made it easy for Hawke by largely eschewing such an approach so that he could portray Labor's spending commitments as evidence of its economic irresponsibility.

Hawke was determined not to let that happen, as he stood alone on the stage of the Sydney Opera House to open Labor's campaign on 16 February. It was the day after Fraser had launched his own campaign in the town hall of Melbourne's middle-class suburb of Malvern, promising more of the same. Hawke's solitary presence was a dramatic recognition by the party that his popularity was the key to its campaign's success. Moreover, this was doubtless how Hawke himself imagined it occurring, with the political messiah looking out over his adoring supporters, with even the future ministers of his government swept up by the enthusiasm of the crowd.

Also present were members of his family, including the ever-loving Clem, along with Hazel, who still hadn't fully appreciated the radical changes that the coming election would bring to her life. Most radical of all was her rapprochement with the soon-to-be prime minister, which was on display for the Opera House audience and television viewers when they stood together, waving and smiling from the stage. She later described how they 'had been re-establishing our sense of partnership' and becoming 'more relaxed and companionable with each other', after years spent living increasingly separate and hostile lives. Now that her husband's life's mission was in sight, it 'felt right', wrote Hazel, who was confident that 'we would work well together'.[13]

It's difficult for an Opposition to overcome all the advantages of incumbency enjoyed by a government, even one led by an arrogant prime minister who'd been unable to steer the economy out of the doldrums. Hawke's popularity was an asset, but wasn't sufficient. He had to allay the reservations that many Australians harboured about his suitability for the high office, while on a more mundane level he had to attract those voters who'd spurned Whitlam in 1975 and stuck with Fraser ever since. In a sense, Hawke was putting the discredited Whitlam and the larrikin union leader to the sword at the same time as he was vanquishing the combative Malcolm Fraser.

It was Hawke the peacemaker and consensus-builder who opened his campaign speech with a commitment 'to reunite this great community of ours, to bring out the best we are truly capable of, together, as a nation, and bring Australia together to win our way through the crisis into which the policies of the past and the men of the past have plunged our country'. He railed against the politics of confrontation, 'which threaten to poison the very well-springs of the national life, the true, decent, Australian way of life'. The verities of the post-war years were in tatters, with falling living standards and declining home ownership. Hawke promised to address all these issues and much more besides. But there would be 'no miracles' and 'no fistful of dollars to be snatched back after the election'. Instead, there would be policies that would bring Australians together in a cooperative effort to boost economic growth without causing inflation. He promised a national summit of trade unions, employers and governments to make everyone aware of the problems and point to possible solutions. There would be tax cuts for low- and middle-income earners, an increase in rent assistance and other social welfare payments, a reduction in the tax on petrol, grants for first home buyers, along with several government works programs to create thousands of jobs. It was to be paid for by combating the tax evasion that had become rife, and by expanding the economy. This was a message of hope, spoken by Hawke with fingers crossed.[14]

With the historical-minded Graham Freudenberg as his speechwriter, Whitlam had appealed in his 1972 campaign speech to the 'men and women of Australia', a phrase first coined politically by Labor's wartime prime minister, John Curtin, many years before. With his own speech also penned by Freudenberg, Hawke harked back to the legacy of Curtin, likening Australia's present economic plight to the country's much more serious situation during World War II, when it was suffering bombardment by Japanese aircraft and submarines and anticipating an invasion. Hawke told his 'fellow Australians' that while they were facing 'a very different kind of crisis, the task and the challenge remain the same – to bring Australians together in a united effort until victory is won'.[15]

There was an authenticity about Hawke's speech that was lacking in his opponent's. Freudenberg had based his oratorical edifice on the historical experience that Australians had had of Hawke, whether he'd been fighting on behalf of ordinary folk or settling disputes that were causing industrial mayhem. Ever since the dismissal of Whitlam, Hawke had been calculating that Australians would crave to be brought back together after the divisiveness of those years. He would embrace all Australians and they would embrace him in turn.

Many of them did. Hawke later wrote of the 'enormous reservoir of goodwill' that he encountered wherever he went. Having watched his parents minister to congregations in the country towns of South Australia and the suburbs of Perth, and having accompanied his uncle Albert as he glad-handed his way around the hustings, Hawke had developed an instinctive feel for political campaigning, which he'd honed over the previous two decades, campaigning mostly on behalf of others. Now it was all about him. And he basked in the public's love and admiration. 'The Australian people are a warm, generous race,' wrote Hawke, 'and I revelled in meeting them in all their various contexts: on the factory floor, in country towns, in suburban shopping malls, in the outback, in the cities, in boardrooms, in pubs, in their homes – everywhere.'[16] It was just how he'd always dreamed it would be, with the path to the Lodge lined with admirers cheering him on. Of course, he couldn't be sure until the votes were counted, but each passing day seemed to make the outcome more certain.

Once again, the climate intervened. The drought had made vegetation across south-eastern Australia so tinder-dry that when bushfires broke out on 16 February, they caused a conflagration that ripped through forests and across thousands of square kilometres of farmland in South Australia and Victoria. Hawke had barely completed his speech at the Opera House before the fires began, creating firestorms that killed seventy-five people, including many firefighters taken unawares when a sudden wind shift engulfed them in flames. Thousands of homes were destroyed, along with hundreds of thousands of sheep, cattle and other livestock. Whole towns were consumed on the day that would be remembered as Ash Wednesday.

The fires were the worst for a century, bringing the shocked country to a standstill. Political campaigning was stopped for several days as the candidates toured the devastated regions and sympathised with the victims. For Fraser, it was a chance to use his prime ministerial authority to coordinate the relief effort, while Hawke visited evacuation centres to commiserate with those who'd been forced to flee their homes. It wasn't a time for political leaders to attack one another, but for Australians to come together in common purpose – a narrative that accorded more with Hawke's campaign than Fraser's. The hiatus in campaigning meant that Fraser was prevented from rebutting Hawke's campaign speech and all the promises contained within it, which caused his campaign to lose even more momentum.[17] Nothing seemed to go right for the prime minister.

A few days after the fires swept across south-eastern Australia, a political storm swept through Western Australia, where the Labor Party secured a 7 per cent swing and 53 per cent of the vote in a state election that saw the young Brian Burke installed as the new premier. It didn't bode well for Fraser's chances at the federal election three weeks later. In a desperate attempt to grab media attention and stoke fears about the economic implications of a Hawke victory, Fraser warned a mass rally in Melbourne that Australians would be better off keeping their money under their beds, because Hawke 'would be robbing the savings of the people to pay for [Labor's] mad and extravagant promises'. Such claims were a familiar conservative trope during elections and had worked well for Fraser in 1980, when he'd claimed that Hayden was intent on introducing a capital gains tax.[18]

The Labor camp was initially concerned that political history would repeat itself and Hawke would be denied victory. This time, though, Fraser's scare campaign smacked of desperation and threatened to cause a run on the banks by frightened depositors. Indeed, the banks were so concerned by this possibility that they repudiated Fraser's dire warning and assured Australians that they had nothing to fear. Even Fraser's own colleagues were appalled, with Howard ringing his staff to ask, 'What the fuck is this money under the beds line?' It made Fraser look like a fool. Yet he repeated the line when he flew on to Adelaide and Perth.[19]

Rather than coming out swinging, Hawke made fun of his opponent. At Richard Farmer's suggestion, he laughed at Fraser's warning, reprising an old Cold War warning about 'Reds under the beds' to say that there would be no room under the bed 'because that's where the Commies are'. Fraser was rattled. And pollsters were finding that voters were marking him down as a result. 'I knew then that Fraser was finished,' wrote Hawke.[20]

For decades, Hawke had been studying the script of his elevation to the prime ministership. His mother had sketched the outline for him as a boy and he'd been following it ever since. He'd always acted as if it was preordained. And for all the drama on the hustings, few were in any doubt about the election's outcome. Certainly not Hawke. The pollsters reported during the campaign that there would be a Labor landslide, and so it turned out to be. Whereas Hayden may well have led Labor over the line, Hawke rode Labor's chariot in a triumphant procession that saw the party sweep to victory with a 4 per cent swing that gave the incoming prime minister a 25-seat majority in the new parliament. Hawke had sold himself to the Australian people as the leader who would drive a dagger through the collective memory of both the Whitlam and Fraser governments. Australians responded with enthusiasm, giving his government a majority that put Whitlam's nine-seat majority in the shade.

Hawke and his entourage watched the count play out on a television in his suite at Canberra's Lakeside Hotel. Clem was there, quietly celebrating his eighty-fifth birthday with a cake, but it was his son who was the centre of attention. Perhaps because the result had seemed a foregone conclusion, there were not the sort of raucous celebrations that had occurred in Whitlam's backyard in 1972, where family, friends, neighbours and local branch members had massed for the result.[21] That would have seemed out of place in 1983, given Hawke was purporting to be prime minister for all Australians.

Two hours after the polling booths closed in the eastern states, the result was clear. But neither leader made a move until the figures began to come in from Western Australia, which only put more seats in Labor's column. Perhaps the biggest vindication for Hawke, and for the MPs who had dumped Hayden, came in the Victorian seat of Flinders, which Labor had failed to win three months earlier and now won with a 6 per cent swing that saw its new MP, Peter Reith, ousted before he'd had the chance to take his seat in parliament. The nature of Hawke's victory also gave cause for satisfaction, with seats falling to Labor in the cities and in the bush. A drover's dog couldn't have done any better than Hawke in rounding up support across the continent. Only the people of Tasmania failed to succumb to his spell, despite the several visits and long speeches to which he'd subjected them.

No matter. Grinning broadly as he emerged from the lobby of the Lakeside Hotel just before midnight, Hawke sped off to proclaim his great victory. Rather than going to the national tally room at the Canberra Showgrounds, where an overflow crowd of well-wishers was awaiting his arrival, he chose to claim victory in the ABC's Canberra studio on Northbourne Avenue. Television had made him, so it seemed appropriate that he should return the favour. Looking down the lens at his national audience, Hawke promised to lead 'a government for all Australians', before telling journalists that 'we're not going to move quickly because ... what the people of Australia want from the incoming government is calmness [and] a sense of assurance'.[22] It was an indication of how he would approach the business of government.

It was only after leaving the ABC studios that Hawke made an appearance at the Canberra Showgrounds. He and Hazel were engulfed by the exultant crowds, before Hawke went from one makeshift television studio to the other, repeating his earlier sentiments and shaking hands with the soon-to-be Opposition leader, Andrew Peacock. Meanwhile, at Melbourne's Southern Cross Hotel, as a hostile crowd booed and jeered outside, Fraser fronted the cameras to concede defeat before breaking down with the emotion of it all as he left the room.[23]

Hawke's big test was about to begin. And he was more than ready for it.

# PART TWO
# Power

CHAPTER SIX

# 1983

Two days after the election, the Hawkes moved into Kirribilli House and held a celebratory dinner at the grand harbourside mansion with its views of the Sydney Opera House. Conscious of the historic moment, Labor's veteran speechwriter Graham Freudenberg marked the advent of the new government with a witty opening line to his after-dinner speech. He'd often visited the prime minister's official Sydney residence during Whitlam's time and now was there for Hawke. 'As I was saying before I was rudely interrupted,' began Freudenberg, before saluting the 'new beginning' in Hawke's life.[1]

While Freudenberg's line might have implied that the Hawke government was going to take up from where Whitlam left off, the grinning prime minister had very different ideas. He'd watched with dismay the disintegration and eventual dismissal of the Whitlam government and was determined that he wouldn't emulate his Labor predecessor in those respects. He also came armed with policies that were designed to avoid the scandals and mismanagement of the Fraser government. A party task force established by Hayden in 1982 and chaired by Gareth Evans had produced recommendations as to how the new government should be run, but it would be up to Hawke to implement them. In the event, his electoral victory and his popularity would allow him to make the government very much his own.[2]

Hawke wanted to be there for the long term, not only to complete the big task of national transformation that beckoned, but also to have Labor accepted as the natural party of government. In the process, he would be able to bask in the adulation of his fellow Australians for a prolonged period. He couldn't imagine that they, or his colleagues, might one day tire of him. And he couldn't imagine a life beyond the prime ministership.

With his commitment to reconciliation, Hawke had made clear that he was not going to take over from where Whitlam's more radical government had left off. Voters didn't want him to do so. The Nobel Prize–winning writer Patrick White thought that Hawke was 'flash' but seems 'right for Australia'.[3] Hawke was the antithesis of Whitlam. Unlike Whitlam, he'd hardly read a serious novel in his life. Importantly, though, he had a closer acquaintance with economics than Whitlam, and had spent more than two decades thinking about how to reshape the Australian economy to meet the challenges that had beset it during the 1970s and which still persisted.

The problem of stagflation was no nearer resolution. Keynesian economics had prescribed government spending to pump-prime faltering economies such as Australia. However, unleashing government spending to reduce unemployment would only exacerbate inflation and undo any benefit of the spending. By the time Hawke became prime minister, a new school of monetarist economists led by Milton Friedman was suggesting instead that governments should cause a gradual increase in the money supply, while also lowering trade barriers and reducing the size of government activity, so as to encourage businesses to take up the slack in the economy without stimulating inflation. Such policies had been embraced by Britain's Margaret Thatcher after her election in 1979, and by the plain-speaking star of second-rate cowboy films Ronald Reagan after he was sworn in as US president in 1981. They were embraced, too, by financial journalists in Australia, along with senior public servants and many Liberal MPs. Hawke was of a similar mind about the need to encourage business spending, boost productivity and cut tariffs. He was also conscious of the need to rein in government spending – which had grown much higher under Fraser as a proportion of GDP than under Whitlam – if he was to retain the confidence of international banks and fund managers, along with the heads of multinational corporations.[4] There was already a state of alarm among these groups.

During the election, the Liberal scare campaign about a Hawke government devaluing the currency and inhibiting the repatriation of foreign funds had caused a flight of capital from Australia, which had put pressure on the country's foreign exchange reserves. Hawke had tried to allay the concerns of foreign investors and deter the speculators, but to little effect. Many preferred to take their money out of Australia until the much-discussed devaluation had occurred. This outflow of funds continued as news of Hawke's stunning election victory was broadcast around the world.

That wasn't his only problem. A government insider had leaked information about the size of the Fraser government's deficit, which had ballooned by 28 February to a predicted $9 billion – more than double the figure that Fraser had told voters. Although he'd been urged by his treasurer, John Howard, to reveal the alarming blowout to voters, Fraser had refused to do so. Ironically, it was John Stone, who'd outclassed Hawke at Perth Modern and beaten him to the Rhodes Scholarship, who now had to inform Hawke about the size of the deficit, which would preclude him from implementing some of his costly election promises.[5]

Back in 1972, a drunken Hawke had shirtfronted Stone at a reception, telling him that he would be among the first to be fired by the incoming Whitlam government. Stone had held onto his job back then and had since risen to become head of the Treasury. Despite his dislike for Hawke, he'd voted for Labor at the election and was pleased to see the end of Fraser and Howard. But he didn't want to see a big-spending Labor government.[6]

The news about the ballooning deficit was so urgent that Stone went to the Lakeside Hotel the day after the election. Perhaps because of their mutual animus, Hawke sent Keating and his economic advisers to meet with Stone in the hotel's darkened bar, which was empty of drinkers and smelled of stale beer. There, Stone told them that the predicted deficit for the 1983–84 financial year had grown to $9.6 billion.[7]

Stone's secret memorandum was political dynamite. It not only exposed the economic profligacy of the Fraser government, but also lobbed a political mortar at the new Labor government. Stone was putting them on notice that massive spending cuts were required. The financial position was 'unprecedented in Australia during peace time', warned Stone, 'as is the level of Government spending'. In two years, they would be going from a balanced budget to a deficit equal to

6 per cent of Australia's gross domestic product (GDP). Stone's memo would make it difficult for Hawke to sack him; it's never a good look to shoot the bearer of bad tidings. Appearances are important for investors and foreign exchange markets, and immediately sacking the head of Treasury would create an impression of instability. It would smack too much of the Whitlam years, and might confirm Fraser's campaign accusation that a Hawke government would paint Australia 'red'. As Keating later recalled, '[T]he last thing we needed to look like was the Beverly Hillbillies arriving again after the economic instability of the Whitlam Government and the further big expenditure blowouts by Fraser and Howard.'[8]

The news of the deficit suited Hawke. During the campaign, he'd talked more about bringing the nation together than about Labor's spending promises, which had been drawn up by Hayden and Willis. Moreover, Hawke had been careful to make his campaign promises conditional on the size of the deficit. Once he had confirmation of that, he could put most of the party's big-spending commitments on hold and blame Fraser.

Hawke could also use the deficit to push back against the Keynesian inclinations of most of his ministers and embrace instead the monetarist inclinations of those colleagues who would come to dominate his government. Those advisers with a Keynesian bent were also replaced with those of more monetarist inclinations. Keating was made treasurer, although he'd made some serious missteps during the election campaign that had caused Hawke to wonder about his ability. According to D'Alpuget, Hawke 'was confident that after the election he could re-promote Willis [into the role] and give Keating some other portfolio'. After all, Willis was a trained economist whose work at the ACTU had given him a good grasp of the country's economic problems.[9]

In the end, despite Hawke's sentimental attachment to Willis – who years earlier had occasionally minded his children, and who in 1963 had accompanied him to the funeral of his baby son Robert – the pull of politics won out. Hawke owed his prime ministership to the support of the New South Wales Right, which was led by Keating and Richardson. When they learned that Hawke was thinking of installing the mild-mannered Willis as treasurer, they made clear that it was not on. Keating had told a journalist on the night of the election that he expected to have the role, and privately warned Hawke that there would be 'massive retaliation' if he tried to shift him, while Richardson said it would be akin to a 'declaration of war' with the New South Wales Right. None of these conversations appears in Hawke's memoir, which claims instead that it was a simple calculation that 'Paul's potential as a publicist tipped my hand in his direction, although with some reluctance'. Once the matter was decided, Hawke claimed, he told the nervous Keating that they would 'do the job together', to give Keating time to get to grips with the position and to surround himself with good advisers from whom he could learn the ropes.[10]

There was no time to lose. Hawke had hoped that the flood of money going offshore would stop once the election was decided. Instead, the Reserve Bank governor, Bob Johnston, warned Hawke that funds were still streaming out in the expectation that the incoming government would be forced to devalue the Australian currency. At the time, the exchange rate of the Australian dollar was set by the heads of the Reserve Bank, the Treasury and the Prime Minister's Department, and was usually moved only in small increments. It was while preparing for dinner on that first Sunday night at Kirribilli that Hawke decided the currency should be devalued by a sizeable 10 per cent, which would assure a big profit to those speculators who'd already taken their money out of the country, while removing the prospect of a profit for those who were still thinking of doing so. The devaluation would also make imported goods more expensive, which would have the effect of increasing inflation, so consumers buying foreign-made cars, television sets and other household goods would be the losers.[11] But Hawke had little choice.

The devaluation would be the first of many changes the Hawke government would make. Some would contravene long-accepted Labor policy and cause controversy when they were implemented, as they had not been put to the people at an election. Sometimes Hawke made changes that had not even been approved by cabinet.

While the money markets kept a close eye on the actions of the incoming government, so too did the security services of both Australia and the United States, which were concerned with what a new Labor government might mean for them and for the alliance.

Hawke had presided over a union organisation that included several members of the Communist Party on its executive, which had led to allegations that Hawke himself was a communist. Indeed, such stories were so widespread in the 1970s that his worried mother had asked him whether they were true. On the other side, many in the labour movement were adamant that the CIA had worked behind the scenes to topple Whitlam, just as it had other governments around the world, and that Hawke was in cahoots with CIA representatives in Australia, who often posed as labour attachés.[12]

Labor MPs also had suspicions about the Australian Security and Intelligence Organisation (ASIO), which had kept many leading members of the labour and anti-war movements under surveillance. Whitlam had established a royal commission into the security services, with a view to having the three branches – ASIO, the Australian Secret Intelligence Service (ASIS) and the Defence Signals Directorate (DSD), each of them responsible to a different minister – combined into a single service responsible to the prime minister. Although Whitlam was sacked before he could implement his plan, it confirmed ASIO's longstanding suspicions about the Labor Party. Now the incoming attorney-general, Gareth Evans, was a committed civil libertarian who supported closer parliamentary supervision of ASIO and its sister organisations.[13] ASIO would soon put the new government to the test.

On the eve of the election, ASIO agents had used concealed microphones to bug the Canberra home of a young Soviet spy, Valery Ivanov, as he plied Labor's former national secretary David Combe with alcohol. The 39-year-old Combe had been close to Hawke for two decades. He'd helped Hawke recruit supporters in South Australia before becoming the party's secretary in Canberra, where he'd overseen the building of a national headquarters, but had also been involved in the ill-considered attempt to secure Iraqi money to finance Labor's 1975 election campaign. After resigning as secretary in 1981, he'd tried unsuccessfully to secure preselection for a Sydney electorate, then established himself as a lobbyist in Canberra, which is where he met the Soviet spy, who was posing as a trade representative.

As well as discussing trade opportunities with the Soviet Union and Combe's conviction that the CIA had been involved in orchestrating the downfall of Whitlam, the lobbyist made clear that he was a man on the make. He boasted of the 'very big money' that would come from his contacts within the federal Labor government and the four state Labor governments. The security service couldn't have been more pleased. In exposing Ivanov as a spy, it would gain kudos with its fellow intelligence services in London and Washington, while at the same time exposing a leading light of the Labor Party just as a new Labor government was intent on reining it in. As Hawke was claiming victory in Canberra, Combe went clutching champagne and cigars to Ivanov's house to celebrate. The victory would make Combe the best-placed lobbyist and political consultant in Canberra, while also providing a Soviet spy with a possible conduit to the highest echelons of the Hawke government.[14]

Hawke was oblivious to this political bombshell as he assembled a small coterie of close advisers and grappled with the machinery of his new government. Hawke allowed Fraser a week to depart the Lodge before he and Hazel moved in. Their previously separate lives were once more entwined, although it took some time for Hazel to come to terms with her new role. For Hawke, it was almost as if nothing had changed. He continued to bet on horseraces, studying the form guide on Fridays with his usual assiduity, whether he was at the Lodge, in his prime minister's suite or even chairing a cabinet meeting. Although he would later say that he and Hazel 'spent more time together when I was prime minister than [during] any other period in our marriage really', he continued to enjoy occasional trysts with several of his lovers.[15] His narcissism demanded it.

Journalist Troy Bramston has claimed, and some of Hawke's predecessors could attest, that living the very public life of a prime minister didn't necessarily prevent sexual dalliances or the maintenance of a relationship with a lover. His 'office wife' and one of his lovers for the last decade, Jean Sinclair, was ever-present, and her flat was not far away. Although Hawke could seclude himself in his office suite, which had couches and an adjoining shower, his staff are adamant that there was little opportunity for him to use it for a tryst without their knowledge. There might have been greater opportunity at the Lodge, where he could have entertained one of his lovers when Hazel was with Rosslyn in Melbourne or visiting Stephen in the Kimberley. It's more likely, though, that his modus operandi was to use his bodyguards to take him incognito to the homes of his lovers, wherever they might be.

'He just expected discretion from everybody,' claimed the head of his security detail. In an attempt to crimp Hawke's sexual proclivities, and to minimise the risk of an intelligence breach and embarrassment to the government, Graham Evans had warned Hawke that the security staff had been instructed to compile a daily report on his activities. But his libido couldn't be contained so easily. As his tourism minister, John Brown, later observed, Hawke was 'terribly indiscreet' as prime minister and 'always wanted to talk to [me] about girls'.[16]

Hazel had come to accept Hawke's affairs and one-night stands, and was just relieved that he was no longer drinking. As she took on the responsibilities that came with being the prime minister's wife, she was left by Hawke to cope as best she could. She told a journalist that she regarded her new position 'as an extension of my position as Bob's wife'. On the first morning in Canberra, as she watched Hawke's car pull away from the Lodge, she felt 'that if I suddenly disappeared, no one would notice'.[17] She'd wanted him to pursue his ambition, but she hadn't prepared for what her own role might be.

The Frasers had left behind a butler, who had charge of the 27-room residence, with its two chefs, four housekeepers and three gardeners. Hazel might have thrown herself into redecorating the place, but she could see no sense in that. She discovered a grand piano in storage, had it restored and moved into the Lodge, and also accepted a supply of books from a publisher to fill a bookshelf, while stipulating that D'Alpuget's biography of her husband not be one of them. For a time, she was at a loose end. The running of the household and the cultivation of the garden were both handled by staff, and although she'd hoped to resume her career as a social worker, that life had ended. Nor was she able to spend as much time with close friends. She bought a puppy and two kittens, but the dog died of distemper.[18]

The Lodge had similar amenities to the Hawkes' Sandringham home, with a swimming pool, tennis court and a billiard table, all of which Hawke relished. They had retained their much-cherished home, expecting they'd be able to go there frequently, as Fraser had done with his grazing property in the Western District, but it didn't turn out that way. In April 1983, Rosslyn gave birth to a baby there, with a doctor and midwife in attendance and Hazel on hand to help. But the house would eventually be let out to tenants, and later sold, when the Hawkes realised that the Lodge would be their home for the foreseeable future.[19]

Hazel soon became consumed by the demands of being the prime minister's wife. Just as she had as a social worker, she found that she could eke out an existence in her own right. She was given a secretary, who was seconded from the public service to deal with the increasing flood of invitations, letters and requests for media interviews, mostly from women's magazines. Not surprisingly, and much to Hazel's annoyance, journalists drew on D'Alpuget's biography for some of their questions. She decided after four months that she wouldn't do any more interviews, but soon changed her mind and began consciously to create a public persona for herself that could complement Hawke's.[20]

Hazel's initial idea of remaining in the shadows was never realistic, especially as she began to be seen as a political asset for Hawke. There were the strenuous overseas trips when she accompanied him to Washington, Jakarta and Paris. She continued with her yoga and developed contacts with local organisations with interests in art, music and social welfare. Among her friends in Canberra was Annita Keating, who'd moved to the capital with her children after Keating became treasurer. By late 1983, Hazel was sufficiently confident in her new role that she agreed to give an Australia Day address at the National Press Club. Annita was in the audience to hear her talk about her experience as a wife and mother, and about the influence on her of feminist works such as Anne Summers' *Damned Whores and God's Police*. Attracting a bigger audience than Hawke had done, she also used the occasion to make some insightful comments about the continuing oppression of Aboriginal people, informed by the times she'd spent with Stephen.[21]

Blanche d'Alpuget, meanwhile, immersed herself in her writing and continued a relationship with a prominent journalist. However much her biography of Hawke had helped him gain the prime ministership, she could only watch from a distance as Hazel took on the role that he'd promised would be hers. Although D'Alpuget was now separated from her husband, she remained in Canberra, where she was appointed a writer-in-residence at the Australian Defence Force Academy (ADFA), which had been established as a college of the University of New South Wales. Since the publication of her prize-winning novel *Turtle Beach*, followed soon after by the Hawke biography, she'd become a writer of some renown in Australia and overseas. Researching Hawke's life had taken her to Israel, which she now wanted to make the setting for her next novel. Although it was little more than an idea when she took up the ADFA residency, D'Alpuget said the novel would be 'about broken dreams and, of course, relationships between people'. Published in 1986 as *Winter in Jerusalem*, it must have been a cathartic book to write, as it is studded with apparently autobiographical references.[22]

Its main character is Danielle Green, a screenwriter and a single mother of a school-age daughter, who is commissioned by a Hollywood producer, Bennie Kidron, to write a script about the Jewish uprising against the Romans, which culminated in the much-commemorated mass suicide of the besieged Zealots at Masada around AD 73. At one point, D'Alpuget has Danielle announce dramatically to an Israeli friend that she is 'through with men! Radical celibacy equals peace of mind.' Despite her best intentions, Danielle falls in love with Kidron, who can be found in his Los Angeles office 'drunk, sober, and in between, several days each week', much like Hawke at the ACTU. Listening to Danielle, her Israeli friend ponders 'the weakness in Danielle's nature that drew her to tainted men'. By the end of the book, her relationship with Kidron has ended, with Danielle listing the stages of her attachment 'through desire, possessive love, anger, hatred, despair, and humiliation', until finally she arrives at a state of equanimity 'that admits only love'. D'Alpuget later described how she drew on Hawke, 'or some characteristic or saying of his', in 'book after book'.[23]

While D'Alpuget was tapping away at her typewriter, Hawke was relishing the role he'd finally achieved after a lifetime of maternal pressure and confident expectation. It wasn't such a long time since there'd been a Labor government, and four of his senior ministers – Hayden, Keating, Bowen and Uren – had previous ministerial experience in the Whitlam government. Hawke had watched as Whitlam struggled to cope with some of his more unruly ministers, who'd waited so long to get into power and would sometimes appeal to the Labor caucus if they were unable to win the support of the cabinet. Hawke put a stop to that by accepting a caucus task force recommendation to have an inner cabinet of just thirteen members (later increased to seventeen), which he chose from the 27-strong ministry elected by caucus.

There was only one woman, Susan Ryan, who was appointed Minister for Education and Youth Affairs. The other members were Hawke's deputy, Lionel Bowen (Minister for Trade), Paul Keating (Treasurer), John Button (Minister for Industry and Commerce), Ralph Willis (Minister for Employment and Industrial Relations), Don Grimes (Minister for Social Security), Mick Young (Special Minister of State), Stewart West (Minister for Immigration and Ethnic Affairs), Peter Walsh (Minister for Resources and Energy), Bill Hayden (Minister for Foreign Affairs), Gareth Evans (Attorney-General) and Gordon Scholes (Minister for Defence). It was this inner cabinet, and its much smaller Expenditure Review Committee (ERC), that met most often and became the decision-making engine of the government.

More importantly, Hawke's inner cabinet included only one representative of the Left (Stewart West) and was composed mainly of like-minded ministers who would support the prime minister in making the difficult decisions that were required to transform the economy and keep Labor in power. Hawke's authority would be almost absolute – which could have been his undoing, had he wielded it without consulting his colleagues and advisers. But he excelled as a chairman. His time as president of the Student Guild Council in Perth and later as president of the ACTU gave him valuable experience in managing board meetings. Also valuable was his overriding impulse to bring people together. Hawke was the complete opposite of Whitlam, said Graham Freudenberg. Indeed, the 'key to his success as prime minister was his role as chairman of cabinet'. Although he was a 'poor parliamentarian', he was 'truly superb' as the chair of cabinet. As Peter Walsh recalled, rather than taking votes, Hawke's habit was to continue the discussion until he determined that a consensus had been reached that was 'accepted by most and [was] not too objectionable to others'. [24]

Although he was a great believer in the importance of the public service, Hawke came to rely upon a praetorian guard of personal advisers, who were installed in the warren of offices that ran off the narrow corridor to his prime ministerial office in the north-eastern corner of Parliament House, which looked across Lake Burley Griffin to the grim edifice of the Australian War Memorial. The advisers were selected based on various criteria, including their amiability and intellectual capacity, but none lasted who did not share Hawke's overriding ambition to restructure the Australian economy by opening it up. The chain-smoking Jean Sinclair was still there but was no longer pre-eminent.

As his principal private secretary, Hawke had long ago decided on a public servant he'd met during a visit to the United States in 1981. At the time, Graham Evans was a counsellor at the Australian embassy and had accompanied Hawke, then a newly elected MP, to meetings with members of Congress and the US administration. Hawke had been so impressed with the cricket-loving Evans that he'd offered him a job once he became prime minister. That was something he'd been prone to do, but this time he followed through and plucked Evans from the Treasury, where he was working in its international division.[25]

In turn, Evans suggested that a cricket-playing economist named Ross Garnaut should be enlisted as his economic adviser. Like Hawke, Garnaut was a graduate of Perth Modern School and was similarly convinced of the need to modernise the Australian economy and open it to the world. Providing political advice were the tough-talking Peter Barron, of the New South Wales Right, and the pragmatic Bob Hogg, of Victoria's Socialist Left, who'd helped to engineer John Cain's election as Victorian premier. As his principal speechwriter Hawke chose Freudenberg, who would also continue writing speeches for Premier Neville Wran.[26]

Some of Hawke's advisers were in offices bereft of windows and little bigger than broom cupboards. But they had ready access to Hawke, whose spacious office was decorated in the garish colours of the 1970s, which made it appear dark and drab despite having windows to the north and east. It wasn't helped by the brown carpet and the walls being lined with dark wood, while the windows had grey blinds with curtains featuring 'a mosaic of brown and orange'. All this was the legacy of Fraser's government. There were bookshelves on one wall, where a spyhole allowed staff to check on whether the prime minister was busy before entering the room. If he wanted privacy, Hawke only had to shift a book and the hole was blocked.[27]

The lobby leading to the prime ministerial office displayed a line of photographs of former Labor leaders, including Hawke's hero, John Curtin; the final image was Bill Hayden's. As he said, Hawke might have felt 'real sadness' about toppling Hayden but consoled himself with the thought that it had been the necessary cost of Labor winning government and of him achieving his destiny. The photographs emphasised the history that now weighed upon his shoulders. He was determined that when it came time for his photograph to be displayed, those glancing at his image would remember that Robert James Lee Hawke had a list of accomplishments as great as Curtin's.[28]

CHAPTER SEVEN

# 1983

On 11 April 1983, just five weeks after the election, Hawke walked into parliament as prime minister. Not into the first sitting of the new parliament, but as the convenor of the National Economic Summit that he had promised voters he would hold. It was part of his commitment to bring Australians together after the fractious years of the previous decade. With representatives from business, trade unions, government and community groups, the meeting was designed to be in stark contrast to the Fraser years and to set the tone for the sort of cooperative country that Hawke hoped to create. He wanted the different groups to acknowledge the deep structural problems afflicting the economy and thereby change the atmospherics around the national conversation, which had been marked for so long by the thunder and lightning of disputation and confrontation. Transforming the economy couldn't be done without that understanding and the tacit cooperation of the community. Hawke aimed to achieve what Fraser had been unable to. And he would do it with the support of his party and the trade unions. Elisha-like, he would utilise the 'mantle of power' that accrues to a prime minister, particularly one who has led his followers out of the political wilderness.

In an early meeting with the full cabinet, Hawke outlined the economic direction that he intended his government to follow, which mimicked the changes happening elsewhere, particularly in Britain and the United States, where conservative governments were ceding much of their power to the financial markets. That wasn't the direction Hayden had intended to take. Nor was it the direction that most of Hawke's cabinet would have chosen. Yet Hawke and his economic ministers (Dawkins, Walsh and Keating) were allowed to have their way. As they filed out of the cabinet room, the science minister, Barry Jones, asked his colleague Michael Duffy how Hawke had managed to achieve agreement despite most of the cabinet wanting to go in a different direction. 'It's all a matter of numbers,' said Duffy. 'There were four of them and only twenty-three of us.'[1]

The economic summit had been Hayden's idea but Hawke made it his own, tying it to his theme of reconciliation and investing it with an urgency that responded to the post-election concern with the budget blowout. Prior to the summit, Hawke had released details of the deficit, along with the damning assessment by Stone of the previous government's profligacy.

On 11 April, four weeks after being sworn in as prime minister, Hawke welcomed the ninety-eight delegates, who were spread around the relatively intimate confines of the House of Representatives, which normally accommodated 128 MPs. Susan Ryan was the only female delegate, although representatives of women's organisations, along with Indigenous and social welfare groups and others were allowed to watch from the galleries.

Rather than holding the summit at the Sydney Opera House or a capital city conference centre, the parliamentary space, with its green leather seats impressed with the weight of politicians from decades past, invested the proceedings with a seriousness they might otherwise have struggled to achieve. The surroundings encouraged participants to believe they were more than just the audience for a political performance by Hawke, who sat at the centre table with his novice treasurer sitting alongside and furiously taking notes. Although the state premiers were there, neither the new federal Opposition leader, Andrew Peacock, nor any of his senior colleagues were invited; their presence, it was thought, would have turned the summit into a fractious political debate.[2] Which would have destroyed the atmosphere Hawke wanted to create.

Hawke left nothing to chance. This seems to have been when the prime ministerial chair in the House of Representatives had several centimetres added to its legs. Hawke was much shorter than his predecessor, Malcolm Fraser, who towered twenty centimetres above him. More importantly, he would be sitting alongside his treasurer, Paul

Keating, who was fourteen years younger and nearly ten centimetres taller. With this raised chair, the television news would appear to show Australians they had a leader whose apparent physical stature, at least when seated, confirmed that he was in charge.

Arrayed around Hawke in the chamber were some of the most powerful people from the business world, state governments, trade unions and several other sectors. While business groups had nominated members, Hawke had added Sir Peter Abeles and fellow Oxford graduate Sir Rod Carnegie, along with several others, including Sir Keith Campbell, who had recommended the floating of the Australian dollar to the Fraser government only to be rebuffed. Although each of the delegates had their own interests and expectations for the summit, Hawke was able to draw on the popular desire for competing sectors to come together in common purpose. Claiming that the nation faced the 'gravest economic crisis in fifty years', Hawke called on delegates to consider their 'wider responsibility to the people of Australia'. It was a high-risk gamble that could easily have failed. However, just as Hawke had hoped, assembling the influential powerbrokers in one place brought the result he wanted. It was an educative process for everyone, producing a widespread realisation that Australia's economic recovery would depend on them acting cooperatively to produce a larger and more prosperous economy, rather than squabbling over the size of their shares of the existing economy.[3]

The ACTU was represented by its new secretary, Bill Kelty, an economics graduate and long-time admirer of Hawke, and by its president, Cliff Dolan. They made clear that the unions had discovered the futility of chasing compensation for higher prices, only to see their gains come at the cost of even higher prices and higher unemployment. Australian manufacturers had learned a similar lesson, having seen their profits eroded and productivity stagnate. Hawke and his former union colleagues had seized upon the idea of an accord, under which unionists would agree to wage restraint in return for the government reinstating the centralised wage-fixing system and compensating workers with a 'social wage', to be received as government payments in the areas of health, education and social security, which would make up for any reduction in real wages. Although it wasn't a party to the accord, the business sector would be rewarded by the government agreeing to an increase in their profit share, in return for moderating its price increases and dividend payments.

During the election, Hawke had promised to create half a million jobs within the first term of his government, with the goal of returning Australia to its post-war norm of full employment. Harking back to a wartime speech made in the same chamber by Curtin, who'd called on Australians to be unstinting in their efforts to prevent invasion, Hawke called on delegates to be just as unstinting in their efforts to meet the current economic crisis.[4]

Despite a few dissenting voices – including that of the Queensland premier, Joh Bjelke-Petersen, who arrived late after earlier saying he wouldn't attend at all and was the only delegate who refused to sign the final communique – the summit ended as a triumph for Hawke. Delegates gave him a standing ovation and agreed with him that the desired economic recovery would 'require restraint in expectations and claims from all sections of the community, except for the impoverished'.[5]

The four-day summit had achieved all that Hawke had hoped for. The various speeches and the government briefing papers had educated delegates – whether they were union leaders, business magnates or state premiers – about the extent of the economic crisis and suggested pathways out of it through cooperation and a concern for the national good. It had changed the political atmospherics. 'Almost everything Hawke achieved as prime minister had its foundation in that week,' Peter Barron later said. That was somewhat of an overstatement, but delegates did leave Parliament House with a more benign view of the Labor government and its leader, and a willingness to consider the national interest when pursuing their separate sectional interests.[6] At least for a time.

Fortunately for Hawke, the summit was held at the nadir of the recession. Autumn rains were already breaking the ruinous drought and bringing smiles to the faces of farmers. There would be an economic boost as soon as that translated into bigger harvests and better prices for their produce. The international economy was also recovering, which would soon generate higher prices for Australian exports. It was a good time to be prime minister. Or it would have been, had Hawke not suddenly been beset by two explosive political issues that threatened to blow up his government.

One had been sparked by a dispute with Tasmania over the damming of the lower Gordon River, which runs through pristine wilderness. The state's Liberal government had already outraged environmentalists by flooding beautiful Lake Pedder, on the upper Gordon, in 1978, and wanted to increase its hydroelectric capacity even more with the construction of another dam further down the river in a World Heritage region, which had been made part of the Franklin-Gordon Wild Rivers National Park in 1982. During the recent federal election, Hawke had opposed the building of any more dams on the river, and he'd visited the state several times to defend the policy. His speeches had been in vain, with Tasmania being the only state to see a swing against Labor. There was a fear after the election that the Tasmanian government would begin work on the controversial dam before the new federal government could have a case against it heard in the High Court.

In order to gather evidence for the case, the attorney-general, Gareth Evans, asked the RAAF to make a high-altitude photographic flight above the isolated site with an F-111 reconnaissance aircraft to ascertain the state of work. Unbeknown to Evans, an F-111 was unavailable and an RAAF Mirage fighter was sent instead. With the low cloud cover on 7 April, workers at the dam site were startled to see the Mirage come screaming across the treetops in an unsuccessful attempt to take clear photographs. Sending a fighter plane on a 'spy' mission against another part of Australia was not a good look, and it couldn't be kept secret. Exposed on the eve of Hawke's economic summit, it brought a shower of ridicule on Evans, who was thereafter known as 'Biggles', the fictional aviator in W.E. Johns' stories for boys, and was depicted as such in countless cartoons.[7]

Hawke was furious. It not only detracted from his summit but smacked of the raid on ASIO's Melbourne headquarters in March 1973 by the newly appointed Labor attorney-general, Lionel Murphy, who was suspected by ASIO of being a Soviet spy. The last thing that Hawke wanted was for his government to be likened to Whitlam's.

While Hawke could publicly brush off the 'spy' flight and lay political responsibility at the feet of his young and inexperienced minister, much worse was to come.

CHAPTER EIGHT

# 1983

Less than two months into his prime ministership, Hawke was visited by the head of ASIO, Harvey Barnett, with news that would shake his new government to the core.

Barnett chose his moment well. It was Sunday 20 April, the day before Hawke's colleagues were due to take their seats on the government benches.

The dapper Barnett had served in the navy during the war, before becoming an arts student at the University of Western Australia when Hawke was there. Barnett, the son of wealthy country shopkeepers, had won prizes for diction and played the organ in the chapel of St George's College, where he'd boarded and acted in the dramatic society. As a spy with ASIS in the 1960s, he'd been based in Singapore and Jakarta, where his work had involved keeping watch on Soviet spies. Now, as head of ASIO, he'd found one in Canberra. The Soviet diplomat Valery Ivanov, he told Hawke, was in the process of recruiting Labor's former national secretary David Combe as a Soviet agent.[1]

Confirming that a spy was posing as a diplomat wasn't alarming in itself. The Australian capital was awash with spies. Expulsion was never considered unless they were engaged in activity that was clearly incompatible with their ostensible role as diplomats or that posed a security threat to Australia. The surreptitious recordings of Ivanov's conversations with Combe, who was in the process of expanding his increasingly influential lobbying company, seemed to provide just such a pretext for expelling him. To ensure that outcome, Barnett had gone straight to Hawke, rather than confiding his fears to his minister, the attorney-general, Gareth Evans, who was more likely to question ASIO's evidence and express concern for Combe's civil liberties. Conscious that his operatives hadn't expelled a Soviet spy in twenty years, Barnett knew that his coup would not only bring ASIO favourable headlines around the world but also help protect it against anything the new Labor government might have in mind for it.[2]

It was much more complicated for Hawke, who had become close to Combe in the 1960s. Back then, Combe was a young political apparatchik in South Australia who'd met him at Adelaide airport and led him around the city's pubs. Over the years, Combe had enlisted political supporters for Hawke in both the ACTU and the Labor Party, and had been a stalwart supporter himself, which Hawke repaid when the Iraqi money scandal erupted and Hawke, as Labor president, allowed Combe to keep his job as national secretary. Later, in the campaign to topple Hayden, Combe had been a supporter of Hawke.

Now, though, things were different. As a lobbyist, Combe had recently upset Hawke by attending a supposedly one-on-one meeting between Hawke and the conservative chief minister of the Northern Territory, who was a client of Combe's. In a passing comment, Combe boasted to Hawke about how much money he was now earning as a lobbyist. It was more than Hawke was earning as prime minister.[3]

Annoyed, and perhaps a little envious, Hawke was receptive to Barnett's warning about Combe's access to the most senior levels of the Labor government. It was a warning the prime minister couldn't afford to dismiss. His instinct for self-preservation pushed him towards cutting Combe loose. However, because of the widespread suspicion of ASIO within Labor's ranks, he couldn't afford to move against Combe without being certain of his ground.[4]

Although Hawke demanded to read the raw intelligence on which the ASIO assessment was based, he readily accepted from the ASIO summaries of the conversations that Ivanov was a spy intent on recruiting Combe as an informant, if not an agent of influence. Which was certainly how it seemed to the agents who listened to the sometimes unclear intercepts. It wouldn't have helped Combe's case that when Hawke was handed the transcript of the drunken discussion, he read comments by Combe that derided Hawke's campaign in Moscow to obtain the release of the refuseniks, lambasted Hawke's relationship with Rupert Murdoch and described his own hopes of profiting from his links to the incoming government.⁵

With the memory of the Iraqi money scandal also in his mind, along with his earlier humiliation at the hands of the Russians, Hawke agreed with ASIO that Ivanov be expelled from Australia. When it was suggested that the Russians wouldn't be happy, Hawke responded: 'Fuck the Russians.' Then, in emergency meetings with the six-member security committee of cabinet, he convinced his colleagues – Mick Young, Bill Hayden, Gordon Scholes, Lionel Bowen and Gareth Evans – to have Combe placed under surveillance and banned from contact with the government. It would mean the end of Combe's burgeoning business as a lobbyist.⁶

As the ministerial head of ASIO, Evans could have ensured that the well-placed Combe would at least be accorded a hearing before being blackballed. However, Evans had been weakened by the Biggles affair and bowed to the new prime minister's determination to be seen by the security services and the United States as strong on national security. In fact, none of the ministers was in a position to challenge a prime minister who'd just been elected in a landslide, and who was determined, as Evans said, 'that this was going to be a Government of absolute integrity [with] no spivvery, no bullshit, no funny business'. As well, Evans believed Hawke had 'this characteristic of wanting to hurt those closest to him as a demonstration of just how seriously moral he was'. That was exactly how Hawke would later justify his actions: these 'excruciatingly painful steps', he said, 'were taken to establish that this was a professional, unsentimental, non-mates Government'.⁷ That wasn't exactly true.

It wasn't only Combe who was caught in the crosshairs of the Ivanov affair. After the security committee meeting, Hawke's close friend and old drinking mate Mick Young confided the gist of its deliberations to Eric Walsh, a fellow lobbyist and political journalist. Walsh then warned one of his clients who was involved in Australia–USSR trade and had Combe as a consultant. Unbeknown to Walsh, the client was also an ASIO informant, which was how Hawke came to hear of Young's indiscretion. Revealing the decisions of the cabinet committee was a clear and serious breach of Young's duties as a minister, even though Hawke had done likewise by advising two associates of the

Labor Party, Richard Farmer and Bill Butler, not to follow through with their plan to join Combe's lobbying business.[8]

Hawke's first instinct (notwithstanding the misleading account of the episode in his memoirs) had been to find a politically expedient way of letting Young off the hook. The two men had had a long and intimate association for decades. Graham Richardson described how Young was 'closer to Hawke than anyone in government'. They'd shared a flat in Sydney prior to Whitlam's election, they'd been 'allies on the National Executive for more than a decade, they ate and drank together, laughed together, went to the football together and rang the SP bookie together. They were mates.' Moreover, Young was too valuable to Hawke as a political operative in parliament and a numbers man in the party.[9]

According to the scenario they cooked up, Hawke would write to Young calling him to account for his action, to which Young would respond with an expression of regret and a promise not to transgress again. The plan only came unstuck when questions were raised by one of Hawke's advisers about whether such a cover-up might breach the Crimes Act. This was sufficient to convince Hawke that Young also had to be cut loose, particularly as the Ivanov affair was creating hysterical headlines and being pursued in parliament by the new Opposition leader, Andrew Peacock, and National Party leader, Ian Sinclair, who thought they had the inexperienced prime minister on the run.[10]

The confidence of the Opposition was buoyed by the results in two by-elections. The first took place on 7 May after the resignation of Malcolm Fraser, which saw his safe western Victorian seat of Wannon retained for the Liberal Party with a 1 per cent swing in its favour. Peacock called this a 'stunning success'. Three weeks later, the relatively marginal Melbourne electorate of Bruce was up for grabs following the resignation of its long-time MP, Sir Billy Snedden. Hawke needed only a 0.8 per cent swing to win it and he campaigned hard. So too did Peacock, who loaded forty of his MPs onto a bus for a day's doorknocking.[11]

Both leaders had much to lose. Hawke had put his popularity on the line with Labor's by-election slogan: 'I agree with Hawke'. But the voters didn't. Despite predictions of a Labor victory in the mainly middle-class seat, there was a 4 per cent swing against the government, which allowed the Liberal candidate, Ken Aldred, to succeed Snedden comfortably. From 1975 to 1980, Aldred had represented the seat of Henty. Now he was returning to parliament and his sights were set on Hawke, who conceded that voters had given him 'a biff on the chin'.[12] Yet he'd been prime minister for little more than two months.

Hawke blamed Paul Keating's mini-budget, which had just introduced a tax on superannuation lump-sum payments and a means test for pensioners aged over seventy, and abolished Fraser's home mortgage rebates. Labor's candidate blamed Hawke for 'failing to properly explain' the superannuation tax. Peacock saw it as a protest by families disappointed by 'a whole string of broken promises' and disturbed by the government's 'general impression of incompetence and incoherence'.[13] The Combe affair would have also played a part.

Neither Hawke nor ASIO emerged unscathed when the media learned of the government's blacklisting of Combe, which sparked protests from within the Labor Party and from an outraged Combe, who declared his innocence. Some Labor MPs planned to show that Combe was not out in the cold by organising a very public lunch with him. Under pressure from caucus and parliament, Hawke referred the matter to a royal commission, confident that it would quell the immediate furore and decide in his favour. To make sure of that, he chose a New South Wales judge, Robert Hope, as the commissioner and a leading lawyer, Michael McHugh QC, who'd acted for him in defamation cases and was the husband of Labor MP Jeannette McHugh, as the barrister for the government. Supposedly a supporter of civil liberties, Hope had been appointed by Whitlam in 1974 to investigate the security services, only to defend their breaches of those liberties. He was now appointed by Hawke to determine whether his recommendations had been implemented, with the Combe and Young issues being added to his remit.[14]

With the media becoming increasingly sympathetic to Combe, and the full ASIO transcripts of Combe's conversations with Ivanov turning out to be less damning of Combe than ASIO had suggested, Hawke was urged to testify so as to change the media narrative and make Combe effectively on trial. Putting the prime minister in the dock was a calculated risk. As a union advocate, Hawke had been in the habit of destroying the testimony of employers' witnesses who took the stand in the Arbitration Commission. Now he was the one who would be facing hostile questions from Combe's counsel, Ian Barker QC, who'd recently created international headlines after successfully prosecuting Lindy Chamberlain, who'd been accused of killing her baby Azaria while camping near Uluru. Although Chamberlain would later be pardoned, she remained languishing in jail as Barker prepared to turn his cross-examining skills onto Hawke.[15]

To prepare the prime minister, McHugh took Hawke through the questions that Barker was likely to ask. It was time well spent. Hawke was helped by his own decision to deny Combe's defence team both the details of the relevant cabinet discussions and the transcript of the drunken discussion between Combe and Ivanov. This effectively tied Barker's hands and shifted the spotlight away from Hawke and his ministers, putting it squarely onto Combe. ASIO intercepts of Combe's phone calls were partially released by the commission, although material that would surely have been embarrassing to Hawke, concerning a meeting he and Combe had with the mafia in San Francisco in 1978, was kept secret. Over three days on the stand in early August, Hawke aggressively defended the expulsion of Ivanov and his government's treatment of Combe.[16]

The royal commission's report on 6 December agreed with Hawke. While Hope concluded that Ivanov had been intent on cultivating Combe as an agent of influence for the Soviet Union, the report absolved Combe of having become such an agent. Combe might have had reason to feel vindicated, but the suspicions about him remained and his lobbying career was destroyed. Unfortunately for Hawke, the issue did not die with the publication of the report. Combe would continue to fight to restore both his business and his reputation. He would blame Hawke for his plight and apply political pressure on him by backgrounding journalists about matters that Hawke would prefer to keep secret. One of those matters was the trip that Combe and Hawke took to Vancouver in 1978, stopping over in San Francisco at the request of Abeles for a meeting with the mafia-controlled Teamsters Union, Although much of the media ignored the story, *The National Times* made a point of reporting it among its many stories on the links between organised crime and politicians, police, the judiciary and business leaders, including Hawke's closest friend, Peter Abeles.[17]

Combe kept up the pressure by having his allies in the party put it on the agenda for the party's following federal conference. Combe's years as national secretary ensured that he had a large measure of goodwill among the delegates, as he moved among them seeking support for a motion that would restore his reputation and his livelihood. In his own defence, Hawke told the delegates that the government 'took the action we believed was necessary and at no time did I or the Government have any animus towards him and there is none now'. Wanting the issue to be finally buried, Hawke backed a unanimous motion that acknowledged the harm done to Combe and his family and declared that there was no impediment to Combe's future employment with the government. In return, it trusted that the former national secretary would show 'continuous loyalty to the Party and the Government'.[18]

Despite the conciliatory wording, neither the government nor the party was forthcoming with sufficient work to restore Combe's lobbying business, which left Combe and his wife bitter about their treatment. Combe's occasional forays into the spotlight would keep the issue alive until John Dawkins, then minister for trade, appointed him in 1985 as Australia's consul-general and trade commissioner in Vancouver, Canada, ensuring his silence for so long as he remained on the public payroll.[19] The issue had been an early test of Hawke as prime minister. While his government had emerged with some of its shine rubbed off, Hawke remained as popular as ever with voters. There were more serious challenges to come.

CHAPTER NINE

# 1983

Amidst all the Combe controversy, Hawke remained as focused as he could be on establishing the bona fides of his government. The National Economic Summit had served that purpose for Australians by showing the Hawke government to be very different from that of Whitlam. While his ministers continued to implement the party's policies in their particular portfolios, Hawke took off in early June on his first overseas trip as prime minister. Clutching a passport that claimed him to be 179 centimetres tall, about six centimetres taller than his actual height, he began with a stopover in Port Moresby.[1] It was a nod to his earlier experience in pre-independence New Guinea as ACTU advocate, but also a reflection of his belief that Australia's security and economic interests lay predominantly in the Asia-Pacific region, rather than being entwined with those of Britain and Europe. That had been the basis of Australia's foreign policy since the 1960s, when Washington had steadily usurped the influence of London in Canberra's corridors of power and Japan had become Australia's major trading partner.

Although he flew on to Jakarta for talks with President Suharto, where Hawke had to navigate the diplomatic difficulties caused by the continuing Indonesian occupation of East Timor, his mind was probably elsewhere. Because his next stop was Geneva, where the ILO was holding its three-week congress. This was where he had held court each year as ACTU president and fallen in love with Helga Cammell, a woman he'd thought seriously of marrying. His visit was 'like a homecoming', he told the hundreds of delegates who gathered to hear him address a special session on 10 June. He was no longer the often-inebriated ACTU president but the sober prime minister who was anxious to speak about the serious issues of apartheid in South Africa and workers' rights in Poland. As the administrative head of the International Federation of Commercial, Clerical and Technical Employees, Cammell was presumably among the audience. Hawke and Hazel weren't in Geneva for long, but there was time, on the eve of his departure for Washington, for him and Paul Keating to dine with Rupert Murdoch, when the government's media and aviation plans were doubtless discussed, before Hawke dashed off to 'meet some old Genevan friends', which may have included Cammell.[2]

While Washington was not Hawke's first stop, it was the most consequential. He was anxious to assure American policymakers and investors that his government would pose no threat to them, and that Australia would remain a reliable strategic ally and a welcome host for American capital. He took Keating along to reinforce the latter message. He wanted American investment to resume its role in the Australian economy, and American defence and security chiefs to be reassured that Australia posed no threat to their country's interests. Hawke was mindful that it was only ten years since the CIA, under the Republican president Richard Nixon, had economically destabilised the left-wing government of Salvador Allende and supported a subsequent coup by reactionary elements of the Chilean army. And it was less than eight years since Whitlam had been deposed. It was fortunate that the expulsion of Ivanov had preceded his visit to Washington. As Hawke would later reflect, '[I]f Labor softness on national security had been of concern to our own security forces or to the foreign services with whom they dealt, those of the US in particular, from Combe-Ivanov onwards that concern was wiped away.'[3]

As ACTU president, Hawke had become used to walking a line between Communist Party union officials and the CIA agents posing as labour attachés with whom he would regularly meet to talk about the union movement. While at the ACTU, he'd also become friendly with the head of the American Bechtel Corporation, George Shultz, who now served as Reagan's secretary of state. That friendship would serve him well as prime minister, when he had to walk a similar line between those in the Labor Party who wanted a more independent foreign policy and his own inclination to keep Canberra largely in lockstep with Washington. While he told the Washington Press Club that his government would 'pursue an independent and self-respecting foreign policy', he made clear that Labor's policy was no different from that of the Liberal Party and would be 'at all times consistent with Australia's international obligations'. And there was no greater obligation than Australia's strategic relationship with the United States, which had seen it become embroiled in costly wars from Korea to Vietnam. Although he didn't echo Harold Holt's cloying declaration to President Lyndon Johnson that Australia would go 'all the way with LBJ', he did say that the two countries would be 'together forever'.[4]

In an implicit disavowal of Whitlam's foreign policy initiatives, Hawke said that his government would have 'no illusions about its capacity to influence global events, and no false notions of our self-importance'. Its contribution to international affairs would be at the edges. As examples, he cited the ongoing conflict in Cambodia as a regional issue where Australia could play a useful role, and the broader issue of disarmament, where Australia would seek to create a nuclear-free zone in the south-west Pacific. This reflected the public opposition to the French nuclear testing on Mururoa atoll. Hawke made clear that it wouldn't affect Australia's continuing export of uranium or the hosting in Australia of nuclear-armed warships. Nor would it impede the work of the several US intelligence bases in Australia, even if their purpose was to support American forces in a nuclear war. He blamed expressions of 'anti-Americanism', rather than the split in the Labor Party, for keeping Labor out of office in the 1950s and '60s, and assured Americans that Labor was 'again the party of Curtin'.[5]

It was a misreading of history by Hawke. While Curtin had certainly sought American help to save Australia from a Japanese invasion in 1942, effectively ceding economic and strategic control of the country to General Douglas MacArthur, he hadn't wanted the constrictive economic and strategic embrace of the Americans to persist into the post-war world. Instead, the Curtin government had wanted to reassert Australia's relative independence within the British Empire, with dreams of Australia even creating a sub-empire of its own in the south-west Pacific.[6]

This episode in Australian history was forgotten during the Cold War, when Labor was accused of being anti-American and reacted by creating the myth that there was an unbroken line between Curtin's wartime alliance with MacArthur and the ANZUS Treaty of 1951. Hawke was not a great reader of history and would have imbibed the myth without much critical reflection. He had a strong emotional attachment to the story of Curtin, who'd given up grog to lead the nation. Hawke had an equally strong attachment to the United States, which probably first took root when he was a boy in wartime Perth as American sailors and airmen strode the city's streets. It was reinforced through the friendships he'd formed during his time in Oxford and his association with conservative American union officials in Geneva, as well as with the succession of CIA agents in Australia. Moreover, he believed that the innate conservativism of the electorate strongly favoured the alliance with America, and he wouldn't disappoint them.

At the same time, Hawke recognised that Australia's economic future lay with the fast-developing economies of the Asian region. In this, he was following the example of Whitlam, who'd opened the way for Australia to establish relations with Communist China before the United States had done so. To mark the ten years since Whitlam's historic move, after which trade between the two countries increased tenfold, Hawke had hosted a visit by the Chinese premier, Zhao Ziyang, who'd been persecuted during the Cultural Revolution and later rehabilitated under Deng Xiaoping to become a leading advocate of free-market reforms. Although the premier had come at Fraser's invitation, it was Hawke who presided over the lunch in parliament house on 18 April, where he hailed the normalisation of Australia's relations with China, looked forward to a reduction of tension between China and other countries, and welcomed a greater expansion of ties with Beijing. Within weeks, China had agreed to allow BHP to begin exploring for oil in the South China Sea.[7]

During the Vietnam War, many Australians had feared a Chinese invasion, never foreseeing that the invasion would turn out to be Chinese officials and business executives eager to secure supplies of Australian resources for their nation's modernisation program. Like his predecessors, Hawke was happy to help. He recognised this as an economic opportunity that could also transform Australia. But it could take decades to play out and he couldn't rely upon the gradual increase in trade with China to solve the seemingly intractable dilemma of high inflation and unemployment that had dogged Australia since the 1970s. At least he had a government that was much more streamlined, disciplined and focused than Whitlam's. And he had a clear idea of what he wanted to achieve.

Soon after becoming prime minister, Hawke had told the National Press Club of his 'long-term commitment to restoring growth to our nation's economy, a commitment to increasing employment, to turning the tide of unemployment, and a commitment to ensuring both that the benefits of recovery are fairly shared and that they are not lost in a new bout of inflation'. He hoped that markets might do for the seemingly intractable problems of unemployment, inflation and economic growth what protectionist policies and governments had singularly failed to do.[8]

In the wake of the election, Hawke had boasted to journalist Michelle Grattan of having a 'well-developed art of delegation', which was how he'd run the ACTU while gallivanting around the world for months every year. Of course, that only works if you're surrounded by good people. Apart from his carefully chosen staff, having a very able cabinet was perhaps Hawke's greatest asset, along with his consultative manner of chairing meetings. As Susan Ryan wryly observed, meetings 'would not conclude until the leader's desired outcome was desired by all present'. The extended discussions meant long and frequent meetings. Hawke's popularity with the electorate helped to ensure that potentially rebellious ministers confined their criticisms to scribbled notes passed across the cabinet table or spoken sotto voce as they left the room. It helped that Hawke didn't attempt to micromanage them. His ministers were expected to get on and implement those Labor policies that were still viable, given the budget situation, and bring well-developed proposals to the cabinet room, which Hawke would carefully read the night before. They had relative freedom to do anything, provided it didn't involve money. As for the caucus, its ability to cause trouble was constrained by Hawke's insistence that the principle of cabinet solidarity had to apply, which meant that any ministers who wanted to argue in caucus against a cabinet decision would have to resign from cabinet. Only one ever did.[9]

Not that the cabinet, or even the inner ministry, was the centre of government power. That was focused instead on Hawke and four of his ministers – Keating, Willis, Walsh and Dawkins – who comprised the powerful ERC. Its task was to review government programs and decide which could go ahead, which had to be cut and which taxes would be imposed to pay for it all. Sometimes Hawke wouldn't attend the ERC himself, instead sending Ross Garnaut to keep a watching brief and report back. Decisions were then taken to the inner cabinet of thirteen senior ministers, where they were endorsed and referred to the full cabinet and the caucus in turn.[10]

Few questioned the ERC's decisions. Health minister Neal Blewett described how they were taken to cabinet with little notice, which made it difficult to organise opposition to them. As for the caucus, according to Blewett, its members were 'so euphoric about getting back into government that it was fairly easy [for Hawke] to lay down the law'. If anyone quibbled about being railroaded, Hawke would point to the deficit as justification. Some ERC decisions were never discussed by the cabinet, let alone by the caucus, before they were implemented.[11]

The floating of the Australian dollar was one example of this. The value of the dollar was set against a basket of currencies by the Reserve Bank, in consultation with the government, each Monday morning. This meant that foreign exchange dealers could reap a quick reward by betting against the value that had been set and then selling off the currency until they forced a devaluation. In the meantime, Australian consumers and businesses would incur the consequent increase in the cost of imports. Hawke had attempted to combat this speculation after the election, when he'd ordered a 10 per cent devaluation, only to see the currency return to its previous value over the succeeding months.

It was well understood that floating the dollar and the concomitant lifting of exchange controls would allow the value of the dollar to be set constantly by the foreign exchange market rather than reactively by the government. The issue had been on the agenda for several years, only to be passed over by Fraser for fear of its possible effects on the cost of the country's imports and prices for its exports. After ordering the initial devaluation, Hawke had wrestled for months with the idea of floating the currency. By October 1983, Hawke decided to go ahead; he was supported by Ross Garnaut and the Reserve Bank's Bob Johnston. Although Keating had long been in favour, he was held back by his Treasury secretary, John Stone, who feared the value of the dollar would be sent skyward, harming the country's export industries. According to Garnaut, it was decided to delay the float until Keating could bring Stone on board.[12]

By 8 December 1983, the last parliamentary sitting day of the year, there was no choice. Speculators were buying up Australian dollars in anticipation of a revaluation. The dollar would have to be floated or another devaluation announced to maintain the competitiveness of Australian exports. Stone remained fearful of Australia losing effective control of its relatively small economy. He warned that its float could cause the dollar to rise rather than to fall, as Garnaut wanted. Both Keating and Hawke were nervous about overruling Stone and facing the political consequences if his fears came to pass. Keating had repeatedly been in Hawke's office for meetings all that day, without a decision being made. Late that night, as the corridors of Parliament House resounded with boisterous partygoers celebrating the end of the parliamentary sitting, Hawke's advisers told him it was 'mad' to hold fire any longer in the face of the mounting crisis. Hawke asked Keating to come back upstairs for a final meeting, during which they agreed to stare Stone down.[13]

Once Keating had advised Hayden, Dawkins, Walsh and Willis of the decision, Hawke called a meeting next morning of the ERC, where Johnston and Stone were asked to present their opposing arguments, even though the ministers were now all of one mind. Stone was wasting his time – as he discovered when Hawke ended the discussion by declaring that the float and the lifting of exchange controls would go ahead. The decision had finally been made.

'You'll regret this,' warned Stone as he left the cabinet room.

While the float did cause a short-term increase in the value of the dollar, just as Stone had predicted, the value abated thereafter, just as Johnston had suggested it would.[14]

Although the floating of the dollar caused headlines, Australians were slow to realise its implications. Hawke's action was as radical as any that Whitlam had taken during his time in the Lodge. The decision cemented the Hawke/Keating decision-making duopoly, while Keating's victory over Stone left the Treasury head mortally wounded and Keating convinced of his pre-eminence as the intellectual engine of the Hawke government. His apprenticeship as treasurer was over.

More broadly, it marked the beginning of a new chapter in the Australian story, one in which the economy would no longer be wrapped so tightly in the comforting blanket of protective regulations, which had sustained its fitful growth for much of the twentieth century. Over time, it would become more exposed to international competition, which would force Australian businesses and workers to become more efficient or face losing custom to their overseas counterparts, particularly the Japanese, whose cars and electronic goods were flooding shops and showrooms.

And floating the dollar was just the beginning. Once that was implemented, Hawke and Keating wanted more parts of the economy to be exposed to market forces in the hope that a more vibrant and outward-looking economy would provide the jobs that the government was committed to creating. Hawke knew that the benefits would take years to become apparent, but confidently expected that he would still be prime minister when that occurred.

CHAPTER TEN

# 1984

The opinion polls during Hawke's first year as prime minister suggested that Australians were happy with their new leader. With the ending of the drought, improving economic conditions and a Hawke-inspired spirit of cooperation replacing Fraser's confrontational style, there was a new burst of optimism. It was given added force when an Australian yacht skippered by John Bertrand won the America's Cup in the waters off Rhode Island in September 1983. Hawke had visited the crew in June and, with Hazel, had been photographed at the wheel as the beaming owner, the England-born Alan Bond, looked on. Bond was a reckless land developer and corporate raider who'd barely escaped bankruptcy in the mid-1970s before being named Australian of the Year in 1978 for his exploits on the water.

Bond's America's Cup challenge was the latest of several he had mounted, hoping that the publicity would boost his international business ambitions and keep him a few steps ahead of his creditors. His boat, *Australia II*, was one of many foreign vessels challenging the Americans. It not only beat off the other challengers but went on to narrowly win the deciding race of the seven-race competition. Millions of Australians stayed up through the night to watch the historic moment. It was the first time in the America's Cup's 132-year history that a foreign boat had won, and Bond was lionised. For the next five years or so, financial cowboys would take the place of sports stars in the Australian firmament. Writer Donald Horne would describe the cup win as 'the greatest disaster to befall Australia in the 1980s'.[1]

Not for Hawke, though. These were his people. He scheduled a cabinet meeting in Perth to ensure that he was present at the Royal

Perth Yacht Club, watching on television with its excited members. As morning broke, and having donned a jacket festooned with the word 'Australia', the ebullient prime minister delighted the dog-tired television viewers by declaring that 'any boss who sacks anyone for not turning up today is a bum'. Although he quickly cautioned that workers would have to work harder in subsequent days to make up for their absence, people only heard the bit about bosses and loved Hawke the more for it. In Canberra, public servants emptied bottle shops of champagne and picnicked on the shores of Lake Burley Griffin. One woman told *The Canberra Times* they were celebrating because 'we are Australians and we are taking the rest of the day off because we work for Bob Hawke'.[2] It was that sort of day.

It wasn't the end of the celebrations. Realising that the historic victory had struck a nationalistic chord, Hawke invited the yachtsmen to visit Canberra two weeks later so that people could express their 'jubilation'. There were formal receptions, a tour of the site of the planned new Parliament House, and lunch at the Lodge. However, he'd timed the extended celebration for 11 November, the day that Whitlam had been dismissed. Hawke might have wanted to shift Canberra's focus away from the Whitlam government's dismissal, but it was also Remembrance Day – honouring Australia's fallen servicemen and women. Hawke's plans provoked a protest from *The Canberra Times*, which thought he should be satisfied with the media coverage he'd 'already garnered ... because of his wish to be present at victories, especially sporting victories'. The RSL, meanwhile, was outraged that Hawke could make time for the yachtsmen on Remembrance Day, but not have time to lay the official wreath at the War Memorial. Sensing a change in the political wind, Hawke immediately tacked, rescheduling his appointments so that he could attend the sombre wreath-laying ceremony as well as celebrate the America's Cup victory.[3]

A month later he flew to South Australia, where a dinner was held to honour John Bertrand. The following day, during a break in a Test match, Bertrand was driven in a lap of honour around Adelaide Oval, while Hawke visited the Australian cricketers in their dressing room before joining Bertrand for lunch. A few days later, he was in Melbourne presenting prizes at the Sport Australia Awards. Hawke was passionate about sport and spread government patronage to different sporting codes for men and women, while also establishing the Australian Sports Commission, through which government funds could be channelled and participation in sport encouraged. As Whitlam caustically observed, Hawke believed there were 'more votes in sport than the arts'.[4]

There was nothing inauthentic about Hawke's embrace of sport, which only added to his public popularity. The Liberals' new leader, the young and debonair Andrew Peacock, shared Hawke's love of sport and also hated losing. He was an only child, a law graduate and a keen womaniser whose first marriage had ended in divorce. Like Hawke, who'd become part-owner of a racehorse with Col Cunningham, Peacock was an enthusiastic participant in horseracing and was often in the winners' circle. Politics proved more difficult. In one of his first polls as Liberal leader, he only managed to secure a 25 per cent approval rating as preferred prime minister, compared to 58 per cent for Hawke.[5]

That poll, in July 1983, also saw Labor retain a commanding lead over the Liberals, 51 per cent to 42 per cent, with the Australian Democrats on 5 per cent. But the demands of the prime ministership seemed to be taking a physical toll on the 53-year-old Hawke, as he dealt with the succession of political crises and resigned himself to this more demanding life. On top of everything, he continued to be dogged by questions about his association with dodgy characters. When he supported an unsuccessful proposal for a casino in Canberra, it was seized upon by newly elected Liberal MP Ken Aldred as offering opportunities for money laundering by organised crime, with suggestions that Hawke was doing a deal behind the scenes to favour the owners of the Wrest Point Casino in Hobart, where he often gambled. Hawke challenged Aldred to repeat the claims outside parliament so that Hawke could sue him. He pointed out that the casino had first been approved by the Fraser government, and that it would boost the ailing Canberra economy and create 'jobs for young women who would not otherwise be able to find employment'. With less than six months as prime minister, his careworn appearance was described by an interviewer in August, who noted the lines on his face deepening to ruts and his mane of hair 'now almost completely silver'. The wise counsel of Hawke's staff helped him cope with the demands of the job, while the tennis court and pool at the Lodge provided outlets for relaxation.⁶ But there remained so much to do and so many political pitfalls to avoid.

As ACTU president, Hawke had been aghast when Whitlam had suddenly announced a 25 per cent cut in tariffs, which had forced the closing of factories that couldn't compete with cheaper imports and caused a drop in support for the government from its traditional voters. While Hawke didn't want to emulate Whitlam's electoral experience, he did want to continue the dismantling of Australia's tariff barrier, while ensuring that the affected workers were supported during the transition. There were thousands of them living or working in his own electorate. And their jobs were all under threat. The coming of jumbo jets had seen Australians return from the street markets of South-East Asia, their suitcases crammed with the cheap clothing and electronic goods that were much more expensive in Australia because of the tariff wall. Workers in the sweatshops of Australian inner cities might want to have their jobs protected, but consumers were the losers. Hawke realised that Australia's economic future would be enhanced if it abandoned those industries that could never be competitive and instead moved up the value chain by supporting industries that required a better-educated workforce and in which Australia enjoyed a comparative advantage. He had to move carefully, though, as he was constrained by the power of the protection lobby among both trade unions and businesses.

The steel industry was the first to be tackled by the industry minister, John Button, with months of patient negotiation with BHP, which wanted to make thousands of its workers redundant; with the trade unions, which wanted the jobs of their members protected; and with the state governments, which wanted to keep the company's foundries operating. The eventual deal guaranteed BHP a minimum of 80 per cent of the Australian steel market and subsidised improvements to its steelworks, and offered workers early retirement rather than retrenchment. It wasn't protection in perpetuity, but support that would expire in several years, in the expectation of a more competitive industry. The steel plan provided a template for other industry plans that Hawke and Button would pursue over the next several years.⁷

The union movement had attended the National Economic Summit and had accepted the Prices and Incomes Accord, hoping that it would provide the promised path out of the economic morass in which Australia was stuck. However, some powerful unions were angered by the prospect of tariff cuts that threatened the livelihood of their members and, by extension, the wealth and power of the unions. Improved productivity in the car and steel industries promised higher profits for shareholders but brought thousands of retrenchments for workers. It's not surprising that some Labor supporters questioned the direction that Hawke was intent on taking Australia.

That opposition had come to a head at the ALP's national conference, held in Canberra in July 1984, when the question of allowing foreign banks to operate in Australia was debated, along with the government's decision to allow the mining of uranium at the recently discovered Roxby Downs copper and uranium deposit in South Australia. Until then, the party had only been prepared to approve existing uranium mines. The issue had recently prompted the resignation from his cabinet of the left-wing stalwart Stewart West. Now the party's policy had to be brought into line with the government's.

Hawke had always argued that Australia had more chance of influencing international debates about nuclear non-proliferation if it was an exporter of uranium. Moreover, any ban on its mining would be resisted by its well-paid uranium miners. As for the admission of foreign banks, Hawke had little time for the four major domestic banks, whose hold on the local financial industry was limiting competition and inhibiting the entrepreneurial instincts of Australian businesses by restricting their access to capital. More competition in the banking space would surely bring easier access to finance for both businesses and individuals. Keating deployed such arguments when he convinced a majority of conference delegates to allow the admission of up to fifteen foreign banks. The proposal for uranium mining at Roxby Downs was also passed.[8]

There was never a risk of the conference turning against Hawke, who'd brought Labor back to government and was riding so high in the polls that he was known as 'Mr 75 Per Cent'. In fact, one poll had him at 78 per cent, a level no post-war prime minister had ever achieved. Australians had good reason to be satisfied with him. Unemployment, inflation and interest rates were all going down, and more than 200,000 jobs had been created. The only serious shadow at the conference had been cast by the still-aggrieved David Combe, who wanted Hawke and his ministers to concede that he had been treated poorly over the Ivanov affair. Which Hawke grudgingly agreed to do.

With the party conference out of the way, Hawke and Keating could proceed with the further deregulation of the economy. There was so much to do, and the prime minister and treasurer were of one mind. Although they would later fiercely dispute which of them should be given the credit for initiating particular changes, neither could have done it without the other. Keating has claimed that he brought ideas to Hawke, who then gave them his political support. This ignores Hawke's commitment, from at least the mid-1970s, to create a more market-based economy.

Keating's claim also ignores the contributions of other senior ministers who were of like mind, such as Walsh, Willis and Dawkins, and of the Reserve Bank governor, Bob Johnston, and Hawke's economic adviser, Ross Garnaut. The government was led by a prime minister and a coterie of powerful cabinet ministers who were all intent on transforming Australia and, by doing so, restoring the Labor Party's reputation for economic management, so that it could once again aspire to be regarded as the natural party of government.[9]

The Accord, with its trade-off between wage increases and government payments, was central to Hawke's success. Health insurance was a big part of that bargain with the trade union movement, with the restoration of a universal, government-funded health insurance system after Fraser had dismantled Medibank. In its place, Fraser had established Medibank Private, which provided health insurance for those who could afford it, but about two million Australians had been left to manage without insurance as best they could. Now Hawke's health minister, Neal Blewett, reintroduced the principle of universal health insurance. Called Medicare, and established with the agreement of the states and territories on 1 February 1984, the scheme provided free treatment for patients in public hospitals and up to 85 per cent rebates on the scheduled fee for a consultation with a doctor. It allowed most people paying for basic cover on their private insurance policies to rely on Medicare instead, which would be paid for partly by an income tax levy.

Since health insurance comprised a significant proportion of the consumer price index (CPI), the introduction of Medicare caused such a big reduction in the medical insurance area of the CPI that it negated the price rises in other areas. Because wages were indexed to the CPI, it brought a break in the inflationary spiral that in turn produced an effective pause in wages growth for six months. Together with the breaking of the drought and the spending in Fraser's expansionary budget of 1982 and Keating's follow-up budget of 1983, the wage pause helped to drive the unemployment rate back below 10 per cent and create nearly half of the jobs that Hawke had promised during his first term.[10] That promise had been predicated on an assumption that his first term would last three years. In the event, it lasted less than two.

The Liberals had forced Whitlam to two early elections and then called two early elections of their own, in 1977 and 1979, when Fraser calculated that he could profit from the disarray in the Labor Party. The public were sick of the cynical abuse of the political process, and Hawke had promised during the 1983 campaign to serve his full term and introduce a referendum for fixed-term parliaments. However, the temptation to capitalise on his popularity became too strong to resist. Hawke saw an opportunity to build a bigger electoral buffer to ensure he remained as prime minister for at least another two terms.

And there was a good, practical reason for an early election.

Fraser's early elections had caused the terms for the House of Representatives and the Senate to no longer coincide. Although the House of Representatives didn't require an election until early 1986, there had to be an election for half the Senate before the end of 1984. Rather than having two campaigns in relatively quick succession, Hawke seized upon the half-Senate election as a pretext for having a simultaneous election for the House of Representatives, hopeful that it would lock in the bigger majority he desired and once again synchronise the elections. Hawke chose to make it a long campaign, believing that it would increase his vote and confident that Peacock wouldn't perform well on the hustings. A long campaign would also give Hawke more opportunities to lap up the love of the voters.

Hawke had much to be confident about. Apart from his own popularity holding up, his government had mostly performed well. The economy was on the mend after a decade or so of lacklustre performance. The Accord with the trade union movement was limiting wage rises and industrial disputes, and allowing the government's economic policies to be more expansionary than they would otherwise have been. Along with his own economic understanding and communication skills, Hawke's troika of economic ministers – Keating, Dawkins and Willis – were restoring Labor's reputation for economic management and for industrial peace. A raft of other reforms had been introduced in quick time, not least Medicare and the beginnings of the industrial reconstruction being orchestrated by Button. A shift in education funding had also begun under the stewardship of Susan Ryan, with a new formula based on need overturning the preference that Fraser had given to the wealthy private schools. The bastions of privilege would still enjoy largesse from the Commonwealth government, but to a lesser extent than government schools.

With the ERC anxious to curb the budget deficit bequeathed by Fraser, there was little immediate scope for radical improvements in social welfare payments. But there were measures that the government could take for the advancement of women following Fraser's dismantling of some Whitlam reforms. Given the demands on the budget, they tended to be measures that wouldn't increase spending. Nonetheless, they were of great and enduring importance.

Women had been crucial to Hawke's electoral success, with Labor for the first time securing about 50 per cent of their vote. Although there were only a handful of women in the parliament, they had a powerful advocate in Ryan, who'd been elected as a senator for the ACT in 1975 with the slogan 'A woman's place is in the Senate'. She was the divorced wife of a diplomat and the mother of two children, and had been a teacher before graduating with a Master of Arts. A member of the Women's Electoral Lobby, she was politically astute and a committed feminist. As an Opposition senator in 1981, she had moved a private member's bill that drew on the United Nations Convention on the Elimination of All Forms of Discrimination Against Women. That had been introduced by the UN in 1979 and ratified by fifty nations by the time Ryan proposed her bill. Under Fraser, Australia had refused to ratify the convention, and his government had likewise refused to support Ryan's bill.[11]

With Labor's election in 1983, that all changed. Hawke had appointed Ryan as minister for education, which gave her a cabinet seat, while also making her assistant minister for women. This ensured that women's issues were discussed in the otherwise totally male cabinet. The former Office of Women, which had been established by Whitlam and then relegated to the outer reaches of the public service by Fraser, was resurrected by Hawke and renamed the Office for the Status of Women (OSW) – and, at Ryan's suggestion, brought within the Department of Prime Minister and Cabinet.[12]

There was no tokenism about this. With Hawke's support, the beefed-up office would have a whole-of-government status, providing advice on all cabinet submissions and proposed legislation. Perhaps more importantly, every government department was required to submit an annual Women's Budget Statement, which reported 'how their policies and programmes affected women'. Most departments also established sections to advise on how the implementation of their policies affected women and what changes were required to improve them. Ryan's bill outlawing sex discrimination was finally passed by parliament in December 1983, in the face of vociferous opposition from conservative women's groups and despite nervousness about the issue in caucus.[13]

With Ryan's strong support, Anne Summers, a leading feminist author and journalist on *The National Times*, was appointed in November 1983 to lead the OSW. It was a sign that the Hawke government was intent on systemic change to foster greater gender equality. That reflected the growing participation of women in the workforce and the political reality in caucus, where fourteen Labor women now sat among the suits. They formed a women's committee, which monitored the actions of individual ministers in answering the needs of women.

On a pragmatic level, Hawke sensed the increasing political power women were wielding and realised that his continuing as prime minister could depend upon their support. On a deeper level, and despite his derogatory attitudes and behaviour towards women in the past, he had imbibed the example of his mother, who had fostered the advancement of girls through education, and he'd been exposed to feminist arguments by his wife and daughters, and by some of his lovers. Summers certainly felt that Hawke had a genuine commitment to the betterment of women.

He told her that this was due to his reading of Simone de Beauvoir's landmark book *The Second Sex* (1949), which had ushered in second-wave feminism. It had inspired a generation of feminist authors, from Betty Friedan, author of *The Feminine Mystique* (1963), to Summers herself. It is doubtful that Hawke had ever read the 700-page book from cover to cover, but some of the women in his life certainly had, and they impressed its arguments upon him. Summers was called upon for advice when Hazel was putting together her Australia Day address for the National Press Club. When Summers arrived at Kirribilli House to meet with Hazel, she wandered into the garden and was taken aback by a greeting from a 'little guy in front of me, wearing nothing but tiny red speedos, his nut-brown body daubed with white zinc'. It was, of course, Hawke dressed in his preferred attire.[14]

By mid-1984, Hawke could afford to be relatively relaxed. The economy was on the mend and the budget was being brought under control by his treasurer and the ERC. Hawke had resisted the urge to engage in a rapid flurry of activity, which had marked Whitlam's first eighteen months in government. Hawke's ministers were introducing policies that implemented many of Labor's election promises, while ditching some that threatened the budget's return to surplus. The sex discrimination law was a case in point. It was a progressive policy that would benefit women and enhance the reputation of the government, while the burden would be borne largely by businesses, many of which were happy to support Hawke's reform agenda and to reap the expected financial rewards.

Some promised reforms fell by the wayside. Much to Gareth Evans' chagrin, Hawke refused to proceed with several important law reform initiatives that had been approved by party conferences. One of these was fixed-term parliaments, which Hawke had promised voters but would have required a referendum. Another was Aboriginal land rights, which would have upset the powerful mining lobby and Hawke's mate, West Australian premier Brian Burke, who was helping to funnel millions of campaign dollars from big business into the party's coffers.[15]

Despite these policy disappointments, Hawke and his ministers had reinvigorated the business of government and changed its direction in several important and lasting ways. This period might not have been as radical as Whitlam's first year and a half, but it was progressive and could claim a level of economic responsibility that Whitlam had never attained.

Indeed, Hawke was on a roll. He'd done the seemingly impossible, restoring economic growth and cutting unemployment and inflation. Stagflation seemed to be at an end. His popularity remained extraordinarily high and Andrew Peacock could not lay a glove on his government in parliament. Despite Hawke's occasional missteps, the loyalty of his ministers was relatively undimmed and another election victory seemed certain.[16]

But Hawke hadn't counted upon a personal crisis, which would throw him into a state of such deep depression that it threatened to bring an early end to his prime ministership.

CHAPTER ELEVEN

# 1984

As the 1 December election approached, Hawke was confident that voters would reaffirm his prime ministership and increase his parliamentary majority despite a slew of embarrassing scandals. One concerned the hapless Mick Young, who'd failed to declare a number of gifts, including a Paddington Bear he'd brought back from overseas in his wife's suitcase, and on which a small amount of import duty was payable. Young had been stood down by Hawke during the Combe/Ivanov affair, only to return to the ministry and cause further headlines with his stuffed toy. The issue played into popular perceptions about the venality of politicians, but was hardly worth the headlines it attracted. Nevertheless, Hawke asked Young to stand down while an inquiry was held, which duly exonerated the former shearer.[1]

Another issue concerned Lionel Murphy, who'd been Whitlam's attorney-general before being appointed by Whitlam as a High Court judge. Police tapes of phone conversations revealed that Murphy had a close friendship with a wealthy solicitor, Morgan Ryan, who'd frequently been Murphy's instructing solicitor in trade union cases in the 1950s before largely giving up the law to become a full-time gambler at racetracks and a paid peddler of influence with the police, judges and politicians. It may have been at the racetrack that Ryan developed links with Sydney's criminal underworld. The bowdlerised transcripts of the police tapes were leaked to *The Age*, which handed them to Attorney-General Gareth Evans on the eve of their publication.

Dribbled out over days in February 1984, the '*Age* tapes' caused a sensation. It was implied that Murphy was part of a web of corruption in Sydney involving senior police, magistrates and the notorious criminal Abe Saffron. The fevered reports of the bugged telephone calls alleged that Murphy had agreed to intercede with judges or magistrates on behalf of drug dealers and other malefactors. If that could be proved, it could have led to Murphy's sacking from the High Court.[2]

The former Labor politician had a well-deserved reputation as a defender of civil liberties, and had been responsible for the passing of landmark legislation, including the Racial Discrimination Act and the Family Law Act, but he'd also caused embarrassment to the Whitlam government with his March 1973 'raid' on ASIO's headquarters after believing that he was being denied information about Croatian terrorism. He was now threatening to cause embarrassment to Hawke's government, and Gareth Evans referred the matter to the director of public prosecutions. The DPP found no evidence of criminal wrongdoing, yet the Liberal and crossbench senators combined to set up a Senate inquiry to determine whether Murphy was a fit and proper person to sit on the High Court. Some Liberal politicians had been pursuing him for years.[3]

The whiff of corruption swirling around Murphy was the latest in a series of allegations, mainly about Labor politicians in New South Wales, which had seen Neville Wran temporarily stand aside as premier in April 1983 after the ABC's *Four Corners* program alleged that he'd pressured the chief magistrate, Murray Farquhar, to have a case against one of his political supporters dismissed. To clear his name, Wran established a royal commission with very restrictive terms of reference that didn't allow the commissioner to examine allegations of systemic corruption. Although Wran was exonerated, Farquhar was jailed for attempting to pervert the course of justice.[4]

The commission's report didn't stop the rumours about Wran, appropriately known as 'Nifty Nev'. Phillip Adams claimed to have been present when 'terrible deals' had been done between Wran and Kerry Packer, with Adams describing Wran as 'the most corrupt figure in the history of Australian politics'.[5] Other stories abounded, being driven partly by Wran's failure to crack down on illegal casinos and clean up the police force, as well as his earlier defence of Farquhar and his reappointment of him in 1978 despite his association with George Freeman, one of Sydney's major crime bosses, who had links to the mafia. There are also the several deals that Wran did that involved government property and contracts that were to the financial advantage of Abeles.⁶

The corruption allegations also caught one of Wran's ministers, Rex Jackson, who was in charge of prisons and had become heavily indebted to SP bookmakers. Jackson tried to dig himself out by taking bribes to release prisoners from jail, only to be exposed when federal police tapped a telephone line on which he was heard negotiating a bribe. The matter was referred to Hawke, who had the explosive information passed on to the New South Wales government – which was where corruption allegations were sent to die. Wran sat on the information until Peacock raised the matter in parliament and details of the police tapes were leaked to the media. Wran denied the need for an inquiry until Jackson was found to have misled the New South Wales parliament. It was only then that Jackson was charged, convicted and sent to prison. Rather than accepting responsibility and cleaning up the mess, Wran blamed the media for the allegations that were besetting him and his ministers.⁷

With his popularity plummeting, and with Hawke's backing, Wran decided on an early state election in March 1984. With Labor controlling sixty-nine of the ninety-nine seats in the lower house, it would have taken a massive swing to topple him. In the event, Wran held on to the premiership despite Labor suffering a two-party-preferred swing of 6.3 per cent and losing eleven seats; Wran suffered a swing in his own electorate of 8.4 per cent.⁸

It was a lesson for Hawke, since Wran's popularity had exceeded even his. Voters might turn against him, too, if the taint of corruption enveloped the federal government or touched him personally. He'd already been forced in late 1983 to brush off suggestions about his involvement with organised crime, after the media reported him visiting a San Francisco cafe owned by Salvatore Amarena, a 'notorious West Coast organized crime figure' with connections to the Florida mafia. The cafe was 'a centre for meetings of organised crime members', including those from Australia, such as Abeles' close friend Bela Csidei and the corrupt New South Wales copper turned international drug dealer Murray Riley. In November 1978, Hawke and Combe had stopped over in San Francisco, where, at Abeles' suggestion, the pair contacted the mafia-connected Rudy Tham, the local boss of the Teamsters Union, who'd been instrumental in resolving labour problems suffered by TNT's American subsidiaries. According to Hawke, it was Tham who directed him to the mafia hangout. The visit had remained secret until Combe exposed it in the wake of his falling-out with Hawke, saying that the pair had spent a 'pleasant few hours' there behind closed doors. When Hawke was questioned about this in November 1983, he tried to brush it off, accusing Peacock and his colleagues of adopting 'McCarthyist tactics and attempting to impute guilt by association'. He claimed that he'd been unaware of Tham's mafia connections and 'would not recognise [him] if I ever saw him again'. It was a 'meeting of total innocence', claimed Hawke during a press conference, before amusing reporters with an imitation – straight out of a gangster movie – of Amarena's accent.[9]

Although he'd managed to brush off these questions, Hawke could never be sure when the spotlight might return to his links with shady characters, particularly given the media frenzy about the *Age* tapes. Phone calls by Abeles appeared on some of the tapes, but were in Hungarian and, on the order of the royal commissioner, were never translated. Hawke couldn't be sure that some of his own phone calls wouldn't emerge to embarrass him just before the next election. Far better to do as Wran had done and call an early election that would have the advantage of once again synchronising the House of Representatives and Senate elections while also giving Hawke a parliamentary majority that would be sufficiently large to ride out any future swings against Labor. Although he refused to listen to the *Age* tapes himself, so as to distance himself from the issue and limit the questioning from journalists and his political opponents, he did ensure that copies of relevant stories in *The National Times* were faxed to him in Canberra rather than have to wait hours for physical copies of the paper to be sent from Sydney.[10]

As a habitué of racetracks and casinos and a patron of SP bookmakers and prostitutes, Hawke knew that he was vulnerable to a potential exposé by a courageous journalist or a speech by a politician taking advantage of parliamentary privilege. The royal commission set up by Fraser in 1980 to investigate the criminal activities of the Painters and Dockers' Union was still proceeding. Commissioner Frank Costigan had discovered much more than Fraser had bargained for. Costigan found that the criminality of the Painters and Dockers ranged from murder and drug trafficking to money laundering and tax-avoidance schemes involving the big end of town, including some with links to the Liberal Party. Tax-avoidance schemes had become rife due to the lax laws of the Fraser government and the indulgence of the High Court.[11]

Caught up in the hearings was the media proprietor Kerry Packer, who was accused in the commission's draft report of involvement in drug trafficking, importation of pornographic videos and even murder, all of which he denied when the report was leaked to the media. Costigan's report recommended that his successor organisation, the National Crime Authority (NCA), continue the investigation of Packer. That didn't happen and Packer was never charged, with Hawke being a stalwart defender of the media tycoon.[12]

The disappearance and supposed murder in 1977 of a Liberal candidate and anti-drugs campaigner, Donald Mackay, from the town of Griffith – the centre of the mafia-controlled marijuana trade – kept organised crime in the headlines as the search continued for the perpetrators. By the time that the inquest on Mackay was held in 1984, a growing number of books had been published about crime and corruption linking police, politicians and prominent businessmen, along with newspaper articles on organised crime, mainly in the Fairfax press.[13]

Bob Bottom, the crime writer who'd given the police tapes to *The Age* and campaigned for years to get governments to tackle corruption, was depressed by the lack of action. In 1979, he'd written a landmark exposé, *The Godfather in Australia*, which claimed that organised crime had become 'a frightening fact of life in Australia', encompassing not only the 'Mr Bigs' who 'appear proud of their criminal associations' but also 'businessmen (some knighted) and politicians' and those who 'hide behind a police badge'. Bottom became an adviser to Wran on organised crime before leaving in disgust at Wran's lack of action. In 1984, he warned that 'organised crime in Australia ... now reaches out into all facets of society, with hardline criminals of the old underworld working hand in glove with politicians, lawyers, accountants, bankers and businessmen'.[14]

When Hawke then decided to wind up the Costigan Royal Commission and replace it with the less powerful NCA, he was vigorously attacked by

Opposition leader Andrew Peacock.[15] Using a parliamentary speech on 13 September 1984, Peacock drew on the mounting public unease about corruption to move a censure motion against the government for closing down the Costigan Royal Commission. He described Hawke as 'a little crook ... who associates with criminals and takes his orders from those who direct those criminals'.[16]

Hawke's continuing association with Peter Abeles and the property developer and aspiring casino operator Eddie Kornhauser was certainly unwise. Over the years, he'd frequently put himself in situations where he'd been paid large sums of money and where favours might be demanded of him in return. After questions were raised about Hawke pressuring the local council to support Kornhauser's attempts to secure a casino licence on the Gold Coast, Hawke told parliament that Kornhauser 'is a close personal friend of mine, and I am proud of it'. Similarly, he maintained his close friendship with Abeles despite being warned by D'Alpuget that she thought the businessman was a crook, presumably after she'd read articles in *The National Times* implying as much. Hawke stood by his friends regardless of the political risks.[17]

Fortunately for Hawke, Peacock was unable to produce any evidence to support his accusation that Hawke was 'a little crook'. Looking on from the gallery was Hawke's 87-year-old father, who was there to give 'moral support' to his son. Clem told journalists that he thought Peacock's allegations were 'baseless' and his speech was 'pathetic'. His son, said Clem, had always been 'honest and straightforward' and 'stuck to the truth'. Peacock's talk of Hawke being 'a *little* crook' was doubly insulting to the diminutive prime minister. After being forced by the Speaker to withdraw his description and amid much uproar from both sides, Peacock suggested instead that Hawke was 'a big crook in a little frame', only to be forced to withdraw once again as Hawke called on him to provide evidence. When Peacock's speaking time expired, the government voted to extend it, only to find, as Hawke had suspected, that an embarrassed Peacock had nothing to add.[18]

Peacock could only point to the corruption in the New South Wales Labor government, and suggest that Hawke, reliant as he was on the support of the New South Wales Right, must also be corrupt, whether by deed or by association. Hawke was able to swat away the empty insinuations. Privately, though, he had reason to be deeply troubled.

He couldn't be sure that evidence of corruption wouldn't emerge to cruel his prime ministership, in the same way that it was eroding Wran's reputation as premier and destroying Murphy's position on the High Court.

Already, questions were being raised about the Sydney judge John Foord, who, back in September 1982, without giving any reasons, had overturned Susan Hawke's conviction for marijuana cultivation and possession. The case didn't make much impact at the time, but two years later, in the lead-up to the 1984 election, journalists asked Hawke whether he had played a role in Foord's decision. That accorded with the ongoing reports about the corruption of the New South Wales justice system and the pressure that politicians had been shown to exert on magistrates and judges. Foord himself would be charged in 1985 and later acquitted with attempting to pervert the course of justice, allegedly at Wran's behest, in a trial involving Morgan Ryan.[19]

While Sue's case created a cloud of suspicion about Hawke's possible involvement, it was Rosslyn who most concerned him. He and Ros had been close when she was a child, only for her to flee their dysfunctional home at the age of fifteen to live as a hippie in New South Wales, where she'd become addicted to heroin. The birth of her first child in 1983 had been a proud moment for Hawke, who kept a picture on his otherwise empty desk of himself holding his grandson, David. All the while, Ros's addiction was taking a terrible toll on her body. Although she spent some time living at the Lodge with her husband and their baby, she was in Melbourne when she was admitted to hospital for the birth of her second child on 1 August 1984. Hazel was there to help after the caesarean birth, which allowed her to see the effect that heroin had had on her 24-year-old daughter, who weighed just 38 kilograms. Doctors told a horrified Hazel of her daughter's limited life expectancy unless something was done. Rushing back to Canberra, Hazel demanded an immediate appointment with her husband, who'd just returned from Port Moresby.[20]

Overwhelmed by the news, Hawke was distraught at being forced to confront the results of his neglect as a husband and father. He later wrote of how he was 'devastated and overwhelmed by sorrow for this beautiful girl ... with whom I had spent too little time when she became a teenager'. As Hazel was ushered out of his office, Malaysia's prime minister, Dr Mahathir Mohamad, arrived for a scheduled meeting with Hawke and Keating, only to have his host break down in tears. While Mahathir offered his sympathy, Keating could see that Hawke had had the stuffing knocked out of him and had fallen 'into a very big hole'. Hawke had revealed his emotional instability in front of his likely successor. Keating would later say that the day marked a turning point in Hawke's prime ministership – that he would never recover the 'leadership and energy' he'd shown during the government's first eighteen months. Others around him conceded that Hawke sank into a state of deep depression for a few weeks or even a few months, but claimed that he continued to perform as prime minister and appeared 'fully restored' by the middle of 1985.[21]

Hawke became even more indebted to Abeles when the transport magnate had a 'distraught and hysterical' Ros flown to the United States, accompanied by the shopping centre magnate Frank Lowy. She was admitted to an addiction clinic in California for several months of successful treatment. It was presumably Abeles who paid for the expensive clinic, as he had for so many of Hawke's other expenses. Meanwhile, Ros's husband sought treatment in Australia, and her two children were moved into the Lodge to be minded by a friend.[22]

Back in 1979, Hawke had suffered such a deep bout of depression that he'd welcomed the prospect of dying from the brain tumour he wrongly believed he had. Similarly, when he'd been misled by Soviet officials into believing he'd successfully arranged freedom for Russian refuseniks, he'd become so depressed that he'd considered suicide. Now he was so 'inconsolable and deeply depressed' that he 'seriously contemplated resignation' so that he might concentrate on 'my daughter's life and my family's happiness'. It was during those dark days that Peacock called Hawke 'a little crook' and *The National Times* published an article asking questions about Sue's acquittal. After eighteen months as prime minister, the pressures on Hawke were proving to be unrelenting.[23]

At the ACTU, Hawke had been able to disappear for an afternoon, a few days or even weeks without being held to account. That wasn't possible as prime minister; all he could manage was the occasional dalliance or his weekend gambling. He might be enjoying unprecedented levels of public approval, but so had Wran before he was enveloped in allegations of corruption. Hawke knew that this could also happen to him.

It was the prospect of his lifelong ambition coming to an early end, as much as the situation with Rosslyn, that caused him to break down in tears when asked about Sue's acquittal at a press conference on 20 September. He told the bemused journalists: 'You don't cease to be a husband, you don't cease to be a father, and my children and my wife have a right to be protected in this matter.' For years, Hawke had been shielded by journalists, most of them men, who'd followed an unwritten rule not to report his gross behaviour, whether it was a drunken interview that a television station decided not to broadcast or the many examples of his public womanising. Some journalists didn't want to cause the downfall of a widely admired leader, while others were deterred by Hawke's readiness to resort to defamation actions. Indeed, he implied at the tearful press conference that he would take legal action if the media continued to probe his family.[24]

Any dark thoughts of resignation were soon set aside when Hawke received an avalanche of supportive messages, including from MPs on both sides of the parliament. Hazel also helped when she agreed to do a television interview that was designed by Hawke's worried advisers to dispel any negative impression that Hawke's tearful press conference might have created in the minds of voters. It was during this interview that Hazel revealed that Hawke's tears were really because of the news about Rosslyn's drug addiction, of which the public had been unaware. She appealed for the family's privacy to be respected.[25]

As a result of Hazel's intervention, and Peacock's failure to press home his 'little crook' allegations, Hawke's standing in the opinion polls was undiminished. He retained a commanding lead as preferred prime minister, while Peacock languished on a miserable 15 per cent.[26] The public support wasn't enough to lift Hawke's spirits in parliament, where it was left to Keating to mount a devastating attack against Peacock as Hawke sat slumped by the despatch box.

Perhaps an election could restore the prime minister's equilibrium by enfolding him in the love of the Australian people. Hawke's advisers predicted that an early election would reinforce Labor's hold on government, helped by a boost to the number of MPs. They thought that Labor could emerge from the election with a majority of forty, up from twenty-five at the previous election. That could ensure at least two more terms for Hawke.[27]

The New South Wales Right had encouraged Hawke to increase the number of MPs in the House of Representatives from 125 to 148, which meant that the Senate numbers had to maintain their existing ratio with the lower-house numbers and be increased from sixty-four to seventy-six. That should have made a forty-seat majority even easier to achieve, particularly given the disarray in the Liberal ranks as John Howard quietly prepared to challenge Peacock for the Liberal leadership. Unfortunately for Howard, Hawke's announcement that the election would be held on 1 December put paid to any chance of that challenge going ahead.

With his customary hubris, Hawke decided that an abnormally long campaign with him at centre stage would make a Labor landslide even more certain. There were expectations, based on polling, that Labor could win as many as 100 seats in the 148-seat legislature, which would make it a landslide of historic proportions. Whereas Fraser's campaign in 1983 had lasted twenty-eight days, Hawke's would go for a mind-numbing fifty-five days.

Hawke was handicapped from the outset, however, when he suffered a painful eye injury while batting in a cricket match against journalists in Canberra. He misjudged a bouncer and the ball hit him in the face, smashing his glasses and sending a sliver of glass into his right eye. Although his sight was saved, he was left in excruciating pain for days, which exacerbated his sour mood.[28]

Had he been his normal exuberant self, Hawke might have been able to win the expected landslide. However, it had only been nineteen months since the last election, and the long campaign tested the patience of the electorate and gave Peacock a chance to erode Labor's support among swinging voters. While Hawke pointed to his economic achievements, which had seen falling unemployment and inflation, Peacock seized upon the government's introduction in that year's budget of an assets test and an incomes test on pensions, along with a 30 per cent tax on lump-sum superannuation payouts. Although the changes had been designed to make the welfare system more equitable, it had opened the door for Peacock to mount a scare campaign about people's savings, and he duly promised that he would repeal the assets test and the superannuation tax if he was elected. The eight-week campaign gave Peacock more time to hammer home this simple message.[29]

With taxation now the central issue of the campaign, Hawke told a Perth radio compere, who'd been prompted by Hawke to ask the question, that he would hold a national tax summit once the election was out of the way. The promise was in line with a decision of that year's ALP conference, which had seen an unsuccessful push for a wealth tax. That had been headed off on the conference floor with a promise to have a review of the tax system after the election. Rather than reassuring voters, the promised review opened the door for the Liberals to claim that Labor planned to introduce a capital gains tax, which was the same scare campaign Fraser had run against Hayden in 1980. Hawke intended that the tax summit would be much like the previous year's economic summit, and that it would reach a similar consensus.[30]

Despite talking to Keating earlier that day, Hawke had given his treasurer no inkling of the summit. Keating was ropeable, later complaining that Hawke's announcement was 'a complete curve ball'. Keating believed that the reform of Australia's complex tax policy was not suited for discussion, let alone decision, in a public forum. In a further attempt to ward off the Liberal attack, Hawke promised that government expenditure, the budget deficit and tax revenue would not be allowed to increase as a proportion of GDP in the coming parliamentary term. As Peter Walsh later observed, this was 'almost meaningless', since they were all at 'record levels' during the previous term and the country's improving economic circumstances would make the promise easy to fulfil.[31]

Hawke launched Labor's campaign at the Sydney Opera House on 13 November 1984, with Hazel, Sue and Clem sitting in the front row. Looking down the lens of the television camera, Hawke called on Australians to 'build upon the great gains' of his government and help him usher in 'a new decade of national unity, national purpose and national progress'. After less than two years in power, there was much to trumpet: from the drops in unemployment and inflation, which had resulted from the Accord with the union movement, to the initiatives in public housing, education, health and the status of women. There was much more besides in his long list of achievements, in which he touted Labor as 'the Party of Growth, Equity and Peace' and promised to 'attack the causes of poverty and inequality'. It wasn't the sort of lofty speech that Whitlam had been prone to deliver. Or the kind of combative pitch Hawke had made to voters with Freudenberg's help in 1983. Neither were there any expensive tax cuts or other bold initiatives that could undermine Labor's continuing repair of the budget.[32] Rather, it was the sort of prosaic presentation that Hawke had been inclined to make at an ACTU Congress. Which meant it was unlikely to get voters excited about its impact on their personal circumstances.

As an indication of Peacock's success in stirring up fear on the hustings, Hawke felt compelled to devote part of his speech to rebutting claims about the assets test on pensioners, pointing out that it would only affect about 2 per cent of pensioners, and that social services inspectors wouldn't be invading the homes of pensioners to tot up their assets. He also responded to Peacock's taunt in parliament about him being 'a little crook' by promising to boost the strength of the Australian Federal Police and commit his government to 'an unrelenting attack on organised crime'.[33]

Repeating the Liberal claims only gave them currency and provided a sign of Hawke's nervousness in his quest to increase his majority. While the polls had convinced him that he could easily win against Peacock, he also wanted to show the Labor caucus that they had to keep him as prime minister if they wanted to remain on the government benches. Some Labor MPs had been shaken by the sight of a tearful Hawke on television and were increasingly impressed by Keating's parliamentary performance and his growing confidence as treasurer.

Hawke was also impressed and leaned on Keating for support during the campaign. He needed as much support as he could get. 'The star performer of 1983 was a real dud in 1984,' recalled Richardson, 'and nothing we did could shake him out of it. His staff were mortified, his mates worried. And his Treasurer was stunned.'[34]

When Hawke was due to speak at a business lunch in a Sydney hotel, he insisted that Keating accompany him. It was reminiscent of Hayden using Hawke and Wran to buttress him during the 1980 campaign. When Keating questioned the optics of it, he was told that Hawke would paint the government's achievements with broad brushstrokes, while Keating should concentrate on the economy. According to Keating,

Hawke's staff were 'worried about his performance on the road, and so I was there to bolster him'. Which he did. After Hawke read his speech to the assembled business executives, Keating launched into an extemporaneous survey of the recovering economy and the economic reforms that he'd helped to usher in. Hawke was not amused when Keating's speech received the better reception, and he was even more upset when Keating noted, as they were leaving the hotel, how well it had gone. 'My friend,' said Hawke, 'you can have this job when I'm ready to give it to you, and that won't be before 1990 at the earliest.' A shocked Keating took this as a warning not to outshine the PM when they were on a platform together. Thereafter, Keating said he would always drop his 'presentation down a notch – more often, a couple of notches'.[35]

Hawke's immediate threat, though, was Peacock, whose dogged campaigning was eroding Labor's support in the opinion polls. As the election day loomed closer, the increasingly confident Liberal leader challenged Hawke to a televised debate. Such events had been an important feature of American presidential campaigns ever since John F. Kennedy had faced off against a sweating Richard Nixon in 1960, but they had never been done in Australia. It was a high-risk gambit for both men, but Hawke could hardly refuse after he'd challenged Fraser to a debate ahead of the previous election only to have Fraser refuse. Despite his lacklustre performance in the campaign to date, Hawke was confident of his prowess on the rostrum, believing that he would be able to show up the weaknesses of his playboy opponent, whom Keating had derided in parliament as 'the sunlamp kid'. They agreed to a ninety-minute debate on the Monday night before the election, with a moderator and a panel of six senior journalists. Because of its novelty, and the fact it would be shown live on all four channels, there was certain to be a huge and captive audience.[36]

The opening statements by both men set the debate's tone, with Hawke sounding flat and nervous and talking in generalities, while Peacock spelled out his principal election commitments and promised to repeal the assets test for pensioners. He also was quick to contest claims made by Hawke about cutting youth unemployment and increasing school retention rates.

It was the issue of corruption that created the most heat. Richard Carleton cited a claim from Paul Landa, the recently deceased New

South Wales attorney-general about whom there'd been serious allegations of corruption and who'd suffered a heart attack just two days before. Prior to his death, the 43-year-old Landa had reportedly complained to the former Labor minister Jim McClelland about the pervasive corruption in the state. Carleton seized upon the comment to ask Hawke when he was going to get involved in tackling corruption.[37]

Hawke tried to dodge the question, telling Carleton that it was unseemly to quote the recently deceased Landa. When that provoked guffaws from the audience, he gave a long-winded response, during which he claimed to have passed on to the New South Wales government any allegations of corruption that had come to his notice. That was hardly an adequate reply, given the stench emanating from that state and its government's apparent protection of the perpetrators. Hawke conceded none of that, though, pointing to what he described as Wran's overwhelming victory in the latest state election as proof that voters had not given any credence to the allegations. In fact, Wran had lost eleven seats.[38]

Hawke might have mentioned his establishment of the NCA, which was meant to continue the work of the Costigan Royal Commission but which lacked some of its independent powers and relied upon state police forces to conduct prosecutions. It also required the approval of a committee of state and federal ministers before it could invoke its coercive powers to demand documents or require witnesses to give evidence. When Peacock pointed to these deficiencies, Hawke could only reply that Peacock had failed to contribute to the parliamentary debate on the bill that created the crime authority.[39]

One journalist tried to put Peacock on the spot by asking whether he stood by his allegations about Hawke being 'a little crook'. When Peacock pointed to the retraction he'd made in parliament, Hawke reminded him that he'd left the allegation about him being 'a big crook' on the parliamentary record.[40]

This prompted journalist Peter Bowers to ask Hawke whether he would clear up the mystery about the theft of US$1000 in cash from a locked briefcase in his Boulevard Hotel suite on 21 February 1982. A copy of the police report, which had been leaked to the press gallery by Liberal MP Michael Hodgman, revealed that the thief also took $3600 in Australian currency and an unknown amount of traveller's cheques. Within two days of the robbery, Hawke had written to the hotel manager claiming that he'd lost a total of $5770 to a thief who had supposedly used a master key. It represented nearly half a year's income for the average Australian worker. Blaming the theft on the hotel's 'negligence', Hawke demanded that he be reimbursed by the hotel. Even though it was an eye-watering amount, it was the American money that sparked the most speculation. Hawke refused to divulge who had given it to him, angrily telling Bowers that his report to the police was sufficient proof of the money's innocent origins.[41]

That didn't satisfy Bowers, who noted that it was very unusual for anyone to be carrying around that much American cash, particularly at a time when there were strict Reserve Bank rules about the possession of foreign currency. He again asked Hawke to explain its origins, which Hawke again refused to do. The money may have come from Abeles, because the TNT boss decided after the robbery to provide Hawke with a driver-cum-bodyguard whenever he was in Sydney, with the formidable figure of private detective Tim Bristow being placed on a $40,000 retainer.[42] Hawke's cack-handed response to Bowers only added to the suspicion that the money might have corrupt origins, when it may have simply been casino winnings from one of his overseas trips.

The issue of the hotel robbery had first been publicised just before the 1983 election in an obscure Melbourne newspaper, *The Toorak Times*, which specialised in the breathless reporting of scandals. The mainstream media either missed the story or decided not to pursue it, other than an obscure paragraph in Sydney's *Sun-Herald* two weeks after Hawke became prime minister. It was six months before *The National Times* ran a report on the robbery, noting that the Opposition couldn't decide whether Hawke should be pursued in parliament over the issue. In April 1984, the combative Liberal backbencher Wilson 'Ironbar' Tuckey zeroed in on the thousand dollars in US currency, suggesting that Hawke's possession of the money had breached the rules of the Reserve Bank. Rather than answering the allegation, Hawke got his finance minister, John Dawkins, to respond.[43]

It was only after Peacock's 'little crook' comment in October 1984 that journalists asked Hawke about the robbery, with the prime minister claiming his 'total innocence'. Picking up on Hawke's sensitivity, the Liberals returned to the fray in parliament. Michael Hodgman walked into the chamber with a folder emblazoned 'Boulevard Hotel', implying that there was much that Hawke was hiding. Hodgman had interviewed the hotel's night manager, learning that Hawke had demanded and received full recompense from the hotel for his loss. When Hawke refused a debate in parliament, Hodgman called him a 'gutless little coward' and warned that the issue would haunt Hawke throughout the election campaign. His persistence saw the Tasmanian suspended from parliament for a week. Hodgman wanted to know why Hawke had so much money on him, why he'd left it in his hotel room and why he couldn't specify the amount of the traveller's cheques or on which bank they were drawn. By refusing to answer these questions, Hawke ensured that they would be raised again during the election campaign, which Peacock did by calling during the leaders' debate for Hawke to 'come clean'.[44]

Agreeing to the leaders' debate had been a mistake by Hawke. In the view of the media, Peacock was the clear winner and now appeared in the public mind as 'a far more formidable figure', while Hawke had been 'tense and edgy in his body language' and 'especially unconvincing' when deflecting the question about the theft from his hotel suite.[45] Of course, their relative performances weren't sufficient to win the election six days later. Hawke remained hugely popular with voters, and his government seemed to have found a solution to the economic problems bequeathed to it by Fraser. He was hardly likely to be thrown out after only being in power for less than two years, based upon uncertainty about Labor's tax plans and resentment by a few wealthy pensioners towards the assets test.

But the voters didn't give Hawke the substantial swing he wanted. Instead of a swing to Labor, his government suffered a swing of 1.5 per cent against it. The enlargement of the lower house had created an extra twenty-three seats, of which Labor only managed to win seven, with sixteen going to the Coalition. In the next parliament, Labor would have eighty-two seats to the Coalition's sixty-six. A disappointed Keating recalled how Labor was thereafter 'looking over our shoulder', unsure whether it would survive the next election. Describing it as 'a dreadful result', Bill Hayden said that 'it looks like the drover's dog has won again but he looks a bit clapped out this time'.[46]

The election was a devastating result for Hawke. The 'magic aura that had surrounded the Prime Minister had lost its brightness', wrote D'Alpuget. As for the now ebullient Peacock, his shaky leadership had been rescued by the unexpected results. He confidently predicted that he would be prime minister after the next election and warned that it was now Hawke who had to worry about his own leadership.[47]

CHAPTER TWELVE

# 1984–1985

Hawke bore much of the responsibility for the 1984 election result. Having such an early election and an extraordinarily long campaign created resentment among voters, with some Labor supporters also made uneasy by Hawke's floating of the dollar and admission of foreign banks. Although the creation of Medicare was welcomed, there had not been the rush of progressive changes that Whitlam had introduced. Labor voters' disappointment might have been responsible for the abnormally large number of informal votes, which jumped from 2 per cent in 1983 to 7 per cent in 1984. Hawke blamed it instead on voters being confused by a change in the Senate voting system, which allowed them to mark just one square to indicate their preference for a party, rather than having to consecutively mark each of the many candidates on the unwieldy ballot paper. He suggested that some voters had mistakenly marked only one square on the ballot paper for the House of Representatives and thereby made their vote informal.[1]

Except that Labor suffered an even worse swing against it in the Senate, where the Coalition picked up five extra seats to Labor's four, with the Democrats gaining two and the Nuclear Disarmament Party one. After less than two years in power, there was clearly dissatisfaction with the Labor government, with Hawke's poor performance in the campaign exacerbating the erosion of support for the party.[2]

The election outcome was fortunate for Hawke in one respect, since it kept Peacock as the leader of a party divided between its diminishing group of progressives and the rising band of economic rationalists led by the former treasurer John Howard. The rivalry between Peacock and Howard would divide the Liberals for a decade and help cement Hawke in power. Hawke's greatest challenge would come from his own side.

Keating sensed Hawke's vulnerability as he struggled to recover from his prolonged bout of depression. While Hawke's authority in caucus was unchallenged after two election wins, his second term as prime minister would see that authority gradually erode as Labor MPs opposed his support for American missile tests in the Pacific.

The so-called MX missiles were designed to be used in a nuclear war against the Soviet Union. They were part of the more muscular approach that President Reagan was taking towards Moscow, which threatened to upset the existing strategic balance and perhaps increase the possibility of a nuclear war. The Fraser government had agreed that American aircraft could be based in Sydney to monitor the testing of these experimental missiles, which were planned to splashdown in the Tasman Sea off the coast of Tasmania. While keeping it secret from his cabinet, Hawke had agreed with the US secretary of state, George Shultz, in 1984 that the tests could go ahead, asking only that the splashdown site be shifted so that it was outside Australia's 200-kilometre exclusive economic zone. When the new defence minister, Kim Beazley, warned Hawke that he'd 'have hell to pay on this', Hawke dismissed his concern. Beazley was right. When the security committee of cabinet discussed the issue on 29 January 1985, Gareth Evans suggested that the Americans be asked to withdraw their request for Australian cooperation. He noted in his diary that Hawke was not amused: 'This question makes the PM, who is nothing if not consistent in his passionate support for all things American, extremely irritable.'[3]

Hawke should have listened to his colleagues. When news of the secret tests became public on 1 February, there was uproar from the many Australians who couldn't countenance the thought of nuclear-capable missiles being aimed towards Australia, while some were fearful that the development of intercontinental missiles with multiple warheads that were designed to destroy Russian missile silos would accelerate the arms race between the two superpowers.

The unrest, coming so soon after the 1984 election, when Hawke had spruiked his government's nuclear disarmament credentials, might have been quickly quelled had Hawke been present in Canberra to hose it down. But he was flying to Washington by way of Europe and was not well placed to allay the anger among Labor MPs who'd been kept unaware of the politically sensitive tests and who now publicly expressed their annoyance. Their anger was shared by the Victorian premier, John Cain, and many stalwart members of the party. Hawke had reached Belgium when the right-wing powerbrokers Graham Richardson and Robert Ray, who were visiting Japan, called him from Tokyo's Imperial Hotel to warn of the rebellion in caucus, where the Left and Centre-Left factions were united in opposing Australian involvement. Even some members of the Right were aghast at the news.[4]

Despite the prior warning from Beazley and Evans, the caucus rebellion caught Hawke by surprise. His deep attachment to the United States and his equally deep distaste for the Soviet Union blinded him to the political peril into which he'd blundered. His initial reaction was to urge Hayden to fight the naysayers in caucus, while Keating cheered him on, perhaps hoping it would erode Hawke's support. According to Richardson, the pretender to Hawke's throne was 'totally gung-ho' and was 'literally telling them all to get fucked'. Richardson and Ray realised the numbers were stacked against Hawke, and Richardson told him so when the prime minister caught the powerbroker on his hotel toilet in Tokyo. During the long and difficult conversation, he told Hawke to back down. Otherwise, it could cost him the prime ministership if a special Labor conference was held and voted against him on the issue.[5]

No more needed to be said, and Hawke informed the security committee of his decision. A sleeping Evans was in Rome when Hawke rang after midnight to give him the news. The government was now in 'an appalling mess', wrote Evans in his diary, although he doubted whether the experience would 'have a salutary effect on Hawke's almost unthinking pro-Americanism'. He was right on that account. Hawke later dismissed the caucus rebellion as 'a bout of residual anti-Americanism and pacifist naivety within the party'.[6]

Had he not backed down so quickly, Hawke feared the issue could also threaten the tenure of the several US intelligence and communication bases in Australia, particularly the Pine Gap base outside Alice Springs. That was not something Washington would have welcomed, particularly after the New Zealand Labor government of David Lange had just forbidden the entry into its ports of any American naval ships that were nuclear-powered or that might be carrying nuclear weapons. Since the Americans refused to declare whether a ship had nuclear weapons, that meant all their ships were effectively banned from entry. Washington responded by suspending its cooperation with New Zealand under the ANZUS Treaty. Although Hawke was concerned that Australia could be similarly treated, he was relieved to discover, on his arrival in Washington, that the Americans accepted his decision without argument.[7]

Indeed, much to Hawke's chagrin, he watched on as Secretary Shultz assured journalists in the foyer of the State Department that the Americans could monitor the tests just as easily from US Navy ships out in the Pacific. On an earlier visit, Hawke had been told that Australian help was vital; now it seemed he'd been conned. He'd lost political skin in caucus for nothing.[8] The Americans were not going to have a major disagreement for fear of threatening their spy and communication bases in Australia. A blow-up might also have led to Hawke's toppling, and a new prime minister might not be so pliable.

As a face-saving measure designed to appease the Americans and reassure Australian public opinion, Hawke had his cabinet and caucus express support for both the bases and the treaty. The missile crisis and a subsequent drop in the value of the dollar were not a good look for Hawke after the disappointing election result. An opinion poll saw his approval rating fall by 8 per cent while only 9 per cent of respondents thought he was doing an excellent job as prime minister.[9] His luck seemed to be deserting him.

Once Hawke's several months of depression came to an end, he gathered his government together and focused on developing a strategy for winning the next election. During a dinner at the Lodge in April 1985, he called on his ministers to exhibit more self-discipline in their media statements, and for his own part promised to reassert himself as a leader by becoming more 'effective, thrusting and purposeful'. Gareth Evans suggested that he'd already begun to do so two days earlier, when he'd addressed a Business Council dinner. Looking on was a bevy of ministers, including Evans, who thought Hawke 'made a good, lively speech, the best I've heard from him for some time, on the economy, devaluation and our responses to the present circumstances'. Hawke wanted to recapture the optimism that had characterised his first term as prime minister, when the ending of the drought, the run of good economic results and the several important reforms he'd introduced had spread good cheer through government ranks. After the 1984 election, the good cheer had been replaced by gloom, which Hawke found difficult to shift. Peacock was now more popular in the opinion polls than him. Hawke would have to turn that around.[10]

The visit of another senior Chinese official, the Communist Party's general secretary, Hu Yaobang, mightn't have lifted Hawke's approval rating, but it gave him an opportunity to create another building block in the future prosperity of both countries. The growing trade between them had seen China become Australia's fifth-biggest trading partner by 1985, up from being the tenth-biggest the year before. Both countries wanted it to grow much bigger. China wanted to develop its iron and steel industry and Hawke was keen that it do so with high-quality Australian iron ore and coking coal. Which was why Hu Yaobang had flown into Perth in April 1985, being met by Hawke before they flew to the Pilbara to inspect an iron ore mine that was about to be developed. Hawke had already given China the green light to participate in its development and take a large percentage of its production. In a sign of the intimacy between the two leaders, the small-statured Hu took Hawke by the hand and walked with him as they talked amiably about the future of their countries' economic relations. It was a future that was beyond the political horizon of both men.[11] Which meant that Hawke would never receive the praise he deserved for helping to establish a trade relationship that would repair Australia's perennial trade deficit and underpin the country's prosperity for decades.

The media might focus on Australia's worrying balance of payments, but voters were more focused on the mix of taxes they were forced to pay and the changes Hawke had in store for them.

During the election campaign, he'd been outshone by both Peacock and Keating. And it was Keating who would again be centre stage during the forthcoming tax summit. With Australians paying a top personal tax rate of 60 per cent and a company tax rate of 46 per cent, there were good arguments for big reductions in both rates and for replacing the lost government revenue with different taxes. Hawke left it up to Keating and his Treasury officials to come up with proposals that could be presented to the summit.

Central to Keating's plan was to shift part of the tax burden from income to consumption. He was following an international move to place a greater reliance upon consumption taxes as a means of raising revenue. Keating wanted a retail tax of 12.5 per cent, which would be offset by the abolition of existing sales and wholesale taxes and by a reduction in income taxes, with the top rate to be 49 per cent. There would also be generous payments to the poor, upon whom the new tax would otherwise weigh heavily. Other tax proposals included the introduction of dividend imputation, which would allow shareholders and superannuation funds to avoid paying tax on dividends received from companies that had already paid company tax on their profits. Another change was the introduction of a fringe benefits tax to stop people from minimising their taxable income by having their employers top it up with tax-free benefits, ranging from the provision of vehicles to the payment of school fees. Lastly, there was a proposal for a capital gains tax so that the profits from asset sales, whether shares or property, were taxed on the same basis as wages and salaries.[12]

After an intense effort over several months, Keating and his Treasury officials were ready to submit their proposals to a weekend meeting of the cabinet. Only then would it go forward to the tax summit in July 1985, when delegates from business, unions and other groups would be presented with three alternatives for discussion: options A, B and C. The last of these was the most contentious, since it was the only one that included Keating's preferred consumption tax. Because it would raise most revenue, it was also the only one that would permit Hawke to announce substantial reductions in income and company taxes. After his electoral setback the previous year, Hawke could see the sense of a consumption tax but declined to give it his untrammelled support, fearing it might lose him the next election. It would have been different had he won his hoped-for super-majority in 1984, but he was now risk-averse.[13]

So were many of his colleagues. Working in the background was Tom Uren, who'd sensed Hawke's prevarication on the issue and Keating's resulting anger with the prime minister. 'That fucking

Hawke,' Keating had told Uren, 'he's such a dynamic decision maker.' Seizing on this, Uren told his colleagues that they 'had to use this to drive a wedge between Keating and Hawke' by 'briefing selected journalists, as well as informing Hawke's office what was going on'.[14]

The rift became clear during the weekend cabinet meeting. Keating watched with frustration as Hawke sat silently during the discussion on the consumption tax, leaving Ross Garnaut to speak on his behalf. 'Bob was sitting in Cabinet like he'd been hit with a formalin dart,' recalled Keating, who found himself arguing the details of the various proposals with Garnaut while Hawke remained mute. It was an exhausting process that went way past midnight on the Sunday.[15]

Although many objections had been voiced, Hawke hadn't put any of them to a vote. That allowed Keating to claim that there was a consensus in favour of his preferred proposal, Option C. Daring Hawke to call his bluff, which could have caused Keating to resign, the triumphant Treasurer led his officials out of the cabinet room to celebrate with champagne. They had 'walked in with a monster proposal', said Keating, and now 'walked out with a Cabinet document reflecting it'.[16] As far as the consumption tax was concerned, they should have left the cork in the bottle.

Although Hawke had allowed the government's submission to include the consumption tax as part of its preferred option, he was lukewarm about the idea. Sitting back as chairman, he'd given free rein to Keating, who tried to cajole and charm his nervous colleagues into the tax cart while Hawke watched on benignly. Keating would later complain about Hawke being in and out of the cart depending on his political whim on any particular day. After the shock of the 1984 election, Hawke feared that the election in 1987 might be his last. Introducing a consumption tax in the face of widespread community opposition could make it so. Peter Walsh agreed, describing it as a 'formula for catastrophe'.[17]

Keating kept at it, but each time he and his Treasury officials walked out of the prime ministerial office, Hawke's advisers would whisper warnings to him about the political risks, reinforcing their arguments with figures from Labor's pollster, Rod Cameron, which showed that the public were strongly against a consumption tax. Keating complained to Gareth Evans that he'd been 'displaced in the PM's affections by his office advisers', whose competence Keating disparaged. Evans agreed that Hawke was 'getting steadily more isolated from real-world concerns – spending all week immersed in his office, his Saturdays beside the phone following the races, and his Sundays absorbing Cabinet submissions with the help of his advisers'.[18]

Hawke had told Keating that he could see the sense of a consumption tax, since it would catch wealthy tax avoiders in its net and allow income taxes to be cut. That should encourage enterprise, grow the economy and bring in much-needed revenue for the government. The poor would be compensated to minimise the tax's regressive nature. However, Hawke couldn't escape the fear that climbing into the tax cart alongside Keating could see them both being led to their political execution at the next election. The tax cart could turn into a tumbril. Not wanting to slap down his treasurer, Hawke gave Keating the go-ahead to sell the tax to the public and the sceptical interest groups, including the ACTU, in the weeks prior to the summit. Hawke did consultations of his own, flying around the country to talk with voters who disparaged the notion of a consumption tax. He expected that Keating would come to recognise it as a lost cause. Urged on by his Treasury officials, however, Keating refused to concede defeat.[19]

The key to success for the treasurer was the ACTU, which would have to convince its members to accept the increase in the CPI that a consumption tax would cause, while agreeing not to seek compensation through higher wages. Business would also have to accept the basket of new taxes, both the ones it supported, such as the consumption tax, and the ones it opposed, such as the fringe benefits tax and the capital gains tax. It was a big ask – too big, as it turned out. The ACTU's Bill Kelty listened to Keating's advocacy but declined to buy what the treasurer was selling.

That became painfully clear when the 160 delegates to the National Tax Summit threaded their way through a throng of police on the steps of Parliament House on Monday, 1 July, while thousands of farmers gathered to protest on the lawn opposite. Many of the delegates had been at the economic summit two years earlier: the gathering included state premiers, leaders of business and trade unions, and representatives of groups, ranging from welfare lobbies to women. Missing was the amity, good humour and desire for consensus that had marked the earlier summit, when a triumphant Hawke had been flush with electoral success and his newly installed treasurer was still coming to grips with his portfolio. This time, Hawke attended as a weakened prime minister, alongside a treasurer who had grown in stature and had a sure grasp of his job.

Both men had miscalculated – Hawke in thinking that an agreement on tax reform could be thrashed out in the glare of television lights, and Keating in believing he could convince the delegates of the merits of a consumption tax. Hawke had to watch a succession of delegates announce from the rostrum their different objections to the three options Keating had presented to them. None favoured a consumption tax, whether it was set at 5 per cent in Option B or 12.5 per cent in Option C. The states were against it, as were the welfare groups and the ACTU, while the recently formed Business Council of Australia declared that it didn't support any of the options. Queensland premier Joh Bjelke-Petersen summed it up, proclaiming to the delight of delegates that Hawke's attempt at consensus had created 'a consensus of opposition in the community', which Hawke confirmed by going outside during a break to address the thousands of angry farmers, only to be booed off the stage.[20]

Keating was angriest of all. Although he'd opposed the summit from the start, Hawke had given him the task of making it a success. He'd gone at it with his customary zeal, intending to build on the historic transformation of the economy that he and Hawke had begun with the floating of the dollar and the entry of foreign banks. But changing the tax mix was never going to be simple, and the introduction of a consumption tax was the most difficult change of all. After going at it with a will, Keating discovered belatedly that Hawke had had a late-night meeting in Kelty's hotel room, where the pair had agreed that the ACTU would oppose the consumption tax. With business also against it, Hawke could safely take the tax off the table. Had he not done so, Hawke later reflected, 'Labor would have lost the 1987 election'.[21]

Keating should have seen this coming but hadn't. Hawke would later claim that his treasurer was 'in the grip of a manic optimism' that made him 'oblivious to the politics of the exercise'. The politics wasn't just about the unpopularity of the consumption tax. It was also about the indecisiveness of a government that had been at loggerheads with itself for months and which had Hawke being lambasted as 'old jelly-back'. According to Phillip Adams, when the delegates gathered at Yarralumla for post-summit drinks, Keating let fly. 'I've never heard a tirade like it; I've never heard such a stream of obscenities and rage, all directed at Hawke.' who hadn't yet arrived. Thirty years later, Keating's anger had barely abated: he complained to Kerry O'Brien that 'Bob should not have sold me down the drain overnight.' The dispute could have destroyed their working relationship, but that was in neither of their interests. Hawke needed Keating's political salesmanship and belligerence in parliament to shore up his government. The treasurer would have to hide his humiliation in the hope that the Labor caucus would eventually see that his contribution to the government was more valuable than Hawke's.[22]

At the end of the summit, Hawke tried to put the weekend's discussions in a positive light. He pointed to the summit's almost unanimous agreement about the need for a national identity card to guard against tax fraud, which would give him the confidence to go ahead with a so-called Australia Card. There was also agreement about the need to reduce marginal tax rates. That was not a surprise, as everyone thought that their income and business taxes should be lower. They just couldn't agree on how the resulting hole in the government's revenue should be filled – which had been the whole point of the summit. Although Hawke had been unable to get agreement on any of the three tax options, he declared that there had been 'majority support' for the principles of 'equity, efficiency and simplicity', which would provide the basis for any tax changes. 'Equity' meant that poor Australians couldn't be disadvantaged by the changes, while 'efficiency and simplicity' meant that any changes would have to produce a positive economic benefit and an improved allocation of the nation's resources.[23]

Hawke also claimed that there had been agreement for a broadening of the indirect tax base and an examination of dependent spouse rebates and family tax allowances. He undertook to draw up a tax package that would also include full imputation for company dividends. Lastly, to the applause of delegates, Hawke tried to dispel the stories about a rift between himself and Keating, claiming that 'no prime minister could have asked for better, closer, more effective co-operation than I have enjoyed with Paul Keating'. The 'effusive congratulation of Paul', wrote

Gareth Evans, was to 'disguise the fact that [Keating] has just had the political equivalent of three-quarters of one testicle cut off'.[24]

The treasurer would have to bury his bitterness and bide his time, because he was now tasked with putting together a package of tax changes that could be sold to his cabinet colleagues and accepted by the community. It didn't stop him complaining to close colleagues that Hawke was 'in a state of drift' and was just a 'lucky mug who doesn't know what he wants to do with the country, what he wants to do with his life, or where he wants to lead the Government'.[25] With the summit behind him and Keating derailed, Hawke had a chance to ponder these questions.

It wasn't just the voters he would have to impress, as Hawke also had to satisfy those Labor MPs who feared that Labor's hold on government might be slipping away. During a cabinet meeting in the wake of the summit, Bill Hayden surprised his colleagues by mounting an 'incredibly strident' attack on the tax option that was supposedly the consensus of the conference. It was a sign of the government being 'in serious danger of falling apart', wrote Evans. As if to confirm that grim prognosis, Hawke demanded that cabinet support the deregistration of the radical Builders Labourers Federation, whose secretary, Norm Gallagher, had been jailed for corruption, suggesting that it could help rescue the government's fortunes.[26]

When Evans cautioned his colleagues against acting precipitately, Hawke slipped him a note warning that the government was 'down to the wire and we should understand that and act accordingly'. With Lionel Murphy having just been found guilty of perverting the course of justice, Hawke had to ensure his own reputation wasn't tarnished by the stench emanating from Sydney, where one Labor minister had been jailed, Wran had been forced to stand aside for three months and Murphy had been dragged through two Senate inquiries and a court case. Hawke could never be sure that an investigative journalist from *The National Times* or *Four Corners* wouldn't one day make allegations about his own historical links to Sydney's criminal underworld, whether it was accepting tips about rigged horse races, playing the tables at one of Sydney's many illegal casinos or enjoying the late-night company of Abe Saffron at one of the several nightclubs he controlled in Kings Cross.[27]

Ever since he'd been the industrial advocate at the ACTU, Hawke had been in the habit of staying in or near Kings Cross, with its boisterous drunks, loitering sex workers, and bulked-up bouncers guarding nightclub doors. Saffron's son claimed to have met Hawke several times, presumably in the company of his father at one of his clubs, when Saffron still enjoyed the protection of corrupt police and politicians and hadn't attracted the level of notoriety that had since become his lot. He had had so much influence within the police force that in 1978 he had them remove his photos and fingerprints from their records. Wielding that influence became more difficult after state and federal royal commissions and media investigations had caused Saffron to be labelled the 'Mr Sin' of the criminal underworld, which prompted the federal authorities to place him under surveillance. That would be difficult, since the ageing mastermind was careful to distance himself from actual criminal activity, using loyal underlings and frontmen to conceal his involvement.[28]

Hawke spurred on the police pursuit of the hitherto untouchable Saffron, whose arrest would establish Hawke's anti-corruption credentials and help shield him from accusations about his own past associations with such characters. In the case of Saffron, their association was sufficiently close for Saffron's son to urge him to call Hawke and ask for the NCA to back off. Anxious to avoid jail, Saffron did so, only for Hawke to refuse to take the call. Doing so could have destroyed Hawke. Instead, Saffron was arrested in a pre-dawn raid in November 1985, with Hawke exulting to colleagues that Saffron was 'now in the net and there is more to come'. Like the US gangster Al Capone, Saffron was arrested for tax evasion after a former associate provided police with two sets of account books, which revealed the income Saffron had failed to declare. After several court cases, he was jailed for three years. He celebrated his first Christmas behind bars by having the dancers from his Les Girls strip club put on a show for his fellow prisoners.[29]

The arrest of Saffron sparked a heated exchange between Hawke and Keating, with the treasurer warning the PM in a cabinet committee that he would come to regret his pursuit of Saffron if it was based upon evidence gleaned from unauthorised police tapes. Although the tapes had led to the jailing of Farquhar and revealed Murphy's wrongdoing,

Keating declared that 'the police are corrupt and should never be given an inch when it comes to telephone tapping', only to have Hawke respond: 'I was right and you were wrong and you'll always be wrong on this issue.' Working himself into a lather, Keating shouted back: 'You were fucking wrong and you'll live to regret it.'[30]

Fellow ministers seated around the cabinet table witnessed the angry exchange with alarm. There could no longer be any doubt about the widening schism between the two powerful pillars that had kept Labor in government. Hawke might have led the party to power in 1983, but the 1984 election had shown that his appeal was on the wane. Labor MPs worried whether the party could survive without the combination of Hawke's charisma and Keating's political salesmanship. The challenge for Hawke would be to keep his increasingly volatile treasurer within the cabinet without sparking a public explosion that could bring the government down.

CHAPTER THIRTEEN

# 1986

By 1986, the now silver-haired Bob Hawke could reflect with some satisfaction on the past three years. Relaxing in the Lodge with Peter Abeles, both puffing clouds of smoke from their Havana cigars, they could only wonder at the relative success of his performance as prime minister.[1] To the surprise of many colleagues, Hawke had been able to make the transition from union leader to national leader. He had brought the managerial style that had served him well at the ACTU to the business of government, giving a relatively free rein to his ministers in the implementation of the party's electoral policies, which they had been largely responsible for developing under Hayden's leadership.

Being prime minister was a lot more difficult than being president of the ACTU. It was harder to avoid the public's gaze, and Hawke was liable to be called to account daily for his government's actions. Yet he could still escape to the home of one lover or another, while his minders waited outside or sat in the next room. And he could enjoy leisure time on Fridays, the racing guide spread across his desk as he phoned trainers and jockeys for the inside running for Saturday's horse races. Of course, there'd been embarrassing missteps and some political disasters, but he'd mostly managed to stare down querulous journalists, and with the assistance of several formidable ministers usually dominated question time in parliament. He was widely regarded as leading a government of considerable talent, and was thought to have largely tamed his wilder excesses. Hazel believed he was a changed man and embraced her position as the prime minister's partner, with all the influence and attention that came with it, creating a highly regarded role for herself that was probably worth a percentage point or two for Labor at the polls.

Although the 1984 election result had been a disappointment, the government wouldn't have to go back to the voters until late 1987. That didn't stop some ministers from saying privately that they were 'fucked', which enraged Hawke when he heard of it. Chomping on his cigar at the next cabinet meeting, he declared with characteristic confidence that they would 'shit it in' when they next went to an election. He warned his colleagues that any more talk of losing would see him sack the offending ministers.[2] That didn't stop the talk, or the private musing about alternative prime ministers.

By now, there was only one clear candidate, Keating, whose handling of the Treasury portfolio was impressing journalists and pleasing his big-business supporters, while his combative style both amused and buoyed Labor MPs in parliament. Not that his performance translated into public support for Keating to become prime minister. Nevertheless, he'd made his leadership ambitions relentlessly clear to his caucus colleagues, who'd been charmed and cowed by him in equal measure. They would be the voters who mattered in any leadership contest.

Following Hawke's desultory performance during the last campaign, it was natural that leading Labor MPs would think of Keating as the person most likely to be their future leader. Hayden had taken Gareth Evans aside at a diplomatic reception in August 1985 for just such a talk, telling Evans that he was 'becoming enormously impressed by Keating' and would 'unequivocally support him for the leadership … whenever the appropriate occasion arose'. Evans alerted Keating to the shifting political ground. Two weeks later, Evans spent the evening with Keating, dining in a restaurant and visiting Annita Keating in hospital after the birth of her fourth child, before going to Keating's home to see his antique clocks and silver. During the evening, Keating poured scorn on 'Hawke's enthusiasm for tacky friendships and vulgar pursuits', which presumably referred to Abeles and Kornhauser and Hawke's womanising. With the prime minister's approval rating still high, though, there was no talk of mounting an immediate challenge.[3]

It might have been different had the Liberals not been so divided. Peacock had out-campaigned Hawke in 1984 but was now beset by a challenger. A dismal position in the opinion polls during 1985 had left him feeling so threatened by a series of headline-making appearances by his dogged deputy, the bespectacled and hard-of-hearing John Howard, that he demanded Howard publicly promise that he would not mount a leadership challenge. When Howard refused, Peacock called a party meeting in September 1985 to declare the deputy's position vacant. It was a strange tactic by Peacock, which Howard turned to his advantage by winning back his position. Liberal MPs clearly wanted the more charismatic Peacock retained as leader while his duller deputy did the policy work. It's unclear, though, how they thought this could be workable, given the strained relations between the two men. Believing that his position was now untenable, Peacock immediately resigned, which allowed Howard to be swept in as leader, although he wouldn't prove any better than Peacock at lifting the party's fortunes.[4]

These machinations would have been reassuring for Hawke, who was struggling to articulate a clear vision of where he proposed to lead the country. He was making the economy more competitive, but the benefits were flowing more to profits than to wages. What was worse, the dollar had been steadily declining at the same time as the prices of Australia's main exports had been dropping to historical lows as the international economy slowed. It meant that Australians were paying more for their imported goods, while foreigners were paying less for Australia's exports, causing a widening trade deficit that threatened to imperil the market's confidence in the government's handling of the economy. And that could spell political disaster for Hawke.

In theory, the floating of the dollar should have ameliorated some of the effects by deterring businesses and consumers from buying increasingly expensive imports, while at the same time making Australian exports cheaper for purchasers overseas. Yet the deficit continued to widen in early 1986 as Australian consumers increasingly bought better-quality Japanese cars and electronic goods, and businesses imported expensive capital goods, such as aircraft bought by Abeles for Ansett, for which there was no local alternative. As for Australian exports, which were mostly minerals and farm produce, they were already cheap due to the oversupply on the world market. But the yawning gap in the current account hadn't yet alarmed the markets or caused headlines that were capable of disturbing the equanimity of voters or Labor's backbench.

That all changed on 13 May, when the previous month's current account deficit was released. It was bigger than analysts had predicted and caused a precipitous fall in the value of the dollar. The deficit was still being digested by commentators as Hawke left for Tokyo the following day. During the flight on his VIP jet, he assured accompanying journalists that there was no crisis. It wouldn't have fitted with the narrative he'd sold to voters at the previous two elections, in which he featured as the maestro who was orchestrating an economic recovery after a decade of downturn. Nor would it fit with the narrative he was planning to sell in Tokyo, where he wanted to strengthen Australia's fast-growing economic ties with Asia's economic powerhouse, not least by attracting wealthy Japanese tourists, and to seek Japan's support for a lowering of tariffs on agricultural produce under the General Agreement on Tariffs and Trade (GATT).[5]

Hawke had a good story to tell the chiefs of Japanese companies, who'd been concerned in the 1970s with the high level of industrial disputation in Australia under his leadership at the ACTU and could now be assured of the relative peace that had become the norm under his prime ministership. At an official dinner, Hawke was buoyed by the remarks of the Japanese prime minister, Yasuhiro Nakasone, who dispensed with traditional Japanese formality to talk of 'my good friend Bob', which played into Hawke's conviction that he had carved out a special place for himself on the world stage and was loved by some of its most powerful leaders.[6]

As he bathed in the apparent adulation of the Japanese prime minister, Hawke was angered to receive alarming cables and phone calls from Australia and be pestered with questions by the accompanying troop of journalists. They were prompted by a seemingly off-the-cuff comment by Keating warning of Australia becoming a 'banana republic' if its underlying economic problems were not corrected – which, of course, was his job as treasurer.

Keating had been addressing a breakfast of business executives at a reception centre in Melbourne, before he was called to the phone for an interview with influential radio talkback host John Laws. He could have reassured Australians about the underlying strength of the economy and the passing nature of the crisis. Instead, he took the opportunity to acknowledge the deep structural problems that decades of reliance on largely unprocessed primary products, combined with a high tariff wall that protected its inefficient secondary industries, had bequeathed. Not surprisingly, having the treasurer warn of Australia becoming a banana republic resulted in headlines around the world, causing Hawke's confidence-building trip to be dogged by stories about the economic crisis at home.[7]

Keating told the media that he would put the matter on the agenda of a forthcoming meeting of the Advisory Committee on Prices and Incomes, which comprised representatives of state and federal governments along with employer and union representatives, prior to Hawke's return. This set off alarm bells for Hawke's political svengali, Peter Barron, who warned that it would allow Keating to play the part of prime minister despite the deputy prime minister, Lionel Bowen, being in charge during Hawke's absence.[8]

Having worked himself into a fury by the time he'd flown on to Beijing, Hawke instructed Keating and his senior ministers to assemble in the cabinet room so that he could assert his authority and dress down his treasurer over speakerphone, later briefing the accompanying media that he'd put Keating in his place. Keating and his allies, meanwhile, described how the treasurer had angrily rebutted the several prongs of Hawke's attack, with Keating telling Hawke that he was acting 'like a chook with its head cut off'.[9] Their starkly different background briefings gave further confirmation of the growing schism between the pair.

Keating's 'banana republic' comment had shocked the money market, causing a sharp drop in the Australian dollar and forcing up the price of imports, thereby thwarting Hawke's attempts to curb inflation and unemployment. The comment also reverberated in the public mind, and would continue to do so for several years. Many took it as an admission of failure by Keating. After all, interest rates had soared to more than 18 per cent, although mortgage holders were protected by a government-imposed cap, which limited their rate to 13.5 per cent. The high interest rates were complicating the government's attempt to kickstart the economy and cut the high unemployment rate, which was still over 8 per cent nationally, and much higher among the young.[10]

What were voters to make of a government whose treasurer thought the country was at risk of becoming a banana republic? Had the three years of wage restraint and the government's attempts to revitalise Australian manufacturing been for nothing? No wonder Hawke was irate and saw the comment as part of Keating's campaign to undermine him. That was possibly a trifle paranoid. John Howard was probably right to regard the banana republic comment as a flippant remark made with no regard to the way it would echo in the Australian community.[11]

Rather than denying the seriousness of the balance-of-payments position, both Hawke and Keating tried to use the market reaction to their advantage. Hawke quickly went on television, telling 60 Minutes that the 'party is over', with Australia 'now in a crisis which is as great as the crisis of war'.[12] His comments were not quite as memorable as Keating's banana republic comparison, but would do the job of showing that he was back at the helm of the wallowing ship. Hawke would now have the task of getting it back on course. To do that, he would have to confront the collapse in Australia's terms of trade.

The solution should have come from the stabilising effect of the floating dollar, but a collapse in oil prices had spread to the minerals that Australia exported, while government farming subsidies in the United States undercut the prices that Australia received for its food exports. It meant that there would be no quick return to higher export prices.

Hawke didn't give up hope. Each day, as he arrived at Parliament House, he would poke his head into the cubbyhole occupied by his newly appointed economic and environmental adviser, the young Craig Emerson, and ask what had happened overnight to the value of the Australian dollar relative to the American dollar. Its precipitous fall in the weeks after Keating's 'banana republic' comment – it reached a historic low of just 57 cents on 28 July – reinforced the impression of a government in crisis. Although this wasn't good for his government's standing, it allowed Hawke to do things that he wouldn't otherwise have been able to do, while he tried to bring the public along for the ride. A carefully staged address to the nation on 11 June saw Hawke explain how the country was receiving $6 billion less for its exports, which meant Australians were living beyond their means. He wanted voters to accept new cuts to their wages and entitlements, while being reassured that he and Keating had the crisis in hand.[13]

It was also important that the confidence of the financial markets was restored. The ERC was tasked with reducing government expenditure by another $1.5 billion in order to produce an even bigger surplus, while Hawke ensured that the trade unions remained committed to the discipline of the Accord, which had seen the wages of their members eroded while the proportion of national income going to company profits steadily increased. He tried to assure voters that the sacrifices he was asking of them would be applied equitably, and that measures would be introduced to supplement the incomes of the poorest Australians.[14]

Photographs of Hawke hobnobbing with his wealthy patrons didn't help his cause, whether it was lolling about in his bathers on Frank Lowy's superyacht off the exclusive Lizard Island Resort in North Queensland, fishing with crooked businessman Laurie Connell off the coast of Western Australia, walking out the back door of a television studio with Rupert Murdoch, or dining in dinner suits with Kerry Packer and Alan Bond. In 1984, Hawke and Western Australian premier Brian Burke had hosted a lunch for the John Curtin Foundation, which brought together politicians and businessmen in an organisation that was dubbed 'WA Inc'. It was designed to funnel money to the state and federal branches of the Labor Party, in return for which state government contracts were doled out to a grab bag of dodgy businessmen.[15]

Foremost among these were Bond and Connell, both of whom, along with Burke, would later be jailed for their various criminal activities. Connell was a notorious fixer of horse races who established a merchant bank, Rothwells, which eventually went broke despite Connell securing financial support from Burke and his successor as premier, Peter Dowding. Connell was fond of telling people that he was mates with Burke and could 'get on the phone to Graham Richardson or Paul Keating [and] I go fishing with Bob Hawke'.[16]

Although Hawke was warned by some of his senior ministers about dealing with these unsavoury characters, there is no indication that he took any notice. Their money could be the difference between winning or losing the next election, while the young Burke was supported by the New South Wales Right as a possible future prime minister.[17]

Hawke had helped some of these businessmen with industrial issues as president of the ACTU and now was in a position to help them even more as prime minister. In the case of Lowy, soon after Hawke had enjoyed Lowy's hospitality on his yacht, he'd chaired a meeting that saw the cabinet decide to sell half of the government-owned Belconnen Mall to Lowy's Westfield. It was more difficult when he was being pulled in different directions as Lowy, Murdoch, Packer, Bond, Christopher Skase and Robert Holmes à Court pressured him to loosen the media laws to suit their separate business ambitions, while two of the biggest newspaper empires – the Melbourne-based Herald and Weekly Times and the Sydney-based Fairfax – wanted laws that would help them fend off likely takeovers. Hawke left it to his hapless communications minister, Michael Duffy, to satisfy the media moguls while protecting media diversity.[18]

Hawke himself was more concerned with creating a media landscape that would facilitate Labor's hold on government. Historically, the media had been mostly hostile towards the Labor Party and its policies. It was important to Hawke that any changes his government made would satisfy the most powerful of the moguls in the expectation they would support Labor, or at least not campaign against him at election time. That meant mollifying Kerry Packer, whose Channel Nine television stations in Sydney and Melbourne had the biggest audiences and who wanted to buy stations in other cities; and Rupert Murdoch, who already controlled newspapers across Australia and aspired to purchase the Herald and Weekly Times, which his father had previously controlled and which owned the biggest-selling newspapers in Victoria and Queensland.[19]

Because of the powerful business interests and the political issues involved, the cabinet discussions were interminable as Hawke sought a way through the morass without losing the support of either his media mates or his cabinet colleagues. For three years, Duffy had successfully defended the principle of media diversity whenever Hawke had tried to change the rules to allow further media concentration. As the cabinet discussions wore on without Hawke giving a clear indication of his preferred changes, an exasperated John Button turned on him, asking: 'Bob, what do your mates want?' The implication of the impish minister was clear. Hawke was trying to do the bidding of his media mogul mates but was struggling to get his ministers to agree on a consensus position that would satisfy Packer and Murdoch.[20]

Neither mogul enjoyed good standing among the public or the party. The allegations against Packer at the Costigan Royal Commission had left his reputation under a cloud despite Hawke's strenuous efforts to defend his 'close personal friend', while Murdoch's role in the fall of the Whitlam government and his adoption of American citizenship had left him in bad odour among the Labor faithful. To reach a resolution, Hawke had the issue referred to a small cabinet subcommittee, which comprised just him, Keating, Duffy and Button. That effectively settled the issue, since Hawke and Keating were of one mind about the historical hostility of the Herald and Weekly Times and Fairfax towards Labor. They blamed the Herald group for nearly losing Labor the 1984 election and were determined to break it up and weaken Fairfax. Duffy and Button were hardly going to roll the prime minister and treasurer.[21]

The solution, devised by Keating, was to change the rules on cross-media ownership so that the proprietors would have to decide whether they wanted to dominate newspapers or television. They couldn't do both. As the treasurer memorably put it, they could be 'princes of print or queens of the screen'. Presumably sick of the issue, and comforted by Hawke's assurance that it was positive for Labor, the cabinet agreed on 24 November. Although Keating's proposal gave the appearance of protecting media diversity, it would exchange the Herald empire for a Murdoch one, resulting in Australia today having one of the most concentrated media landscapes in the Western world.[22]

After Keating met with Murdoch in New York and advised him of the pending change, the mogul quickly struck at the Herald and Weekly Times, making an offer that its board couldn't refuse. Despite counteroffers from Holmes à Court and Fairfax, it was Murdoch who celebrated that Christmas, folding his father's former newspaper empire into his own much larger one, which now stretched from London to New York.

Even though Murdoch now controlled a majority of Australia's morning newspaper circulation, Hawke couldn't have been more pleased and raised no impediment to the deal. He'd always regarded the Herald and Weekly Times as the bastion of the Melbourne establishment, publishing a 'violent, virulent anti-Labor journal'. Now the group was in the hands of Murdoch, who, Hawke was confident, would support him at the next election. It would have been Hawke's worst nightmare for it to have fallen into the hands of Fairfax, with its recent penchant for investigative journalism and its publication of the so-called *Age* tapes. He could count on Murdoch being protective of Abeles, whose management of the jointly owned Ansett and Ansett Worldwide Aviation Services was producing the profits that would help Murdoch finance the takeover of the Herald and Weekly Times and achieve his expansion plans in the United States and Britain. In fact, it was Abeles who arranged the sale of Murdoch's television and radio stations, along with the Adelaide *News* and the Brisbane *Sun*, to Frank Lowy, who celebrated with a dinner at his Point Piper mansion attended by the Hawkes and the Murdochs, as well as the New South Wales Labor premier, Barrie Unsworth.[23]

Meanwhile, courtesy of the Labor government, Packer's television interests had doubled in value, with the new media law allowing him to sell the Nine network to the avaricious Bond for $1 billion, with Bond adding the stations to those he owned in Adelaide, Brisbane and Perth. The new law also allowed Skase to control the Seven network, and Frank Lowy the Ten network. A few years later, when Packer bought the Nine network back from Bond for a fraction of the previous sale price, Australia's greatest gambler would famously say that 'you only get one Alan Bond in your life'. Packer could also justifiably have said that you only get one Bob Hawke in your life, because the coup couldn't have occurred without Labor's media law facilitating it. The prime minister also ensured that Packer was cleared of the Costigan allegations and wouldn't face further investigation by the Royal Commission's successor organisation, the NCA.[24]

When Packer organised a celebration of his network's sale to Bond in April 1987, it wasn't appropriate for Hawke to be there in person. But he couldn't resist being there remotely. Filmed in the garden of Kirribilli, he dismissed the 'unjustified innuendos, slanders [and] malicious gossip' that had been directed at Packer. 'And it was all untrue,' declared Hawke – who also pointedly reminded Packer that 'loyalty is a two-way thing'.[25] With an election in the offing, and Packer still retaining an influential magazine business, Hawke was anxious to keep Packer onside. He never knew when he might need to draw on his links to the different media moguls to protect him from the sort of allegations that were besetting Lionel Murphy at the High Court and that had caused Neville Wran to resign as New South Wales premier in July 1986.

Both Murphy and Wran had watched their careers unravel. After evidence from the Chief Magistrate of New South Wales, Clarrie Briese, Murphy had been found guilty of attempting to pervert the course of justice in trying to protect his 'little mate' Morgan Ryan, the corrupt solicitor who worked for Abe Saffron. Murphy was acquitted on appeal, but only after he made an unsworn statement from the dock, which saved him from being cross-examined but wasn't an edifying look for a High Court judge.[26]

Wran, meanwhile, had been a staunch defender of Murphy. He'd threatened to sack Briese for testifying against Murphy, and declared before Murphy's second trial that his friend was innocent. The latter of these outbursts led to Wran being fined $25,000 for contempt of court.[27]

The allegations against Murphy continued in the media and in parliament, where Hawke reluctantly agreed to a Senate inquiry to determine whether Murphy was a fit and proper person to sit on the High Court. Although Hawke had described the proposed parliamentary inquiry as 'a prostitution of parliament', he had relented when the Australian Democrats and Coalition senators combined to support it. Three Labor senators were added to the committee, with Labor's Michael Tate appointed as chairman, in the hope that he would ensure Murphy was cleared of wrongdoing. Instead, Tate sided with the non-Labor senators, deciding that Murphy's behaviour, although not criminal, was not 'fit and proper' for a judge of the High Court.[28]

When reports suggested that Murphy's fellow High Court judges would refuse to sit with him, Hawke established another inquiry to recommend whether or not parliament should sack him. He had to tread warily, as some members of caucus thought the allegations warranted an inquiry regardless of the political risks to the government, while others were just as adamant that Murphy was the innocent victim of a witch-hunt. In the end, Hawke appointed a parliamentary commission of inquiry, composed of three judges, to consider the many allegations. If the judges decided against Murphy, the parliament would be empowered to take the unprecedented step of forcing him to step down.[29]

It was in the midst of this inquiry that Murphy was diagnosed with inoperable bowel cancer. Dealing with the disease would be his final trial. Determined to return to the High Court for one or two final cases, Murphy sent Wran to Canberra to discuss it with Hawke and the acting attorney-general, Gareth Evans. Both men were shocked by Wran's news, although Evans was conscious that it made their dilemma easier. Hawke thought he might be able to wring some political advantage by keeping Murphy's medical diagnosis secret until Howard and his colleagues had a chance to attack his return to the High Court. Once they'd made 'unmitigated cunts of themselves', said Hawke, the news of Murphy's diagnosis could be released to Howard's discredit. Even Wran thought Hawke's suggested strategy was 'too neat', and it was dropped. Anyway, the news of Murphy's illness quickly leaked to the media.[30]

Hawke had wanted Murphy to retire in the hope he would disappear from the headlines. He asked the governor-general, former High Court judge Sir Ninian Stephen, to suggest such a course to Murphy. But the crusading law reformer didn't want his career to end in public disgrace and insisted on his right to continue sitting. Which he did, while the news of his medical diagnosis caused the commission of inquiry to be brought to an abrupt end. Among the allegations that would die with Murphy was the claim that he had interceded with Wran to get the government-owned Luna Park leased to a company controlled by Saffron, and that he had money secreted away in Swiss banks. The several state and federal royal commissions into corruption and organised crime had failed to uncover the full extent of the multifarious connections between organised crime, big business, corrupt police and customs officials, judicial officers and politicians. Now the three judges comprising the commission of inquiry had also failed.[31]

Murphy managed to deliver a final written judgment for the High Court on 21 October 1986, before dying in Canberra that same day. Several weeks before, he had visited the Lodge with his wife, Ingrid, where the couple had Sunday lunch with the Hawkes before Murphy and Hawke retired to the study. According to Murphy's former press secretary, George Negus, he 'was capable of brilliance and foolishness almost in the same breath'. While his brilliance had resulted in important contributions to Australia's political and judicial systems, his foolishness had eventually brought him undone. He had no one to blame but himself. His tangling with ASIO as Whitlam's attorney-general had created powerful enmities and harmed his political reputation. But it was his relationship with Morgan Ryan and Abe Saffron that would have destroyed his career, had his illness not intervened.[32]

Looking across at Murphy, Hawke saw someone with 'the sad, warm eyes of a charitable man at peace with himself'. Perhaps that was because Hawke had agreed that the government should grant Murphy a generous $750,000 to cover the legal fees he might have incurred in the several court cases and inquiries. It was a massive amount for a man who was earning about $250,000 a year and had a rich portfolio of property and other assets, and for whom a public appeal had been launched to cover his legal expenses.[33]

After Murphy's death, Hawke told Australians to forget about the allegations of Murphy's corruption and links to organised crime and concentrate instead on Murphy's 'magnificent ... achievements'. He tried to keep the allegations against Murphy secret in perpetuity but was forced by the Senate to do so for only thirty years.[34] Anyone publishing the allegations before then could face jail. Meanwhile, Hawke introduced laws to ban the unauthorised tapping of telephones and to make the possession of tapes or even transcripts a jailable offence, which had the desired result of causing police forces to destroy tapes they'd made in the past. It wasn't until June 1987 that the federal government passed a law allowing police to tap telephones, but only for offences involving sentences of at least seven years' jail.[35]

Wran also had questions to answer, but his sudden resignation as premier in July 1986 meant they too were unlikely to be answered. The premier had survived one royal commission, which had duly exonerated him because he'd written its highly restrictive terms of reference. The several other state and federal royal commissions had now come to an end, leaving just the relatively weak NCA as the principal investigator of organised crime. The NCA could only act against individuals after getting a reference to do so from a committee of federal or state politicians, and specific charges would have to be identified before an investigation could begin. Open-ended investigations, which could have brought the Packers and the Abeles of this world within the purview of the NCA, were prohibited. Frank Costigan had recommended that the NCA take over his partially completed investigations, particularly into Saffron and Packer. Hawke was only prepared to sanction an investigation into Saffron, which would see him charged with defrauding the taxation department. He would never be charged for his criminal dealings in vice, gambling and drugs. Most of his confederates in the world of business, politics, police and the judiciary also escaped being charged.[36]

Despite his murky connections to that world, Hawke's narcissism encouraged him to think of himself as relatively invulnerable to attack by his detractors. Yet the years of newspaper reports emanating from the *Age* tapes and the subsequent inquiries had cost him politically. On the one hand, there were the claims of corruption involving Wran and Murphy that had threatened to embroil Hawke. Then there was his grudging support for the parliamentary inquiry into Murphy, which upset those in the Labor Party and the legal fraternity who admired Murphy's work on law reform and could not believe he'd been involved with Sydney's underworld.

It was presumably for this reason that a mix of cheers and boos erupted from the audience when Hawke walked into the Sydney Town Hall for Murphy's state memorial service, while Wran was cheered enthusiastically. As Hawke sat there among the dignitaries, listening to the panegyrics, he might well have hoped that the combination of Murphy's passing, Wran's retirement and the establishment of the NCA would end the years-long public focus on corruption and organised crime. But drug-war killings continued to capture the headlines, while the Donald Mackay inquest in 1984 and the subsequent trial of one of his murderers in 1986 shone a light on the power of the drug lords and the rotten state of politics and policing in New South Wales. That seemed to be confirmed when a Sydney sex worker named Virginia Perger claimed to have cavorted in a 'Love Boat' on the harbour with senior state and federal Labor figures. The boat was owned by Joe Meissner, who had been implicated in a brutal attack on the state Labor MP Peter Baldwin. Meanwhile, popular books on organised crime continued to be published, and investigative journalists from the ABC and the Fairfax-owned *National Times* continued to pursue stories about political corruption.[37]

From 1978 to 1981, the editor of *The National Times* was the Walkley Award–winning Evan Whitton, who shifted to *The Sydney Morning Herald* and went on to publish several landmark books on corruption and organised crime. His successor was Brian Toohey, who continued Whitton's focus on corruption by publishing reports from the United States that linked Hawke and Abeles to the mafia. Detail was later added to these by an aggrieved David Combe. Articles about the theft of the US dollars and traveller's cheques from Hawke's Sydney hotel room added to rumours of his involvement in corruption and possible links to organised crime. His steadfast refusal to explain his possession of the money and his threats of libel action to silence journalists seemed only to confirm such suspicions.

While Hawke was jockeying to replace Hayden in 1982, *The National Times* had run a front-page story about Hawke's links with prominent businessmen, specifically his relationships with Abeles and Kornhauser and the suggestion that he might be used to serve their interests if he became prime minister. The paper's later reporting of the *Age* tapes further infuriated Hawke, who lashed out at Toohey and *The National Times* at any opportunity, telling the Labor caucus that the paper had 'lied and lied', and that the claims about political corruption involving Wran were part of an 'orchestrated attempt to try and create ... an impression of impropriety' based on 'unfounded' allegations.[38]

After Wran had initially dismissed the tapes as 'phoney' before reluctantly accepting their authenticity, both Hawke and Wran tried to shift public and media attention to the legality or otherwise of the police taping of private telephone conversations, rather than allowing the focus to be on the possible criminality that had been exposed, including by Wran himself, who'd refused to act against illegal casinos. Gareth Evans was similarly dismissive, describing the taping as one of the most 'illicit, illegal and despicable affairs in Australian history'. Under Toohey's editorship, *The National Times* journalists Wendy Bacon and Marian Wilkinson ploughed on in the face of Hawke's threats – and despite Toohey and Bacon being charged by the New South Wales attorney-general with contempt of court for publishing an article about the corrupt prisons minister.[39]

Hawke's links to various media moguls helped prevent critical stories about him and his associates, particularly Abeles, from reaching a broader audience. Bacon noted how *The Wall Street Journal* published a front-page report about Abeles' payments to mafia-controlled accounts in the Cayman Islands, only for it to be ignored by most of the Australian media. That ensured there was little criticism when the government appointed Abeles to the board of the Reserve Bank. Like the knighthood he had allegedly purchased from Wran's corrupt predecessor, Robert Askin, Abeles' appointment to the sensitive and high-powered position would enhance his status in the business community, and possibly help him conceal the secret transfers of ill-gotten gains that he was said to have made to Swiss banks.[40]

Hawke would later be confronted with claims that Abeles had been recorded on a car phone instructing an employee to transfer a large amount of Australian money into United States currency in order to take advantage of an expected drop in the value of the Australian dollar. Now that he was a board member of the Reserve Bank, where he was privy to confidential information about movements in the exchange rate, this currency trading raised serious ethical questions about Abeles' suitability to be a board member. When questions were asked by the Opposition, Hawke put off any response for several months and then simply said that he had 'absolutely no reason at all to doubt in any way the integrity of Sir Peter Abeles'.[41] Allegations about Abeles were left to accumulate in the vault of the NCA, where they seem never to have been subject to serious investigation.

So long as media criticism was largely restricted to *The National Times*, with its relatively small circulation, it was unlikely to erode Hawke's popularity among voters, which had been built up during his time at the ACTU, when he'd engaged television audiences and intimidated interviewers with his angry rejoinders and implied threats of defamation actions. There'd only been a handful of reporters covering the trade unions, and Hawke had most of them under his thumb, writing stories that glorified his role as the industrial peacemaker. As an MP, with the advice of Peter Barron, he proved himself to be just as adept at handling the press gallery of more than a hundred journalists. As soon as he became prime minister, he dispensed with the doorstop interviews of which Fraser had been fond, insisting that journalists and TV crews not beset him with questions when he was stepping out of his car or walking up the steps of Parliament House. Instead, they should keep their questions for the press conferences that he promised to hold. The press gallery readily accepted this arrangement, which allowed Hawke to describe it as an agreed 'rule' and to push past any journalists who tried to break it by pestering him with questions.⁴²

The ABC proved more difficult to manage. The current affairs program *Nationwide* was fronted by Richard Carleton, the journalist who'd goaded Hawke after Hayden had been deposed. That interview had exposed the fury that always lurked just below the surface of the then putative prime minister. His advisers were right to suspect that his eruption on *Nationwide* had cost him support from swinging voters, who likely wondered about Hawke's emotional stability. His expected landslide at the election was contained to a swing of less than 4 per cent. The experience with the 'impertinent' Carleton had caused Hawke to refuse to appear on *Nationwide* during his government's first term.⁴³

But it wasn't only Carleton who annoyed him. During an interview on ABC morning radio in Sydney, the host, Jane Singleton, asked Hawke a question about party factions that he didn't want to answer. Rather than changing the subject, Singleton terminated the interview, telling him it would be 'a waste of taxpayers' money' to go on. The ABC would blame poor ratings for later sacking her.⁴⁴

To Hawke, there was a pattern of impertinence by ABC presenters, which was compounded when *Four Corners* made the startling allegation in April 1983 that Wran had intervened in the trial of a friend, leading rugby league official Kevin Humphreys, who was alleged to have defrauded club funds to pay his gambling debts. Rather than being jailed, Humphreys had been let off with a fine and a good behaviour bond by the corrupt chief magistrate Murray Farquhar. When the program was aired, Wran immediately denied the allegation, appointed a royal commission with narrow terms of reference and sued the ABC for defamation, which effectively prevented further discussion of the allegation because it was now sub judice. Although Wran was exonerated by the royal commission, Farquhar was sentenced to four years' jail. As for Wran's defamation action against the ABC, the secret settlement reportedly resulted in no damages being paid, other than the reimbursement of the premier's legal costs.⁴⁵

These results allowed Wran to portray himself as the victim of a political witch-hunt orchestrated by the ABC and the Fairfax press.

He tried to bring Fairfax to heel by offering to make it a partner with Murdoch and Packer in the lucrative Lotto organisation, only for Fairfax to decline for fear it would create a conflict of interest. When it was clear that Fairfax would continue its investigations of corruption, Wran instructed that no government advertising was to be placed in Fairfax papers.[46]

Whenever he was asked, Hawke defended Wran. According to Hawke, the New South Wales premier 'is clean. He is straight. He is incorruptible.' Similarly, he had defended the former ACTU executive member and New South Wales Labor powerbroker John Ducker when allegations surfaced in early 1984 that he had been paid $50,000 to arrange a casino licence for a Chinese-Australian restaurateur who had Abe Saffron as a silent partner. Hawke was quick to dismiss the allegation, declaring that Ducker 'is my friend. I trust him. He is a good man.' Indeed, Hawke had already appointed Ducker to the Qantas board, while Wran had made him a member of the New South Wales Public Service Board. Without conclusive evidence, and with the Chinese-Australian businessman refusing to testify, no charges were ever brought against Ducker.[47]

As for the ABC, Hawke had to tread warily, since the publicly owned broadcaster had some powerful defenders in the Labor caucus, not least Michael Duffy, and much public support besides. That didn't stop Hawke and Barron meeting in April 1984 with the ABC's newly appointed managing director, Geoffrey Whitehead, to complain about the ABC's treatment of the Labor Party and the Wran and Hawke governments. It was the *Four Corners* program 'The Big League' that had helped to uncover the widespread corruption in New South Wales. Who knew where the focus of these investigations would next be directed? Hawke let Barron lead the attack on Whitehead, only to have the ABC chief defend the corporation's independence. Although Hawke hastened to assure him that he respected its independence, he was determined to do what he could to tame it.[48]

That would not be easy. Even if the ABC board was stacked with political appointees, there was no guarantee that they wouldn't become defenders of the ABC's independence. Hawke still seized the chance when the ABC chair, businessman Ken Myer, resigned in April 1986. Two candidates for his position soon emerged. One was the head of the

New South Wales Rail Authority, David Hill, who'd been a member of Wran's staff before being appointed by the premier to the authority. His candidature for the ABC chair was favoured by the New South Wales Right, which wrongly assumed that the well-connected and politically astute Hill could be counted upon to prevent any further exposure of corruption within their ranks.[49]

The other candidate was Brian Johns, the Penguin publisher and political journalist who'd been an adviser to both Whitlam and Fraser and was the favoured candidate of the Centre Left. Which wouldn't have endeared him to Hawke. But Abeles was pressuring Hawke not to appoint Hill, with whom he'd had a falling out. His pressure put Hawke in a bind, since his position remained reliant on the continuing support of the New South Wales Right.[50]

Rather than making the choice himself, Hawke left it to Duffy to decide. In the event, both sides were satisfied. Duffy recommended that the forty-year-old Hill should be appointed as chair of the ABC, while Johns should be made the managing director of SBS. Although Hawke was pressured by Keating and Duffy to amalgamate the two organisations, sparking protests from ethnic communities, the Senate blocked the amalgamation. Meanwhile, after two months as chair, Hill pressured the managing director to resign in the wake of a critical auditor-general's report. Then, with the approval of the board, and with a nod and a wink from Hawke, he promptly stepped into Whitehead's shoes without the board advertising for other applicants.[51]

Just as he had with the railways, the supremely confident Hill would be running a major media organisation despite having had little media experience. He would quickly remove most of Whitehead's senior managers and bring a concentration on ratings, believing that an increased audience for ABC programs, particularly Australian-produced ones, would help to insulate the organisation's budgetary allocation from cutbacks by efficiency-minded ministers. The surviving senior executives were left mindful of the need to please the new managing director and not upset Hawke or his ministers.[52]

Although Hill might try to defend Hawke from attack by ABC journalists and program makers, Hawke would be unable to quell the rising tide of disquiet among supporters who felt his government was betraying hallowed party principles and threatening to privatise iconic institutions that had been established by previous Labor governments. As 1986 drew to a close, it wouldn't be long before Australians had the opportunity to pronounce judgement on Hawke and his government.

CHAPTER FOURTEEN

# 1987

Sitting in the summer sun on the verandah of Kirribilli House in January 1987, casting an occasional glance at the passing tourist boats, Hawke would have been disturbed to read his political obituary in the *Times on Sunday* (as *The National Times* had become). According to the report, he was going to resign from parliament if he lost the next election, which was due within a year. Even if he won his third election in a row, which no Labor prime minister had ever done, he was expected to retire soon after.[1] Either way, he would be gone.

Although Hawke would later deny it in his memoirs, this was what he'd told voters during the 1984 campaign, and what he'd implied to journalists and confided to his likely successor, Paul Keating.[2] If he followed through with his promise, it meant that he had, at best, three years left as prime minister. That wouldn't do. Looking wistfully across the harbour towards the Opera House, the scene of several of his political triumphs, Hawke would have realised how much he would have to give up if he stepped down. Far better to pull off an electoral win that might overshadow the last campaign and confirm for the doubters that he was Labor's best hope for retaining government into the future.

Just days after the *Times on Sunday* article, Hawke told *New Idea* that his was the best of Australia's post-war governments, including those of Chifley, Menzies and Whitlam, and that he was confident of winning the next election. Rather than resigning soon after that poll, he told the publication's mainly female readership that he would continue serving until he'd completed seven or eight years as prime minister. Only then would it be 'time to make way for someone else'. That would take him beyond the 1990 election.[3]

So far, Hawke had led a charmed political life. Less than three years after entering parliament, he'd become Labor leader. Within weeks of toppling Hayden, he'd beaten Malcolm Fraser and become prime minister. At his next electoral test, he'd faced off against Andrew Peacock, who later confessed that he wasn't sure he wanted the top job. Hawke couldn't imagine doing anything else. He also couldn't imagine anyone else doing a better job than him. Keating had staked a claim to the leadership, but the work of treasurer was testing his health. He was often off sick, arrived late to meetings or didn't attend at all. This gave Hawke a justification for staying longer than he'd previously promised, and for weakening Keating's claim by suggesting that there were other ministers who were just as qualified to succeed him.

The Opposition, meanwhile, was being led once again by the doughty John Howard, who lacked charisma but had an astute political mind. Fortunately for Hawke, Peacock was still lurking, ready to pounce if Howard sank further in the polls. While the divided Opposition worked to Hawke's advantage, he was aware that the faltering economy could cause voters to set aside any reservations they harboured about Howard.

The coming election was on Hawke's mind when he flew off on another visit to the Middle East and Switzerland, this time to address the World Economic Forum in Davos as part of Australia's campaign to reduce agricultural subsidies in Europe and North America, and to discuss peace in the Middle East during visits to Jordan, Israel and Egypt. At the Western Wall in Jerusalem, the lapsed Congregationalist inserted a folded paper wishing, or perhaps praying, for an historic third term.[4]

Fortunately for Hawke, his VIP jet landed back in Canberra a day after Joh Bjelke-Petersen announced an audacious bid to overthrow Howard and become prime minister at the next election. With the backing of John Stone, controversial historian Geoffrey Blainey and a clutch of dodgy Gold Coast businessmen, the 76-year-old Queensland premier and corrupt peanut farmer had become deluded after his state election win in November 1986. The stunning victory had gone to his head, causing the plain-speaking premier to dream of leading a Quixote-like march on Canberra to snatch the prime ministership from Hawke at the next federal election. He told Hawke to 'make the

In 1982, the Hawke family enjoyed their last Christmas together at their Sandringham home. (Steve and Ros at the back, Sue, Hazel and Hawke in front). *(JCPML, Hazel Hawke Collection)*

A cigar in one hand and the other wrapped around a woman's waist, Hawke is photographed at a charity lunch in January 1980, a few months prior to giving up alcohol. *(Are Media Pty Limited / Woman's Day)*

Wondering whether he'd been right to leave the ACTU, a pensive Hawke in his electorate office after his first weeks adjusting to life as an Opposition MP. *(Sydney Morning Herald, Kevin Schrieber)*

The Fairfax media company earned Hawke's continuing enmity after the investigative journalists of the *National Times* raised questions about his close links with Eddie Kornhauser and Peter Abeles. *(Fairfax)*

Gambling was one of Hawke's passions, whether in casinos or at the racetrack. He was at Flemington when his part-owned horse, Buoyant Bird, won a race on Melbourne Cup Day, 1980. *(The Age, Tony Feder)*

The sport-loving Hawke surrounded by well-wishers at Manuka Oval in Canberra. *(BHPML)*

An ebullient Hawke and a rather overwhelmed Hazel are swallowed up by the cameras in Canberra's national tally room on the night of the 1983 election. *(NAA)*

Chin forward, Hawke has all the answers when he first fronts the media as prime minister, while treasurer Paul Keating listens and learns. *(NAA)*

The height-conscious Hawke poses with the diminutive John Button and the rest of his newly sworn-in cabinet on the steps of Government House. *(NAA)*

While the political stage in Australia was being dominated by the Ivanov crisis, Hawke headed for Washington in June 1983 for his first outing on the world stage, where he was greeted with a flurry of flags by President Reagan. *(BHPML)*

Alan Bond was on hand in Newport, Rhode Island, to explain how his yacht was being prepared for the upcoming America's Cup contest. Hawke told the yacht's captain, John Bertrand, to 'destroy the bastards', which Bertrand and his crew did, much to the delight of Hawke and millions of Australians. *(NAA)*

After Gough Whitlam's Medibank scheme had been gutted and then abolished by the Fraser government, one of the first acts of the Hawke government was to reinstate it, changing its name to Medicare. It would be one of the most enduring legacies of his government. *(Sydney Morning Herald)*

In 1984, Hawke presides over a lunch in the garden of the Lodge. (Left to right, Ros, Matt Dillon, Clem Hawke, Bob Hawke, Paul Keating, Annita Keating and Hazel Hawke. *(JCPML, Hazel Hawke Collection)*

Caught among the crowd on a visit to China in March 1984, Hawke pursues his vision of developing closer economic ties between the two countries. *(NAA)*

The start of something big. With premier Brian Burke on the far right, Hawke hosts the general secretary of the Chinese Communist Party, Hu Yaobang, on a visit to Western Australia in 1984, when China made its first purchase of iron ore. The death in 1989 of the reforming Hu was partially responsible for sparking the Tiananmen Square demonstrations. *(BHPML)*

Corruption had become endemic in Australia, with networks of influence linking organised crime bosses, businessmen, police, judges and politicians. When the New South Wales premier Neville Wran came under pressure over allegations of corruption in 1985, Hawke was his staunchest supporter. *(Geoff Pryor/NLA)*

During the 1985 tax summit, an estimated 45,000 angry farmers descended on Parliament House, shouting down Hawke when he tried to appease them. Their display of anger helped to ensure that there would be no consumption tax. *(NAA)*

In November 1986, Hawke visited Kakadu National Park as part of his campaign to court the environmental vote at the 1987 election. The strategy proved crucial to Labor's success. *(BHPML)*

While Hawke took a leading role in the campaign against apartheid in South Africa, cartoonist Geoff Pryor pointed to his failure to make a similar stand on behalf of Indigenous Australians. *(NLA, Geoff Pryor)*

During a visit to Israel in January 1987, Hawke had talks with the far-right prime minister, Yitzhak Shamir, who made it clear that he was adamantly opposed to a Palestinian state. The visit marked a turning point in Hawke's attitude towards Israel. *(NAA)*

In May 1988, Hawke spoke at a welcoming ceremony in Melbourne for Soviet refuseniks, warning that Israel needed to pursue peace with the Palestinians if it wanted to survive as a democratic Jewish state. A furious Isi Leibler, his legs crossed, looks on. *(NAA)*

During the Bicentenary, the Aboriginal leader Galarrwuy Yunupingu presented Hawke with the Barunga Statement, which called for recognition of land rights and the negotiation of a treaty. Hawke promised a treaty by 1990. It's still waiting to be done. *(NAA)*

Look over there! After spending Australia Day 1988 on Sydney Harbour, Prince Charles wrote to Hawke admiring his ability with the binoculars to 'spot a good cleavage from a hundred paces!' *(News Ltd)*

Striking pilots and their families confront Hawke during the 1990 election campaign. *(The Age)*

Adopting his long-time Hawke persona, Max Gillies glad-hands his way among the well-connected audience at the annual grand final breakfast in the Southern Cross Hotel, only to be bopped sharply on the nose when he came face-to-face with Hawke. *(The Age)*

As the Cold War came to an end, Hawke had a long, one-on-one meeting with the reforming Soviet leader, Mikhail Gorbachev in November 1987. It was a sign of the influence Hawke enjoyed as Australian prime minister. *(BHPML)*

After eight years as treasurer, Paul Keating had finally had enough of playing second fiddle. *(Sydney Morning Herald, Peter Morris)*

Hawke takes his leave. After narrowly fending off Keating's first challenge, a majority of the Labor caucus decided that continuing disunity would destroy the party's slim chance of winning the 1993 election. *(Sydney Morning Herald)*

Playing the clown for the camera, Hawke reports from war-torn Somalia for Kerry Packer's *60 Minutes*. The unsettling experience helped to convince him that a career in the media was not for him. *(BHPML)*

An emotional and humiliated Hawke is caught between his wife and her close friend Janet Holmes à Court who had just launched Hazel's memoir with some cutting remarks about Hawke's record as a husband. *(Sydney Morning Herald, Quentin Jones)*

Love was in the air. Bob and Blanche on their wedding day in July 1995. *(Sydney Morning Herald, Andrew Meares)*

After a close friendship of nearly thirty years, a distraught Hawke takes the weight of Peter Abeles' coffin in 1999. *(Sydney Morning Herald, Robert Pearce)*

Along with Blanche, Paul Keating and Julia Gillard, Hawke waves his walking stick in acknowledgment to the crowd of Labor supporters at the 2016 federal election campaign launch. *(Sydney Morning Herald, Alex Ellinghausen)*

On the balcony of their Northbridge home in March 2019, Hawke goes through his regular morning routine of cryptic crosswords, hoping that it will ward off dementia. *(BHPML)*

best of it while you are there because you won't be there much longer'. Brandishing a populist 25 per cent flat tax policy, the malevolent spectre of Bjelke-Petersen appeared over Canberra.[5] Hawke's mother was right. Her son really was blessed.

In the first few months of 1987, Bjelke-Petersen's mad plan saw his Queensland National Party try to blow up the coalition that held the federal Liberal and National parties together, with Nationals MPs being instructed to withdraw from the Coalition party room. John Stone's participation in the attempted putsch lent some credibility to the Queensland premier's economic policy, which had otherwise been widely derided as 'voodoo economics'. It seemed for a time that the high-profile leader of the National Farmers Federation, Ian McLachlan, would join the Queensland crusade, but he thought better of it when the Queensland Nationals failed to get sufficient colleagues in other states to join them.[6]

The political divisions were not just within the National Party and between the Nationals and the Liberals, but also within the Liberal ranks as well. Peacock was hankering to retake the leadership and thought a partnership with Bjelke-Petersen might help bring that about, describing Bjelke-Petersen's crusade as 'a God-driven and abiding duty to drive the Hawke government from power'.[7]

With polls showing that both Bjelke-Petersen and Peacock were more popular than the Opposition leader, Howard became so insecure that he sacked Peacock as his deputy on 23 March. He had no choice: Peacock had been taped talking on a car phone with the Victorian Liberal leader, Jeff Kennett, during which Kennett confided that he'd told Howard, 'You're a cunt, you haven't got my support, you never will have.' Peacock responded in a similar vein – only to see their private diatribe against Howard splashed across the pages of the Melbourne *Sun*. In a desperate attempt to keep Nationals MPs onside and reduce the momentum of Bjelke-Petersen's campaign, Howard steered his Liberal colleagues further to the right, throwing overboard some of his party's more liberal inclinations and ditching a few of his more liberal ministers. He still couldn't keep the two parties together. On 28 April, he was forced to announce the end of the Coalition. The two parties would go their separate ways ahead of the election.[8]

Hawke couldn't believe his luck. It was 'the stuff of which Labor dreams are made', wrote Graham Richardson. Some of Hawke's advisers, although not Richardson, urged him to call an early election to take advantage of the disunity among the party's opponents. Most of his colleagues, however, were urging him to see out the term. Hawke had already forced them to an election in 1984 after less than two years in power, and they didn't want to face the trouble, expense and political risk of another early poll. Hawke's close call in 1984 caused him to be similarly cautious.[9]

By this time, though, Hawke had lost some of his closest and most experienced advisers: Peter Barron, Graham Evans, Bob Hogg and Geoff Walsh. That might explain why he agreed to be interviewed by radical investigative journalist John Pilger on 4 March 1987. The British-based Pilger had been commissioned by the ABC to do the interview for *The 7.30 Report* to mark the fourth anniversary of the government's election. Any one of Hawke's former advisers would likely have recommended against doing the interview. In their absence, it was left to Barrie Cassidy, recently recruited to Hawke's office from the ABC, to impress upon Pilger the importance of it being a relaxed interview, and Cassidy set out the most comfortable chairs in Hawke's office to ensure it was so. The interview was far from that.[10]

A hostile Hawke arrived late and dealt brusquely with Pilger, telling him to 'get on with it'. His available time had shrunk to just twenty-two minutes. If Hawke was expecting to use the interview to promote himself for the coming election, Pilger had other ideas. With the impatient prime minister tugging at his earlobe, the journalist asked about the disillusionment among loyal Labor voters who 'no longer regard you as a Labor government – they say you're a businessman's government'. As Hawke's fury rose, Pilger asked why there were more children living in poverty than ever before, why he'd allowed Murdoch to take control of most Australian newspapers, and why he hadn't yet done anything about Aboriginal land rights. Hawke had had enough. Ripping off his microphone and storming off, he snarled at the bemused Pilger: 'You've had your time! You asked the wrong questions on the wrong issues. You should learn!'[11]

Fortunately for Hawke, the interview was edited down to just eight minutes and didn't show him walking out mid-interview. The next day, Hawke demanded an apology, although an ABC inquiry revealed no wrongdoing by Pilger or the producer and no need for an apology. Nevertheless, Wran attacked the interview on Sydney radio and Hill, who had been overseas at the time, apologised on his return. This kept the issue alive as Pilger defended himself, supported by a group of prominent academics and writers, along with former Labor minister Jim McClelland.[12]

Hawke's office was acutely conscious of the critics who said that the government was betraying traditional Labor values. Pollster Rod Cameron had picked up on this from his interviews with voters, and had urged Hawke in late 1986 to 'RETURN TO BASIC LABOR VALUES' if he wanted to win the next election. Hawke had scheduled a cabinet meeting in Chifley's birthplace of Bathurst for March 1987, which could have done just that. His advisers urged him to assure Australians that he knew they were doing it tough and would commit his government to protect them and improve their lot, as Labor always did.[13]

Hawke refused. Instead, he told his staff that the government had to challenge the past rather than being 'captives' of it. Australia's economy needed further radical transformation if it was going to break free from its historical reliance on the roller-coaster of volatile primary produce prices and not be hamstrung by the practices and outmoded beliefs of the past. Unless change was instituted, argued Hawke, the country would become worse than a banana republic. 'Fuck the past. Or the past will fuck you,' he told his advisers, describing the ALP's history as 'both an inspiration and a dragon to slay'. His government had been on a path of radical reform rather than a process of 'tinkering' with the economy or providing 'cuddly blankets' to shield people against the harsh winds of international competition. It was tough love designed to encourage Australians 'to do the best for themselves'.[14]

In Bathurst, he told the Labor faithful that his government was breathing 'new life into' the party's 'inherited principles' and 'applying them anew to the task we face today'. With police guarding the doors, his audience had to strain to hear as local college students rapped on the windows with coins to protest the imposition of administration fees. They would have been even angrier if they knew Hawke was intent on doing away altogether with free university education.[15] But the prime minister wasn't going to let their anger divert him from leading the Labor Party down his chosen political path. He had to hope that its members and voters would follow.

Hawke was attracted to the idea of holding the election as late as possible, fulfilling the promise he'd made to voters in 1984. By holding it in early 1988, it would coincide happily with the start of the Bicentenary celebrations. But there were calls urging him to go much earlier. Graham Freudenberg was one of those who pressed the prime minister to take advantage of the disarray in the Coalition ranks and avoid the likelihood of living standards slumping later in the year. The once-in-a-lifetime disarray was unlikely to get any worse, they argued, while the coming fall in living standards could give Howard an election-winning edge. They wanted an election in April 1987. And Hawke might have entertained such a date, since he is reported to have rung Murdoch on 22 March to tell him of the date he had in mind and ask for Murdoch's support – to which Murdoch was said to have responded: 'Well, Bob, what's in it for me?' That wouldn't have endeared him to Hawke after the government had just allowed him to take over the Herald and Weekly Times, and might have given Hawke pause. As would Keating's desire for Hawke to wait until he'd presented a planned economic statement to parliament in May, confident that it would give the government a platform from which to launch a mid-year campaign. However, a winter election was usually avoided for fear of it going against the government of the day. To appease Freudenberg, Hawke promised that he wouldn't call the election until he'd first consulted him.[16]

But Freudenberg was in Sydney and the pressure on Hawke became too intense. Some of it came from his own office, where staff were keen to push their wavering boss off the fence. Amid his continuing indecision, a relentless avalanche of speculative media reports threatened to undermine the tentative economic recovery. The reports were also causing a political distraction that made him look weak. And so Hawke announced on 1 April that he wouldn't call the next election until his government's term had run its course. His declaration, which he quickly regretted, suggested that the election could be held as late as early 1988. Hawke presumably hoped that it would make him, rather than Keating, look to be in charge of his government's destiny.[17]

While his announcement stemmed the media speculation, Hawke's categorical statement infuriated his advisers. An angry

Freudenberg, who hadn't been consulted, sent a telegram from Sydney accusing Hawke of having 'broken his word'. He was not alone in thinking it was 'politically stupid' for Hawke to close off his options when it wasn't necessary. Freudenberg feared Howard would now have time to repair the deep rifts within the Coalition. The delay also committed Hawke to an election timetable that could coincide with a further deterioration in the economy, rather than with the short-term recovery that Hawke and Keating were hoping to engineer. Almost as soon as he'd made the announcement, Hawke began crab-walking his way back. He was soon out among the voters laying the groundwork for the next election, while his senior ministers remained in Canberra to decide the detailed savings that would go into Keating's economic statement.[18]

Much to Keating's chagrin, Hawke appointed the Left's leader, Brian Howe, to the ERC, so that the faction would be involved in the decisions to cut spending on various welfare measures. Sixteen- and seventeen-year-olds would have their unemployment benefit halved, while assistance for those who stayed in school would be increased. This would have the advantage of creating a more educated workforce, thereby lifting productivity, while also removing many young people from the dole queue. 'Restraint with equity' was the watchword of Keating's statement on 13 May. All told, there would be $4 billion worth of cuts to the deficit, made up of reductions in spending combined with revenue gained from non-controversial asset sales. The statement was designed to reassure the money markets so that there would be no electorally damaging slide in the dollar. As an envious Howard noted in his memoirs, 'Hawke continued to govern decisively', while he had to grapple with the challenge posed by Bjelke-Petersen and Peacock.[19]

On 27 May, just two weeks after the economic statement, and with the opinion polls improving for Labor, Hawke took the plunge. It wasn't just a matter of catching Howard on the hop as he was being beset by Bjelke-Petersen. The Queensland premier and some of his fast-money mates were themselves being beset by a media investigation into the corruption that had become a hallmark of their state, and of Australia more generally.

Once again, it was the ABC's *Four Corners*, along with *The Courier-Mail*, which exposed the criminality that had become commonplace under Bjelke-Petersen. It was Chris Masters who fronted the *Four Corners* program, titled 'The Moonlight State' and broadcast on 11 May. It was Masters who, four years previously, had revealed the parlous state of corruption in New South Wales, when the exposure of fraud in rugby league had led to the unravelling of a web linking police, judiciary, politicians, businessmen and organised crime figures. Now Masters had Queensland in his sights.

The program exposed links between corrupt police and the crime figures who controlled illegal casinos and brothels, along with SP bookmaking and drug trafficking, in Brisbane and on the Gold Coast. With the elderly Bjelke-Petersen visiting Disneyland in California, the acting premier reacted by announcing an inquiry, which, after some hesitation, was given to the independent-minded barrister Tony Fitzgerald QC, who expanded the government's limited terms of reference. Hawke had links with some of the figures who were likely to feature in the Fitzgerald inquiry, such as the race-going Russ Hinze and the dodgy developer Eddie Kornhauser, whose Gold Coast casino proposal he'd supported. The inquiry could see Hawke dragged into the spotlight, much as Murphy had been in New South Wales. Far better to have the federal election out of the way before the Fitzgerald hearings began.[20]

Hawke timed the poll for 11 July. This was just thirty-one months after the last one, and was designed to coincide with tax cuts that would boost the take-home pay of many voters. Because the Senate had twice rejected the legislation for the proposed Australia Card, he would make it a double dissolution. That would force all senators to face the voters, and mean that a joint sitting of both houses after the election might provide the numbers to introduce the Australia Card.

Hawke was leaving nothing to chance. He couldn't afford to, since the opinion polls still had the Opposition marginally in front. Hawke had to retrieve some of the seats he'd lost in 1984, thereby reaffirming himself as a vote-winner for the party and reassuring himself that he continued to enjoy the regard of his fellow Australians. That was the reason for his pre-election trips around the country, during which he gauged the public mood and connected directly with voters.

The depression that had dogged him during the 1984 campaign, and for months afterwards, had lifted. He was spurred on by the challenge of the coming contest and the improving prospects of electoral success. Yet he knew it was going to be a tough fight, and later confessed to having been 'a little frightened' when he made the decision to call the election. Australians were experiencing poorer living standards because of the lower prices being paid for their exports, and because of the Accord that was keeping a lid on real wages growth. In contrast, profits were exploding and Hawke's businessmen mates were distinguishing themselves with conspicuous consumption and deals, fuelled by foreign debt, that saw them gobble up established businesses, from breweries to television stations and newspapers.[21]

The campaign would last just over seven weeks, about the same length as in 1984. There would be plenty of time for Hawke to get among the Australian people to argue his case for re-election, while Howard tried to drive a stake through Bjelke-Petersen, whose crusade was insufficiently advanced when the election was called. As the premier's supporters fell away, Howard flew to Brisbane so that his rival could publicly acknowledge that his crusade was over and he would join with Howard to campaign against Hawke and his 'socialist' policies. Despite his claims for months that he would be standing for a House of Representatives seat so that he could become prime minister, Bjelke-Petersen now revealed he wouldn't be a candidate. Nevertheless, his tax policies would feature when a bowdlerised version was put forward by Howard, while his presence on the campaign trail only reminded voters of the destabilising role he had played – and could conceivably still play after the election.[22]

As soon as Howard announced his tax policy, promising a massive $7 billion reduction in the tax take, Hawke concentrated his campaign on blunting its appeal. He had insisted that the advertising agency owned by one of his wealthy mates from the racetrack, John Singleton, should run Labor's campaign, despite Singleton having been a founder of the short-lived libertarian Workers' Party in 1974, and being a party to Whitlam's defeat in 1975. Singleton had built a successful advertising agency during the 1970s, using ocker slang to appeal to ordinary Australians. After selling out for a handsome profit, he later established another agency in the 1980s, which was similarly down-market. Given the appeal of Bjelke-Petersen's populist crusade to disaffected voters, Hawke was right in thinking that the larger-than-life Singleton was the appropriate adman for the times, able to attract the attention of those Labor voters who'd been drifting away from a party they were struggling to recognise as theirs.[23]

With Howard's promised tax cuts in his sights, Singleton roped in friends from Newcastle to play the part of an average couple who questioned where Howard would find the money for the tax cuts. What essential government services would have to be cut, or axed completely, to pay for them? Wendy Wood played the part of an average housewife with a working-class accent who asked Howard where the money would be found. Will it be from cuts to Meals on Wheels? Or to home nursing? Or to pharmaceutical benefits? Or to Medicare? Or through closing childminding centres? Although the Liberals soon dubbed her 'Whingeing Wendy', the relentless ads were so successful that they made voters wonder whether Howard could deliver his promised tax cuts without inflicting pain on vulnerable Australians.[24]

That doubt was reinforced when Keating pounced upon a massive mistake in Howard's figures, which showed that his revenue would be short by more than a billion dollars. Howard took several days to respond, eventually conceding that his figures were wrong, albeit not by quite as much as Keating had claimed. He didn't help his campaign by rolling out a made-up motto at the Liberal launch – 'Incentivation'. It was meant to combine his party's attachment to incentives and to motivation, but was derided by Hawke for sounding 'like something you do to cats'. In contrast, Labor's campaign centred on a song that celebrated the government's achievements to date and called on Australians to stay the course. The television ad showed Wendy Wood and her husband walking up a forested mountain track as the soundtrack played:

We're on our way;
We're on the right track;
Australians have always been good at fighting back.
With a little more strength and patience we'll see Australia right;
Nothing worth having ever happens overnight.

Together:
let's stick together,
let's see it through.

We gotta keep on holding tight;
To that great Australian dream;
Nobody ever got anywhere;
Changing horses in mid-stream.

Together:
let's stick together,
let's see it through.

Hawke hoped the patriotic refrain would 'send a tingle up the spine of the nation'. In turn, Australians had to hope that Hawke had a vision to see them through.[25]

He set out his vision during the launch of the party's policies on 23 June. The event was held at the Opera House rather than at a suburban town hall, which allowed Hawke to make a grand entrance, crossing the harbour from Kirribilli House on board the Admiral's Barge, with Hazel by his side. The choice of venue and conveyance may have reinforced the view among some disillusioned Labor supporters that the party had become the home of the nouveau riche and the glitterati. In fact, the plan was to take a campaign photo of the relaxed couple against a stunning backdrop. Hawke's entrance was also designed to lift his spirits in a way that battling through Sydney traffic in a car would not do, with his advisers hoping that the effect on the prime minister would be palpable for television viewers. Image was everything.[26]

But the organisers couldn't prevent Hawke's passage across the harbour from being upstaged by a peace activist paddling a kayak. Nor could they prevent Hawke from making the grandiose promise that the extra, means-tested funding in Labor's policy for those receiving the family allowance would ensure that 'no Australian child will be living in poverty' by 1990, the time of the next election. After more than four years of Labor in power, there were an estimated three-quarters of a million children living in poverty. It was simply impossible to promise that none of those children would still be living in poverty by 1990, since no government could ensure that parents would direct the additional allowance to their children's benefit.[27]

Hawke later denied that he'd gone off-piste, pointing out his mistake had been to leave the grandiose phrase in the official script rather than to say that no child *need* live in poverty. In fact, he repeated the commitment during a post-election speech at the Victorian state Labor conference on 23 August, when he talked of the government's 'goal of eliminating child poverty in Australia by 1990'. His promise – which had brought cheers from the Opera House audience – would cause him embarrassment for years to come, and would see him held to account at the next election for his government's inevitable failure to achieve that ambition.[28]

Hawke contrasted Labor's limited spending commitments, which were balanced by cuts elsewhere, to Howard's lavish promise to cut taxes by a historically massive amount, while not stipulating what programs would have to be cut to fund the necessary reduction in revenue. It was a big risk by Hawke. Voters could easily have been tempted by the Liberals' largesse, and might not have been worried about the broader effects. In fact, many of them were tempted, or at least were tired of the Labor tag team of Hawke and Keating, who were still grappling with the country's seemingly intractable economic problems.

Every reform to the economy, whether it was the floating of the dollar or the entry of foreign banks, had been kyboshed by a fresh challenge that left many Australians worse off. The collapse in the terms of trade had been the latest challenge to the confidence that voters had placed in Hawke's economic management at two successive elections. Now, as he faced his third election, he was asking them to be patient and to 'stick together' as their real wages and living standards went backwards under the discipline of the Accord. The increase to the family allowance and other social welfare payments was meant to compensate for the decline in real wages and portray Labor as the party of fairness and equity, which was somewhat contradicted by the conspicuous consumption of Hawke's uber-rich friends who had prospered from his policies.

Hawke didn't help matters when he was photographed in the middle of the campaign sitting between Kerry Packer and Alan Bond at a business dinner, where he described Packer to the well-fed audience as a 'great Australian' and his 'close personal friend', and lauded the moguls as friends of Labor. Packer and Abeles were poker-playing mates from the 1970s, which strengthened Packer's links to Hawke. Although Packer wasn't as close to him as Abeles, the two men were knockabout larrikins who shared a love of gambling, sports, women and drink. More importantly, Packer wasn't averse to using his media to support Hawke at election time.[29]

Flying off to Perth several days later, Hawke lunched with some of the fast money men who'd attached themselves to the Labor premier, Brian Burke, in whose office they gathered. One of the fastest was Laurie Connell, who'd profited from the massive inflow of foreign money that Hawke had let loose by opening up the Australian financial system. Connell had made his start in Queensland, where the corrupt politics of the Sunshine State had allowed him to convert a menswear chain into a merchant bank, before he shifted to the similarly corrupt politics of Perth, where he planned to build a $30 million riverside mansion with the money he'd defrauded from his bank. The racehorse-loving Connell used the lunch in Burke's office to lobby Hawke about a proposed tax on gold, promising that he and his businessman mates would make big donations to the Labor Party if the tax was dropped.[30]

Hawke sought support from other voters by making headline-grabbing announcements about the environment. Richardson had been urging this on Hawke for the past year, partly to attract younger and single-issue voters whose preferences might compensate for the continuing fall in Labor's primary vote. During the campaign, Hawke went at it with a will, conscious that this support could mean the difference between success and failure. Protection of the environment didn't have much purchase with traditional Labor voters, who were more concerned with 'hip-pocket' issues and were unlikely to be swayed by environmental questions that could be portrayed as threatening their jobs or their savings. Powerful mining and other business interests could also be counted upon to oppose any environmental measures that threatened their profits. Yet the hard-headed Richardson seemed to have had an epiphany when he visited the environmental campaigner Bob Brown in 1986, with Brown showing him the damage that was being done by the logging of pristine forest areas in Tasmania.[31]

Hawke's supporters in caucus were probably more concerned with the economy than with the environment, but because of Richardson's powerful position in the New South Wales Right, Hawke had to take him seriously. To satisfy both sides, and to rope in swinging voters in marginal seats, Hawke decided to protect four high-profile areas that would resonate with voters: Tasmanian forests, Kakadu, North Queensland rainforests and Shelburne Bay on Cape York. Once they were placed on the World Heritage List, the federal government would be able to override whatever the relevant states or territories might want to do in those places.[32]

The prime minister tasked his adviser Craig Emerson with doing a secret deal with the Wilderness Society and the Australian Conservation Foundation, seeking their support for this agenda so that the government would not be assailed by demands to protect the many other areas that were threatened by development. Hawke told Emerson that he wouldn't 'agree to the greenies having an infinitely elastic agenda'. Once the deal was done on the areas that he was capable of protecting, he wanted their unqualified support – which they readily gave.[33]

Although the opinion polls during the campaign had mostly predicted an easy Labor win, they tightened ominously as election day came closer and Howard's promised tax cuts attracted increasing support. Although Hawke had performed well on the campaign trail, he refused to risk a debate with Howard for fear that it would elevate his opponent, as it had done for Peacock in 1984. Some voters likely saw his refusal as a sign of Hawke running scared and would have marked him down accordingly.[34]

Some would also have reconsidered their support if the *Times on Sunday* had published a damning feature on the Hawke government written by Brian Toohey. It played into the trope of Hawke's betrayal of Labor values. Whereas one in five Australian children were now living in poverty, the richest two hundred Australians had seen their wealth increase by more than 200 per cent since he had come to power. While workers had seen their pay reduced, 'the rich had never had it so good', wrote Toohey. Some of those fortunes came courtesy of the Labor government, which had allowed a concentration of media ownership that had benefited Packer and Murdoch, while other fortunes came courtesy of speculative activity rather than from building job-creating businesses. Despite the Costigan Royal Commission, 'the tax avoidance industry is flourishing', Toohey wrote, with the lifting of Reserve Bank checks allowing money to flow relatively freely to secret bank accounts offshore.[35]

Fairfax took fright at the prospect of laying into Hawke during an election campaign, which would have brought more of the government's anger down on the company. It instructed editor Robert Haupt to spike the story, which caused him to resign in protest. Toohey responded by starting his own magazine, *The Eye*, which promised to publish 'stories the big boys won't print'. The first issue, in July 1987, led with Toohey's denunciation of the Labor government. Called 'The Death of Labor', it was accompanied by a photograph of Hawke leering at a woman's bare midriff.[36] Although the feature would have reinforced the concern among some readers about the Hawke government, the limited readership of the new magazine ensured it had no impact on the election.

An opinion poll one week out from the election had Labor and the Coalition just 1 per cent apart. If Howard had maintained his momentum, Hawke would have lost. Indeed, the initial results on election night caused some observers to call it for Howard, with psephologist Malcolm Mackerras declaring that the Coalition would win a sixteen-seat majority. He wasn't the only commentator to be caught out. It was the first time that country votes were reported at the same time as city votes, which made the early voting for Labor look lower. As a result, the initial results showed Labor losing sixteen seats and winning only one. But a final effort by Hawke and a blitz of Labor ads had kept them alive – just.[37]

Despite Hawke's hopes, the result was tighter than the last election. In fact, the first-preference vote saw Labor suffer a 1.65 per cent swing against it, putting the Liberal and National parties narrowly in front. However, on a two-party preferred basis, the swing against Labor was less than 1 per cent, which gave the government 50.8 per cent of the vote and saved Hawke from the ignominy of defeat. Rather than losing any of his sixteen-seat majority, the opposite happened. Although Howard secured a swing of 1 per cent, he lost four seats when the Labor vote failed to fall in the seats where he needed it to.[38] It gave Hawke a history-making third election victory – he remains the only Labor prime minister to have achieved this.

Hawke's prayer at the Western Wall had been answered. Once again, his mother had been right: he really was blessed. That was the impression he gave late on election night at the Hyatt Hotel in Melbourne, with his father, Clem, there to witness another of his victories. Hawke didn't acknowledge a tearful Hazel, despite her standing alongside, until she put her arm around him. That prompted him to tell the crowd: 'I feel this arm coming around me and I am pleased to say it's been coming around me for 35 years.' He described his wife as 'a great mate and a great campaigner'. Earlier in the year, he'd told *Woman's Day* how surprised he was by the extent to which Hazel had 'blossomed and developed' as the prime minister's wife. And three weeks after the election, he took Hazel on holiday to north Queensland aboard Frank Lowy's superyacht.[39]

Although he'd won the election, Hawke hadn't been able to stop another slide in Labor's primary vote, or prevent the loss of two Senate seats. Overall, the results suggested that voters were tiring of him and his policies. It was in safe Labor seats that the party lost most votes, while it gained some support in more marginal seats. Hawke had to hope that the Labor caucus would be sufficiently buoyed by the small increase in its number and not focus on the continuing decline in the primary vote. He also had to hope that Keating wouldn't hold him to his commitment to retire before the next election.[40]

Hawke had now been prime minister for longer than any other Labor leader except Ben Chifley, whose record he would surpass within weeks. Despite the narrowness of the 1987 election win, Hawke seized upon its historic nature like a drowning man clutching at a rope. If he won the next election in 1990, he would also move past three conservative prime ministers, leaving only Menzies' record of eighteen and a half years. Labor was also in power in every mainland state except Queensland. Regardless, Hawke realised that he was closer to the end of his prime ministership than the beginning. With Keating claiming to anyone who'd listen that he was providing the ideas and the policy direction for the government, prime minister in all but name, it was important that Hawke be seen by caucus and his cabinet, as well as by voters, to be holding the reins. Or he might not be leading the government by the time of the next election.

Urged by his new political adviser, journalist and lawyer Bob Sorby to make bold moves, Hawke told his colleagues that he planned to hold a referendum to have four-year terms, and would conclude a treaty with Australia's Indigenous peoples during the coming Bicentenary. He also announced big changes to the machinery of government, confident that caucus would not block him in the wake of his election win.[41] Without consulting the cabinet, he reduced the number of departments to sixteen, with fourteen assistant ministers being appointed to share the administrative burden. 'He seemed to take the view that he was the Emperor,' observed John Button, who continued as industry minister.[42]

Some of the changes made administrative sense, such as the merging of foreign affairs and trade, but others proved more problematic, with the lines of responsibility between the senior and junior ministers sometimes unclear. Graham Richardson was made environment minister in the hope that he could continue to make the issue an electoral plus for Labor. Kim Beazley got defence, while Gareth Evans was shifted to the sensitive portfolio of transport and communications, which dealt with the powerful media proprietors and some of the privatisation initiatives that Hawke was planning to force through. Evans' fiefdom included Qantas, Australian Airlines, Australia Post and Telecom, as well as the government railway and shipping line. Hawke instructed him to begin the prolonged process by corporatising their structures in preparation for their eventual privatisation.[43] That would be difficult enough; winning the political argument would be much harder.

The progressive Susan Ryan, the government's only female minister, was dumped as education minister after she'd fought Hawke's plan to introduce fees for university students. According to the economic rationalists in the ministry, the Whitlam-era measure of free university education had mainly benefited the children of rich parents, who would have been able to pay the fees anyway, rather than encouraging poorer students to get a degree. It was widely regarded as one of the most important initiatives of the Whitlam government, but was blasted by Hawke, who'd never paid a university fee in his life, as a scheme that forced working-class taxpayers to fund free degrees for the wealthy. It was a populist argument that was contradicted by the figures Ryan presented to her colleagues. But Hawke and his colleagues rolled her in the ERC, which planned to reintroduce fees as part of the 1985 budget, only to have Ryan roll Hawke and his supporters in caucus, which voted against the proposed fees.[44]

Hawke saved face by imposing a $250 administration charge on university students in the 1985 budget, and then, with the support of most of his ministerial colleagues, pounced on Ryan as part of his post-election reshuffle, making her special minister of state, effectively condemning her to political purgatory. It wouldn't have looked good to dump her altogether, but she was henceforth a diminished figure in his government. Back in 1977, she'd angered him when she snubbed his sexual advances at the Perth conference, and now she'd angered him again by successfully appealing to caucus. Her replacement as education minister, John Dawkins, would do what Ryan could not countenance. The lesson wouldn't have been lost on her fellow ministers.[45]

It would prove more difficult for Hawke to get the party behind his plans for the privatisation of public enterprises. He began by telling delegates at the Victorian Labor conference in August, and later at the ACTU Congress, that his government's agenda was much more ambitious than the one he'd set out during the election campaign, which had mostly talked in generalities. To promote future jobs growth, productivity and prosperity, the agenda for the coming term would now encompass the sale of any enterprise whose continued control by the government couldn't be justified.[46] This was something Hawke had floated in 1983, only to be shouted down by the party, and something Howard had promised to do if the Liberals won the election. Now, with the authority given him by a third election win, Hawke would raise it again with a caucus that was much more amenable to the idea, even though the Labor Party's platform opposed privatisation. As did the unanimous vote of the ACTU Congress, with delegates upset at Hawke for likening them to supporters of the White Australia policy.[47]

But the many opponents of privatisation couldn't coalesce around any particular proposal, because Hawke hadn't nominated which enterprises he hoped to sell. Was he eyeing off the big ones – Australian Airlines, the Commonwealth Bank or Telecom, with their tens of thousands of employees? The sale of any of those could lead to job losses and price rises for consumers. Hawke wouldn't say. He assured the Victorian conference that he just wanted to start a debate.[48]

Hawke was particularly sensitive about the possible sale of the government-owned Australian Airlines, previously known as Trans Australia Airlines, for which Peter Abeles had been pushing. Although Ansett, owned by Abeles' TNT and Murdoch's News Ltd, was the bigger airline with more modern aircraft, there was a belief that the government ownership of Australian Airlines gave it an unfair advantage. Speculation about this had increased after Hawke announced that the two-airline agreement would end in 1990. The cosy duopoly had been created by Menzies in 1952 to prevent competitors emerging to challenge the forerunners of Ansett and Australian Airlines. It was another part of Australia's heavily protected economy that Hawke wanted to dismantle. Consumers were meant to be the winners when greater competition was introduced by the ending of the agreement, while the privatisation of Australian Airlines would save the government from having to modernise its ageing fleet.[49]

With Hawke re-elected, Abeles prepared for the imminent competition by having the government prevent any new airlines from having access to the existing domestic terminals. One potential new entrant was the regional carrier, East-West Airlines, which had signalled its ambition to become a national airline. It had recently begun flying between Sydney and Melbourne, offering cheap fares that had undercut Ansett's. According to a former TNT executive, Abeles had been bugging the phones and boardroom of East-West Airlines before swallowing the airline whole, taking out the upstart competitor and extending Ansett's regional reach. Abeles wanted to emulate in the air what TNT had achieved with its trucks, ships and trains, dominating land and sea transport in Australia and carving out a sizeable position across the world. His first wife had described Abeles as a compulsive eater, and it seemed that nothing could sate him. It wasn't for nothing that he was nicknamed 'the Beast of Budapest' – and he relied on Hawke and other politicians to feed his ambitions.[50]

It wouldn't be easy. Hawke had to convince the caucus, the party and voters if he was going to succeed in selling Australian Airlines, while ensuring that Abeles, as a principal beneficiary, would not be examined too closely by the media. Over the years, *The National Times* had run stories about Abeles and his corrupt activities, only to see them mostly ignored by the rest of the media. With that masthead's demise, it was now the ABC's *Four Corners* that had Abeles in its sights.

It wasn't long before Hawke heard about the program, which was being prepared by former *National Times* journalist Marian Wilkinson, and tried to have it stopped. He had to tread warily. *Four Corners* had begun in 1961 and was modelled on the BBC's long-running *Panorama*, which set the benchmark for current-affairs programs. Clement Semmler was the executive who'd established *Four Corners*, with a remit 'to expose issues that were swept under society's collective carpet'. He wanted it to be 'relentlessly outspoken about issues such as the treatment of Aborigines, political corruption, women's rights, and so on'. In doing so, it had upset a succession of governments. Semmler recalled how Robert Menzies had once confronted him, complaining that 'the sole purpose of that wretched program on the ABC is to discredit me and my government'.[51] Now it was Hawke's turn to be upset. Again. How could he be sure that a program about Abeles wouldn't expose embarrassing details about their relationship?

When the ABC chairman, Bob Somervaille called at Hawke's office in late August to argue for additional funding, Hawke had the *Four Corners* story at the front of his mind. He told Somervaille that *Four Corners* was 'a nest of vipers' and that 'we don't fund the ABC to do stories on Peter Abeles'. He'd already cut the ABC's funding by 8 per cent the previous year and was clearly threatening to make additional cuts. He further warned Somervaille to ensure that defamation lawyers vetted the program before it was broadcast, otherwise legal actions might be launched – not just by Abeles, but by Hawke as well.[52]

Hawke might have expected that appointing the former Wran staffer David Hill as ABC chairman and then as managing director would provide him with some protection. But Hill's presence had not shielded him from the Pilger interview earlier that year, about which Hawke was still angry. As was Paul Keating when Hill met with him to ask for additional funding. According to journalist Alan Ramsey, the treasurer told Hill: 'We've had enough of you cunts. It's now [a] full frontal attack. We fucked Fairfax, now it's your turn. And if you think I'm dirty on the ABC, you should hear what Old Silver [Hawke] thinks of you.' With the future of the organisation apparently at stake, Hill and the ABC board immediately launched the 'Eight Cents a Day' campaign, which sought to explain the per capita cost of the ABC to Australians. It was so successful that Hawke was forced to back off and the ABC was promised extra funding. In the event, though, and partly because of inflation, that extra funding was not forthcoming in real terms.[53]

The *Four Corners* program was scheduled to be broadcast on 2 November 1987, about the same time as Evan Whitton published a second edition of his book *Can of Worms*, which detailed the many links between organised criminals, businessmen, politicians, police and members of the judiciary. It carried prominent photographs of Abeles and his criminal associate Bela Csidei, along with an album of mostly bent cops, judges and businessmen. It noted how Hawke had strongly defended Wran and Ducker from allegations of corruption, and how he had dealt with the allegations against Murphy. Although Whitton didn't link Hawke to Abeles, there was plenty of published material that had done so, including a sensational new book, *The Crimes of Patriots: A True Tale of Dope, Dirty Money, and the CIA*, written by American journalist Jonathan Kwitny, which exposed some of the links between Abeles and the American mafia. With all this in mind, it's not surprising that Hawke was uneasy about what *Four Corners* might expose, since it had the potential to send him on a Wran-like trajectory into political oblivion.[54]

But his concern was misplaced, as the program focused on the deregulation of the airline industry and the likely privatisation of Australian Airlines. Wilkinson revealed how Abeles had amassed such great political influence that TNT was able to embark on a massive program of expansion by paying off the corrupt New South Wales premier Sir Robert Askin. When Askin retired, Abeles had dealt in a similar way with the now retired Wran, who was just as generous in extending taxpayer largesse to TNT and integrating TNT executives into the government's transport-related enterprises. Wran was rewarded in turn when a company he chaired was given Ansett's cleaning contract. At the same time, Abeles was corrupting some of the officials of the Transport Workers' Union in Australia, while paying off the mafia in America to ensure industrial peace there. Although the program detailed the close relationship between Hawke and Abeles, no mention was made of the money and goods that Abeles had sent Hawke's way over the years. With no explosive revelations about Hawke, Abeles was able to swat away any suggestion that their relationship was anything more than an innocent friendship.[55]

Acting within the tight constraints of Australia's defamation law, the program simply questioned how Hawke could be impartial when he was chairing cabinet discussions about aviation policy, in which his friend Abeles had such a direct interest. Hawke could have avoided any conflict of interest by absenting himself from such discussions, but refused to do so. As usual, Hawke regarded the question as a reflection on his integrity, telling journalists that he and his cabinet 'will discuss the future of aviation policy with the full integrity that we discuss all issues'.[56] Although the program further embittered Hawke towards the ABC, it could have been a lot more damaging. Abeles' reputation was retrieved somewhat when the Murdoch-owned *Australian* newspaper named him as its Australian of the Year.

Hawke would have been buoyed on hearing that the ABC's proposed offer of employment to investigative journalist Wendy Bacon, formerly of *The National Times*, was withdrawn on the order of ABC management. With Hawke having allowed most of the media to come under the control of Murdoch and Packer, naively believing that the two press barons were 'mates' of the Labor Party, the government continued to face criticism from the fiercely independent Fairfax newspapers. That independence was so jealously guarded that the Fairfax board refused to direct its editors as to the political line they should take or the articles they could publish. At the same time, the board was so shocked by the evidence of Askin's corruption that it instructed *The National Times* 'to put the maximum available resources into following up the story and publishing the facts, not only about Sir Robert Askin but the corruption of other politicians and police – particularly those still living and working in Sydney'.[57]

It was this instruction that had allowed *The National Times* to expose the activities of organised crime figures, together with the corruption of politicians, police, judiciary and business leaders. Articles about crime and corruption had won prizes for the paper's journalists but had not produced profits for Fairfax or won the company any friends in Canberra. When Fairfax executive Max Suich visited Hawke in September 1986 in a vain attempt to soften his antipathy towards the journalists of *The National Times*, the prime minister was unrepentant, calling it 'a bastard of a paper'. His antipathy towards Fairfax was partly based on prejudice against 'old money', which the Fairfax family represented, and partly on frustration at the company's refusal to do deals. That intransigence cost Fairfax dearly, as it came under attack from state and federal Labor governments and had its expansion plans thwarted by government diktat. It was good news for Murdoch and Packer, who were seen as being inside the Labor tent and privy to the government's media proposals, which allowed them to plan accordingly.[58]

In a meeting with Suich, Keating was said to have been 'very blunt about the fact that the NSW right are "deal makers" and that they provide favours to "our crowd" in return for favours given'. In an effort to stem *The National Times*' losses and perhaps soften the antipathy from Hawke and his colleagues, a new editor had been appointed in January 1986 to replace Brian Toohey, and the paper was rebranded first as *The National Times on Sunday* and then as *The Times on Sunday*. But there was little let-up in its focus on corruption.[59]

So far, Hawke had been able to brush away the imputations of his own corruption, helped by the overly protective defamation laws and supportive media proprietors. He was more concerned about the economy, the health of which would likely determine his political longevity. Keating's budget in September 1987 provided him with a pleasant surprise, revealing that an improvement in the terms of trade, along with cuts to government expenditure and the additional revenue provided by the capital gains and fringe benefits taxes, had brought the budget back into balance. It seemed that the sacrifices of the previous few years and the changes wrought by his government were finally bearing fruit. Wealthy Australians couldn't have been happier. They were happier still when Labor allowed negatively geared landlords to claim tax deductions for their rental properties, which would help house prices to spike and force interest rates to rise in response.[60]

Many of the changes had boosted the bank balances of wealthy Australians and they looked forward to more of the same as the stock market continued its five-year bull run, climbing to perilously high levels before suddenly collapsing on 19 October. As Australian stockbrokers watched the overnight action on Wall Street, they saw the Dow Jones index fall by more than 22 per cent – the biggest one-day fall in its history. When the share market opened in Australia, it fell even harder, losing 25 per cent of its value. By the end of the month, the losses would extend to 41 per cent. The collapse cast a pall over the government's recent good news, but Hawke didn't panic – at least initially.

He was in the middle of an international tour that had taken him to the United States for a meeting with Secretary of State George Schultz, and then to Vancouver for a meeting of the Commonwealth heads of government. He next flew to Dublin for talks with the Irish government. Accompanied by the Taoiseach, Charles Haughey, he went with Hazel to watch an international football match between Irish and Australian teams at the famous Croke Park, where the crowd roared a welcome and, much to Hawke's disappointment, the Australian players were beaten by the home team. The defeat was quickly forgotten among the 'merriment and song' in his hotel room. At a press conference the following day, Laurie Oakes asked him cheekily how it felt 'to go to a football match and not be booed?' Which made him 'furious for days', recalled Oakes. While others asked him why he wasn't heading back to Australia to deal with the stock market crash, Hawke still had to tour rural Ireland, seeing where the forebears of Labor legends John Curtin and Ben Chifley had come from. Then he and Hazel flew off to Geneva, where he met with Peter Abeles for a successful night of gambling at a nearby French casino – where a bemused Hazel fanned herself with a $5000 chip – before it was back to Geneva, where Hawke gave a speech calling for a reduction in American and European farm subsidies.[61]

When he finally returned to Australia, the first signs of financial trouble were being felt by the debt-laden companies that had grown enormously in size since he'd become prime minister. Cheered on by Hawke, they'd gobbled up strong cashflow businesses, largely courtesy of the foreign and domestic banks competing for their business. They were led by shifty entrepreneurs like Alan Bond, whose massive political donations had done so much to finance the electoral campaigns that had kept Hawke in power. Their activities came to symbolise the extravagance of the decade, with several of them later ending up behind bars or forced to flee the country.

One was Laurie Connell, who had been photographed fishing with Hawke at Exmouth. Now the stock market collapse had caused his Rothwells bank's cheques to bounce and his business to face bankruptcy. Backed by the Western Australian government, other entrepreneurs who feared for their own fortunes were corralled into contributing hundreds of millions of dollars to the ailing bank in the vain hope that it could be kept solvent. It was just one of many dominoes that would fall over the next few years, threatening the economic recovery that Hawke had been cultivating since 1983. Breathless headlines about the takeover of long-established businesses were replaced by headlines about heavily indebted companies on the verge of collapse. With many billions of dollars of bank lending at risk, there was a fear that the stock market crash was the harbinger of another depression. The Reserve Bank kept interest rates relatively low to encourage economic activity, not realising that the economy had absorbed the shock of the stock market crash and was being pushed along at an unsustainable speed.[62]

While Keating tried to manage the economy, unsure of where it was heading or how best to control it, Hawke's attention was elsewhere. Having confirmed his supposed political supremacy at the 1987 election, and revelling in the regard of the Australian people, he now wished to confirm his supremacy on the international stage and revel in the regard of his fellow leaders. The trip in October to North America and Europe had only been the beginning.

With Russia pursuing a policy of greater openness under Mikhail Gorbachev, Hawke saw a chance to continue his long campaign on behalf of the refuseniks. Flying to Moscow in November, he was escorted into an ornately decorated room in the Kremlin for a meeting with the Soviet leader. It was meant to be brief, but it ran for more than three hours. With just a foreign policy adviser present, Hawke claimed later that he and Gorbachev 'seemed to click immediately' and 'the conversation flowed like quicksilver'. In his mind, few could resist his charms; Gorbachev was just one of many world leaders whom he would claim to have beguiled. During their talk, he handed over the names of twenty refuseniks and asked that they be given exit visas.[63]

The omens looked good, but Hawke's humiliating failure in 1979 had almost destroyed him. He didn't want to make an announcement, only to be caught out again by a combination of his naivety and Russian perfidy. Although he held a reception at the Australian embassy for the refuseniks, he was reluctant to raise their hopes before receiving confirmation from the Russian authorities. In the event, he was informed that exit visas for several of the refuseniks would be granted. It was 'the substantial fulfilment of a long-held dream', wrote Hawke, noting that it 'helped to erase the nightmare of 1979'. He could return victorious, confident that his meeting with Gorbachev would be acclaimed by the Jewish community and regarded favourably by caucus and by most voters.[64]

Hawke's plea on behalf of the refuseniks was just one of the issues he raised with Gorbachev. He also sketched out a plan for peace in the Middle East, which was something he'd done several times before in the naive belief that he somehow held the key to a settlement of the long-running dispute. In pursuit of his plan, he asked Gorbachev to pressure the Palestine Liberation Organization into recognising Israel's right to exist as a Jewish state within secure borders, while he promised to pressure Israel and the United States into supporting the right of a Palestinian state to exist alongside Israel within similarly secure borders.[65] Unfortunately, neither Hawke nor Australia had the strategic heft in the Middle East or the diplomatic influence with Israel and the United States to bring peace to the Middle East. For the time being, he would have to be content with his minor achievement in getting exit visas for a handful of refuseniks.

Despite the disappointment, Hawke continued to seek the applause of an international audience. Hobnobbing with leaders of the superpowers would impress Australian voters, while any international achievements would add to his political legacy.[66] That legacy would be enhanced during the coming Australian Bicentenary commemorating the arrival of the First Fleet, a year of celebrations that was to include the opening of the new Parliament House by the Queen.

CHAPTER FIFTEEN

# 1988

Although the planning for the Bicentenary and the new Parliament House had been initiated by the Fraser government, it was Hawke who would be at the centre of the celebrations. As he proudly related in his memoirs, it was his name that was on the foundation stone of the new parliament. The year didn't begin well, however. In response to public apathy, the government's Bicentennial Authority was forced to launch a $10 million campaign to encourage a greater sense of excitement.[1]

A central part of the celebrations involved a travelling exhibition displayed in huge tents that were transported on specially built pantechnicons. Sponsored by the mining behemoth BHP, the massive trucks would spend the year touring the country, beginning at the Wodonga Showgrounds on a wet New Year's Day. Hawke was scheduled to launch the exhibition, but the small crowd was forced to wait under lowering skies before his late-arriving aircraft finally landed. While he and Hazel were mobbed by starstruck teenagers, a passing thunderstorm caused young girls dressed as swans to lose their feathers. They might have fared better as ducks. The stormy weather didn't help the attendance, with the exhibition being met with a large measure of public indifference, despite the advertising campaign.[2]

This was perhaps because the Bicentenary didn't mark the foundation of the nation and was increasingly seen as a contested historical space. Whereas the United States Bicentennial of the mid-1970s had celebrated American independence, Australia was celebrating the arrival of a convict fleet in 1788, when Governor Arthur Phillip had claimed just the eastern part of the continent for Britain. In doing so, he dispossessed its original inhabitants, whose ancestors had been there for more than 60,000 years.

The impact on the Indigenous inhabitants of that act of dispossession made both Hawke and Hazel ambivalent about the celebrations. It also caused the eminent historian Manning Clark to refuse Hawke's invitation to attend, and prompted thousands of Indigenous Australians to gather in Sydney to protest on Australia Day, when a flotilla of tall ships from across the world was set to sail down the harbour.[3]

There might have been a replica of HMS *Endeavour* among those ships if Alan Bond had had his way. The previous year, he'd promised to build a replica as a bicentennial gift to the nation. When the project was announced, Hawke had stood alongside a beaming Bond, who sported a captain's hat at the site in Fremantle where the ship was to be built.[4] As the repeated looter of cash-rich businesses and notorious avoider of taxes, Bond would have been more aptly dressed in a pirate's hat.

In the event, the construction took longer and was more expensive than Bond had anticipated. Like many others, Bond's heavily indebted businesses suffered a body blow from the Wall Street crash of 1987, when the value of his companies' shares tumbled. Just a few weeks after the crash, he tried to deceive the market and his creditors and shareholders by doing the art deal of the century, buying Vincent van Gogh's painting *Irises* for the auction record price of US$54 million. Not only could he not pay for the purchase, he lacked sufficient funds for the *Endeavour*, which wasn't launched until after the Bicentenary and after Bond's plundered companies had gone broke. Despite voters' concerns about Hawke's relationship with such businessmen, Hawke strongly defended his backing for 'the Alan Bonds of this world'.[5]

It would have been a historical anachronism to feature the *Endeavour* during the Bicentenary, as Cook's vessel had called at Botany Bay eighteen years before the First Fleet arrived. Then again, the flotilla of sailing ships from several nations wasn't meant to represent the arrival of the First Fleet. Nevertheless, a separate initiative involving a re-creation of the First Fleet was organised by people wanting to celebrate the nation's British origins. With Hawke watching on with

Prince Charles and Princess Diana from a naval ship, the fleet of tall ships and the melange of sailing ships mimicking the First Fleet tried to avoid collisions with the thousands of power boats that jostled for the attention of the nearly 3 million onlookers crowding the shores of the picturesque harbour. Later, in a handwritten letter, the future king expressed his admiration for Hawke's ability with binoculars to 'spot a good cleavage from a hundred paces!', although the 39-year-old prince maintained that he'd 'found better ones that you did …'.[6]

In a counterpoint to the celebration on the harbour, and telling a dramatically different story, Indigenous Australians from around the country marched in protest, bearing Aboriginal flags and demanding that their rights as the original inhabitants of the land be recognised and respected. A few months before, Hawke had established the Royal Commission into Aboriginal Deaths in Custody, and he now promised that a treaty or compact would be concluded before 1988 was out. Australians had to recognise, wrote Hawke, 'that two hundred years of European settlement comes after forty thousand years of Aboriginal history'.[7]

After winning his third federal election, Hawke had been advised to quickly make any bold initiatives that he had in mind, because there was no telling whether he would ever win a fourth. Bold initiatives might also convince doubting voters that he had a vision for the country, rather than just for the economy. Although a treaty would have been just such an initiative, and the Bicentenary offered the perfect opportunity to do it, Hawke couldn't bring it off.[8]

Indigenous Australians had to be content with incremental changes that paid some regard to their demands without unduly upsetting the economic interests or national feelings of non-Indigenous Australians. The status of Ayers Rock (Uluru) was a case in point, where Aboriginal land rights were extended to include the rock. Although the title of the land was given over to the local Anangu people, they signed the rock over to the national parks service on a 99-year lease, while taking a majority of seats on its management committee. Despite the change of ownership and it being a sacred place, climbing the rock would not become off-limits to non-Indigenous Australians. Hawke could have emulated Whitlam's ceding of Wave Hill station to the Gurindji people in 1975, when he symbolically allowed dirt from his hand to drop into the hand of the Gurindji leader Vincent Lingiari, a watershed moment for the land rights movement. The handing back of Uluru, which was culturally significant in different ways to all Australians, could have been another such moment, providing a step on the path to Hawke's promised treaty. But he hadn't been sufficiently bold to pass national land rights legislation after the Western Australian government and the mining industry ganged up against him. And he hadn't attended the signing ceremony at Uluru in 1985, which was done instead by the governor-general and the minister for Aboriginal affairs.[9]

The opening of parliament by the Queen on 9 May 1988 provided another moment in which Hawke could have redefined the nation and its changing relationship with Britain, and reflected on its past and future relations with Indigenous people. However, he shied away from doing that. In 1984, he'd endorsed 'Advance Australia Fair' as the national anthem, after it had been introduced by the Whitlam government and then changed back to 'God Save the Queen' by the Fraser government, only to be chosen in 1977 as the national song in a government survey. While officially accepting the people's choice of anthem, Hawke wouldn't entertain the notion of having a new Australian flag that omitted the Union Jack, or of making Australia a republic. Nor would he adorn the walls of the new Parliament House with the sort of historical texts that grace the Lincoln Memorial in Washington. The architects had hired Manning Clark to suggest such texts, but only four were used, none of which were contentious or reflected an Aboriginal viewpoint.[10]

With Aboriginal protestors assembling outside Parliament House to loudly complain about the lack of progress on land rights and a treaty, the only history that was made that day – apart from the formal opening of Parliament House – came when Hawke accompanied the Queen to the races at Canberra Racecourse and loudly leapt up from his seat beside the Queen to celebrate a win.[11] The resulting photo caused his critics to berate him for disrespecting Australia's regal visitor, but there was no keeping the excitable prime minister down.

There were little more than a handful of female MPs in the audience when the Queen opened Parliament House. Hawke's caucus remained overwhelmingly male, and would still be so even at the end of his years in power. Yet his government did make meaningful changes to the position of women. During her time at the Office for the Status of Women, Anne Summers found Hawke to be a willing supporter of initiatives designed to improve women's prospects and act against discrimination. These were issues about which he felt deeply, not least because he was conscious of being prime minister courtesy of strong female support, despite having made minimal progress on equal pay and none on female representation on the ACTU Executive or at ACTU Congresses during his time as president.[12]

It was different now. Hawke needed the votes of women if he was to remain prime minister, and women had great expectations for his government because of the policies developed under Hayden and pushed in parliament by Susan Ryan and influential pressure groups like the Women's Electoral Lobby. As the Whitlam government had, Hawke was able to use the public service and government enterprises as pacesetters for the advancement of women, and used parliament to pass laws against discrimination and sexual harassment in the workplace. His government also ratified the UN Convention on the Elimination of All Forms of Discrimination Against Women. Fraser had signed the convention in 1980 but baulked at ratifying it. Once the Hawke government had ratified it in July 1983, it gave impetus to a range of legislation and initiatives to promote equal opportunity.[13]

In 1986, the government established the Human Rights and Equal Opportunity Commission, with Hawke also pushing an affirmative action law through parliament that relied on the voluntary support of big business to increase female participation and promotion in the workforce. Those businesses that resisted could be named and shamed in parliament, and even denied government contracts. Abeles was prepared to take that risk in relation to Ansett, until Hawke pressured him to comply. However, the prime minister didn't push for affirmative action to get more female candidates preselected for safe Labor seats, or indeed for any seats. That wouldn't happen until 1994, after Hawke had gone. But a National Agenda for Women was launched by Hawke in early 1988 to accelerate progress towards equality, while Quentin Bryce was appointed as the Sex Discrimination Commissioner in 1988.[14]

Other measures introduced by the government – whether it was to boost subsidies for childcare, to encourage children to stay longer at school or to increase the number of women at university – had dramatic benefits for women. Between 1983 and 1988, the percentage of girls completing high school increased from 44 per cent to 70 per cent. An increasing proportion were going on to university, where they had fee-free education until 1988, when Hawke finally succeeded, after pushing Susan Ryan aside, in instituting his vexed Higher Education Contribution Scheme.[15]

Under this legislation, students would pay no up-front fees while attending university, but repayment would be demanded once their post-university income reached a certain level. In the meantime, they would incur interest on the fees until they were paid back. Hawke was happy to take the credit for these initiatives, which were both productivity-enhancing for the economy and vote-enhancing for Labor at election time, but didn't place any significant additional burden on the budget. It helped that the Liberal Party opposed the idea of women's equality and anti-discrimination measures, causing further division within its ranks and impelling one frontbencher to resign from the shadow ministry in protest.[16]

Whether these progressive changes produced any improvement in Hawke's own attitude towards women is debatable. One of the young secretaries in his office had cause for concern when, accompanying Hawke's party on a visit to Townsville, she was told to go to the prime minister's hotel room to pack away the dirty clothes that he'd left scattered about the place. 'I thought this was rather odd,' she recalled, 'that someone like me would have to pack a grown man's bag.' But she obeyed the instruction to 'pick up his dirty underwear', ensuring that she 'picked up a shirt and [then] picked up some underwear and threw them in the bag'.[17]

More than dirty underwear was being uncovered in Brisbane, where the hearings of the Fitzgerald inquiry were exposing the depth of corruption in that state. Hawke's close friend Eddie Kornhauser was in the dock because of his links to the crooked police commissioner, Sir Terry Lewis, who testified that the so-called 'Minister for Everything', Russ Hinze, had sought to conceal reports of Kornhauser's links to the mafia so that he could get a casino licence. As a result of the inquiry, Lewis would soon exchange his knighthood for a fourteen-year jail sentence, while Hinze and several other former cabinet ministers would face charges. Hinze had been pressured by Kornhauser to arrange government approvals for his property developments, as well as the casino licence that would underpin the profits of his Paradise Centre on the Gold Coast. After being loaned $250,000, Hinze had supported Kornhauser's casino proposal and influenced the local council to support the Paradise Centre development, while Kornhauser had used Hawke to ensure that the state Labor Opposition wouldn't raise any objections. It was all for nothing. A rival casino proposal, which had the support of Bjelke-Petersen, won the day.[18]

When Kornhauser's several payments to Hinze were exposed by the Fitzgerald inquiry in March 1988, Hawke defended Kornhauser, calling him 'an honourable man'. He didn't reveal that Kornhauser had once tried to compromise him when Hawke was at the ACTU, and thereafter seems to have had Hawke securely within his web of influence. Although the Fitzgerald inquiry saw Kornhauser charged with corrupt dealing with Hinze, he was acquitted after an eight-week trial, with the jury accepting the defence argument that it had been a loan between friends. In the wake of the acquittal, *The Sydney Morning Herald* observed that 'Bob Hawke and Russ Hinze are breathing easier this weekend.' In fact, the racehorse-owning Hinze would die of bowel cancer before his own trial could be concluded – which would allow Hawke to breathe even easier.[19]

The report about Hawke and Kornhauser appeared in the last issue of *The Times on Sunday*. With the paper's demise, and the gutting of the heavily indebted Fairfax media empire after the young tyro Warwick Fairfax tried to buy the family business, Hawke might now be relatively safe from the attention of investigative journalists. But neither he nor Abeles was safe from having allegations raised in federal parliament about their links with the mafia. Nor could Hawke escape the critical attention of voters.[20]

While the disarray among the Opposition ranks had helped Hawke win the 1987 election, two by-elections in early 1988 revealed a serious loss of support. The first took place on 6 February after Chris Hurford, who'd been dumped by Hawke as minister for community services, resigned from the relatively safe seat of Adelaide in return for Hawke appointing him as Australia's consul-general in New York. His place in the cabinet was taken by Hawke's close supporter Robert Ray, who was made Minister for Home Affairs. Although Hawke threw himself into the campaign to retain the Adelaide seat, he didn't help his chances when he raised the possibility of introducing timed local phone calls. It became the main issue of the by-election, which effectively made it a referendum on economic rationalism. Hawke's charisma couldn't overcome the widespread opposition to the possibility of timed calls. There was also the matter of his arrogance, which had been on display when he answered a question about privatisation from a female journalist. 'Aren't you a clever little girl,' he'd sniped. He never liked being challenged, particularly by a woman. But there was something else underlying his anger, suggested social researcher Hugh Mackay. 'The more the voters slip beyond [Hawke's] grasp, the more cocky, defiant and arrogant he sounds,' wrote Mackay. Although Labor was always likely to lose the Adelaide seat, there was a swing against it of 11 per cent on the primary vote and more than 8 per cent after preferences, which saw the seat taken comfortably by the Liberal candidate.[21]

While that loss was expected, Hawke was more confident about a by-election seven weeks later in the traditional Labor seat of Port Adelaide, which had been held by Mick Young before he'd been forced to resign after yet another political embarrassment, this time over his handling of political donations. Hawke accused the media of having 'driven from public life a great man'. The circumstances of Young's resignation wouldn't help the Labor campaign, even though the party's candidate was a local primary school principal whose forebears had long lived in the electorate. Labor's traditional supporters would have the opportunity to vent any anger they might harbour towards Hawke's embrace of economic rationalism and his support for the privatisation of public enterprises. Although Labor held the seat, it suffered a 14 per cent swing on primary votes and 11 per cent after preferences.[22]

It wasn't the only worrying result for Labor in early 1988. The New South Wales state election was held on 19 March, with Labor losing in a landslide, while a by-election for a state seat in Perth saw a two-party swing against Labor of 23 per cent. The Perth seat had become vacant after the soon-to-be-disgraced ex-premier Brian Burke was appointed by Hawke as ambassador to Ireland. Another state by-election that same day in Perth saw a 15 per cent swing against Labor. Taken together, the results were worrying for Hawke. He'd always argued that his popularity made the Labor government impregnable, and that he needed to remain as prime minister for that reason.[23] That position was now increasingly difficult to sustain.

Hawke's popularity among the Jewish community was also tested when several thousand members of the community gathered at Melbourne's Arts Centre on 17 May to welcome a group of fifteen refuseniks who'd been given exit visas by Gorbachev. Isi Leibler had flown them from Israel to celebrate the partial success of his and Hawke's long campaign to free those Jews who wanted to leave the Soviet Union. Many thousands remained there, and Leibler was continuing his campaign to secure exit visas for them. On stage as an honoured guest, Hawke was presented with a human rights award for his efforts. He responded with his familiar commitment to Israel – only to then liken Israel's treatment of the Palestinian people to South Africa's treatment of its Black citizens. The audience couldn't believe what they were hearing.[24]

Although Hawke had been campaigning on behalf of the refuseniks for more than a decade and was Israel's staunchest defender in the Labor Party, he had also been doing what he could to encourage a peaceful accommodation between the Palestinians and Israelis. He'd done so in 1987 in a speech at the Hebrew University in Jerusalem, when he'd called for an international conference that would see both sides recognise the rights of the other. But the First Intifada had erupted that same year, causing conflict to roil across the Occupied Territories as Palestinians sought freedom from Israeli rule. Instead of coming together, the two sides were moving further apart, and Hawke's hopes of being a peacemaker in the Middle East were being dashed.[25]

His sentiments seem to have been influenced by Shimon Peres, a founding father of Israel and leader of its Labour Party, who was then the Israeli foreign minister after having previously been prime minister. Peres feared that the nation's original principles and its future as a Jewish state were being put at risk by its army's occupation of the Palestinian territories. Echoing Peres, Hawke warned his Melbourne audience that demography would reveal a Palestinian majority in the combined territory of Israel and the Occupied Territories. This would mean the end of Israel as a democratic state, since it could only remain as a Jewish state when the population became primarily Palestinian if it kept the Palestinians in a condition of subservience, much as Black South Africans had been kept subservient under apartheid.[26]

The effect of Hawke's dire warning was to drive a wedge between him and Australia's Jewish community and to end his formerly close relationship with Leibler, who reported to the Israeli government that Hawke 'has illusions of grandeur and is obsessed with a belief that he is destined to become an arbitrator to achieve a peace settlement in the Middle East'. Despite taking his crusade to Washington and New York in June, where he met with President Reagan, addressed the US Congress and talked with Jewish lobby groups, Hawke's hopes for peace would be in vain.[27]

For a time, Hawke seemed similarly doomed in his push to privatise public enterprises in Australia. They were mostly the proud legacy of successive Labor governments, from Andrew Fisher to Gough Whitlam. While the enterprises paid some of their profits to the government, they often required substantial injections of capital from a government that was increasingly loath to provide it. Hawke had met with opposition from the party and the union movement when he announced his privatisation plans after the 1987 election. Unions were anxious about the jobs of their members, while party members were protective of institutions set up by previous Labor governments. Although Hawke was cagey about which enterprises he had in mind, two leading members of the Left faction in caucus, Stewart West and Brian Howe, said they would particularly oppose the privatisation of Australian Airlines and the Commonwealth Bank. The issue was to be debated at the biennial ALP conference in June; Hawke would have to win over the delegates if he was to move forward with his plans.

The Labor Party gathered at Wrest Point Casino, beside the Derwent River in the Hobart suburb of Sandy Bay. The casino was familiar territory for Hawke, who had often played at its blackjack tables. It was in his suite that he greeted Bill Hayden after the foreign minister flew in direct from a visit to Norway.

Hayden had heard of Hawke's predilection for prancing around naked so that onlookers could admire his body. Gareth Evans and Keating had gone to the Lodge one hot day, sweating in their suits, to find 'Bob in the nude'. Such stories did the rounds of Canberra political circles. So Hayden wasn't as taken aback as he might have been when a naked Hawke walked into the suite's lounge room, still wet from the shower and towel in hand. 'He looked reasonably fit', recalled Hayden, 'springing into the room with all of the bounce and confidence of a boxer from one of the lighter weight divisions', although sporting an appendage that was 'far from impressive' despite being 'displayed with such evident pride and satisfaction'. As the prime minister spread himself on the couch to hear the report from his foreign minister, Hayden fought to keep himself from laughing out loud at the 'entertaining idiocy of the act'.[28]

Hawke should have been glad-handing the delegates and stitching up deals that could produce the party platform that he wanted. Without the approval of the delegates, his government wouldn't be able to proceed with the privatisation of public enterprises during this term of parliament. He'd floated the idea in 1984 and been smacked down by caucus and the party. When Howard took it up and made it Liberal policy, Hawke had bitterly denounced 'selling off the great and efficient national assets, like the Commonwealth Bank, Telecom, TAA, Qantas', telling the party faithful who'd gathered in Bathurst in 1985 for the Chifley Lecture that it would be 'the height of economic irrationality'. Now he'd changed his tune and convinced the cabinet to go along with him, arguing that the government couldn't provide the much-needed capital for these businesses without threatening its spending on social programs. Hawke later explained how 'there were a lot of historical sacred cows that needed to be slaughtered. And so, it was a process of culling the herd.'[29]

Transport minister Gareth Evans was instructed to provide proposals to sell off 49 per cent of Australian Airlines and Qantas. In March 1988, he suggested that the two government-owned airlines should be amalgamated with Air New Zealand, which would create an airline of sufficient size to compete with the large international airlines that dominated the aviation world. Once merged, Evans proposed, the new airline should be publicly floated, which would provide the capital needed to modernise its ageing fleet of aircraft. It would also allow the enlarged airline to compete more effectively with Ansett in the Australian market.[30]

That idea wasn't welcomed by either of Ansett's influential owners, Murdoch and Abeles. The latter insisted on conditions being imposed that would undercut the advantages of the merger. Evans would have to devise a new proposal, with Graham Richardson advising the Qantas chairman, John Menadue, that there 'will have to be enough for Peter [Abeles] in any proposal to get Hawkie on-side'.[31]

Whatever Abeles might have wanted to get out of the privatisation of Australian Airlines and Qantas, the party faithful assembled in Hobart were having none of it. As Labor's most successful prime minister, Hawke might have interceded to push his privatisation agenda. But the numbers would have gone against him and he didn't need the humiliation. Rather than voting him down, the delegates referred the question to a committee for further examination.[32] Hawke could take some solace that he might yet win the day at the next conference, in two years' time. Provided that he was still prime minister then.

With each passing month there were more questions about Hawke's retirement and the Labor leadership succession. Some months before, Hawke had visited veteran political journalist Alan Reid, whose career in the Canberra press gallery had begun in 1937. Reid had known many prime ministers and had written stories that had contributed to the demise of several. Now the heavy smoker was on his death bed and offered his advice to the last prime minister he would know, telling Hawke that his big challenge would be arranging a seamless transition to his successor.[33]

Hawke didn't want to think about a transition, let alone a seamless one. There was too much to lose. There were the power and the adulation and all that came with them. Not least his occupation of the Lodge in Canberra and Kirribilli House on Sydney Harbour, where he could disport himself poolside in his red budgie smugglers and wave to his admirers on passing boats. He also wanted time to tour the capitals of the world, building on the relationships he'd created during his five years as prime minister. There were discussions to be had to get fairer markets for Australian exports, there was the push for nuclear disarmament agreements, there was the campaign against apartheid in South Africa, and there was the need to cement closer relations with Australia's Asian neighbours. Although he couldn't envisage his retirement, Hawke said that he planned to remain as prime minister until sometime after the next election, due in 1990, which he believed that only he could win. After that, he said, he would carve out a new career on television, where he'd been a ratings winner as an interviewee for the last two decades. Keating watched all this with mounting frustration.[34]

There is a limit to the life of any government, and Keating could see that Hawke was intent on leaving him just the fag end of this one. He warned colleagues that he might leave parliament if Hawke didn't agree to a handover during the current term. But Hawke still had the numbers in caucus, with Richardson ensuring that most of the powerful New South Wales Right, as well as the Left, remained behind him. That made it easy for Hawke to call Keating's bluff, which he did in the most inflammatory way possible in the immediate aftermath of Keating's sixth budget, delivered on 23 August 1988.

For Keating, this was the culmination of six and half years' hard work that had left him drained. Boosted with antibiotics to cure a chest infection, he reported a big surplus and a buoyant economy, predicting that inflation would fall the following year to just 5 per cent and there would be tax cuts for wage earners in July 1989. It was the budget that would 'bring home the bacon', he trumpeted. A few weeks later, Hawke too had a rush of blood to the head, promising that Australians 'can look forward to improvements in their living standards from both wage increases and tax cuts'. Keating wanted this budget to be his swansong as treasurer, as he hoped to take over as prime minister before the next budget was due.[35]

Hawke had other ideas. He used the post-budget interviews to ruminate on the rumours of Keating threatening to step down as treasurer, and perhaps from politics. He surprised journalists by telling them that Dawkins would be just as good as treasurer, and that Beazley would make a good prime minister.[36]

This was a red rag to the Keating bull and set off alarm bells in caucus, which wanted the election-winning duumvirate of Hawke and Keating to remain intact. After all, it was Keating who'd restored Labor's reputation as a competent economic manager, partly by explaining the intricacies of the economy in terms that people could readily understand. Although Hawke could read a prepared speech better than Keating, he had a tortuous manner when speaking off the cuff and had developed, according to Richardson, 'the hectoring style of a parson giving a sermon', which was perhaps learned from listening to his father in the pulpit or from his time arguing the ACTU case at the Arbitration Commission. For the sake of the government, the appearance of harmony had to be restored. Under pressure from Richardson, a television interview was arranged so that Hawke could lavish praise on Keating and acknowledge that he 'would make an admirable prime minister'.[37]

Keating was not appeased. When Richardson rang him on a car phone, Keating lashed out about Hawke and refused Richardson's suggestion that he meet with Hawke to paper over their yawning rift. A transcript of their intercepted conversation was soon circulating in Canberra, prompting Hawke to respond in kind with an angry telephone call to Keating.[38] Whatever friendship they'd had was at an end. Not that either of them wanted voters to realise they were as disunited as their Liberal opponents.

Hawke believed that the continuing disunity in the Liberal ranks, as well as the disarray among the Opposition after the Bjelke-Petersen madness, would ensure at least two more election victories for Labor. Keating had no such confidence and feared that Hawke's proposed retirement after the 1990 election would leave him with less than one term as prime minister. Calling Hawke on 26 August, Keating complained that Hawke had clearly decided to stay on as prime minister until the early 1990s and that 'I can go to buggery as far as you're concerned'. Their widening rift threatened their political futures. With Keating wrongly claiming to have the support of many colleagues in the caucus and a majority of the cabinet, it was vital for Hawke that they reach a rapprochement. He convinced Keating to meet with him at the Lodge.[39]

It wasn't just Keating who wanted Hawke to settle on a departure plan. Fellow ministers Button, Walsh and Dawkins were all pressing him to agree on a succession timetable, with Button telling a television interviewer on the morning of the meeting with Keating that the two rivals should come to an agreement. He'd said the same thing a year earlier. Back then, he just wanted to stabilise the relationship so that it could continue for the good of the government. Although he didn't say so publicly, Button now hoped that Hawke would hand over to

Keating during the current term. Dawkins was more forthright, fronting Hawke in his office to tell him that he should resign in favour of Keating, which Hawke dismissed as an attempt by Dawkins to replace Keating as treasurer.[40] As Keating was coming to realise, Hawke was never going to leave of his own accord. His narcissism impelled him to stay, cemented in place like a gargoyle on the roof of Kirribilli House.

It was a risky game that Hawke was playing. Keating had talked of leaving politics if Hawke didn't make way for him. Hawke had called his bluff, only to be forced by Richardson to back down and make peace.

It was in this context that Hawke attended the traditional grand final breakfast, which was organised each September by the North Melbourne football club. Hawke had been the guest speaker in his first year as prime minister. Now he was back at the swanky Southern Cross Hotel, sitting alongside other leaders, past and present, of politics and business, when in strode his doppelganger, the comedian Max Gillies, glad-handing his way through the crush as Hawke was wont to do at election meetings. Although Hawke had smiled his way through an appearance with Gillies on *Parkinson in Australia* in 1983, Gillies had made a career out of poking fun at Hawke's narcissism, and the embattled prime minister was in no mood to be upstaged at the breakfast when he was hemmed in by Australia's great and good and being beset by Keating. When Gillies finally reached the high table and bent in to say g'day, he recalled how Hawke grabbed his hand and 'pulled me down so that our heads were nose to nose', keeping him there until photographers had got into position to capture the shot. Finally releasing the comedian, said Gillies, 'he playfully bops me on the nose', as if in jest, but 'with just enough force for the pain to last the 10 minutes' of Gillies' performance at the lectern.[41] Hawke might have wanted to do as much to Keating.

The party couldn't afford for the partnership to be torn apart in public acrimony – especially when there was further evidence of voters turning against Hawke.

In October 1988, when a by-election was held in Bill Hayden's Oxley electorate, the swing against Labor was much greater than expected. Hayden was retiring after Hawke had agreed to make him governor-general. For Hawke, it was a way of atoning for his earlier overthrow of Hayden, which had cruelly denied him the possibility of becoming prime minister when he was on the cusp of achieving it. Voters didn't share Hawke's guilt. For many, the appointment of a serving politician to the lucrative sinecure was yet another example of Hawke providing 'jobs for the boys'.[42] They expressed their displeasure at the by-election.

Oxley was one of the safest Labor seats in the country, meaning it could experience a sizeable swing and still be held by the government. The usual by-election swing against a government averaged 5 per cent, with perhaps another 3 per cent lost because of Hayden's personal following. When the votes were counted on the night of the by-election, the swing against Labor was 12 per cent. The safe Labor seat had become a marginal one. *The Canberra Times* thought the result was 'ominous' for the government, warning Hawke that he 'will have to do better, both to protect his flanks from his Treasurer and to hold on at the end of next year'. For now, 'the tide is still running against him'.[43] It placed additional pressure on Hawke to reach a settlement with Keating that would hold until after the next election.[44]

For years, Hawke had made contradictory suggestions about how long he would remain as prime minister. Each time it was done to keep rivals at bay, particularly Keating. But his best defence against his rivals was always his high standing in the opinion polls and his successive election wins. Keating might disparagingly refer to Hawke as 'Old Silverback', likening him to an ageing gorilla of the kind people had become familiar with on nature programs, but there was general acknowledgement that the still fit and relatively popular leader could not yet be toppled. Nevertheless, Hawke couldn't be sure that Keating wouldn't one day do to him what he had done to Hayden.

Hawke also had to stop the repeated stories about the succession, which were destabilising his leadership and his government. One way was to agree with Keating about a handover several years in the future. Although Keating wanted to become prime minister during the present term, there was little support in caucus for that, and the treasurer had no way of making it happen without destroying the government. Bill Kelty had made that clear in September, when he said that Keating would be the unanimous choice of caucus to succeed Hawke, but only after the next election.

For all his disappointment at the delay, Keating wanted Hawke to make a clear commitment to such a timetable. Not as a throwaway comment in a women's magazine or as a remark to a select member of the press gallery. He wanted an unequivocal commitment by Hawke, made in person and in front of witnesses. Which was an indication of how seriously their relationship had deteriorated. Peter Abeles was suggested by Hawke as a suitable witness. Although Abeles was a 'mate' to both of them, such was the closeness of the relationship between Hawke and Abeles that Keating wanted Bill Kelty there as well. None of their parliamentary colleagues would be there, nor would they be told of it. That fact would anger some Labor powerbrokers when they learned of the agreement much later. The pact was kept secret from both the party and the public for fear that it might cause Hawke to be seen as a 'lame duck' prime minister.[45]

The meeting was held at Kirribilli House, just before dinnertime on 25 November 1988. Without the presence of Abeles and Kelty, it could easily have ended badly. Hawke certainly had misgivings about the meeting, which would lock him into a succession process that he didn't want. If not for Keating's unquenchable ambition, he would remain as prime minister until the public had tired of him. Not that he could envisage that happening. Keating had already provoked Hawke by suggesting that he might stay on as treasurer when he became prime minister, implying that it would be easy to do both jobs. Hawke was incredulous, telling Keating that he had 'no idea, no idea at all of what's involved in being prime minister'. It made Hawke wonder whether Keating was up to the task and whether he was right to agree to the succession at all.[46]

That may have been why Hawke delayed the meeting for six weeks, until he was finally prompted by Kelty. For the prime minister it was like going to the dentist. Sitting across from Keating in the drawing room at Kirribilli, he couldn't help pointing out their relative rankings in the eyes of the electorate and offering some advice 'about what leadership involved' – which included turning up to meetings on time and treating colleagues with respect. The meeting might have ended with Keating storming out under the darkening clouds of a brewing Sydney thunderstorm, but their separate interests demanded they reach an accommodation. They were equally invested in Labor winning the

1990 election: a loss would scupper both their careers. After a bit of toing and froing, Hawke promised to step down after that election and before the end of 1991, thereby 'clearing the way' for Keating. But he couldn't end the meeting without adding a proviso: if the verbal deal became public, Hawke would not honour it.[47]

Keating was under no illusions about Hawke's intentions. It was all about creating political peace in the lead-up to the 1990 election. Hawke was buying time. If Keating wanted the prime ministership, he would have to wrest it from him.

CHAPTER SIXTEEN

# 1989

The end of the Bicentenary was a happy time for Hawke. After concluding his secret pact with Keating, he could look forward to remaining as prime minister, perhaps for as long as he wanted. He'd looked his challenger in the eye and stared him down. Barring the unexpected, he was likely to be safe for at least the next three years, and perhaps much longer, if he could keep Keating on a tight leash and maintain his massive lead over John Howard in the opinion polls. With the opening of the new Parliament House, Hawke was also able to luxuriate in the new and expansive prime ministerial suite, with its modern appointments instead of the dated decoration and furniture of what now became known as Old Parliament House.

On a personal level, Hawke had resumed his relationship with Blanche d'Alpuget in late 1988. She'd divorced her husband, with the pair meeting, often with Abeles' assistance, at various rendezvous in Sydney, where she now lived. While Hawke would pretend to staff that he was going off to meet with Abeles, and D'Alpuget sometimes wore a disguise, rumours of their casual liaisons soon did the rounds. But there was no talk between the pair of it becoming a permanent relationship, so D'Alpuget continued her ongoing affair with a former colleague with whom she was very much in love – as Hawke discovered after ASIO intercepted a phone call between D'Alpuget and the journalist in question. Meanwhile, his frequent dalliances and relationships with other women continued as before, with Hazel being apparently happy to play the part of the prime minister's wife whenever they slept under the same roof. His sobriety made Hawke easier to live with, while her public role helped to compensate for the continued infidelities, which she had come to accept.[1]

In warding off Keating, Hawke had assured his challenger that the disarray among the Opposition ranks would keep Labor in power until at least the 1996 election. There was considerable force in Hawke's assessment. The conflict between Howard and Peacock had resumed. Even though Howard had expelled Peacock from the shadow ministry for supporting the 'Joh for Canberra' campaign, his former deputy still enjoyed support from a sizeable minority of their colleagues, who encouraged him to stand as deputy after the 1987 election. Despite the continuing disunity this would inevitably create within Liberal ranks, he easily beat ten other candidates for the position.[2]

Even though the Liberals' ramshackle coalition with the National Party had been patched up, Hawke couldn't have been more pleased. Not least because another strong challenger for the Liberal leadership had appeared, which opened the possibility of a three-way tussle. The newcomer was the wealthy businessman John Elliott, who'd built a debt-fuelled empire based largely on beer. Younger by two years than both Howard and Peacock, the chain-smoking tough talker was a generous donor to the Liberals, which had helped him become the party's treasurer, and then federal president after the 1987 election. He announced his aim of standing for a safe lower-house seat at a by-election prior to the 1990 election, and declared that Peacock would never be leader again. Had Elliott been elected to parliament, his presence in Canberra would have ensured continuing ructions within Liberal ranks. As long as he kept that option open and remained an unrestrained political commentator as Liberal president, Howard would have to keep looking over both his shoulders.[3] And that meant he had less time to take on Hawke. That wasn't his only problem.

The changing ethnic make-up of Australia after World War II had seen the country's Anglo-Celtic predominance gradually shrink as new ethnic groups arrived to create a more diverse population. The initial groups recruited for Australia's post-war farms and factories were largely blue-eyed immigrants from Britain and northern Europe. When their numbers declined, Australia was forced to look elsewhere, with shiploads coming from the countries of the Mediterranean, particularly Italy and Greece. As the White Australia policy was progressively dismantled, the barrier against Asian immigrants was cautiously lifted.

Hawke had been ACTU president during the 1970s, when Vietnamese refugees began arriving, and he had opposed their admission, even trying to make it an issue during the 1977 election campaign. They came anyway. Tens of thousands fled in boats across the South China Sea to Malaysia and Indonesia, with some reaching as far as Australia. Many perished en route. To bring order to the flow and alleviate the humanitarian crisis, the Fraser government began taking thousands of Vietnamese from the refugee camps and flying them to Australia. As with the Chinese in the previous century, the Vietnamese tended to live in inner-city communities, where their presence disconcerted some Australians. Historian Geoffrey Blainey gave voice to these fears in 1984, when he argued that the flow of Vietnamese refugees was testing Australia's tolerance for newcomers. Blainey found an eager audience among conservative Australians and was lauded by many members of the Liberal Party. During the Bicentenary, he'd warned that Australia was in danger of becoming a 'cluster of tribes' – an argument Howard adapted for electoral purposes in an effort to mobilise those Australians made uneasy or angry by the transforming face of Australia. He began attacking multiculturalism and calling for cuts in Asian immigration.[4]

Hawke watched his opponent crawl out onto this dangerous political limb before he took a chainsaw to it in August 1988, accusing Howard of 'cynical opportunism' and moving a motion in parliament in support of a bipartisan, non-discriminatory immigration policy. In a blow to Howard's authority, six of his own MPs either voted against him or abstained. He pressed ahead anyway, adding a specially commissioned song to his 'One Australia' campaign that called on Australians to 'teach our sons and daughters what it means to be a true Australian'.[5]

Partially beaten back by Hawke on the immigration issue, Howard tried to undermine Hawke's still considerable popularity by associating him with corruption. Despite the exposure of some of his close associates, the Liberals had struggled to tar Hawke with the corruption brush. In 1984, Peacock as Liberal leader had only made a fool of himself when he'd called Hawke a 'little crook' and then been unable to back it up. Other Liberal MPs had tried and failed since then, with Hawke being protected in parliament by the Speaker, who disallowed questions that were unrelated to Hawke's responsibilities as prime minister. It was perhaps a sign of Howard's desperation when he launched yet another assault on Hawke at the end of the parliamentary year in 1988. This time, it came from Hawke's long relationship with Eddie Kornhauser.

In April 1980, six months before being elected to parliament, Hawke was staying on the Gold Coast with the multimillionaire, who was then constructing the Paradise Centre, a mixed development of shops and two apartment towers strategically located on the beach in the heart of Surfers Paradise. During Hawke's stay, Kornhauser had meetings with Gold Coast councillors to seek various approvals for his project, with Hawke joining Kornhauser and the councillors at the adjoining Surfers Paradise Hotel, also owned by Kornhauser and where Hawke was staying. Over lunch in his friend's private quarters, the developer pressed his plans upon the members of the council's planning committee, with Hawke saying that Kornhauser had his support and urging that they 'look after Eddie'. It was only after the Fitzgerald inquiry started to investigate corruption in Queensland, with Kornhauser being a major focus of attention, that one of the councillors referred to Hawke's role.[6]

Jack Egerton had become a member of the Gold Coast council in 1979, after earlier being expelled from the Labor Party for accepting a knighthood from Malcolm Fraser for services to the trade union movement. Egerton had risen through the trade union movement before becoming a powerbroker on the ACTU Executive and Labor's federal executive. Although his knighthood had put him beyond the pale in Labor eyes, Egerton's account of the meeting with Hawke was supported by another councillor, Betty Diamond, who had been present at the lunch.[7]

Insinuations about Hawke's relationship with Kornhauser had been raised earlier that year, after the Fitzgerald inquiry into official corruption revealed that Kornhauser's name appeared several times in the diary of Queensland's corrupt police commissioner, Terry Lewis, in 1981–82. It was suggested that, in his campaign to get a casino licence for his Gold Coast property, Kornhauser was pressuring the police commissioner to remove any references to criminal associations that might otherwise debar him from securing the licence. Hawke was unmoved by the reports, telling journalists that the diary entries were not proof of wrongdoing, that Kornhauser was a close friend of long standing and assuring Jana Wendt on *A Current Affair* that he had 'no reason to believe he's other than honourable'.[8]

With the new allegations from Egerton, Hawke tried to shut down any discussion in his usual way, by threatening defamation actions against Egerton and any media organisations that reported Egerton's claims. In the event, after conceding the gist of Egerton's allegation, he only proceeded against the Murdoch-owned Queensland Newspapers. He also tried to downplay his relationship with Kornhauser, telling a press conference on 30 November that he 'used to see him on the odd occasion' but no longer 'see very much of him'. Once the defamation action had been started, Hawke could dismiss any questions from journalists by saying it was before the courts. He tried doing the same in parliament when several Liberal MPs raised the matter. He refused to answer and instead challenged them to repeat their questions outside parliament so that they could also be sued.[9]

Kim Beazley backed the prime minister up, saying that legal constraints caused Hawke to be cautious in answering the allegations. When the Opposition tried to table the letter from Betty Diamond, which would allow the media to freely report it, the government refused it leave to do so, which prompted the Opposition to move a censure motion against Hawke. This would customarily bring on an immediate debate, but the government gagged it.[10]

The issue couldn't be suppressed that easily. Later that day, when an amendment to the National Crime Authority Act was being debated, Liberal MP Neil Brown read Diamond's letter into Hansard and suggested that the allegations should be referred to the NCA. Although that was never done, the letter could now be reported by the media without fear of Hawke launching another defamation action.[11]

Now that corruption was making headlines again, Howard launched another censure motion against Hawke, claiming that he'd misled parliament with his vague rejection of the Opposition's questions about the luncheon and his expression of support for Kornhauser. According to Howard, Hawke had been 'less than truthful with this Parliament' – which was hardly the basis for a censure motion.[12]

It was only now that Hawke conceded that he had attended the luncheon nearly nine years before, and that he might have said something 'favourable of Mr Kornhauser'. But it was only done, he said, because Kornhauser had been the subject of criticism on the Gold Coast that had been 'expressed in the most unacceptable anti-Semitic form' and his 'natural inclination as a friend [was] to speak positively of Mr Kornhauser whenever Mr Kornhauser was the subject of discussion'. That was another implicit warning to Howard to be wary of making allegations linking Hawke with Kornhauser, or else he, too, could face charges of antisemitism.[13]

Amid the confected hoo-ha, more allegations were raised by the Opposition. One suggested that Hawke had met in a Brisbane motel with Kornhauser and Hinze, together with Clyde Holding and the state Labor leader in November 1981, to discuss Kornhauser's application for the Gold Coast casino licence. However, after consulting his office diary, Hawke told parliament that he had no record of any such meeting. Holding agreed, while Hinze said he was 'about 99 per cent sure' he hadn't been there. Another MP asked Hawke whether Kornhauser had given $50,000 to the campaign to overthrow Hayden in 1983, only to have the Speaker rule the question out of order. Meanwhile, Liberal MP Ken Aldred asked the government to release the transcript of the Commonwealth Police questioning of the mafia informant Jimmy 'the Weasel' Fratianno about Abeles, only to be refused because it might damage relations between Australian and American law-enforcement agencies.[14]

Wild shots were being swung in every direction but none had hit home. Even so, Hawke didn't escape unscathed. His threats of defamation actions against anyone asking questions prompted *The Canberra Times* to comment: 'What a demeaning sight to see our Prime Minister hide behind the wigs and gowns of lawyers, threatening to sue for defamation anyone who dared say anything nasty about him.'[15]

Defending his reputation and shoring up his popularity in the opinion polls was one thing. It was much more difficult to shore up the economic recovery that Hawke and his ministers had laboured so hard to encourage. After the stock market crash of 1987, the government and the Reserve Bank had combined to keep interest rates relatively low, in the belief that the fall in stock prices would drag down the economy and cause a 1930s-type depression.

They were wrong. The economy had been largely unaffected, which meant it was boosted unnecessarily by low interest rates, which began to re-create the inflationary spiral that had dogged the country for more than a decade. At the same time, there was an investment boom, with the banks lending to all-comers as they fought for market share in the new deregulated world. The fall in export prices had also reversed, causing even more money to wash through the economy. By early 1989, inflation was back above 7 per cent and rising quickly.

Once the mistake was realised, a swift about-turn was made. A tightening of credit was engineered in an attempt to take the heat out of the economy. It would have had more effect if Hawke and Keating had been open about what they and the Reserve Bank were doing – that they'd been mistaken and the public should curb their spending. But neither man was adept at mea culpas. Not when they'd been proclaiming for several years their prowess as economic managers. When interest rates finally started to be lifted, they had to raise them much faster and much higher before they began to have the desired effect of slowing economic activity. House prices were booming and workers were demanding, and often getting, wage increases that went beyond the limits of the Accord. To try to rein in the exuberance, particularly in the housing market, interest rates were put up by 6 per cent over just fifteen months, which hurt homeowners and sent some indebted businesses bankrupt. Had Hawke consulted his cabinet, rather than relying upon phone calls and meetings with Abeles, he might have been better informed about the evolving economic conditions and could perhaps have mitigated some of the worst effects of the coming catastrophe.[16]

It wasn't just interest rates that punctured the exuberance in the economy. The speculative bubbles that had developed as a result of the financial deregulation were just waiting to be popped. The back-slapping developers who'd gorged on the freely available bank debt and who'd been lauded by Hawke as they swallowed up iconic businesses with strong cashflows, both at home and abroad, discovered that their revenues struggled to cope with the higher interest rates now demanded by their creditors. Some owed so much that the banks quaked at the prospect of calling in the debts, leaving the colourful businessmen to meet their increasing interest payments as best they could. It often meant looting the businesses they controlled and using creative tax-avoidance strategies.

Alan Bond was the epitome of this, presiding over an empire that controlled many of the world's breweries, along with businesses ranging from the Chilean telephone system to Australia's most profitable television network, New York's Hotel St. Moritz and an Oxfordshire manor house and village. One of his last initiatives was the establishment of Bond University on the Gold Coast. His international business success, combined with his winning of the America's Cup, had cemented him as an Australian folk hero, with Hawke being one of his loudest admirers. Bond had responded with generous donations to the Labor Party and was involved in the corruption of its Western Australian branch.[17]

It all began to unravel for Bond in late 1988, when he started buying shares in a British conglomerate controlled by the powerful businessman 'Tiny' Rowland, who knew Bond was desperate and technically insolvent and responded with an international publicity campaign to destroy him. It was during this campaign in early 1989 that journalist Paul Barry produced a *Four Corners* program that revealed how Bond's empire was being kept afloat by the fraudulent misuse of company funds, and by deception of both its shareholders and the tax office. Despite the exposé, Bond's empire was so big and sprawling that he was able to sell off a succession of assets and rob associated companies to satisfy his bankers and shareholders before he was finally declared bankrupt in 1992; he was later stripped of his honours and sentenced to jail.[18]

Although Hawke had associated himself with Bond and others of that ilk when they were successful and able to support Labor with donations, he left them to swing when the vultures started circling. There is no mention of Bond in Hawke's memoirs and, other than a photograph of a celebrating Hawke at the Perth Yacht Club, there is not even a mention of the America's Cup. Other businessmen who profited spectacularly from Hawke's deregulation of the financial system, and fell from grace just as spectacularly – Christopher Skase, Laurie Connell and George Herscu – were given similar short shrift.

Kornhauser and Abeles were different. They were both much closer to Hawke, and had been for much longer. Hawke did what he could to support Kornhauser when he was under investigation by the Fitzgerald inquiry and being harried by the media. After all, it was Kornhauser who'd organised the funding of the Hawke forest in Israel and been supportive in other ways, while Abeles had been a constant friend, arranger of dalliances, employer of Hawke's former girlfriends and financial supporter for nearly two decades.[19] That was why, when Hawke pushed ahead with the deregulation of the aviation industry, he tried to ensure that Abeles, a half-owner of Ansett Airlines with Rupert Murdoch, was not adversely affected.

Ansett and its associated international aircraft-chartering business had been goldmines for Abeles and Murdoch. In the Australian domestic market, Ansett dominated its government-owned rival, Australian Airlines. The lucrative cashflow from the rapidly expanding businesses had helped cement Abeles in place as the richly remunerated head of its parent company, TNT, and allowed TNT to become an international transport company. It also helped finance Murdoch's debt-laden takeover of the Herald and Weekly Times, as well as his expansion into the media landscapes of Britain and the United States. The imminent ending of the two-airline agreement in 1990 could have endangered that cashflow, had Ansett not had Hawke's protection. He ensured that Australia would not have open skies, which would have allowed international airlines to carry domestic passengers, and secured fifty-year leases of the government-owned airport terminals for Ansett and Australian Airlines, effectively preventing any future airline from posing a serious challenge to their control of the domestic market.[20]

But both airlines were still facing problems. Abeles had equipped Ansett with too many different types of aircraft, which hampered their interoperability on domestic and international routes, while Australian Airlines was burdened by old aircraft and a refusal by the Hawke government to make a sufficient capital investment to allow it to compete seriously with Ansett. Both airlines were also hampered by cost structures that had been allowed to grow under the two-airline agreement. Apart from the aircraft, the biggest cost was the crew, who'd used industrial action over the years to demand ever higher salaries. With Hawke's help, that was about to change.[21]

The US president, Ronald Reagan, had shown Hawke the way in 1981, when he sacked air traffic controllers en masse after they struck for higher wages. Their union was smashed and employers in other industries were emboldened to react just as aggressively when confronted by industrial action. Britain's Margaret Thatcher did likewise with coalminers and other workers, and supported Murdoch's peremptory sacking of print workers when he moved his newspaper business from Fleet Street to Wapping, assisted by the trucks of Abeles' TNT. The lessons learned in these disputes were now going to be applied in Australia, where Abeles and Murdoch wanted to transform Ansett into a leaner and more productive airline that could defend its dominance in what was soon to be a partly deregulated domestic market. All that schmoozing by Abeles and provision of benefits to Hawke over nearly two decades would now reap its richest reward.

The Australian Federation of Air Pilots (AFAP) made it easy for Abeles when it advised its members in December 1988 of its intention to seek higher salaries and better conditions after being held back for several years by the Accord, warning that it would use its powerful position and threat of industrial action to ensure success. That had always worked in the past, when the pilots' demands were usually accepted after a short burst of industrial action, with the heavily protected airlines simply increasing their fares to pay for them. Passengers were the losers, but their numbers increased anyway, growing sixfold during the decade. This time, the pilots' ambit claim included a 30 per cent increase in salaries. Their real incomes had been going backwards and inflation was again rising. With Abeles being paid millions as Ansett's chief, and politicians having just been awarded a 30 per cent salary increase, the pilots were in no mood for compromise.[22]

Neither were Abeles and Hawke. On 15 August, the two men met to lay a trap for the pilots. Also at the meeting were Ralph Willis and Ted Harris; the latter had become friends with Hawke during his ACTU days, when Harris was the head of Ampol and regularly played tennis with him. It was Harris who now enjoyed Hawke's patronage, securing several government appointments. The ACTU's Bill Kelty also phoned in.[23] Although each man had different interests, they were united in their determination to defeat the pilots.

When Hawke later explained his harsh handling of the pilots, he portrayed it as a life-or-death struggle for the future of the Accord, by which unions had agreed to practise wage restraint in return for the government providing improvements in the 'social wage', such as in health benefits and family allowances. But the social wage wouldn't totally reimburse workers for the toll that inflation and wage restraint had taken on their income. It wasn't meant to. Rather, it was designed to gradually deflate the level of wages so that exports of Australian manufactured goods would become more competitive on world markets. It was also meant to stop the wage-price spiral that had powered inflation since the mid-1970s. After presiding over a militant union movement that had increased the workers' share of the national pie, Hawke was now doing the opposite as prime minister, ensuring that a greater share went to profits.

While Hawke wanted to defend the Accord, Harris and Abeles wanted to reduce the cost base of their airlines in case the ending of the two-airline agreement brought competition from new rivals.

Bringing on a blue with the pilots would improve the productivity of the airline industry and boost the profits of the airlines, while also shifting the blame for their operational woes away from the government and Abeles and placing it all on the pilots.[24]

Hawke was spoiling for a fight. He had been enraged when pilots opposed his plan in July 1983 to tax superannuation lump-sum payments. Because they had to retire relatively early, pilots relied on the payments to finance their long retirement or buy a small business to make a post-career living. In protest, they held stop-work meetings and banned any flights to Canberra for four days, prompting Hawke to lambast them as 'a highly paid, greedy, self-centred group of people, unconcerned with the welfare of the rest of their fellow citizens'. Although the tax went ahead, the actions of the pilots and the support from several other unions forced Hawke to partially back down – which made him more than ready to take on the pilots six years later, as they prepared for the regular renegotiation of their agreement with the airlines.[25]

Abeles was also ready for them. In 1986, he'd sacked baggage handlers who'd grounded Ansett flights and only re-employed those who would agree to have a no-strike clause in their contracts. Now he was going to do the same with his pilots. He'd appointed Ian Oldmeadow, the ACTU's airline affairs officer, as Ansett's head of industrial relations, along with Len Coysh, the former executive director of the pilots' federation, which 'created extremely tense employer–employee relations within Ansett'.[26]

Oblivious to the resistance they would encounter, the pilots held stop-work meetings in February 1989, which instructed the AFAP to withdraw from the latest version of the Accord when it ended in June, and then take whatever action was required to make up for the reduction in real income they had incurred since 1983. Once they had detached themselves from the Accord, the federation held discussions with Australian Airlines, expecting that they could reach an agreement that could then be imposed on Ansett and other airlines. When the government-owned Australian Airlines refused to deal, the federation submitted claims to all the airlines and held stop-work meetings from 11 to 14 August to seek support for an industrial campaign. It was on the following day, prior to any industrial action, that Hawke met with Abeles and Harris in Canberra. He described in his memoirs how he 'personally took control of the Government's resistance to the Federation's claim', although the minutes of the meeting suggest that Abeles was calling the shots.[27]

It was certainly Abeles who set out the strategy, which was to manipulate the dispute so that the pilots' award could be suspended and the pilots forced, under threat of losing their superannuation, to sign individual contracts. Once that was done, said Abeles, the government and the airlines could 'really take them on'. The hard-won improvements in their conditions that pilots had gained over the years would be dispensed with. Hawke confirmed with Kelty that the ACTU wouldn't stand in the way of Abeles' strategy, which would make the pilots subject to the punitive provisions of common law. Hawke also agreed with Abeles' suggestion that the government should not levy the normal airport charges during the coming dispute. This would save millions for the airlines and allow them to keep paying their other workers, thereby ensuring that the dispute didn't widen. Everyone at the meeting was adamant that no quarter be given to the pilots, with increasingly extreme measures being suggested to destroy the union and bring the pilots to heel. Although Hawke would later claim that his government 'did not want a fight', that was what the meeting was intent on creating. 'Use instruments which hit hard,' concluded Hawke, telling Abeles and Harris to 'hit as hard as you can, quick as you can, carte blanche from me'. That was what Abeles wanted to hear. Hawke even asked Kelty whether the ACTU would object to using the penal clauses of the Crimes Act against the pilots.[28]

As the dispute developed, Hawke went much further. Two days after the secret meeting in Canberra, the president of the AFAP, Brian McCarthy, directed his members to fly only between the hours of 9 a.m. and 5 p.m. It was a creative tactic that had worked in the past without bringing the airlines to a complete stop, but it didn't work this time. McCarthy had walked into the trap set by Abeles and Hawke. The Arbitration Commission immediately threatened the AFAP with the cancellation of its awards unless the industrial action was stopped by 21 August. When the federation refused to comply, the airlines sent letters to their pilots threatening them with the sack if they didn't lift their work bans. While a minority complied, most pilots stood firm, confident that the airlines would crumble, as they had so often in the past. This time, though, the pilots were confronting a solid phalanx of the airlines, the ACTU and the government.[29]

Just how solid was shown on 23 August, when the airlines grounded their planes and locked out their pilots. Hawke instructed the air force to fly domestic passengers around the country and authorised overseas airlines to pick up domestic passengers. Hammering the pilots fast and hard, the next day saw the airlines issue writs under the Trades Practices Act against the federation and its officials, along with some individual pilots. This tactic had been used in the notorious Dollar Sweets dispute in 1985, in which a young Peter Costello had established his political reputation.[30]

The pilots were in a bind. Fearful of losing their homes and their superannuation, they were told by their legal adviser that their best option was to resign. Some 1647 pilots promptly did, believing that it was also the best way of bringing the dispute to a successful conclusion. But this was just what Hawke, Abeles and Harris wanted them to do, as it dealt the AFAP out of the discussions and allowed the airlines to recast their staffing levels in any way they wanted. With the strikers no longer being employees of the airlines, Hawke declared that the dispute had ended. To further pressure the strikers into signing individual contracts, they were instructed to hand in their cherished pilots' uniforms, while management pilots were instructed to abandon their desks and resume flying. Hawke agreed to expedite changes to the immigration rules to allow the recruitment of strike-breaking pilots from the United States, but that would take time and not produce many pilots. Neither measure was sufficient to get more than a small fraction of the aircraft back into the air.[31]

With the tourist industry in trouble and regional businesses going bust, the big battle was for public opinion. Hawke told Australians it was a 'national emergency' and used the politics of envy to turn them against the strikers, describing the pilots as greedy and elitist and threatening 'Australian life as we know it'. They were no more than glorified bus drivers, said Hawke, and if they won, 'the whole wage system is dead and Australia is dead'. With News Limited owning half of Ansett, Hawke had the help of the Murdoch papers, which splashed overblown stories on their front pages of pilots being chauffeured in stretch limousines to five-star hotels. The striking pilots wondered which of their colleagues were enjoying such largesse, because it certainly wasn't them.[32]

While denigrating the pilots in the media, Hawke tried to win over some of the strikers by sending them letters, writing as 'Australian to Australian' and warning that their action was threatening 'the future welfare and hopes of every Australian family, including, of course, your own'. He made clear that the pilots' claim 'will not be allowed to succeed'. Neither would they all get their jobs back, because the government and the airlines were aiming for higher productivity, which would mean a much smaller number of pilots flying much longer hours. Also in their mailboxes were new contracts from the airlines, which the pilots read with dismay, since many of their hard-won conditions had been removed. The pilots were told to sign them or 'never fly as airline pilots in Australia again'. When the AFAP proposed that its members return to work while negotiations took place, Hawke refused to consider it.[33]

Hawke wasn't seeking a negotiated settlement between the workers and the employers, as he'd done many times as ACTU president, but to break the strike and force the pilots back to work on terms dictated by Abeles and Harris. The pilots didn't understand that he held all the aces:

they had to be broken, for the benefit of Abeles and the productivity of the aviation industry, but also as a lesson for the many other workers who were tiring of the Accord and the cost it was having on their living standards. It was also for his own benefit, since Hawke feared that the collapse of the Accord could cost him the election in 1990. And that was worth the heavy cost to taxpayers and the economy, particularly the tourist industry, as foreigners chose to travel elsewhere rather than be left stranded at an Australian airport or be forced to clamber aboard a lumbering RAAF Hercules cargo plane.[34]

In demeaning the pilots, however, Hawke also demeaned himself. Colleagues had witnessed his temper whenever one of them dared to defy or challenge him. He'd played the aggressive union leader as ACTU president, when such behaviour had seemed to suit his position. But it had appalled his political advisers when he'd rounded on journalist Richard Carleton during the 1983 election campaign, and it appalled Graham Richardson when Hawke 'savaged' an MP from the New South Wales Right during a caucus meeting. In this case, Hawke clearly thought that Australians would be envious of the pilots' pay scales and conditions, only to find that many voters were dismayed by his vitriolic attacks on the pilots and their union. It was difficult to reconcile his carefully cultivated image as a conciliator with the angry prime minister who deployed the armed forces to crush a strike and destroy the lives of those who dared to oppose him.[35]

There was some pushback when the Transport Workers' Union refused to fuel the air force planes, and when some international pilots refused to carry domestic passengers on their aircraft. Hawke compounded the public unease when he lashed out at a 74-year-old pensioner at a shopping centre in Whyalla. Amid the glare of the television cameras, the pensioner had asked Hawke to justify the generous salaries of politicians when compared with the relative pittance paid to pensioners, only to have Hawke berate him as a 'silly old bugger' who didn't know what he was talking about. When the switchboards of talkback radio stations lit up with calls from outraged listeners, Hawke quickly sent an apology to the bemused pensioner, who said he hadn't been wearing his hearing aid and was oblivious to the insult. Labor pollster Rod Cameron warned Hawke in November 1989 that his behaviour was causing voters to see him as 'an angry, snarling, alienating confrontationist'. That could cost him the next election.³⁶

To repair the damage, Hawke struck a more conciliatory stance, urging the airlines not to pursue the millions of dollars in damages that had been awarded by a court against the AFAP and its leaders. And he went on a media blitz to make his case to the Australian people, even agreeing to be interviewed by his old sparring partner, Richard Carleton, who was now fronting Channel Nine's popular *60 Minutes* program. That didn't turn out as well as he might have hoped, after Carleton provoked a testy response by questioning Hawke's handling of the strike and suggesting that he'd become a tired leader, which Hawke was quick to deny. In a more successful attempt to patch up his image, he told the National Press Club in December that it 'grieved me more than I can say' that he 'wasn't able to play that role' of 'trying to get people together'. Of course, he could have done, had he not dismissed out of hand the attempts by the pilots in September and October to negotiate a return to work and a settlement of the dispute.³⁷

Ultimately, the dispute had played out according to the design created by Hawke and Abeles, who was set on refashioning Ansett as a leaner and meaner flying machine. With Hawke's support, and millions from the taxpayer, Abeles certainly succeeded in that aim – and received more than $5 million as a performance bonus. As Hawke declared triumphantly in his memoirs, the dispute had allowed Ansett to rid itself of more than four hundred pilots, while compelling the remainder to lose many of their former conditions, ensuring that Abeles could double the average flying hours of his pilots. Although the industry was gradually restored during 1990, the productivity gains had come at a huge cost. Apart from the economic impact, many Australian pilots were forced either to relocate overseas to find work or leave the industry altogether. Abeles refused to re-employ any pilot who'd spurned the new contracts, while Australian Airlines only re-employed twenty of them.³⁸

The 1989 pilots' dispute left many voters with a more jaundiced view of Hawke. He'd claimed that it was all about defending the Accord, but it wasn't clear anymore that the Accord was producing the desired economic outcomes, as inflation resumed its rise, unemployment and interest rates increased, and the balance-of-payments deficit ballooned. In Victoria, the Labor government of John Cain had been swept up by the debt-fuelled mania that was bankrupting the paper billionaires, leaving Victoria's state savings bank teetering on the brink of insolvency. Keating's warning about Australia becoming a banana republic seemed more prescient than ever.

CHAPTER SEVENTEEN

# 1989

On 7 December 1989, two days before Hawke's sixtieth birthday, he appeared before the National Press Club in Canberra to reflect on his time as prime minister and set out his vision for Australia's future. It was primarily economic. He wanted Australia to be a 'modern, growing' economy, freed from its old protective instincts and its historic dependence on primary exports, an economy that would be 'outward looking' and enmeshed with the 'dynamism of Asia and the Pacific'. But it was also about the quality of life, creating a country with a commitment to social justice, to the protection of the environment and the promotion of 'a tolerant, multicultural, egalitarian society'. His vision included 'a self-reliant Australia' that would speak with 'an independent voice' and help to shape the world.[1] It was a great vision for the next generation. The problem was that the present generation, despite the positive economic and social improvements introduced by the government, had seen a fall in their real wages. Under the Accord, they were meant to be compensated by additions to the social wage through such measures as universal healthcare and family welfare payments. But rises in unemployment and interest rates were leaving too many people worse off, which didn't bode well for the next election.

After Hawke's three terms as prime minister, swinging voters might be questioning his ability to cure the nation's ills. But the Opposition wasn't offering a viable alternative. Howard had been a lacklustre leader who'd appalled some of his own colleagues by opposing multiculturalism and flirting with the idea of making race a criterion for immigrants. For a time, his leadership was threatened by the Liberal Party president John Elliott, who planned to swap his lucrative business career for a shot at the prime ministership before thinking better of it. Elliott's withdrawal from the field didn't protect Howard for long. Those disaffected MPs who'd been traipsing to Melbourne to meet with the businessman simply transferred their support back to their former failed leader, Andrew Peacock, who'd lost to Hawke in 1984. With Peacock's secret blessing, the Howard-haters mounted an undercover campaign to bring him down. It culminated in a party room ballot on 9 May that saw Peacock securely reinstalled as leader. That same day, the Nationals also overthrew their leader, replacing the 59-year-old Ian Sinclair with the 38-year-old Charles Blunt.[2]

The overthrow of Sinclair and Howard had caught Hawke unawares. He would have to face off against Peacock for a second time, this time leading a tired government that was running out of ideas, and with voters increasingly disenchanted with him.[3]

With the election looming, Hawke wrote to his ministers in November 1989 asking for policy suggestions that he could take to the voters. Industry minister John Button urged Hawke to push ahead with the further cuts to tariffs that were scheduled for 1992, along with measures to boost Australia's international competitiveness and productivity. He also suggested that Hawke embrace the notion of a goods and services tax (GST), which Keating had proposed at the 1985 tax summit, only to have Hawke kill it off. Adopting the proposal now would 'completely wrong-foot the Opposition', argued Button, which was divided on the issue, and would find favour with a majority of voters.[4] However, such a move might also have wrong-footed the government, since it would have contravened Hawke's 1987 promise not to introduce a GST. Moreover, his quashing of the tax proposal had caused a bitter dispute with Keating. Now that their relationship had calmed down, Hawke would risk that dispute being brought back to life if he made the tax part of his election platform. And that would risk his chance to win an unprecedented fourth term as a Labor prime minister.

There were many suggestions from other ministers, some of which Hawke wasn't anxious to acknowledge. Like many ministers, Peter Walsh was despondent about Hawke's chances at the forthcoming election. After nearly seven years in power, he thought, the government had a 'stench of decay', and with interest rates at 17 per cent and the balance-of-payments deficit doubling, the country was about to be swamped by an 'economic crisis' much worse than in 1986. Walsh was so concerned in March 1989 that he'd told Hawke he was going to resign, only to be convinced by Dawkins that this would provide evidence to voters of that very decay. So he agreed to hold off until after the 1990 election.[5] The crisis was coming nonetheless.

Hawke couldn't countenance the prospect of rejection and sought ways to avert the apparently inevitable electoral disaster. He seemed certain to lose a swag of seats in Victoria, South Australia and Western Australia, where Labor state governments were on the nose. Hawke would have to make up for this elsewhere, and that would be a big challenge. His best hope was to reuse the strategy the party had perfected at the previous election, which was to pick up second preferences from voters in swinging seats whose main concerns were environmental. That had got Labor over the line in 1987, despite its first-preference share of the vote going down.

As environment minister and Labor's numbers man, Graham Richardson was adamant that it could work again. He advised party activists that the environment had risen to second place on the list of voters' concerns. That made an appeal to environmental concerns the only strategy that had a chance of working amid the deteriorating economic circumstances and the dire political position of the Labor state governments. On occasion, this would mean Hawke would have to choose to protect the environment rather than to create additional jobs. Whenever that choice had to be made, Hawke found himself facing staunch opposition from many of his senior ministers, including Peter Walsh, John Dawkins, John Kerin and John Button. Much to Button's chagrin, it meant the end for a planned paper mill in Tasmania, and made a planned gold and platinum mine at Coronation Hill, near the Kakadu National Park, a matter of fierce contention within cabinet, particularly as Hawke had previously given a green light to BHP, the mine's powerful owner. After fevered discussions over many days, Richardson came up with a compromise that vastly expanded the national park while leaving the planned mine just beyond its border, with a decision on the mine itself left to another day.[6]

The expansion of Kakadu proved popular with voters, despite overwhelming criticism from the media and big business. The decision captured the public imagination much as the Franklin River had done in 1983. Not many jobs were at stake at Coronation Hill, while its mining might threaten the pristine waters of the rivers that ran through Kakadu.

The Murray-Darling River system was also the focus of Hawke's attention, as he strove to portray Labor as being more protective of the environment than the Liberals. The increasing salinity of Australia's biggest river system was creating newspaper headlines and television stories that brought the environmental degradation of the continent home to city voters. Voters in Adelaide didn't have to be told, since the unpalatable water from the Murray-Darling was piped into their homes, impelling many of them to use bottled water instead. The solution to the salinity and to land erosion was to plant more trees – one billion of them, Hawke told a special media event on the banks of the Murray. That made for a good headline. But, looking through the trees, there was not a forest of money to support the planting and other measures that needed to occur over ten years. Just $520 million was to be allocated over that decade, which was hardly sufficient to redress a problem that had been two centuries in the making.

That wasn't the point. It just had to be sufficient to get the environment on the front pages of newspapers, to ensure that Labor was still seen as having the greatest commitment to protecting the environment. Not that it would do much to stem the remorseless landclearing that was destroying wildlife habitats and increasing Australia's contribution to global warming. Although he described himself as being 'reasonably green', Hawke wouldn't put global warming on his government's political agenda. Most of his ministers wouldn't countenance it. When Richardson suggested doing something to limit Australia's emissions, he was said to have been 'ferociously and successfully opposed by Keating'. Nor would Hawke do anything to threaten the expansion of the fossil-fuel industries, which were regarded as being fundamental to Australia's prosperity.[7]

For Hawke, as it had been for Fraser, it was about protecting iconic places that were important to the Australian sensibility, whether it was the Great Barrier Reef, the Daintree Rainforest, the Murray-Darling or Kakadu. It was about appeasing the concerns of the environmental constituency and its important lobby groups without overly upsetting the powerful mining or farming lobbies.

One such issue was perfect for Hawke's political purposes. For some years, the various nations with territorial claims in Antarctica had been negotiating a treaty that would set the conditions for oil drilling in its surrounding seas, as well as for mining onshore if that ever became feasible. Oil companies had already begun drilling successfully in Arctic seas and wanted to do likewise in Antarctica, where massive icebergs posed a great threat to any such operations. It was a continent that had long captivated the public imagination after early explorers brought back photographs and films of its pristine environment. People were captivated anew when television programs hosted by the likes of David Attenborough brought the Antarctic and its wildlife into their living rooms, thereby creating a constituency that would press for its protection from the ravages that oil companies were liable to wreak upon it.

Public desire to protect the Antarctic environment intensified in January 1989, when the Argentine navy ship, *Bahia Paraiso*, carrying a shipload of tourists, was holed by a reef off the Antarctic Peninsula, spilling about 640,000 litres of diesel and causing untold damage to the area's ecology. Just two months later, the supertanker *Exxon Valdez* ran aground off the coast of Alaska, releasing at least 38 million litres of crude oil along more than 2000 kilometres of isolated coastline. It was an environmental disaster. The clean-up was still proceeding as nations prepared to sign off on a convention to govern mining in Antarctica, which would give a green light to American oil companies.[8]

Foreign minister Gareth Evans brought the draft convention to cabinet for approval in April 1989, expecting that it would be rubber-stamped and Australia would fall in with all the other Antarctic nations by ratifying it. After all, the convention had been six years in the making and had the support of Richardson and most of the cabinet. But it didn't have the support of Hawke, who later claimed to have been 'staggered' that weekend at the Lodge, when preparing for the cabinet meeting, to discover that Australian officials had been leading the international discussions that had produced the convention. Nor did it have the support of Keating, who'd argued against it the previous year and now urged Hawke to propose that Antarctica be declared a world park that would be kept sacrosanct for science and in which mining would be forever prohibited. This was what Australian and international environmental organisations and leading figures were demanding, including Greenpeace, which had established its own base in Antarctica to amplify its demand, and the eminent French oceanographer Jacques Cousteau. Even the Liberal Party was against mining in Antarctica, as were the Australian Democrats and a majority of the Labor caucus.[9]

It was misleading for Hawke, as he later did, to portray his conversion to the anti-mining cause as if he were leading the pack. France had already announced it wouldn't ratify the convention and the Australian Senate had passed a motion against ratification. Nevertheless, his passion for the cause was genuine and took his cabinet colleagues by surprise. Evans couldn't see how Hawke would be able to convince the Antarctic nations, including the United States and Britain, to reverse course on a convention they had all agreed upon. But he hadn't counted upon Hawke's determination. Without Hawke's intervention, it almost certainly would have been a lost cause. He used a visit to France to form an alliance with the French premier, Michel Rocard, and together convinced the president, François Mitterrand to authorise a long campaign to bring the other Antarctic nations on board. Hawke would later describe his refusal to ratify the mining convention as one of his proudest achievements as prime minister.[10]

With the Liberal Party in agreement, there was little political downside to Hawke's stance on Antarctic mining. Australian companies had no interest in mining on a continent where ice could be kilometres deep, or in drilling for oil offshore where passing icebergs would pose a constant peril to their rigs and environmental damage was costly to clean up. For Hawke, the political gains would come from those voters who couldn't bring themselves to support either of the two major parties and would instead give their first preference to a party such as the Australian Democrats. As at the 1987 election, it was their second preference that Hawke wanted. So long as he could convince them that the environment would be safer under Labor than under the Liberals, he would get their support.

The party's pollster, Rod Cameron, advised: 'Every time we talk about the environment, our vote goes up.' Hawke just had to keep talking about the protection of iconic locations and making grandiose statements, with little funding attached, about caring for the land. He would succeed so long as he didn't upset the miners or the farmers, or the majority of his ministers who were wary of environmental measures that might have economic implications – and so long as the media gave sufficient prominence to his environmental announcements. But journalists were increasingly disinclined to do this in 1989, sensing the smell of political death about Hawke and his increasingly exhausted ministers.[11]

As Australians coped with rising interest rates and inflation, not many people would have noticed Hawke's achievement in barring the oil drillers from the Antarctic, his pressuring of the South African government on apartheid, or his involvement in the establishment of the Asia-Pacific Economic Cooperation (APEC) in January 1989. The multilateral forum began as a meeting of officials from twelve Pacific nations and only became a high-powered meeting of national leaders after Hawke's retirement, which allowed Keating to claim the credit for it. Yet the grouping reflected Hawke's conviction that Australia's economic destiny lay with the nations of North Asia.

At the time, that mainly meant Japan, but Hawke recognised that China would soon be the powerhouse of Asia, which was why he'd appointed his economic adviser, Ross Garnaut, as Australia's ambassador in Beijing. It was also why he was heartened by the democratic demands of Chinese students in April 1989, and then became distressed when those demands were crushed several weeks later by the tanks of the People's Liberation Army in Tiananmen Square, destroying for a time his expectations of China's gradual economic liberalisation.

The student uprising had been partially sparked by the death of the former general secretary of the Chinese Communist Party, Hu Yaobang, who'd been a leading economic and political reformer and become close to Hawke as they sought to cement closer economic relations between China and Australia. Hu had fallen foul of his more conservative politburo colleagues and been demoted in January 1987 for not cracking down on earlier student demonstrations. Now, the news of his death and the subsequent massacre combined to leave Hawke distraught. After reading detailed cables from the Australian embassy about the massacre, Hawke fronted the media with tears streaming down his face. Without consulting his cabinet, he told a packed memorial service in Parliament House's Great Hall that any of the tens of thousands of Chinese citizens then in Australia could extend their visas if they felt threatened by the crackdown in their homeland. Eventually, more than forty thousand of them would become Australian citizens. Yet he ensured that relations with China returned to normal as soon as was decently possible.[12]

Hawke was nearing the end of his third term as prime minister but felt fitter than his sixty years. In this, he was helped by his decade-long abstention from alcohol, and more recently by following Hazel's example in keeping to a relatively healthy Pritikin diet, which emphasised fruit and vegetables, whole grains, fish and lean meats – although his valet would frequently circumvent the diet's strictures to satisfy Hawke's cravings. In an interview with Blanche d'Alpuget to mark his birthday, Hawke said he was 'happier than ever before in his life'. He might have stopped his copious drinking, but he continued to smoke Cuban cigars, even after the shift to the new Parliament House, where smoking was banned.[13]

With the opinion polls looking dire during 1989, Hawke had occasion to puff away with more vigour after Labor's Wayne Goss won a thumping victory in the Queensland state election on 2 December, gaining a 24-seat majority that brought more than thirty years of increasingly corrupt conservative government to an end. It was a bright spot in an otherwise dark political firmament, which had seen Labor's popular premier in South Australia, John Bannon, almost tossed out by voters just a week earlier.[14]

Despite the turnaround in Labor's fortunes in Queensland, Rod Cameron advised Hawke on 4 December that his value as prime minister had been undermined by his demeanour during the pilots' strike. With interest rates heading towards 20 per cent amid widespread economic gloom, Cameron thought that Hawke's chances of winning the next election were 'not much above zero'. From being the party's main asset, Hawke had become a liability. Labor would be lucky to get 40 per cent of the primary vote.[15]

Hawke's advisers were divided as to how he could escape the political doldrums in which the Labor ship was caught. The prime minister had to hope that Andrew Peacock would again fail to get his measure, and that Keating would keep to his promise not to launch a leadership challenge.[16]

CHAPTER EIGHTEEN

# 1990

It was the beginning of a new decade and Hawke had much to ponder. He had made history as a Labor prime minister. No other Labor leader had ever won three elections in a row, and none had been prime minister for as long as him. And none had had their father present at the celebration of each election victory. That, sadly, would be no more. If Hawke won the federal election due in 1990, Clem would not be there to share in the joy. On 23 December 1989, he'd died at the age of ninety-two, having suffered a stroke several months earlier. After the death of Ellie, Clem had moved to Adelaide to be close to his extended family, and nearer to his son in Canberra. For a time he lived in the same aged-care facility as his brother Albert, a former West Australian premier and Hawke's political mentor, who died in February 1986 after pulling out the tubes that had kept him alive.[1]

Hawke and Hazel had gone to Adelaide for Albert's funeral. Now they were back there for Clem's, along with other family members and a bevy of government ministers. Hawke had already shed tears on television when commenting on his father's grave illness, and he had no more to shed at the funeral. In reflecting on his much-loved father, he made his oft-repeated comment that Clem had imbued him with the belief that 'we are in this world not just to advance our own interests but we owe an obligation to our fellow human beings'.[2] If Hawke was to fulfil his obligation to his fellow human beings, and also advance his own interests, he had to win the upcoming election.

That might have been more difficult if not for the continuing disarray within the Opposition ranks. Whereas Hawke and Keating had kept their intense rivalry largely under wraps, the Liberals were burdened with two men, John Howard and Andrew Peacock, who struggled to keep their ambition in check for the good of the party. Howard and Peacock had ideological differences, too, which reflected the Liberal Party's swing to the right. While Howard provided leadership for the growing number of right-wingers who admired the policies of Margaret Thatcher and Ronald Reagan and wanted Australia to emulate them, he lacked the charisma to bring the public along with him. He tried to compensate for this by appealing to the fears of those who were troubled by the pace of immigration from Asia and by the embrace of multiculturalism by successive governments, both Labor and Liberal, since the days of Whitlam. Howard wanted post-war migrants to assimilate and adopt an Australian identity, and for the pace of Asian immigration to be slowed.

Mixing the two issues had opened the way for Hawke to suggest that Howard wanted to return to the days of the 'white Australia' policy, and allowed him to call on parliament to express its continuing support for a non-discriminatory immigration policy. When Howard insisted that his colleagues vote against Hawke's motion, four Liberal MPs crossed the floor to vote with Labor. Howard had opened the door for Peacock to mount, in May 1989, yet another successful challenge.[3] When Peacock's supporters then boasted publicly about their secret plotting prior to the coup against Howard, it was more manna from heaven for Hawke.

Few of Hawke's colleagues gave him much chance of winning the 1990 election, whenever it was going to be held. Governor-General Bill Hayden confided to the Queen during a visit to London that the Labor government would suffer 'an electoral disaster'. Hawke's image as the consensus leader had been damaged by his snarling attacks on the pilots, which had also wrought untold economic damage. People were hurting and it wasn't just the pilots. Interest rates were at an all-time high and unemployment was rising. Hawke had to finesse an election victory in the face of his plummeting popularity and Labor's declining share of first-preference votes. A pre-election report by the party's federal office, based on the findings of its pollster, made for grim reading. 'If we believed what our research was telling us,' wrote environment minister Graham Richardson, 'we would have gone off to slit our wrists.'[4]

But elections weren't just a contest between parties. They had become partly presidential in nature, and the diminutive figure of Hawke in his elevator shoes still communicated an image of sufficient strength and competence to put Peacock in the shade. He'd also been convinced by his adviser Craig Emerson and Richardson to use Labor's better credentials on the environment as its winning hand. It had become the number two issue in the minds of voters, and Labor had a commanding lead over the Liberals. The environment, rather than the economy, would have to be key to Hawke's success. He'd spent the previous year amassing environmental credits with voters by extending Kakadu National Park, while keeping open the possibility of allowing mining at Coronation Hill. Provided sufficient environmentally conscious voters in swing seats preferenced Labor rather than the Liberals, success could still be his.[5]

The election was set for 24 March, with the campaign to last just five weeks. Hawke wouldn't bore the voters witless, as he had with the last two long campaigns. He would project an image of strength, postponing a prostate operation to avoid any intimations of his mortality. With the public increasingly perceiving him as arrogant, it was also important that he didn't give too many opportunities during the campaign for that damaging perception to be reinforced. His advisers couldn't afford Hawke to be besieged by any more 'silly old buggers' tossing critical comments at him when he was glad-handing his way through a suburban shopping centre in the glare of television lights. As his speechwriter Stephen Mills recalled, Hawke's itinerary was carefully 'designed to minimise spontaneous and direct contact with the voters in favour of tightly controlled media exposure'.[6]

As the prime minister jetted from one electorate to another, he would give the appearance of immersing himself in the love of Australians; in reality, he was skipping across the surface of their hardening regard, careful not to be sucked down into it. During the last campaign, he'd asked voters to stay the course with him as he and Keating righted the economy, promising prosperity for their families and an end to child poverty by 1990. The return of prosperity was receding into the distance as stratospheric interest rates, reaching 20 per cent or more, tightened the budgets of families with mortgages, while his Family Allowance Supplement and other social welfare measures couldn't ensure that there would never be any Australian children living in poverty. Both those promises now hung from his neck like dead albatrosses. All the while, looming in the background was Keating, not fully realising that Hawke now had a steely determination to remain in the Lodge (and Kirribilli).[7]

The rivalry between Hawke and Keating might have dominated the 1990 campaign had the Liberals not had an intense rivalry of their own, and had Keating not kept his ambition in check. Some ministers who wanted to see a peaceful handover between the pair tried to suggest that such a handover might have already been agreed upon. John Button had floated as much in 1987, and he did so again in February 1990 when asked by a journalist whether an agreement had been reached. 'I suspect incidentally they have,' said Button, before adding that he didn't actually know. Hawke was furious when he heard of his minister's unhelpful comment, which could cause some voters to have second thoughts about voting Labor if they were going to end up with the unpopular Keating during the term of the next government.[8]

In an attempt to staunch the talk, Hawke insisted that he was going to serve out the full term if re-elected. In a meeting of cabinet, he called on Keating to confirm that there was no handover agreement in place. 'If you say so,' said Keating, which must have raised eyebrows around the cabinet table.[9] Yet nobody in cabinet or caucus, other than Hawke and Keating, had an inkling of their Kirribilli agreement, and none of his colleagues had an interest in stirring up talk of a leadership challenge, which could only cruel Labor's chances at an election that was certain to be closely fought.

Had the Liberals been able to combine the urbane charm of Andrew Peacock with the policy smarts of John Howard, they might have had a leader who could take on Hawke and win. But they'd overthrown Howard and were stuck with Peacock, which would make the 1990 face-off a re-run of the 1984 one. The Liberals had tried the slogan that 'a vote for Hawke is a vote for Keating', only to have Keating respond that 'a vote for Andrew Peacock is a vote for Andrew Peacock'. It was a great rejoinder, causing the Liberals to abandon the idea.[10]

Although Hawke had won the 1984 election, he hadn't done well in the televised leaders' debate. And when the votes were counted back then, Labor suffered a 2 per cent swing on first preferences. Hawke had to ensure that his debonair opponent didn't get the better of him again. At the same time, his advisers impressed upon Hawke the need to curb his volcanic temper, which was always bubbling beneath the surface. Try as he might, he let his temper take control at two early events, only to see his outbursts featured on the television news.[11] It wasn't a good look.

Just a week into the campaign, Hawke tried to put all this behind him when he was ushered into the ABC studios in Sydney on 25 February for the 'Great Debate' with Peacock. It was an all-male affair, with journalist Paul Murphy acting as moderator and four political journalists posing the questions. It was a Sunday night, and a big television audience was guaranteed to watch the re-match between the two combatants of the 1984 election.[12]

Hawke had hunkered down at Kirribilli, in much the same way as he used to do in his Sandringham home before a crucial wages case, absorbing the policy details and deciding on his tactics. He didn't practise for the debate with someone taking the part of Peacock. Supremely confident, he relied on himself and took no notes into the debate, wrongly believing that Peacock was going to do the same until being advised otherwise just before the event. No matter. Hawke's confidence served him well when he stood at his lectern, looking across at the slightly nervous Peacock, whose lectern was weighed down with a bulging folder. Hawke's luck held, as it often did, when he won the toss. He called on Peacock to make the opening pitch so that Hawke would be the one to close the debate at the end.[13]

Their pitches couldn't have been more different. Whereas Peacock described a heavily indebted country and an economy 'on the brink of collapse', where the next generation would suffer a lower living standard than that of their parents, an even-tempered Hawke painted an optimistic picture of a nation that had paid off government debt and was being transformed into a productive, export-oriented economy that promised higher living standards for all, albeit with wages being tightly controlled. The present high interest rates, argued Hawke, reflected an economy where demand was greater than expected, but that would soon be back under control. He had a stronger argument to make about the government's achievements in education and healthcare, and was more across the details and the arguments than

Peacock, who declined four times to ask follow-up questions and often spoke in woolly generalities. The media judged Hawke the winner, as did his relieved advisers. Peacock implicitly conceded the same when he challenged Hawke to another debate once their election policies had been released. Hawke declined.[14]

When it came time for the campaign launch, however, Hawke struggled to make a compelling pitch for re-election. He'd asked voters at the last election to stay the course, promising that his economic policies would bring inflation, interest rates and unemployment back down and give the nation an economy that was more productive and outward-looking. Now the economy was overheated and looked to be headed towards a recession, so that argument couldn't be run a second time. Instead, on 8 March, with pilots and their families protesting outside, Hawke tried to make it all about leadership.

The launch was at Brisbane's Lyric Theatre rather than Sydney's Opera House, since Labor's re-election would hinge on securing a swag of seats in Queensland to offset the heavy losses expected in Victoria and Western Australia. While Victoria was a basket case after the collapse of its state-owned savings bank, the party would be helped in Queensland by the election three months earlier of the popular Labor leader, Wayne Goss. In Western Australia, some hope was provided by the political 'cleanskin' Carmen Lawrence taking over as Labor premier after the scandal-ridden years of Brian Burke. But Hawke placed most hope in a re-run of the previous election, when environmentally minded voters in marginal seats were asked to give their second preferences to Labor. One of the VIP jets was placed at the service of the environment minister, Graham Richardson, who used it to criss-cross the continent, blitzing the local media everywhere he landed. He later recalled how he'd 'flogged the environment message during every waking moment' and was there in the Lyric Theatre to hear Hawke's campaign launch.[15]

Voters might have become critical of his government's economic policies, but Hawke knew they had even less confidence in Peacock's ability to manage the economy. 'This is not a time for slogans or hollow rhetoric,' Hawke told the Labor faithful in Brisbane and the millions watching on their television sets at home. Rather, 'it is a time for leadership. It is a time for substance.' He also promised

Australians a bright future for them and their children, as tens of thousands more completed secondary school and went on to university or technical college. Many of these were young women, who were offered a big increase in childcare places and the promise of employer-provided superannuation in their retirement. While the benefits of the government's tough decisions to transform the Australian economy were still to be fully felt, Hawke concluded with a vision of 'stronger national prosperity from a world competitive economy – greater financial security for families – a ladder of opportunity for all Australians – unshakeable protection of the national environment'. Twelve times during his speech, he'd addressed his audience as 'my friends', hoping they would respond in kind by regarding him as the leader who had their interests at heart. That was given more substance by having Hazel alongside him when he acknowledged the standing ovation at the end.[16]

Over the last two weeks, Hawke was kept to his tightly scripted campaign. His advisers got the media to ignore the constant presence of protesting pilots and kept Hawke to carefully arranged photo opportunities with the very young and the very old, which were designed to get a smiling Hawke on the nightly news. Despite his caution on the campaign trail and his expressions of confidence about the result, the outcome remained unclear in the context of a deteriorating economy in which businesses were going bust, interest rates were squeezing households, and the aviation and tourism industries were still struggling to recover from the war on the pilots. There was also the issue of corruption, which had stained the reputation of several state governments and caused allegations to be made against Hawke and some of his ministers. 'Scarcely a week goes by,' Governor-General Hayden informed the Queen, 'without some new disclosure of official corruption.' It was a culture in which 'everything has a price and can be bought, including favours', and in which 'smart operators prosper [and] only mugs get caught'.[17]

On the eve of the election, Peter Walsh and John Dawkins were in Fremantle having 'a boozy lunch' with some of their staff, anticipating that it could be their last such occasion. Both ministers were convinced that the government 'would lose the election narrowly', which would throw most of their staff out of a job.[18]

That same day, Russell Braddon was in Sydney. The bestselling author had squired the young Hawke around London back in 1953, but now Braddon didn't seem able to connect his wide-eyed companion with the grizzled prime minister on the television. He wrote to his London agent suggesting that the election 'should have been a doddle for the Opposition. (Hawke has made a thorough cock-up of everything) but Peacock's so ludicrously inept & conceited & full of bluster that he'll be lucky not to be pipped at the post.'[19]

While Braddon formed his view from watching the leaders on television, Graham Richardson had formed his view on the streets of the capitals and from mixing with locals in country towns, which led him to believe that Hawke would win. He was so convinced that he placed sizeable bets on it. The last week of the campaign pressed home the constant message underpinning Labor's preference strategy, with their advertisements telling minor party voters that 'the real choice for Democrat and Green voters is who you want to be Prime Minister of Australia – Bob Hawke or Andrew Peacock? If you care about the environment, if you care about the future of Australia, your [second] preference choice must be Labor. Put the Liberals and National last.'[20]

On election night, a quietly confident Richardson was in the national tally room in Canberra commentating for Channel Nine. The early signs didn't look good, as Labor's primary vote slipped to a new low of just less than 40 per cent against the Opposition's 43.5 per cent. Even the hapless Arthur Calwell had done better in the disastrous 1966 election, when he'd fought a principled campaign against Australia's involvement in the Vietnam War. Hawke had won 49.5 per cent of the primary vote in his first election, but it had been all downhill since then. The latest swing against Labor on first preferences was 6.5 per cent, which could have been dire for Hawke. He might have mimicked the ignominy of Calwell's loss, had his poor primary result not been buoyed by the second preferences of those who gave their votes to the minor parties but couldn't bring themselves to give their second preferences to Peacock.[21]

Although Peacock still received more than 50 per cent of the two-party-preferred vote, he didn't receive it in the seats where he needed it. He was also held back by the National Party, which had just suffered a stunning defeat in the Queensland state election amid evidence of widespread corruption and now lost five of its federal seats, including that of its ineffectual young leader, Charles Blunt. Labor lost seats in Victoria but picked them up in other states. Even in Western Australia, where the corrupt practices of 'WA Inc' had rocked Labor's reputation, the party narrowly held the seats it had expected to lose. Although the early returns made the final result difficult to pick on election night, the following days saw a number of closely fought seats falling Labor's way. In the end, the government emerged with eight fewer seats, which still left Hawke with a nine-seat majority in the 148-seat parliament.[22] His luck had held.

As Braddon observed in the wake of the 1990 election, Hawke had won 'not because anyone wanted him but because all the minor parties ... directed their preferential votes ... to Labour (not Hawke) rather than Peacock (not the Liberals)'. When Freudenberg mentioned the 'marvellous' win to Whitlam, the party grandee suggested to his former speechwriter that the more appropriate word was 'miraculous'.[23]

Indeed it was. The results showed that Australians had been tiring of Hawke and were looking for a fresh face and fresh solutions to the worsening economic conditions. Peacock's second election loss allowed just such a fresh face to finally appear. Rather than going back to Howard to replace Peacock, the Liberals chose a flashy young economist who'd had extensive experience working for business and government, including for the Reserve Bank, before being elected to a safe Sydney seat in 1987. The charismatic John Hewson, with his penchant for Ferraris, might be able to do what the tag team of Howard and Peacock had signally failed to do at three elections.

Hawke felt he might have lost the 1990 election if Howard had remained as Liberal leader. Now he had to contemplate his prospects at the 1993 election, when the economy would be in the doldrums and he would be sixty-three and facing off against the 46-year-old Hewson. That can't have been a comforting thought.

For seven years, Hawke had presided over a party that was in a state of electoral decline. Yet he had been largely instrumental in ensuring it retained its hold on government. At the same time, his hold on the party was weakening. Some of his colleagues were openly urging him to hand over the prime ministership to Keating, while the factional leaders openly defied the re-elected prime minister by insisting on their choices for the ministry. Senate leader John Button also defied him, refusing to accept the offer of the high commissionership in London and insisting on remaining as industry minister, even though he had decided that this term would be his last. Hawke mostly agreed to the factional choices, despite his advisers urging him to resist the factional deals and choose a ministry that would revitalise the government and be best for Australia.[24]

Finance minister Peter Walsh added to the pressure on Hawke, telling journalists in some post-election reflections that the country was 'living on borrowed money and borrowed time', which contradicted the line that Hawke and Keating had pedalled during the election. Walsh claimed that Australia's 'profound economic problems had not been adequately recognised, let alone dealt with', and that they needed to be confronted by a ministry that was elected on the basis of talent rather than on factional allegiance. 'It was a cheeky attempt to seize the policy initiative for the next term,' recalled Walsh, 'and it failed.'[25]

The acerbic Walsh had nothing to lose. He'd considered resigning the previous year, only to be talked out of it. Now he wanted to swap the finance ministry for the big-spending ministry of community services so that he could take a razor to it. Hawke refused. Had he agreed, it could have cost him the prime ministership. His economic strategy since 1983 had involved shrinking the wage share of national income and boosting the profit share, which was meant to encourage businesses to create more jobs while the government picked up the slack with a range of social welfare payments. Walsh would have tried to reduce those payments or do away with some of them altogether. When he was refused the position, he resigned from the cabinet and sat on the backbench.[26]

He wasn't the only one to be upset by the make-up of the new ministry. Of greater political importance was Hawke's refusal to let Richardson have his preferred ministry of transport and communications. Having helped to craft the electoral strategy that had just given Hawke his victory, Richardson expected to reap his reward when Hawke doled out the ministries. As a powerbroker of the New South Wales Right, he'd also been instrumental in Hawke's toppling of Hayden and had been a leader of Hawke's praetorian guard ever since. He was confident that his choice of ministry could not be denied by a grateful prime minister. Hence his shock when Hawke offered him anything but the powerful portfolio that he most prized.[27]

Instead, Hawke offered him a succession of other ministries, in the hope that one of them might satisfy him. He was so desperate to appease Richardson that he offered him the defence ministry, which he'd already offered to Senator Robert Ray, the leader of Victoria's right wing. When Ray refused to give up defence, Hawke had to go back to Richardson and tell him he could no longer have it. Richardson, who was forced to accept the role of minister for social security, was left secretly sharpening his knife for the leadership struggle to come, in which he could now be counted among the Keating camp.[28]

Amid all the ministerial changes, deputy prime minister Lionel Bowen also stepped down, allowing Keating to step up in his place as the heir apparent.[29] Everything seemed to be falling into place for Keating. Under the Kirribilli agreement, Hawke had agreed to resign during the current term so that Keating would have sufficient time prior to the next election to live down his failures as treasurer and build up his popularity as prime minister. However, during the election, Hawke had promised Australians that, if they elected him again, he would see out the term. He couldn't do both.

CHAPTER NINETEEN

# 1990

Clem Hawke had lived long enough to see his son's elevation to the prime ministership and victory at two subsequent elections. Now that Clem was gone, there was no parent left for Hawke to impress. He arranged for his mother's ashes to be brought from Perth to lie alongside those of his father in the suburban cemetery in Adelaide. In some ways, the couple had lived separate lives. Now their son had brought them together forever. Neil had also been buried there. The simple plaque listed their names and life spans, before ending with:

> Devoted Parents of Neil and Bob
> Thanks For Two Wonderful Lives.[1]

With his parents gone, Hawke would have thought about his own mortality and what he might do in his post-political life. Those thoughts of mortality would have been reinforced that April, when he led an official delegation to commemorate the seventy-fifth anniversary of the World War I battle at Gallipoli.

The commemoration marked a watershed in how Australians regarded that long-ago conflict. The diminishing ties with Britain and the nation's involvement in the Vietnam War had caused Australians to be much more critical of their nation's participation in World War I, and of the right-wing Returned Services League. The 1969 British film *Oh! What a Lovely War* had lampooned and lambasted in equal measure the strategic direction of the conflict, setting the tone for how it had come to be viewed in the 1980s, when protestors became a regular feature at Anzac Day marches. Some of the servicemen who'd experienced the senseless slaughter on the Dardanelles Peninsula, at the Western Front and in the desert of Palestine shared the jaundiced view of the conflict. But the ranks of those who'd fought in World War I were thinning out at each Anzac Day march. The seventy-fifth anniversary of the Gallipoli landings would provide an opportunity to honour their service and sacrifice on the beaches where they'd first fought their way ashore.

Accompanying Hawke to Turkey was the new Opposition leader, John Hewson, and fifty-eight of the last surviving Anzacs, all of them aged over ninety, along with their carers. Graham Freudenberg had written a Gettysberg-like speech inspired by thoughts of his own father, who'd been at Gallipoli. With the veterans assembled in front of him, and having walked along one of the trenches, Hawke was overcome by the moment. His recently interred father might not have been at Gallipoli – he'd refused to serve in that war – but Hawke would have remembered the desperate sense of loss that he'd felt as a teenager when Clem served as a chaplain during World War II, albeit at a camp near Perth. Much as Clem had officiated at Anzac services in the country towns of South Australia, bringing rural communities together in quiet remembrance, Hawke provided a similar service on the actual battlefield, firstly on the beach at Anzac Cove and later that day at Lone Pine. He would do it for the nation as a whole, with the ABC's cameras providing a live broadcast of the commemoration.[2]

The fact that Hawke was standing on Turkish soil, made sacred by the blood sacrifice of the eight thousand Australian soldiers who'd fallen, set the tone for his two speeches. There was no glorification of the conflict. 'For us,' he said, 'no place on earth more grimly symbolises the waste and futility of war – this scene of carnage in a campaign which failed.' He paid tribute to the sacrifice that the Turks made in defence of their homeland, and lauded their military leadership. And, of course, with the fifty-eight Australian survivors seated in front of him, some of them distressed by the trauma of it all, he praised the Australians who'd responded to the call to fight there. Their commitment to the new nation of Australia remained as relevant today as it did then, said Hawke, intending that the hundreds of young backpackers in the audience, along with the millions watching the live broadcast at home, would take note. There was a sense that the solemn occasion represented the passing of the baton of national responsibility from the old veterans to those young Australians who might one day be asked to make a similar sacrifice. Lastly, the prime minister paid tribute to the Anzac legend and the changing meaning it had for Australians, which he distilled down to the sense of mateship that allowed the Australian soldiers 'to see it through'. Wiping away tears, he returned to sit beside Hazel; he would later say that he was 'moved beyond measure' by the experience.[3]

It was around this time that Hawke confided to Craig Emerson that 'he was considering going into business and was preparing to hand the prime ministership to Paul'. Then he thought better of it, telling Emerson soon after his day at Gallipoli that he'd 'changed his mind about handing over to Paul'. After praising the Anzacs for answering Australia's call and exhorting his fellow citizens to commit themselves to Australia, he could hardly abandon the nation as it slipped towards recession. He could not forsake the party without a fight, which would mean abandoning the government and the party to Keating, whose standing in the polls did not encourage confidence in his ability to keep Labor in power.[4]

Hawke had lived his life for this time, imbued with the idea of his own greatness. He would not walk away of his own accord without some greater prize in the offing. Talk of going into business was a daydream conjured out of cigar smoke and was unlikely to provide the power and satisfactions of being prime minister. Holding on was his best option, which he could construe as being for the good of the party and the country.

Of course, it would mean going back on the Kirribilli agreement, with all that would mean for his relationship with Keating and the stability of his government. He would have to keep his decision secret and try to string Keating along for as long as possible, as he had been doing for several years. Hawke was confident that he still had the numbers in caucus and that Keating would be loath to announce a challenge, which he would be likely to lose and which could see him sidelined by another challenger appearing from the political shadows. For the time being, Hawke could safely deflect any pressure from Keating. The Kirribilli agreement didn't specify a date for the handover, just that it would occur during the present term.[5]

And there was so much for him still to do. Ever since 1987 there had been plans to reshape Australia's telecommunications market, but it had taken years for Hawke to overcome resistance from within the party and the trade union movement. It wasn't until after the 1990 election that the discussions became more concrete, and also more heated, between Keating and the new communications minister, Kim Beazley. Whereas Keating wanted to see more competition between several players, Beazley wanted just one new company to compete with the government-owned Telecom, with its 87,000 employees. Round and round the arguments went for months. Eventually, with Hawke looking on benignly, Beazley won the argument in cabinet, prompting a furious Keating to storm out of the room, calling it 'a fucking second-rate decision by a second-rate government'.[6]

Also on the chopping block were the government-owned Australian Airlines and Qantas, with cabinet approving a selldown of its interest in both airlines. The issues caused a furore in parts of the party that were determined to oppose any government move that breached the Labor platform against the privatisation of government enterprises. In announcing the cabinet decisions, Hawke had to bat away suggestions by journalists that the government had been afflicted with 'paralysis'. But that impression was only reinforced by the necessity for him to call a special party conference to approve the required change to the party platform.[7]

The conference delegates who met in Canberra on 24 September 1990 were more receptive to privatisation than they might otherwise have been because, just a month beforehand, part of another government enterprise had suddenly been sold. When the State Savings Bank of Victoria found itself bankrupt at the end of the credit-crazy 1980s, it posed a serious threat to the stability of the country's financial system, which Keating quickly solved by having the government-owned Commonwealth Bank step in to buy it. Cabinet agreed to fund the $2 billion purchase by selling 30 per cent of the Commonwealth Bank, a venerable institution described by *The Canberra Times* as 'the greatest sacred cow among government business enterprises'. The bank had been established in 1911 by Labor prime minister Andrew Fisher and had grown to become a central bastion of the nation's banking system. Once its partial sale had been accepted, the proposals before the special conference appeared much less momentous.⁸

Although the Labor Left remained furious at cabinet's decision about the bank, Hawke was able to argue that taxpayers should no longer be forced to finance the huge capital costs required to modernise Telecom and provide Australian Airlines and Qantas with the new aircraft they desperately required. He also lauded the benefit of breaking the monopolistic hold that Telecom exercised over telecommunications and claimed that the proposed asset sales would raise $3 billion, which could be spent on the nation's infrastructure. Abeles wouldn't be the beneficiary, said Hawke, since Australian Airlines would become a much stronger competitor to Ansett. A majority of the delegates duly fell in behind Hawke and approved the sale of Australian Airlines and up to 49 per cent of Qantas, but the pilots' strike had left the airlines in such a parlous state that their quick sale was unlikely to reap the promised reward for the government.⁹

The debate over privatisation had been messy politically for Hawke, and the resolution of the issue was unlikely to win him many votes. Those Labor supporters who believed he was betraying the party's traditions had additional cause for their conviction, while the voters being adversely affected by the deteriorating economic conditions were looking increasingly towards the young Liberal leader, John Hewson, to provide answers to their plight. By July 1990, Hewson was outpolling Hawke. The 'Mr 75 Per Cent' from 1984 had become 'Mr 37 Per Cent'. Yet Keating's approval rating was even lower, and no other Labor MP came within cooee of Hawke or Keating.¹⁰

A majority of caucus members had trusted Hawke to lead them to four successive election victories. Despite some nervousness among Labor MPs about the post-election slump in the opinion polls, and the honeymoon period that Hewson was enjoying among voters, there was little indication that the caucus wouldn't put their trust in him for a fifth time. Hawke was relying upon that sentiment. He'd used the Kirribilli agreement to ensure a stable leadership team in the lead-up to the 1990 election and to delay his final reckoning with Keating. That reckoning couldn't be delayed for much longer. He certainly wanted to remain as prime minister, but he would need to keep the support of caucus if he was going to stare down Keating. And caucus would only support him if he represented their best chance of another victory. That meant lifting his poll numbers from the depths to which they had sunk.

As the tide of Hawke's popularity continued to recede, and as economic conditions worsened, it had seemed that the prime minister could be facing the end of his political career. Fortunately for him, the luck that had served him so well throughout that career continued to hold. Not this time because of some half-crazy Queensland premier, but because of some half-crazy dictator from half a world away.

The Iraqi president, Saddam Hussein, invaded neighbouring Kuwait on 2 August 1990, quickly overcoming its defenders and incorporating the small country as a province of Iraq. It led to international condemnation and a demand by the United Nations that Iraq withdraw. Hundreds of Westerners, including many diplomats, were held hostage; Australians were among them. Acting under the aegis of the United Nations, a coalition led by the United States imposed a range of sanctions to pressure Saddam into withdrawing. The sanctions would be enforced by a naval blockade that would prevent the export of Iraqi oil by sea. It was inevitable that Australia would make a contribution to the international coalition.

Rather than waiting to be asked by the United States, Hawke rang President George H.W. Bush on 10 August to offer two frigates and a fuel supply ship to serve alongside the Americans in the Arabian Sea. His enthusiasm may have been partly inspired by reading William Manchester's latest volume on the life of Winston Churchill, which covered the period from 1932 to 1940, when Churchill was most bellicose in his speeches about Germany. Hawke didn't want to appear that bellicose. He told Bush to say that Australia was asked by the United States to make a contribution, rather than that Australia approached Washington to be involved. That was how the matter was portrayed both to the public and to the cabinet, with Hawke telling journalists he hadn't initiated the phone call. In reality, he wanted to take a leading role in order to curry favour with the Americans and to ensure that a strong multinational coalition confronted Saddam Hussein. But he had to tread carefully, since he was seen by some Australians as an American lickspittle. Keating, for his part, wanted the most limited contribution to be made.[11]

With the sanctions likely to soon be replaced by military action, with all the political risks that would involve, Hawke saw an opportunity to deploy his negotiating skills to avert such an outcome. Hawke had made such suggestions before in relation to the Arab–Israeli conflict, but Australia was not a Middle East player, and Hawke could hardly portray himself as a peacemaker when he was so passionately committed to the Israeli cause and so closely connected to the Americans. This time, he spoke to President Bush about the possibility of asking Jordan's Crown Prince El Hassan bin Talal to intercede with Saddam, in the hope that he might be offered something that would *allow* him to withdraw without being humiliated. That was as far as it went. Although Bush gave him some encouragement, Crown Prince Hassan didn't believe that Saddam would willingly give up the rich prize that was now in his grasp.[12]

Playing the part of peacemaker on the international stage could have brought Hawke applause from an Australian audience. Now it looked like he would have to play the riskier role of leading the nation in a distant war, much as John Curtin had done nearly fifty years before. And that could cruel Keating's chance of replacing Hawke according to the timetable they'd agreed at Kirribilli.

It might have been so much easier if Hawke had pursued a career in business or the law, where his retirement would not have been the subject of constant speculation, and was less liable to pressures beyond his control. But his mother had chosen this path for him and he would follow it for as long as he was able. Hawke might well have had such thoughts as he watched the fireworks explode from a barge anchored off Frank Lowy's harbourside mansion at Point Piper. It was the billionaire's sixtieth birthday bash and the rich and the powerful were out in force, with an orchestra taking over the tennis court to entertain the hundreds of guests. Hawke was reported to have made an emotional speech in honour of his long-time friend and supporter, but he later said that was a figment of a journalist's imagination.[13]

Presumably, Lowy didn't know of Hawke's deal with Keating. But Abeles knew, and so did Kelty. Hawke had to find a way of slipping out of the political trap he'd laid for himself, as his impatient treasurer pressured him to name a date for the handover and Hawke repeatedly told journalists that he planned to stay. When D'Alpuget had interviewed him for a feature article to mark his sixtieth birthday, he'd told her that he would remain as prime minister until 1993, which would mean he would be spending a decade as prime minister, after having spent a decade as ACTU president and a decade as ACTU advocate. That might have seemed like a neat outcome to Hawke, but it wasn't a timetable that Keating could accept: Hawke's resignation needed to be within the next twelve months if Keating was to have any chance of establishing himself as prime minister and improving his poll numbers. Both men were conscious that governments don't last forever; Keating already thought he had little chance of winning the next election. Hawke, of course, thought that only he could lead Labor to victory.[14]

It was across this gulf of understanding that a frustrated Keating met with Hawke on 9 October to press the prime minister to make good on his promised timetable. The earlier feelings of friendship between the two men had been replaced by barely concealed enmity, as Hawke sought to hold onto his position and Keating sought to unseat him, now with the active assistance of Graham Richardson. In July 1990, Hayden had confided to the Queen that Richardson was working to have Hawke replaced by Keating 'sometime before the end of the next calendar year'.[15]

After being fobbed off by Hawke for several years, Keating was now convinced he had no time to lose. Although he was concerned about the deteriorating economy, fearing it was worse than his officials were reporting, he wanted to chance his arm nonetheless. After all, if Hawke held on and lost the next election, it would see the young Hewson installed as prime minister, which could destroy Keating's chance of ever winning the top job. Yet he couldn't openly challenge Hawke, since he didn't have the numbers in caucus. Keating could try to pressure Hawke to go, but he had no way of forcing him. Most of the caucus felt an obligation towards Hawke and still believed that he remained their best chance of them retaining their jobs after the 1993 election.[16]

Confident in that knowledge, and aware of the movement that was building against him, Hawke once again sent Keating from his office with a vestige of hope that he might yet stand down. This time, Hawke suggested that he might resign after the next Commonwealth Heads of Government Meeting (CHOGM), to be held in Harare, Zimbabwe, in a year's time. After welcoming Nelson Mandela to Australia following his release from twenty-seven years' imprisonment in South Africa, the meeting in Harare could be seen as a fitting end to Hawke's work to end apartheid. Another year would also give him time to complete his work on new financial arrangements with the state governments. Keating was unimpressed, particularly after he was assured by Gareth Evans that the Harare meeting was 'bullshit' and of no importance.[17]

If there was to be a war with Iraq, it could pose political risks for Hawke if it led to the preventable loss of Australian lives. Then again, the brief Falklands War had been the making of Margaret Thatcher, cementing her in 10 Downing Street for the rest of the 1980s. Playing the part of commander-in-chief was unlikely to extend Hawke's time at the top through the 1990s but it was likely to improve his poll numbers, which could be sufficient to ward off the possibility of a challenge from Keating.

Hawke was going to need something, because the economy was no longer a strong suit for Labor after Keating announced that Australia was now officially in recession. The irrational exuberance of the 1980s had come to a shuddering halt, with several of Hawke's wealthy supporters scrambling to escape their creditors. Keating and Hawke had been in denial about the worsening economic conditions despite tales of woe being told by voters to MPs in their far-flung offices.

As Australians struggled to keep their businesses afloat and worried about how they would fund their next mortgage payment, the snappily dressed treasurer tried to put his best gloss on the bad news, telling journalists on 29 November that it was 'a recession Australia had to have' – as if Australians, rather than the government or its profligate mates, were to blame for their present misfortune. The inflammatory phrase, which seemed to show no empathy for the misfortune Australians were suffering, would dog Keating for the rest of his career. He and Hawke would bicker over whether Hawke had approved the statement prior to its release. But it didn't matter. The damage was done, primarily to Keating's reputation rather than to Hawke's. Opinion polls now showed Kim Beazley, rather than Keating, to be the preferred successor to Hawke.[18]

It was in this context – and little more than a week after Margaret Thatcher had been forced out as British prime minister, and after Hawke had told the Perth radio host Howard Sattler that he would lead Labor to the next election – that Keating gave full vent to his frustrations. Hawke's comment to Sattler meant he would breach the secret Kirribilli agreement. Keating hit back at an annual press gallery dinner, where dressed-up journalists and politicians hobnobbed in a convivial atmosphere to mark the end of the political year, once the last stories had been filed and the last insults had been hurled across the despatch boxes. Keating was the guest speaker And the audience was in for a treat. Everyone there knew that Keating had been pressuring Hawke to retire and had been assiduously recruiting colleagues to his cause. This was therefore an opportunity for the treasurer to reveal whether he had the makings of a prime minister and to make his pitch to the press gallery.

Traditionally, such speeches were not meant to be quoted by the half-pissed scribes, whose mouths were agape as Keating launched a fusillade of political grapeshot at Hawke, his government and all that he stood for. Keating told the startled journalists, who scrambled for pen and paper, that Australia had never had a leader who could compare with the great American presidents, Washington, Jefferson, Lincoln and Roosevelt. The wartime Labor leader John Curtin, much admired by Hawke, was nothing more than a 'trier', said Keating. Although Hawke was never mentioned by name, the implication was clear, particularly after Keating described himself as the 'Plácido Domingo' of Australian politics. While the renowned tenor always learned his lines, the 'very emotional' Keating was reading with little apparent forethought from some hastily written notes on a drink coaster.[19] It was no less powerful for that.

Hawke quickly learned what Keating had said. So did the public, once the details were published. Keating later denied that the speech was intended as an attack on Hawke, explaining that it was done in the immediate aftermath of the death of a senior Treasury official with whom he'd been close. Chris Higgins was only a few years older than Keating and had collapsed from a heart attack during a run the previous evening. His untimely death was reminiscent of the death at a relatively young age of Keating's father, who died while on a walk near his Sydney home. Keating couldn't be sure that he wouldn't go the way of his father before his political career reached its culmination.

Although Hawke was ropeable once he heard the details and then saw them printed on his birthday in the Fairfax Sunday papers, he was also relieved. He had wanted an excuse to renounce the Kirribilli agreement and now felt that he had it. He called Keating to a meeting in the prime ministerial suite on 10 December, where he spent more than three hours giving his treasurer a lesson on Labor history, during which he defended Curtin and suggested that Keating's performance proved him unready for the nation's leadership. Leaning back in his chair and puffing on a cigar, with staff watching on a closed-circuit screen, a relaxed-looking Hawke brushed away suggestions from an 'aggressive' Keating that he had taken the speech as a personal attack, and accepted Keating's assurance that no offence had been intended. But the gloves were now off. Hawke told Keating that the Kirribilli agreement 'was now very much in issue'.[20] Later, both sides backgrounded journalists, who could smell blood in the water.

The following day, after speaking with his advisers, Hawke held a press conference at Parliament House where he was pestered with questions. All equivocation was now gone, with Hawke declaring that he would 'lead the party to the next election [in 1993] ... with the intention of going through that term' to the following election, in 1996. If he did, Keating would have no chance of becoming prime minister, since neither man thought Labor could win two more terms. Keating was fine with that, said Hawke, claiming that he'd apologised for his speech and agreed to see out the current term as treasurer.[21]

The commitment to stay for five more years had been urged on Hawke by Richardson, who'd played the part of peacemaker, also urging Keating to walk into Hawke's office and begin with an apology and an explanation that his derogatory remarks about former leaders were only referring to those prior to Hawke. Nobody believed any of that – neither Hawke nor Keating, and certainly not the journalists, who had mostly tired of Hawke and favoured a change of leader. Richardson had told Hawke that this was also the view of a majority of caucus, which was somewhat of an exaggeration. But Richardson pressed on, suggesting to Hawke that his best course of action was to quietly resign before Christmas, rather than wait for the inevitable challenge by Keating and a humiliating loss in caucus.[22]

Time would tell whose bluff would work.

CHAPTER TWENTY

# January–June 1991

By January 1991, Hawke and Keating were preparing for the challenge that now seemed inevitable. With Hawke having declared his intention to remain in power for another five years, Keating had to bring things to a head or give up altogether.

Under the terms of the Kirribilli agreement, the 62-year-old Hawke was meant to resign by the end of the year. Clearly that was not going to happen. Sitting out in the summer sun at Kirribilli, the prime minister took confidence from the many expressions of support he'd had from colleagues. Although Richardson had thrown his support behind Keating, much of the New South Wales Right still supported Hawke, along with much of the Left. If it was put to a vote, he was still sure to win decisively. He could expect that the voting margin was likely to increase in tandem with the expected improvement in the economy, which should also result in improved poll numbers. And it was his poll numbers that had allowed him to wrest the Labor leadership from Hayden in 1983. Nearly eight years on, a recovery in his public standing would surely keep the prime ministership from Keating's grasp. If Hawke could buy sufficient time, a leadership challenge by an unpopular usurper would become impossible.

Keating wasn't about to let that happen. Hawke had made the Kirribilli agreement conditional on it being kept secret. If it became public, Hawke said, he would no longer abide by it. For two years, other than confiding in a few key staff members, Keating had kept to this commitment. Even when Richardson switched from Hawke to Keating in March 1990, he wasn't told of the secret pact. Not, that is, until 28 November, a week before the Plácido Domingo speech, when Keating finally told his principal supporter of the agreement.[1]

Keating had held a meeting with Kelty and Abeles, who'd been the two witnesses to the Kirribilli agreement, with a view to having them pressure Hawke to make good on his commitment. While Kelty took Keating's side, Abeles prevaricated. When Richardson learned of the outcome, he concluded that Abeles 'was obviously preparing the way for Hawke to rat on the agreement'. Keating's Plácido Domingo speech, and the ways he had tried to excuse it during a meeting with Hawke, had given him just the excuse he needed. In his memoirs, Hawke said that Keating's 'whole performance strengthened my belief that he was not ready for the leadership.' And strengthened '[my] conviction that I was better equipped to lead the party and ... had a much better chance of leading it to victory at the next election than Keating.'[2]

There would be no new meeting of the Kirribilli participants. Hawke had fobbed Keating off, or stared him down, so many times now that he believed he could do it again. He wouldn't do a Hayden and be forced out without a public challenge from Keating and a vote of the caucus, where he held the upper hand.

That hand was strengthened on 18 January, when the coalition against Saddam Hussein launched its military operation to expel the Iraqi occupation forces from Kuwait. Not only did this allow Hawke to play the role of war leader, resulting in a lift in his poll numbers, it made it more difficult for Keating to launch an open challenge while Hawke was seen to be directing Australian forces in a distant conflict. For Hawke, the war bought time. And nothing is more valuable to a politician than time.[3]

Keating later claimed that he would have become prime minister by the end of 1990 had Saddam Hussein not invaded Kuwait. That is a stretch. Hawke was vulnerable, but not that vulnerable. By the end of 1990, the Iraqi forces were still ensconced in Kuwait and the three Australian ships were helping to enforce the sanctions rather than engaging in open hostilities. It wasn't until mid-January 1991 that the coalition forces, acting under UN authority, began attacking the Iraqi occupiers with the intention of pushing them out of Kuwait. It was then that Hawke announced that the Australian vessels would take part in the 'armed action' and that parliament would be recalled on 21 January for two days of debate about the war. It was the first time since the Vietnam War that Australian forces had been sent into battle, and the first time since World War II that they would see action so far from Australia. Although a small number of MPs used the debate to oppose the involvement or express their misgivings, most backed Hawke's motion of support for the Australian forces. Cabinet members were briefed each morning by the Chief of the Defence Force – as if there was much to say on a daily basis about the actions of the small Australian contingent. Keating thought it was a farce and stopped attending.[4]

There was no telling how long it would take the coalition forces to expel the Iraqis. Although Saddam Hussein had been given until 15 January to withdraw, the land offensive didn't begin immediately. With the aircraft of the coalition forces bombing Baghdad and pummelling the occupying Iraqis, while Iraq unleashed missiles on Israel and Saudi Arabia, there was talk of a possible peace deal, brokered by Gorbachev, to avoid an all-out war. Sensing that the Americans wouldn't seriously consider any counterproposal from Saddam, Hawke was concerned that the Soviet Union might use its veto at the Security Council to remove the United Nations cover for the coming ground operation. That could make Hawke politically vulnerable if he continued Australia's involvement regardless, particularly as Keating didn't share Hawke's enthusiasm for the conflict and thousands of Australians had taken to city streets in anti-war demonstrations.[5]

In the event, Hawke's fears were unfounded. The coalition ground forces, without any Australian contribution, were unleashed on 24 February and quickly sent the Iraqis scurrying back over their border, where their long convoy of armoured vehicles and troop-laden trucks was largely destroyed by the attacking aircraft. The fighting was all over by 28 February. The distant battle couldn't have gone any better for Hawke. He'd puffed himself up as a war leader without actually going to war in a meaningful way. His other battle was much closer to home.[6]

In Keating's view, Hawke was using the Gulf War to delay the coming leadership contest. As soon as the war started, recalled Keating, 'Bob wrapped the flag around himself and went into the bunker'. His putative successor was having none of it. He'd been fobbed off too often. Although he supported Australia's involvement in the coalition, he wasn't going to let the conflict divert him from his offensive against Hawke. Nobody could tell in January how the war was going to go, how long it would take to expel the Iraqis or how many casualties Australia would suffer in the process.[7]

It was in this context, and in the midst of the air assault on the Iraqi forces, that Hawke asked Keating to meet with him in his office on 31 January. He was feeling strengthened by the war and wanted to put Keating back in his box. He repeated to Keating what he'd told journalists in December: he intended to remain as prime minister until after the next election. Although he agreed with Keating that this would mean breaking the Kirribilli agreement, he said that he was only doing so because he had a better chance than Keating of winning the election. He was doing it for the sake of the party.[8]

Keating disputed this, predicting that Hawke was 'dead meat' and was destined to lose in 1993, and he pointed to the steady decline in Labor's primary vote over the last four elections. Hawke hadn't been able to turn that around and wouldn't be able to do so at the next election, which meant Labor would lose. Keating said that only he had a chance of improving Labor's first-preference position – which Hawke dismissed out of hand. There was no argument in Keating's armoury that could convince Hawke to go. Even when Keating let it be known that he wouldn't preside over another budget and would retire from parliament if he wasn't made prime minister by mid-year. If he carried out his threat, that would end the successful political partnership that had kept the government in power for nearly eight years.[9]

Neither threats nor appeals were capable of moving Hawke, who was confident that he retained the support of a majority in caucus as well as a majority of voters. The only slight sliver of hope for Keating came when he suggested to Hawke that he should resign with his dignity intact once the Gulf War was won. It would be a moment of triumph, a time when Hawke would be able to claim that he was going of his own volition rather than being forced out. 'I'm prepared to think about that,' said Hawke.[10]

Not surprisingly, Keating wasn't satisfied; he'd heard it all before. But he couldn't do anything about it. Hawke's position had strengthened. Any challenge against him would now be considered 'an act of sedition' by their wavering colleagues, complained Keating. Once again, Keating's window of political opportunity had slammed shut. He was determined that it wouldn't stay shut, berating Hawke as 'Napoleon without a hat'. The good fortune that Hawke had enjoyed through most of his life was shared with the Australian forces in the Middle East. While the Iraqis were quickly routed, setting fire to hundreds of Kuwaiti oil wells as they went, they had lost tens of thousands of their countrymen, as opposed to little more than a hundred personnel from the coalition forces. There were no Australian casualties at all.[11]

The satisfaction Hawke felt at this outcome was soon tempered by a return to normal politics. Once again, political corruption was the issue that threatened to ensnare him. There was always a danger that a royal commission called by the new Western Australian premier, Carmen Lawrence, to inquire into the activities of the dodgy businessmen and politicians, known by the media as WA Inc, would catch Hawke and perhaps some of his federal colleagues in its net. One of the most explosive allegations at the royal commission claimed that Hawke had promised just prior to the 1987 election, at a fundraising lunch hosted by Premier Brian Burke and attended by Laurie Connell, Alan Bond and other business identities, to ditch a proposed gold tax if the businessmen would make massive, secret contributions to the federal Labor Party. In the wake of the lunch, nearly a million dollars was transferred to Labor's National Secretariat in Canberra.[12]

Burke had since resigned as premier, but had then been appointed by Hawke as Australia's ambassador to Ireland and the Holy See, and planned to make a career for himself in the federal parliament once he'd finished his posting to Dublin. He'd formerly been considered by the New South Wales Right as a possible future prime minister, and he still entertained such thoughts himself. That ambition evaporated when he returned to Australia to give evidence at the royal commission in April.[13] It was extraordinary to have a serving ambassador answering questions at a royal commission into his possible wrongdoing.

There were calls for Burke to be sacked, or at least step down, but Hawke refused to force him to do so. Things only got worse when details of Burke's financial dealings were revealed. (As a result of these disclosures, he was sentenced in 1994 to two years gaol for defrauding his travel allowance and sentenced again in 1997 for defrauding Labor Party funds, although he was later released after appealing the conviction.) While Hawke avoided holding a press conference, he couldn't avoid question time in parliament, which was now televised. The chamber erupted in uproar when Hawke tried to deflect questions from Opposition leader John Hewson about Burke and about his own relationships with the Perth businessmen. The media added to the pressure by publishing photographs of a beaming Hawke standing alongside Connell, Bond and the others, and perched on a fishing boat off the Western Australian coast with Connell and Richardson after the 1987 election.[14]

Initially, Hawke fumbled his defence by providing misleading answers to parliament. At first, he said that he couldn't have given an assurance at the lunch because the gold tax hadn't yet been discussed by cabinet. Then he had to walk that back, telling parliament later that night that he'd already made assurances on several occasions prior to the fundraising lunch that there would be no gold tax. That proved, said an apologetic Hawke, that the donations made after the lunch were not connected to anything he might have said at the lunch about the gold tax. Although it showed that he'd promised there'd be no gold tax well before the lunch was held, he did announce an extension of the tax-free period on the morning of the lunch, and conceded he might have discussed the gold tax during the lunch. It was all done, he later admitted, to save four vulnerable Labor seats.[15]

Ironically, when Hewson leapt on Hawke's answer, accusing him of misleading parliament, it was Keating who sprang to his leader's defence, mounting a devastating attack on the Opposition leader. Keating's parliamentary performance demonstrated both his value to the government and Hawke's depreciating value. Hawke needed the double act to continue. But that was about to change.[16]

Even though Burke finally resigned at the end of April and the royal commission declined to call Hawke as a witness, the political effects were dire. Because of the miasma of corruption swirling around Labor, together with rising unemployment, the party was 'stuffed' at the next election no matter who was leading it, wrote Tony Wright in *The Canberra Times*.[17] Such predictions only made Keating more determined than ever to bring on a challenge, come what may. He knew that his chances of winning the next election as prime minister would be zero if he couldn't get the prime ministership within twelve months. He had to topple Hawke while there was still time for him to become sufficiently popular prior to the poll.

Keating was convinced that he could have won sufficient caucus votes in December 1990 to beat Hawke, but the war had changed the political dynamic. Now he would have to take one shot in the hope of seriously wounding Hawke and gaining sufficient momentum to take a second, successful shot within months. It didn't matter what Hawke now did or said, Keating's course was set: he would declare a challenge before the parliament rose for the midwinter break.

Perhaps because he wasn't expecting to win at the first attempt, Keating made little effort to recruit undecided colleagues to his cause. Richardson didn't help by having qualms about how an unsuccessful attempt to topple Hawke would be viewed within the party and by voters generally. Even a successful attempt would open Keating and his close supporters to criticism. After all, such a thing had never been done before to a Labor prime minister, let alone one who had led them to four election victories in a row. And choosing Keating would be a big risk. As the treasurer who purported to be able to work the economic levers to produce a recovery, he'd become a lightning rod for all the attacks on the government by those badly affected by the recession. His approval rating was dire and there was no guarantee he could turn it around by replacing Hawke as prime minister. But his supporters had little choice but to follow him into the valley of political death, hoping that his boldness and bravado would see them emerge on the other side with their careers intact.[18]

For Hawke, there was the confidence that came from having a sizeable majority of the caucus on his side. Some saw him as offering the only chance they had of winning the next election, thereby preserving the government's legacy – and their jobs. Several were kept in the Hawke camp by order of party powerbrokers, including Bill Ludwig, the trade union heavy from Brisbane, who threatened the preselection of Queensland Labor MPs who were thinking of supporting Keating. Others couldn't bring themselves to turn against such a successful Labor leader. For every MP who sidled through Hawke's door to suggest that he go before he was pushed, there were more who reinforced his firm resolve to remain. When the prime minister was asked by Jana Wendt on Channel Nine what he would do if a delegation of MPs tapped him on the shoulder, he responded defiantly: he would tell them, 'I'm not going.' He would only agree to go if he thought Keating had a better chance than him of winning the next election. And that wasn't going to happen, even after the short-lived lift in Hawke's poll numbers slowly subsided from a month-long high of 50 per cent. That counted as a poor number for a leader who'd formerly been 'Mr 75 Per Cent'. And it only got worse, sliding to 28 per cent in April, while Labor's support also dropped to 28 per cent, which would mean a Liberal landslide at the next election.[19]

While Hawke took comfort from Keating's worse approval numbers, he also began thinking about what his post-politics life might look like. He had Hazel secretly inspect harbourside houses, finally finding one on a steep block fronting Middle Harbour. It would be a peaceful idyll, a place where he might be able to enjoy his privacy and experience some semblance of the pleasure he'd had at Kirribilli House. He also fixed on a new career, believing he could become a television interviewer who could draw upon all the contacts he'd made over the previous two decades as a leader of the trade union movement and prime minister. Hawke's purchase of the property in July 1991 for $1.23 million, helped by a mortgage from the Commonwealth Bank, was a sign of his recognition that his time as prime minister would be over some day. But not too soon, since it would need to be renovated before it became the dream home that he and Hazel had in mind, and they had nowhere else to go in the meantime. So it would be wrong to suggest that the house purchase was an implicit indication from Hawke that he was preparing to hand over the prime ministership to Keating. It's much more likely that he was preparing for the possibility of losing the 1993 election, by which time his new house could have been ready for occupation.[20]

In the midst of the Gulf War, Hawke had used his strengthened position to dismiss his treasurer's talk of succession. But Keating wouldn't go away – and this time it was he who forced a meeting with Hawke, once the New South Wales election on 25 May was out of the way. He'd been urged on in recent weeks by constant speculation in the media, with an editorial in *The Canberra Times* insisting that any challenge 'must happen soon, because it would do the party no good to sacrifice Mr Hawke on the eve of an election'.[21] With just one more week of parliament before MPs dispersed for the winter recess, it was now or never as far as Keating was concerned.

Richardson might have been Keating's main organiser, but he was concerned about how an unsuccessful challenge might affect his own career. He'd met with Hawke late on Wednesday, 29 May, to warn that the Kirribilli agreement would be revealed if Hawke refused to honour it. A supremely confident Hawke was unconcerned, reminding Richardson of 'his special relationship with the Australian people', only to receive a curt response from his former long-time ally, who'd seen the best and worst of Hawke over the years. 'Don't peddle this bullshit to me,' he'd said, and confirmed that the challenge would be on. Although Hawke was confident of having a large majority of caucus behind him, he asked Richardson what Keating might settle for, telling him that he would 'think about things overnight'. That led nowhere, with Hawke telling Richardson the following day that he was 'prepared to consider this question on my overseas trip but you should know that I don't think I'll be changing my mind'. Keating wasn't going to be fobbed off with another vague commitment. He'd made it known from the start that he would be coming one day for Hawke's job. He'd also made it known to Hawke that there'd be no back-stabbing: he would tell him to his face. That day had finally arrived.[22]

Hawke couldn't quite believe it when Keating pushed his way into his office at 5 p.m. on 30 May to announce that he was going to challenge him for the party leadership. Richardson had suggested to Hawke that the challenge could be days, months or even a year away, even though he knew Keating was intent on getting into the Lodge in June. Eschewing confrontation and trying to buy more time, Hawke told his headstrong deputy to sit down so they could have a discussion, suggesting that he 'would think about having another round of conversations about transition arrangements' once he returned from his imminent trip to Europe.[23]

It was too late for that. Keating knew that if he gave in again to Hawke's usual mix of blandishments and threats, his campaign would be at an end. Moreover, journalist Laurie Oakes had been primed by Richardson with the details of the Kirribilli agreement and was set to tell Australians about it on the evening news. It would be a big scoop, and Keating thought the revelation would cause voters and Labor

MPs to look askance at a prime minister who'd reneged on a solemn undertaking. That might be worth a few extra caucus votes, he hoped. Keating demanded Hawke bring the matter to a vote at the caucus meeting the following Tuesday.[24]

Hawke's organisers had been keeping tabs on the likely votes in the 110-member caucus, which had not seen any recent shift in numbers from the Hawke column to the Keating column. With caucus expected to split seventy to forty, they were determined that Keating be given no time to organise any wavering MPs to vote for him. If those numbers bore out, Keating would be left shy of the psychologically crucial 40 per cent.[25]

The newspaper headlines on Friday, 31 May were dominated by the shock news of the Kirribilli agreement and Keating's challenge. Journalist Paul Kelly thought in retrospect that Keating had made a serious error by not allowing the news of the agreement to be absorbed by the public and the caucus for a few days before announcing his challenge. It meant that it couldn't have the desired effect of eroding Hawke's support prior to a challenge. Keating had also undercut himself in caucus by declaring in parliament just a few days previously that the party's leadership would only be open when Hawke said it was, which suggested that it was up to Hawke whether or not he resigned. By challenging a few days later, Keating seemed to be reneging on this declaration of his own, which made it harder for him to play the part of Sir Galahad in the coming contest.[26]

While each side took to the trenches, Hawke felt he had the upper hand. Although Keating wanted a vote to be held during Tuesday's caucus meeting, it was Hawke who decided when caucus meetings were held and what their agenda was. He was desperate to hold onto the seventy MPs whom he'd been counting in his column for the last several months, and to deny Keating's supporters the chance to entice them away. Rather than wait until Tuesday, as soon as he received Keating's challenge he announced that a caucus meeting would be held the following morning at 8 a.m. And when the meeting got underway, he further loaded the dice in his favour by calling on Keating to move a motion declaring the party leadership vacant, which would be decided on the voices and not by secret ballot.[27]

Keating adroitly sidestepped this trap by reminding Hawke what Hayden had done when he'd first been challenged by Hawke in 1982.

He'd stepped down as leader and brought on a secret ballot for his position, which Hayden had gone on to win. Momentarily disconcerted, Hawke calculated that his best move was to persist with his demand, only for Keating to refuse to move Hawke's desired motion until the following Tuesday. Amid the rancour and confusion, the meeting was closed.[28]

Hawke had made a serious miscalculation: by denying caucus a secret ballot, he had revealed his sense of insecurity. That wasn't a good look for a leader. After urgently conferring with Robert Ray and others, he tried to retrieve the situation by calling on Labor MPs to reconvene for another meeting at 10 a.m. Anxious not to be outwitted by the old fox, Keating told his followers to leave Canberra, while Hawke had messages about the meeting sent to the government drivers taking MPs to the airport. Keating remained at Parliament House, as he and Hawke were due to attend a premiers' conference that day and the party's National Executive on the Saturday, but he refused to attend the hastily called caucus meeting. Only about seventy MPs showed up, so there was no point having a vote. Hawke tried to gain a minor advantage by calling the caucus meeting for Monday morning, rather than Tuesday.[29] The drama was turning into a farce.

The embattled prime minister hid out at the Lodge over the weekend, refusing to do media interviews so as to avoid answering questions about the Kirribilli agreement. That left the floor largely to Keating, who promised to lead a government with 'direction, strategy, *esprit de corps*, enthusiasm and, dare I say it, where necessary, excitement'.[30]

The party apparatus supported him. ALP secretary Bob Hogg, who'd formerly been one of Hawke's advisers, had told the prime minister back on 24 May that it was time for him to resign before he was removed by caucus or the voters. He believed it was for the good of the party if it was to have a hope of winning the next election. Despite his great admiration for Hawke when he was a staffer at the ACTU, Bill Kelty had delivered the same message. Hawke refused to listen. Now, after the meeting of Labor's National Executive on Saturday, 1 June, Hogg told a press conference what he'd told Hawke in private: that Keating was capable of winning the next election, and that Hawke could not endure the instability that an unsuccessful Keating challenge would cause.[31]

With Hawke occupied by the premiers' conference and the National Executive, and hunkering down at the Lodge, MPs could ponder Hogg's intervention and the political consequences of an unsuccessful challenge. Keating's loss would be the government's loss, since it would remove one of its two major pillars and ensure months of media speculation about when a second challenge would occur. Hawke had to defeat Keating so decisively that a second challenge would be out of the question. That didn't happen.[32]

The seventy votes Hawke thought he could count upon were reduced in the secret ballot on Monday, 3 June, to sixty-six, while Keating received forty-four. Each side tried to portray the result as a victory, but Keating was the more relaxed combatant. He was retiring from the contest relatively unscathed and, having resigned as treasurer, could remove the heavy burden of office that he'd shouldered for the last eight years. From the backbench, he would be able to look down upon the verbal sparring between the wounded Hawke and the sprightly Hewson, who was energised by the divisions among his opponents. Although the media was rooting for Keating, and would continue to do so, he said he wouldn't be mounting another challenge. 'I had only one shot in the locker, I fired it and the result is there for all to see,' Keating declared to the media. He would later say that 'walking out and walking away' was uppermost in his mind at the time.[33]

Keating wasn't believed about the number of shots in his locker, and there was no walking away. He only needed twelve MPs to change their vote for him to emerge the victor. That was something that Hawke well realised. He might have used the moment to retire, rather than waiting to be winkled out, but he dismissed the suggestion when it was made to him by his departing press secretary, Barrie Cassidy. 'You're just tired,' he told Cassidy, whereas Hawke still had the fight to lead his fractious government into whatever the future might hold.

CHAPTER TWENTY-ONE

# June–December 1991

The prime minister knew that his continued survival depended on his own performance and that of the minister whom he'd appointed to replace Keating as treasurer. Rather than Ralph Willis, who missed out once again, Hawke chose the minister for primary industries and energy, John Kerin. As deputy prime minister he appointed the Left's Brian Howe, a rather dour Methodist minister who'd served as minister for social security. With Kerin and Howe, there'd be none of the excitement that Keating had promised the caucus. However, if Kerin proved to be a competent treasurer and able to guide Australia out of the recession, it might work for Hawke. Howe's appointment was a sign of Hawke's newfound reliance on the Left and his lack of trust in the New South Wales Right, which had brought him to power and kept him there for the last eight years.[1]

Hawke had been looking forward to a trip to Europe and London, where he was due to address trade and disarmament conferences and receive the freedom of the city of London. That would no longer be happening; it was the keys to the Lodge and Kirribilli House that he was more interested in retaining, and for that he would have to remain in Australia to shore up his position. Instead of jetting off to Europe, he would be going to Hobart for the Labor Party's centenary conference, marking a hundred years since its origins in the labour disputes of 1891. The conference would give delegates the chance to discuss some of the issues that had vexed the government, from privatisation to uranium mining and media diversity.

In the days before the conference, Hawke holidayed at the recently built Mirage resort in Port Douglas, formerly owned by the notorious

Christopher Skase, a high flyer of the 1980s who'd subsequently crashed to ground under the burden of the pilots' dispute and his massive debts and fled to Spain. Shortly before Hawke stayed at the five-star resort in late June, Skase had been found by journalists living in luxury on Majorca, much to the annoyance of his aggrieved creditors, who would never see most of their money again. By chance, Keating was also at the Mirage resort, although he wouldn't cross paths with Hawke.[2] There wasn't going to be a rapprochement.

It was only Hawke who flew south to Hobart's Wrest Point Casino, where the devoted Jean Sinclair was waiting. She'd been with Hawke since his election as president of the ACTU and had followed him to Canberra, where her flat had been a place of escape and her advice a boon. She was described by Graham Freudenberg as 'a river of calm'. Now the 51-year-old Sinclair was dying of lung cancer. Hawke's world was falling apart, but he tried to hold it together in Hobart with a stirring speech, patched together in his hotel suite shortly beforehand, which celebrated Labor's role in building modern Australia and its mission to 'set the agenda for the future of Australia'. He would have raised some eyebrows with his claim that 'no Labor government has been more faithful to Labor's true traditions' than his. How could it be otherwise, asked Hawke in a part of the speech he wrote himself, since he was the very embodiment of the Labor movement, having led its industrial wing and then its political wing?[3]

After his years at the top of the ACTU and the nation, Hawke's messiah complex was bordering on becoming a God complex. It was part of the narcissistic disorder that had been fostered by his parents and his time in the Congregational Church, and was given full vent in this self-written speech that he delivered at the Hobart conference. Presumably still smarting at Keating's Plácido Domingo comments, he used the speech to reaffirm his place in the Labor pantheon – although he suggested that he was head and shoulders above the other Labor prime ministers – and to declare that he and his government were going to win the next election.[4]

For Hawke, the conference was a success. As leader, he'd portrayed an image of strength and optimism while avoiding the divisive issues that sometimes caused Labor conferences to descend into unseemly uproar in front of the media. He'd also avoided any mention of the recent challenge by Keating. One of the few embarrassing moments came when the vote for the next national president ended in a tie after one delegate marked his vote with a cross rather than a tick. As the factions bickered, Barry Jones conceded in favour of the Right's Stephen Loosley, even though Jones would otherwise have won. That peaceful outcome ensured that the Right and Centre Left preserved their power on the National Executive. The divisive issue of uranium mining also failed to detonate, with the present party platform, which allowed the existing three uranium mines, left unchanged. If it had come to a debate, Hawke had indicated he would have pushed for more mines to be opened, as he had on previous occasions, which would have brought the fury of many delegates down on him. By avoiding a debate, Hawke emerged unscathed.[5]

Neither Keating's challenge nor the conference in Hobart had much effect on the opinion polls, which continued to show Hawke as the preferred prime minister compared to Hewson, and had Labor within striking distance of the Liberals. These were some of Hawke's best poll figures for the year. Who knew – he might yet hold off a second challenge from Keating. When journalists asked him whether he'd have Keating back in the cabinet, Hawke dismissed it out of hand, saying his cabinet was already full of competent ministers.[6] But the plain fact was that none of them could match Keating on the floor of the parliament.

Hawke didn't need to be reminded that it had taken two votes, spaced nearly nine months apart, for him to topple Hayden as Opposition leader. It would be much harder for Keating to topple a historically successful prime minister. He had to hope that Hawke and his ministers would stumble so disastrously that the caucus would feel impelled to support a second challenge. That seemed a long shot in the wake of the centenary conference, when Hawke had joined a local choir at a celebratory dinner to lead delegates in the singing of 'Solidarity Forever'. But after the delegates went home at the end of the conference, Hawke was left to lead a caucus that was becoming increasingly dissatisfied with his leadership.[7]

It didn't help when he insisted at the first cabinet meeting since beating off Keating's challenge that the government ban the mining of Coronation Hill. Rather than pointing to the possible environmental effects on Kakadu National Park, he drew on the traditional beliefs of the Indigenous owners, who held that a sacred spirit dwelling within Coronation Hill should not be disturbed. He would later say that he 'just had a deep, deep feeling about that'. He'd disappointed his son, Steven, when he'd failed, after pressure from the mining industry and the Western Australian government, to introduce the promised treaty with Indigenous people. Perhaps this would partially atone for that. Hawke was so adamant about it that he was prepared to stake his leadership upon it. 'You do things that are right, just got to be done,' said Hawke. He was supported by past and present ministers for Aboriginal affairs and the results of an inquiry into the substance of the traditional belief. And he was not for shifting. The cabinet could hardly call his bluff after caucus had just endorsed his leadership, so it went along; a defeat of Hawke in cabinet would have been a humiliation. Nevertheless, none of the cabinet members doubted that Hawke's authority had been seriously eroded, or that some of those who'd voted for him just days before were already regretting their decision. There was even talk of the caucus overriding the cabinet, but nothing came of it.[8]

After upsetting pro-mining MPs from the Right and Centre Left factions, Hawke then upset his new-found supporters from the Left when Kerin brought down a budget in August that included a co-payment to be imposed on Medicare patients, which undercut Hawke's conference speech about Labor being the party of compassion and the Liberals being the party that wanted to dismantle Medicare. The co-payment was driven by the dire economic conditions, which were set to see a budget deficit for the first time in three years. The impost would fall hardest on the poor, which made most of the caucus inclined to oppose it. Their views made no difference, as Hawke wasn't going to brook any opposition. In a frenzy of phone calls, MPs were told that 'it would look bad for Hawke' if he were rolled in caucus.[9]

In the last months of the Whitlam government, Bill Hayden had designed the Medibank scheme, which had since become Medicare. Now, looking on from Yarralumla, he saw the imposition of a co-payment as 'an intolerable proposition for Labor culture', and suggested that it was the measure that 'finally sealed Hawke's downfall'. It also made it more difficult for Hawke to argue against John Hewson's proposal for a goods and services tax, which would fall mainly on the lower and middle classes unless compensatory measures were introduced to counterbalance its regressive effects. Had he still been treasurer, Keating might have been able to send the policy to the political knacker's yard. But he wasn't going to help the cranky prime minister in his tussle with the young merchant banker. He was also hampered by his own enthusiastic support for a goods and services tax at the tax summit in 1985. Keating was content to bide his time, allowing the dismay within caucus to develop while trying not to have it spill over into damaging displays of party disunity that might destroy his chances of winning the 1993 election, should he become prime minister.[10]

There was no certainty that a second challenge would ever be mounted. Richardson went even further, privately telling Hawke at the Lodge in August 1991 that he wouldn't be challenged 'provided you don't make any mistakes'. The following month, he assured Hawke on radio that there definitely wouldn't be a challenge. Hawke wouldn't have been fooled. Both he and Richardson knew that as soon as Keating could be sure of gaining a majority of votes in caucus, he would bring on a vote. In the meantime, Keating had to play a careful game, waiting for Hawke to stumble so badly that the handful of caucus members he required would switch their votes. For his part, Hawke and his number-crunchers had to keep their supporters securely onside.

Their campaign wasn't helped when Hawke and Hazel flew off to Harare for CHOGM. They spent part of the two-week trip at a hotel at Victoria Falls, and it was there that journalist Tony Wright encountered Hawke on the hotel verandah, finding that he was 'crotchetty to be so far removed from the plotting'. Hawke had relished such meetings in the past, where he could act as an equal with his Commonwealth counterparts, particularly Britain's Margaret Thatcher, and pursue his passionate campaign for the dismantling of apartheid in South Africa. Now, though, the Cold War was over, Nelson Mandela had been released and apartheid would soon be a thing of the past. With Mandela present at the conference, Hawke could announce a winding-back of the sanctions that the Commonwealth had imposed on South Africa, which he could count as a historic victory. But it was the battle in Canberra that was occupying his mind.[11]

And that battle came to a climax on 21 November, when John Hewson released *Fightback!*, the economic policy the Liberals would take to the next election. Like a rabbit in the headlights, Hawke was transfixed. Although Hewson's policy document was more than 600 pages long, it was reduced in the public mind to its central proposal, a 15 per cent goods and services tax, combined with reductions in other taxes. It was pitched as a 'plan to rebuild and reward Australia' and promised 'jobs and growth'. What was there not to like about that? The media mostly embraced it, as did many voters.[12]

Whereas Hawke had been beating Hewson in the polls as preferred prime minister, now their positions reversed. In 1983, Hawke had promised to rescue Australia from the economic morass into which it had been led by Fraser, only to lead it into an even deeper one. Those who were drowning in mortgage debt with historically high interest rates, or searching vainly for work, or spruiking for reluctant customers, were attracted by Hewson's pitch. Although Richardson told an interviewer on the night of its launch that 'every time you put your hand in your pocket, John Hewson's hand will be in there with yours', Hawke went quiet. Rather than acting as choirmaster to a chorus of similar criticism, he took the unimaginative and roundabout route of looking for mistakes in its arithmetic, which would take his officials days to do.[13]

The *Fightback!* package would be Hawke's undoing. Whereas Keating would have dismissed it with a withering phrase, Hawke sent it off for analysis, which created a political void that Hewson was happy to occupy. Labor MPs were left to shake their heads in dismay, knowing that Keating would have handled the challenge very differently. Hawke even made a plea for Keating to do so from his backbench eyrie. That was never going to happen. If the party wanted Keating to demolish *Fightback!*, the caucus would have to make him prime minister.[14]

It was six months since Hawke had defeated Keating's challenge. In that time, Hawke had been telling anyone who'd listen that Keating had called Australia 'the arse-end of the world' and had threatened to decamp to Paris if he wasn't made prime minister. The implication was that only Hawke loved Australia, and only Hawke was loved in turn by Australians.[15]

His claims about Keating were more than misleading. Like Hawke, Keating's lifelong ambition was to be prime minister of Australia, and by early December 1991 he was close to achieving his aim. Hawke's approval rating, which had risen to 50 per cent as the missiles cascaded on Baghdad, had now slumped in some polls to about half that figure. Hewson was much higher in the polls than both Hawke and Keating, and the Liberals were 12 per cent ahead of Labor. It was clear that Hawke couldn't prevent the government from suffering a devastating defeat at the next election, while Keating offered a slim chance.[16]

To pressure the caucus, Keating let it be known that he would resign from parliament if he wasn't made prime minister by December. He'd already invested in a piggery in country New South Wales and expected to become a businessman. As if to emphasise his intentions, he emptied out his parliamentary office, planning to resign from parliament at the end of January. He believed that he'd have little chance of winning the next election if he didn't become prime minister by Christmas.[17]

It wasn't only the intimation of his political mortality that was pressing in upon Hawke. He'd watched for months as Jean Sinclair had sickened and died. He'd been so distraught that he was unable to deliver the eulogy at her Melbourne funeral in September 1991. Two months later, Hazel feared that she too was stricken with cancer. She had an exploratory operation on her abdomen, which gave her the all-clear but still required her to spend ten days in a Sydney private hospital. She was discharged on 28 November and planned to recover at Kirribilli House, just as Hawke was facing renewed pressure in Canberra to resign.[18]

Many in Hawke's position might have decided they'd had enough, and might have used their wife's health as a reason to bow out after a successful career. Not Hawke. Since childhood he'd never taken well to losing, and he wasn't about to walk away from a fight with Keating when he firmly believed that he was the only one who could win the next election for Labor. The problem was that fewer and fewer of his colleagues agreed with him, particularly when he and Kerin had no effective rejoinder for Hewson's *Fightback!* package. In a desperate move, reminiscent of Hayden's last-ditch appointment of Keating as the Opposition's Treasury spokesman, Hawke announced the dumping of Kerin as treasurer in favour of Ralph Willis, while Kim Beazley was made finance minister.[19]

The sacking of Kerin spoiled everything for Hawke. It occurred after Richardson had met with Hawke to recommend that Kerin be sacked, as he'd botched a news conference during which he confirmed that Australia was in its fifth quarter of recession, and then confessed that he didn't know that the acronym 'GOS' stood for gross operating surplus. His performance made the flummoxed treasurer look like a fool, which prompted Richardson's meeting with Hawke. When Richardson's recommendation was leaked to the media, the resulting headlines forced Hawke's hand.[20]

On 7 December, *The Canberra Times* asked, 'Beginning of the end?', while Hewson demanded that Hawke call an election so the people could decide. On 12 December, the front page screamed, 'Hawke "is finished"'. Hawke had hoped to survive until Christmas and then announce a major ministerial reshuffle in January, which he could present as being akin to a new government, shorn of its time-servers and soon-to-be retirees.[21]

Fearing that Hawke was taking the government down with him, a delegation of his staunchest supporters, including Beazley and Evans, met with Hawke first thing on Thursday, 12 December, and called on him to resign, both for the sake of the government and for himself. They suggested there be a handover to Keating on 15 January, so that Hawke could make a dignified exit after hosting the visit of President George H.W. Bush. As was his habit, Hawke stalled and then told them later that day that he was determined to fight any challenge. Incredibly, they let him get away with it. Even though they knew he was leading them into an electoral abyss, they pledged to support him in any vote against Keating. It did not matter, as other Hawke supporters indicated they were prepared to switch sides. Keating finally had his opening, just as his Christmas deadline approached. A desperate Hawke described his opponents as 'terrorists'.[22]

The only chance for the caucus to gather before Christmas was on 19 December, when Hawke had called the House of Representatives back for a day to consider legislation on political advertising that had been passed by the Senate. It was a fateful decision. In the run-up to that day, the usual Christmas festivities were held for the press gallery and parliamentary staff. Amid the celebrating, the pressure from the Keating camp and some of Hawke's key supporters continued to urge the prime minister to retire without a vote having to be held, as the tally was shifting towards Keating.[23]

On 16 December, Beazley went to the Lodge to make another effort to shift him, but it was fruitless. During the discussion, Hawke happened to mention that Hazel was recovering from her recent operation for an ovarian cyst. Anxious to assure Beazley that he wouldn't use this as a reason to retire, he fetched Hazel from her bedroom so that she could confirm for Beazley that she 'wanted him to bat on for ever'. Unfortunately for Hawke, it wasn't Hazel's opinion that counted. The opinion polls were swinging decisively to Hewson and the Liberals, making a Labor victory in 1993 under Hawke look impossible. On 17 December, a new poll had the Liberals in front by 21 percentage points; Hawke's approval rating was abysmal at 26 per cent.[24]

It was in this context that Keating prepared to strike. Although Hawke was still begging for more time, suggesting he wanted a couple of months before retiring, Robert Ray warned him that Keating now had a majority of the caucus behind him. On 18 December, most of the Labor MPs gathering in Canberra attended the caucus Christmas dinner, hosted by Hawke at the Lodge. Although Keating and Richardson stayed away, it was an awkward affair, as Hawke learned that he would be presented with a petition calling for a special caucus meeting to decide the leadership. Ray counselled him to accept his certain defeat with all the dignity that he could muster. Hawke said that he would 'go with grace', although he hadn't given up on winning.[25]

This time, he wouldn't try to arrange the meeting in ways that would favour his survival. There would be no early-morning meeting to catch his opponents on the hop, and no show of hands to pressure the waverers not to desert him. A few MPs had feared that Hawke might in desperation drive off to Yarralumla and ask Hayden to prorogue the parliament for an early election, which would lock him in place. But he was sensible enough to realise that he would lose such an election. A caucus vote was different – he still believed he had a chance. He wouldn't go meekly, as Hayden had, and would use every last minute to call and cajole those MPs who he thought might support him. Keating and Richardson did the same, staying up much of the night.[26]

On 19 December, as the tense day wore on, Richardson feared that some of Keating's votes were slipping away. Hawke, in case he lost, had daughter Sue come from Sydney to be there with Hazel and Ros. Because he'd called the meeting for 6.30 p.m., the caucus first sat through a last question time for the year, during which Hawke showed pluck under pressure and the new treasurer, Ralph Willis, showed that he just might be able to take on Hewson and *Fightback!*. But it's unlikely that the pair's performance shifted any votes back to Hawke. One vote he would have got was that of Gareth Evans, but the foreign minister was on an official visit to Indonesia. Hawke declined to call him back and Richardson refused to give him a pair.[27]

This time, Hawke opened the caucus meeting by standing down as leader and calling for nominations; both he and Keating were candidates. Some MPs chose to mark their ballot papers in the seclusion of a booth at the back of the caucus room, while others did so openly to assure their colleagues. With a touch of gallows humour, Hawke showed Keating his paper, and his challenger reciprocated. Of the 107 caucus members in attendance, fifty-six voted for Keating and fifty-one for Hawke. Although the result was tight, Neal Blewett said the numbers didn't reflect the sentiment in caucus, with 'the great majority of members [believing] Hawke was no longer viable as prime minister'.[28]

It was an emotional moment for all concerned. Keating had almost given up on becoming prime minister and was saddened by the manner of it happening, although Annita later reminded him that 'Bob's fiddled you around for years. There was a justice about all this that just had to be.' It had gone much more smoothly than many had anticipated. The expected bloodbath had been avoided. Keating was anointed as Labor leader, telling the caucus that he 'had big shoes to fill' and promising to build on the policies of the Hawke government, and to restore 'unity and harmony'.[29]

For his part, Hawke pledged not to utter a word of criticism against Keating and his new government. The outgoing prime minister received a standing ovation from both the caucus and, later, the House of Representatives, before he headed to Government House to hand in his resignation to Bill Hayden, the person he'd toppled as Labor leader and denied the prime ministership. He couldn't stop himself from telling Hayden than he would have won if only he'd had another day to round up the extra votes. Had that happened, wrote Hayden in a letter to the Queen, 'it would have been like a condemned man escaping the gallows because the rope broke'. The execution would still have gone ahead. Accepting his fate, Hawke told journalists that he wanted to be remembered 'as a bloke who loved his country, and still does, and loves Australians, and who was not essentially changed by high office'. Amid the tears and some cheers, there was much embracing and consoling among Hawke's staff, many of whom now faced an uncertain Christmas.[30]

The new year would also usher in an uncertain time for Hawke. He betrayed some sense of this when he faced the press for the last time as prime minister. With Hazel sitting beside him, he noted that he would now be 'a considerably poorer man'.[31] In fact, within a year or two, he'd be richer than he'd ever been before, and living a life of considerable luxury in a mansion on Sydney Harbour.

# PART THREE
# Postscript

## CHAPTER TWENTY-TWO

# 1992–1994

This wasn't how it was meant to end. Right up until his downfall, Hawke had believed he could hold on. He had refused the entreaties of Keating and Richardson, and even of his closest supporters, to go quietly and with his dignity intact. The centenary conference of the party would have been an ideal time for him to have done so. It would have allowed him to leave with the acclamation of the party that had given him so much and which he'd led back into government for a historic four consecutive terms. Or perhaps after the visit of President Bush, which didn't have quite the same symbolism. He'd refused every suggestion and was now at the end of his political career with nowhere to go.

He didn't even have anywhere to live. He planned to rebuild the home that he and Hazel had bought at Northbridge, but they'd put a tenant in to help pay for the massive mortgage. He had no clear plan for how to pay for it all, now that he was no longer receiving a prime minister's salary. As he complained to journalists on the day of his overthrow: 'My income stream has been diminished. I have considerable debts and I'll have to start thinking about how I'm going to meet those.' As always, he just knew that, somehow, he would be able to.[1]

While he considered his options, the Hawkes would have, courtesy of Keating, a last Christmas at the Lodge, surrounded by their closest friends, along with some of their children and grandchildren. Long-serving advisers and other staff who'd have to find new jobs also called by. And there was one last New Year's Eve bash under a marquee in the garden.[2]

It was a difficult time for the couple. Hawke's close mate John Singleton let them stay in his harbourside home at Birchgrove while he was away in January, after which they would have to find somewhere else. Hazel, who was completing a memoir that she'd been working on for more than a year, was still recuperating from her operation the previous November and so wasn't in much of a state to resist when they conferred at Singleton's house with the architect designing the renovation of their Northbridge home. The extent of the renovation, combined with his natural ebullience, prompted Hawke to suggest that the existing house be demolished and a new one built in its place. This would add vastly to the time and expense: the two-month renovation would turn into a two-year build that would take all their savings and earnings to finance.[3]

The pressure of this might have been the cause of Hawke's grim-faced demeanour when he and Hazel attended the Australian Open tennis later that month. Or it might have been because he was seated in the same row as some of his former cabinet colleagues. Neal Blewett described in his diary how they were 'all seated when Hawke arrived, modishly attired in an apple-green jacket, with Hazel. I secured the most wintry of acknowledgements, and Ros [Kelly] – whose legs Hawke literally stumbled across both coming and going – no acknowledgement at all.'[4]

Back in Sydney, the couple shifted from Singleton's house to the swanky Ritz-Carlton hotel in Double Bay, across the harbour from Northbridge. They were given a special deal with free accommodation, which had been negotiated by the celebrity agents International Management Group, with which Hawke was now associated. Hazel still felt unwell. When doctors investigated, they discovered she had a tumour at the base of her brain, which fortunately proved to be benign. It meant more time in hospital, where it was removed on 17 February, and another long period of convalescence. Even more hospital time was needed a few months later when it was discovered that the operation had caused fluid to leak from her spinal cord. This required nearly two more weeks in hospital and further months for recovery. The still vigorous Hawke would not have envisaged spending his retirement years with a wife suffering from a succession of ailments and complaining, after her operation, of cognitive decline.[5]

The discovery of Hazel's tumour gave him a reason to announce his retirement from parliament. It would end the ignominy of him being shifted from his prime ministerial suite to the distant backbencher's room that Keating had vacated after toppling him. That was aggravating enough, as was the idea of sitting on the backbench and watching his successor take on Hewson. Retiring from parliament would allow him to get out and start making the money he needed to earn if he was going to deal with his debts. He complained to a journalist that he'd 'been in public life for 33 years and I've not made a quid in that time'. That wasn't exactly true, of course, and the many Australians suffering under the recession would have taken issue with his self-pity. But the annual declaration of his pecuniary interests that he'd made to parliament during his prime ministership do support his oft-repeated claim that he wasn't driven by a desire to accumulate wealth.

To accord with the rules for ministers to prevent conflicts of interest, there were no shareholdings and no company directorships. His assets were properties that were jointly owned: the family home in Sandringham, the flat he'd bought in Canberra that was rented out for a time after he became prime minister, and an investment property in the Melbourne suburb of Aspendale. The couple had bought the two-bedroom Aspendale house, located just a stone's throw from the beach, a few weeks after the 1983 election for $39,000. It was rented out before being sold two years later for $70,000. After the Canberra flat and Sandringham home were sold, the proceeds were placed in bank deposits before some was invested in another Canberra house in 1987 to accommodate Ros. That was sold in 1991, about the time they bought the harbourside house in Sydney. Something that was never included on his list of pecuniary interests, and which could well have caused a conflict of interest, were the various defamation actions he launched against media companies.[6]

Although Hawke was comfortably situated with his superannuation from the ACTU and the parliament, he'd only been in parliament for eleven years and now faced having to finance the building of a harbourside home and finding a new career. He'd already set up a web of shelf companies and a trust to handle the income he hoped to make and to keep tax to a minimum. As a start, the International Management Group arranged a well-paid interview on the top-rating

*A Current Affair*, hosted by Jana Wendt. It was in the warm embrace of Channel Nine's studio lights that he announced his retirement, rather than following the conventional course of announcing it at a meeting of caucus, or perhaps to the parliament or at a press conference. He told Wendt that his much-anticipated retirement was due to Hazel's health challenges. 'That poor lady has had a helluva year,' he said. He also signalled that his retirement would mark the end of any relationship with Keating: 'That relationship was one that arose in government', said Hawke, 'and the relationship ended in government'.[7]

Although Neal Blewett conceded that Hawke couldn't have gone on as a backbencher, he 'found his consummate television performance distasteful'. A cartoon in *The Canberra Times* poked fun at Hawke, showing him dressed like Liberace while Wendt asks him why he hasn't criticised Keating during the interview. 'That'll be another ten grand,' says the agent hovering behind him.[8]

The cartoon was a sign of how Hawke would be seen by a section of the public made churlish by his constant appeals for sacrifice and his apparent disinclination to make them himself. Despite his professed attachment to the Labor Party, his resignation would be bad news for Keating, which was perhaps partly the point, since it would cause a by-election at a difficult time for the party. In the event, his seat was lost to an independent candidate, Phil Cleary, who based his campaign on Hawke's betrayal of Labor values.

Hazel completed her memoirs and her book was launched in November 1992 in front of an invited audience at the Bennelong restaurant at the Opera House. A lot of her friends were there, including Connie Benn from the Brotherhood of St Laurence, along with many politicians and several of Sydney's rich and powerful, including Abeles, Lowy and Singleton.

The 62-year-old Hawke began the proceedings by likening himself and Hazel to a pair of 'strong, vigorous plants whose growth and development in this jungle of life have been, as I would put it, intertwined together'. Then, while he looked on admiringly, it was time for businesswoman Janet Holmes à Court to do the formal launching, during which she referred to Hazel's 'tumultuous and traumatic marriage'. As Hawke's benign equanimity faded to quiet fury, Holmes à Court described how Hazel, prior to her husband becoming prime minister, 'felt inadequate and [was] treated as such'. Indeed, 'there are many of us here today who can't believe you stayed in your marriage for so long'. She noted how Hazel had been such an asset to Hawke when he was prime minister, despite 'a rival' writing to Hazel to say that she 'would have to be hidden if Bob ever became Prime Minister'.[9]

Like the trooper she was, Hazel acknowledged the 'challenges' she'd faced in her life and put a more positive spin on the years before Hawke had become prime minister, describing how 'Bob was carrying me along with him on his spirited and highly motivated life's path', during which 'we have learned a great deal'. Bob, she said, 'is a great Australian' whose 'essence is generous and outgoing', and she wanted her book to be seen as 'a love story'. She ended her speech as she'd ended the book, by looking forward to their new life together at Northbridge. She described how their house 'will hang on the slope of the hill, a dangle of rooms embracing the northern sun and the view of sparkling blue water', where the 'birdsongs of the bush [would combine with] the clinking of rigging on the masts of boats'. She expected that their life there would provide 'another kind of contentment'. They had 'gathered just a touch of moss', she wrote, 'but not nearly enough to stop us rolling busily, contentedly, on … in our little bit of magic'.[10]

The final phrase was one that Hawke had once used when referring to the house. Although he gave Hazel an apparently warm embrace at the end of her speech, the event had humiliated him in front of his friends and former colleagues, while the building of their new home was already poisoning their relationship. His dream home was turning into a nightmare.

Whereas Hazel had originally proposed that they should live in the existing house once it had been renovated, Hawke was conscious of the mansions in which some of his friends lived. He'd said that 'the ostentatious display of wealth … doesn't appeal to me', and his Sydney home wouldn't have an imposing street presence or be classed as a mansion. But it would be resplendent with some of the flashy accoutrements of a five-star hotel to which he could invite those same wealthy friends and distinguished visitors from overseas. Hazel had to comply. From the narrow one-way street, there would be little sign of the splendour that lay behind the wide garage door that stretched across much of the frontage. Once the existing house was demolished, the design of its replacement on the steep block provided many grounds for disagreement as its cost escalated.[11]

The arguments didn't end after they finally moved into the home in late 1993, despite Hazel putting a good gloss on it for a well-paid photoshoot in the *Australian Women's Weekly*, saying that 'it's a good place to be'. The reality was different. Hawke had begun drinking again, and the angry outbursts that had been commonplace were heard once more by concerned family and friends. They weren't just about the building of the house, but also because of Hazel's suspicions about his continuing infidelities. Hazel had been useful to him when he was aspiring to be prime minister, and later serving in that role, adding a crucial percentage point or two at election time. Their relationship had been rekindled at the Lodge, but now he wouldn't be facing any more elections, and any intimate moments were complicated by her health challenges. The cognitive decline and headaches that she experienced after her spells in hospital no doubt tested their relationship.[12]

Shortly before his resignation from parliament, Hawke embarked on a new life in business with the help of a financial adviser and accountant. The money he'd got from the sale of the Sandringham home in the early 1980s had been kept in banks and partly used to purchase the flat in Canberra, where Hawke had lived briefly as a backbencher before moving to the Lodge; he'd later let Ros and her family live there. The real estate boom of the late 1980s had largely passed him by, leaving him poorly placed to buy a house in Sydney, let alone knock one down and build anew. It meant that he had a mortgage of more than $1 million, which he had no way of servicing with the salary of a backbench MP.

Hawke's retirement gave him a lump sum of nearly $500,000 and a yearly income of nearly $50,000, indexed for life. He would also receive a staffed office in Sydney, a Commonwealth car and driver, and first-class domestic air travel for himself and Hazel. A publishing contract for his memoirs gave him $200,000, while the sale of the Canberra flat brought in more. But he needed much more to reduce his debts and set himself up for the lifestyle he wanted to enjoy.[13]

It was also about proving to himself – and to his detractors – that he could rise from the ashes of his political career to become a success in business. He'd tried to become a media megastar for Packer's Channel

Nine and failed to find the success or fulfilment that he'd sought. Perhaps this was because he didn't enjoy subsuming his own ego for the sake of interviewing other prominent people, such as when he covered the 1992 UK election for *60 Minutes*. Or the following year, when he was asked by the ABC to appear with South Africa's Bishop Desmond Tutu, who was staying with Melbourne's Anglican archbishop Keith Rayner, who chanced upon Hawke during the making of the program. Rayner recalls how he 'happened to come into the room where Bob was sitting quite alone and looking quite disconsolate and out of sorts', leading Rayner to conclude that Hawke 'was upset because the main attention was being lavished on Tutu and not enough on him'. In fact, according to D'Alpuget, he was depressed and feeling 'absolutely lost' after leaving politics. Apart from not being the centre of attention, there were the dangers Hawke encountered reporting on the famine in Somalia, which he found 'very scary'. He was so moved by the plight of the people that he donated his fee to a local hospital.[14]

Instead of a new career in the media, his post-retirement life would be built on the contacts he'd made overseas, mainly in China but also in South-East Asia and the Middle East. Making more than a hundred trips to China, he would become one of the conduits for Western businesses wanting to trade in China and elsewhere, and for Asian investors keen to do business in Australia. Which had been a theme of his government. When he'd visited China in May 1986, he'd told a welcoming banquet of the great progress that had been made in the thirteen years since diplomatic relations had been established, in expanding trade between the two countries and forming joint ventures. Hawke's recognition of the potential of the economic relationship had been seen in his appointment of his economic adviser, Ross Garnaut as ambassador to China in 1985. When Garnaut returned in 1988, Hawke commissioned him to write a report that would suggest additional ways in which both business and government could accelerate the development of economic relations with the nations of north-east Asia. By the time Hawke launched the report in November 1989, he could celebrate the outward-looking country that his government's policies had helped foster and look forward to the economic opportunities that would flow to it as a result. The Tiananmen Square massacre had been a bump in the road. Now, as a private citizen, with his wealth of contacts, he could strengthen the linkages that he'd helped create between China and Australia, to the benefit of both countries.[15]

He was not just a facilitator for other people but also did deals of his own. One of these involved the purchase, for $7.5 million, of a three-storey office building in Melbourne's Collins Street, formerly the headquarters of *The Age* and now mostly leased at a high rent to Telecom, with its basement occupied by a cinema showing X-rated movies. Hawke bought it in September 1993 with a property investor and bookmaker friend Peter Bartholomew, apparently on behalf of a syndicate of Asian investors. How much Hawke earned from this lucrative deal is unclear, but the annual reports of his companies reveal him earning nearly $2 million during 1992–93, which was more than all the money he'd made as prime minister. Some of this income was from speeches or public appearances, but most was from introductions or contracts he negotiated on behalf of Australian and international businesses that required a well-placed facilitator to introduce them to the powerbrokers of the expanding Chinese economy. Hawke was their man. And he was keen to show that he could do it. His former staunch supporter Gareth Evans couched it in terms of Hawke's race to be rich, which he described as 'tacky', but he had to do something to support his family and his lifestyle.[16]

After being toppled as a four-time election winner, Hawke had to contain his feelings as Keating was victorious in the 1993 election – the one Hawke had argued only he could win. It was only at the last minute that Hawke had deigned to let Keating know he would be attending the campaign launch, after which he predicted Keating would lose. How galling was it, then, for Keating to prove him wrong. Even though Keating feared on the morning of the election, 13 March 1993, that he was destined to lose, Graham Richardson assured him that he was headed for an unexpected win against the odds and should start writing his victory speech. The early result from Tasmania, which didn't have daylight savings time and so was an hour ahead of the east coast, revealed that Labor had won three extra seats in the island state and the government was destined to prove the opinion polls wrong and be returned.[17]

Nationwide, there was a 5.49 per cent swing to Labor on first preferences, the first time such a large pro-Labor swing had happened since 1983. Labor ended with eighty seats, two more than Hawke had secured in 1990. An exultant Keating, having outdone Hawke, declared it to be 'the sweetest victory of all'. Describing it as a victory for the 'true believers', Keating was determined to celebrate it with a dinner in parliament's Great Hall. Hundreds lined up outside, clasping their $100 tickets as they waited to file in. While Keating and a select few were seated prominently on the top table, the country's longest-serving Labor prime minister was relegated to one of the many other tables, where he sat mostly grim-faced as he endured Keating's night of triumph. For Hawke, it was a night of humiliation, which he would only remedy by achieving success in his newly chosen field, and by writing a history of his government that would put Keating back in his place.[18]

Hawke's memoirs would put on record his achievements as prime minister and rebut the claims by Keating that he was the driving force of the government after the 1984 election. Some of Hawke's former staff helped him, while government-paid staff in his office in Westfield Tower typed the drafts. He'd long ago resumed his relationship with Blanche d'Alpuget, who was brought in to help with the final editing in early 1994. When *The Hawke Memoirs* was launched at the Museum of Contemporary Art in August that year – timed, somewhat ironically, for Father's Day – both Blanche and Hazel were in the crowded hall and were full of praise for the book. Reviewers were not so kind, noting the overly self-referential text. It was a memoir that took self-aggrandisement to a new level, even for a politician. Sales suffered as a result, even though Hawke reprised his love affair with the Australian people, touring shopping centres around the country to sign copies.[19]

According to publisher Heinemann, 75,000 copies were sold, which was about equal to Hazel's book. That wouldn't have pleased Hawke. Its sales were also dwarfed by Whitlam's previously published memoirs, which sold about twice as many. He'd told his publisher that it had 'better make lots of money', and it did, bringing him around $1 million. But that wasn't its only purpose. Hawke used the book to direct sprays of venom at Keating, whom he accused of opposing the Gulf War and of describing Australia as 'the arse-end of the world' – charges that played to the popular perceptions of Keating as being arrogant. These accusations were vehemently denied by Keating, both at the time and later. But some mud stuck, and presumably hurt Keating's chances at the 1996 election, as Hawke doubtless intended.[20]

Despite the critical reviews of the memoir, D'Alpuget suggested that it would take its 'rightful place in Australian letters when the dust of floccinaucinihilipilification settles'. ('Floccinaucinihilipilification' is a jocular term meaning the action or habit of estimating something as worthless.) That might have been a subtle rejoinder to Hawke's comment at the launch that spelling was not one of her strengths. The book faced heavier headwinds when Hawke and Hazel announced in November 1994 that they were getting a divorce. Hazel had endeared herself to Australians, and many did not take kindly to the news that her philandering husband was walking out on her. Their magical retirement together was not going to happen.[21]

CHAPTER TWENTY-THREE

# 1995

Blanche d'Alpuget would later say that the death of Hawke's long-time lover Jean Sinclair had caused her to have visions in which Sinclair urged her to get closer to Hawke. He'd rekindled his relationship with D'Alpuget while he was still prime minister, but there was no talk of marriage during their surreptitious trysts. It wasn't something he considered until he was suddenly confronted with the possibility of losing her altogether. That happened in June 1993, when she was a passenger on a small seaplane that crashed on a flight to the Great Barrier Reef, where she was collecting material for an article for *The New York Times*. She and her fellow passengers were lucky to escape with their lives, swimming to safety through a window on the sinking aircraft. Hawke was phoned by a mutual confidant and given the news, which was the catalyst for his decision that, finally, he would marry his long-time lover.[1]

He'd told D'Alpuget back in 1979 that he couldn't walk away from Hazel, the mother of his children, who'd borne so much else besides. Even though he'd then made a marriage proposal to D'Alpuget soon after, he'd pulled out of it for the sake of his political career. When questioned in 1989 about his tumultuous relationship with the popular Hazel, he was adamant that she understood that his behaviour 'was part of a pretty volatile, exuberant character and she knew my love for her had never changed. I have always loved Hazel – always.' But he no longer did so. He realised that it was Blanche he now loved.[2]

His arguments with Hazel had again become heated and she was less inclined to accept his wandering ways. She was also dismayed when he went back on the grog. It happened in a Double Bay restaurant in 1993, when friends and family were celebrating Hazel's birthday. Depressed by the fractious state of his marriage and the lack of a clear career before him, Hawke was prevailed upon to celebrate Hazel's birthday with a glass of champagne. And another, and another, only to become drunk for the first time in thirteen years. He was still inebriated when he met secretly with Blanche, who was appalled by his backsliding. She didn't want their relationship to be marked by bouts of drunkenness and the unbridled behaviour that came with it. He promised that he could keep it under control. Which he mostly would.[3]

Hazel had been a supportive companion during his years at the ACTU and in parliament, but she had little interest in accompanying him on his business jaunts, not least because of her health problems. As Hawke explained to an interviewer, she 'didn't really have an interest in the business consultancy type of thing', which 'involved an enormous amount of travel overseas and she didn't come'. Although he was fit and healthy, Hawke couldn't be sure how much more life he had to live, and realised that he would only be truly happy with D'Alpuget. She could accompany him on long-haul flights and buoy his moods.[4]

Ironically, it was Hawke who had a fit of jealousy in late 1994, when D'Alpuget was flying into Hong Kong to meet him after completing a work assignment in Pakistan. When her plane failed to arrive, she explained that it had been cancelled. Hawke refused to believe her, suggesting that she'd been engaged in a dalliance. He was so distraught that he broke off their relationship. It was only after checking with the Pakistani ambassador in Canberra, who rang the control tower in Peshawar, that he found her flight had indeed been cancelled.[5] Their relationship was back on.

This was confirmed when the breakup of his relationship with Hazel was announced on 29 November 1994, and his relationship with Blanche was plain for all to see when the couple were photographed holidaying on Berrara Beach, south of Sydney, in January 1995.[6]

That was good for another highly paid media exclusive, this time on Channel Nine's *60 Minutes* and in the pages of *Woman's Day*. Being filmed in bath robes and bathers brought the ageing couple few admirers and enraged Hawke, who felt he'd been betrayed by the magazine and announced that the $200,000 fee for the story would be donated to charity. Public sympathy was very much with Hazel, who was voted as one of 100 'national living treasures'. (Although the list was updated over the years, Hawke never made it.) The love between the betrothed couple was certainly real, but its graphic depiction couldn't help but remind audiences of the long-suffering Hazel, who had given so much, only to be spurned.[7]

The wedding of Hawke and D'Alpuget took place on 23 July 1995, in the familiar surrounds of the Ritz-Carlton hotel in Double Bay, in front of 150 guests, including the ever-present Peter Abeles and Kim Beazley, who'd become Keating's deputy prime minister, as well as other friends from politics and the racetrack. A gaggle of journalists and photographers snapped the happy couple. It was no ordinary wedding. With Blanche in a cream wedding dress and Hawke resplendent in a white jacket and black bow tie, the ceremony was performed by a former Protestant minister, Dutch-born Mario Schoenmaker, who claimed to have clairvoyant gifts and became the mystical leader of the Independent Church of Australia. Turning his back on traditional church structures, he had written *A Short Occult History of the World* and *The New Clairvoyance: Deeper Perspectives on the Aura and Reincarnation*. It's not clear how much the besotted Hawke, who had long described himself as agnostic, believed any of this, but Blanche was training to be a priest of the church. The ceremony certainly marked a radical departure from Hawke's marriage to Hazel, which had been conducted by his father in a Congregational church. After the service, the couple and their guests were taken to the reception in a vintage double-decker bus, presumably directing a disparaging glance at protestors who were loudly objecting to Hawke's business activities in Burma.[8]

Meanwhile, the divorce with Hazel had been finalised after much negotiation. Hazel had developed a limited income stream of her own, from the sales of her book and other books that would follow, and from a three-year publicity deal with an Australian pharmaceutical company for their pain relief products. With her partnership with Hawke over, it was he who left their Northbridge home in late 1994 until the division of their assets was finalised. Hazel had helped him to pack and 'put him in a warm soothing spa'. They had lunch together with Sue and her husband, before Hazel drove Hawke to a temporary abode. It was agreed that he would buy her out of the home and she would go to a place of her own, which she eventually did late the next year, moving into a modest three-bedroom home in Middle Cove.[9]

According to one of Hazel's closest friends, Vera Wasowski, the 'marriage to Bob was a torment, but she loved him – even on the day of his marriage to Blanche'. But she didn't go to his wedding. Instead, her children arranged a 'Liberation Party' at the Northbridge home for the same day. They had gone to the wedding, but Sue and Ros had been dressed in black to mark their displeasure. Others, wrote Wasowski, left the wedding 'after the "vows" (an ironical word to use when you're talking of Bob) to come to Hazel's party'.[10]

Life would be dramatically different for both of them. While Hazel threw herself into working on behalf of charitable organisations, much like the ones she'd formerly represented, Hawke toured the world with D'Alpuget for six months every year, doing deals. Until she tired of the frequent travel. One deal closer to home was to have the soon-to-be married couple photographed for colourful spreads in the Packer-owned *Australian Women's Weekly* and *Woman's Day* and a *60 Minutes* program on Channel Nine for which they were reportedly paid a combined $500,000.[11]

The media exposure didn't help Hawke's reputation, since it reminded people again of Hazel, the woman he'd spurned, whom they held in high regard. No matter how often Hawke and D'Alpuget professed their love for each other, which was clearly evident, the public support for their relationship would always be less than fulsome. Which was frustrating for Hawke, who also had to deal with the reactions of his children and with accommodating himself to a new wife who had ideas of her own independence, insisting after a time on having her own bedroom and briefly walking out after one of his drunken episodes. As it had been with Hazel, and despite his promise to keep his drinking under control, his drunkenness remained a source of tension.[12]

Although Hawke did charitable work of his own and continued to support the Labor Party at election time, he was consumed by his business dealings, some of which were less reputable than others. Sometimes, he seemed to have trouble discerning the difference. When a questionable associate or arrangement was pointed out by a probing journalist, Hawke's usual reaction was to brush it off angrily as being of no account. He was, as biographer Troy Bramston observed, 'easily attracted to riches' and didn't look too closely at whose hand was holding out the money, whether it was a triad-related businessman in Hong Kong, the promoter of a casino in Pakistan or a Saudi-linked businessman for whom he acted as best man and who was later jailed.[13]

Nor did Hawke shrink from pressing his questionable business interests onto his political contacts. One was the former Queensland premier Peter Beattie, who would take the call because it was Hawke only to find that 'he would be talking about some fucking Chinese guy'. Many others would answer his calls or agree to a meeting but ignore the proposals he was making, which were usually on behalf of Asian businessmen seeking advantage. Presumably, Hawke was paid regardless of the outcome. And there must have been occasions when backdoor deals were struck with state or federal politicians on behalf of Hawke's clients.[14]

Throughout his career, Hawke had difficulty recognising those who were trying to take advantage of him. Then again, even when he was warned, as he had been about Abeles, he often pressed head anyway if there was a buck to be made or some other satisfaction to be had. The rotund Hungarian had schmoozed Hawke since their first meeting in 1970, inveigling himself into Hawke's affections with gifts and support that played to Hawke's ego. Hawke had done what he could to smooth any industrial troubles, even meeting with American mafia leaders on Abeles' behalf. As prime minister, Hawke returned Abeles' many favours by having him appointed to the board of the Reserve Bank and throwing the government's support behind him in his tussle with the pilots, despite the initial, heavy cost to the Australian economy. His final favour may have been having Abeles made a Companion in the Order of Australia in June 1991.

Hawke had usually been defensive about Abeles, whom he described as his closest friend. Abeles was not wealthy when they first became friends, Hawke countered, and he wasn't going to abandon their friendship as Abeles became wealthy. This was nonsense. Abeles was a wealthy and powerful businessman in 1970 and became much more so because of his close friendship with Hawke. That friendship also became closer, if that was possible, when Abeles acted as the intermediary between Hawke and D'Alpuget, providing a place where they could meet for trysts away from the gaze of the public and the media. When he and Hazel were staying at the Ritz-Carlton, she was living nearby in Woollahra, with Abeles helping to ensure that the news of their resumed relationship stayed secret.[15]

By the time of Hawke's resignation as prime minister, Abeles was also losing influence. The twin pillars of his power had been Ansett and TNT. Because of his mismanagement, both companies were in such trouble by the early 1990s that he was eased out. Had Hawke remained as prime minister and been able to help protect him, Abeles might have been able to hold on a bit longer. Divorced from his major business interests, Abeles became a director of one of Hawke's companies and, in turn, was helped by Hawke to establish businesses overseas. It didn't stop the soft-talking Hungarian from trying to strengthen his links to Keating, telling Bill Kelty 'that he had seen Bob Hawke recently and had been shocked by his hatred of Keating'.[16]

But Abeles' days as a political consigliere were numbered. In early 1999 he was diagnosed with pancreatic cancer, and died on 25 June at the age of seventy-five. After hearing that his friend didn't have long to live, Hawke rushed back to Sydney from a meeting in Melbourne, arriving in time to kiss the forehead of the unconscious powerbroker. At Abeles' crowded funeral in a Woollahra synagogue, attended by Beazley, Kelty, Wran and Lachlan Murdoch, a tearful Hawke delivered the eulogy before helping carry the heavy coffin to the hearse. His passing, said Hawke, 'leaves a void that can never be filled'. He'd been the closest of friends, as well as a supporter and confidant. As he had been to several other aspiring political leaders over the years. In reporting the death, the ABC noted that there remained a 'number of unanswered questions surrounding his business dealings'. Which remained murky, as his first and second wives fought in court over his substantial estate.[17]

Each funeral of a contemporary brought Hawke's own mortality to mind. And how he would be remembered. His reputation had been damaged by his reneging on the Kirribilli agreement, by the manner of his leaving office, by his divorce from Hazel and by his post-political business dealings. It had also been damaged by the early 1990s recession, which had left one million Australians unemployed. Bill Kelty, despite being close to Keating and having supported his leadership challenges, had retained a deep affection for Hawke. In the lead-up to the March 1996 election, he was concerned that the tattered reputation of the former prime minister was affecting Labor's electoral prospects.

When the mining company Conzinc Riotinto tried to dispense with unionised labour in late 1995, sparking a bitter industrial dispute that spread to the coalmines and the docks, Kelty saw an opportunity to revive the Hawke of his ACTU days. This was the Hawke whom the young Kelty had grown to love when he'd started his own career at the ACTU. But he wasn't loved by Keating, who wrongly believed he'd settled the dispute himself before flying off to Osaka for a historic meeting of APEC. He could only look on from afar as Hawke took centre stage at the industrial commission in Sydney. ACTU official Greg Combet helped brief him on the case, before Hawke took his familiar place at the union table, with Blanche sitting alongside and massaging his neck. Union officials who'd become disenchanted with Hawke when he was prime minister applauded the reappearance of the Hawke of yore. Keating wasn't impressed, suggesting to journalists in Osaka that even the French mime artist Marcel Marceau could have convinced the judges.[18]

These sporadic skirmishes would continue for years, denying Hawke the respectful retirement that he believed to be his due.

CHAPTER TWENTY-FOUR

# 1996–2019

The battle by Hawke to establish his legacy as a union leader and prime minister was complicated by his successor's apparent determination to have his achievements overshadow those of Hawke. Sometimes it was implicit, when Keating confronted issues that Hawke had shied away from. Whereas Hawke had embraced the Gallipoli legend, based on Australian troops fighting at Britain's behest in World War I, Keating embraced the legend of the Kokoda Track in World War II, when Australian troops were fighting for the direct defence of their own country. That opened the door for Keating to question Australia's continuing subservience to Britain. When the Queen visited Canberra, the suavely attired Keating broke with royal protocol by gently placing his hand on the monarch's back to guide her towards waiting guests, an action that provoked a vitriolic reaction from the British press. It was something the larrikin Hawke would not have done.[1]

Nor had Hawke been prepared to put an Australian republic on the political agenda, whereas Keating announced there that would be a referendum to let Australians decide the issue. The polls suggested the proposal would pass, with Keating hoping that its advent could be timed for the beginning of the next millennium. The High Court's historic *Mabo* decision allowed him to confront the issue of Aboriginal land rights, bringing all the stakeholders into the difficult discussions that led to the court's ruling being given legislative effect. Land rights was another issue that Hawke had largely squibbed during his nearly nine years as prime minister.[2]

Although Keating had been in power for less than half the time of Hawke, he was regarded by many observers as having made a bigger impact on the direction of the nation. When Keating also claimed to have been the driving force of the Hawke government during much of its time in office, it made for an ongoing dispute that would wax and wane as each man made claims about his contributions to the government.[3] It would have been better for Hawke to have left it alone. Keating had certainly driven many of the economic reforms in the final five or six years of the Hawke government, but it was Hawke who'd given them shape and impetus when he became prime minister and protected them with his popularity.

Not all of these came without considerable cost. The entry of foreign banks had been a mixed blessing. Rather than promoting entrepreneurship and improving productivity, their presence had distorted the economy by creating a debt-fuelled boom that encouraged spivs and shysters like Alan Bond to put together business empires, which collapsed like houses of cards at the end of the decade, when historically high interest rates left them defenceless. Several of these spivs, whose support Hawke had sought, ended up in jail, as did some of those caught up in corruption and organised crime in the 1980s. Many others should have been in jail but escaped because of half-hearted attempts to investigate their activities. Hawke lived on the edge of this world. It was inhabited by some of the people with whom he was associated at the racetrack or to whom he owed debts, whether political or financial. After Bond was released from jail for fraud, Hawke didn't shy away from appearing alongside him in 2013 to celebrate the thirtieth anniversary of Bond's America's Cup win.[4]

When asked to name his major achievements as prime minister, Hawke sometimes struggled. In a speech in 1998 to mark the establishment of the Bob Hawke Prime Ministerial Library at the University of South Australia, he focused on his commitment to the politics of consensus rather than division. When pressed to provide examples of his achievements, he often pointed to the banning of mining in Antarctica, which was agreed in June 1991. He'd certainly done much to bring this about, staring down his cabinet and the American and British governments, but Keating had also played a role in putting it on the agenda and was keen to claim the credit. Other environmental initiatives were partly driven by the need to shore up Labor's declining primary vote with the second preferences of environmentally minded voters. In seeking their support, Hawke acknowledged the environmental crisis but never did much to avert it. Which was a sensible political calculation. Neither his colleagues nor the broader electorate would have borne without protest the political or financial cost that was required to make a meaningful impact on the continuing environmental degradation of the continent. Although the government was aware of global warming and the threat it posed, Hawke and his colleagues shrank from imposing a carbon tax on emissions when the matter came before cabinet in 1991.[5]

Nor did he stem the increasing inequality in Australian society or the increasing irrelevance of the trade union movement, which lost much of its membership and some of its influence during the years of his government, as smaller unions coalesced into behemoths that settled comfortably into the new corporatist environment. Hawke had more to boast about with regard to the position of women, having introduced laws against discrimination and lending his authority to changes for which his minister, Susan Ryan, had been campaigning for years. These had also been incorporated in policy documents that had been prepared during Hayden's time as Labor leader, and that Hawke brought forward as prime minister. Other policies in the fields of education, health and social welfare also resulted in dramatic improvements in the lives of Australian women, with school retention rates and higher education participation rates creating real momentum towards gender equality. This would have made his late mother particularly proud.

Hawke's achievements were shared with his ministers. He was more of a manager than a visionary leader, and was fortunate in having a group of intelligent colleagues who could suggest and implement progressive policies in their portfolios. Just as he'd expected his staff at the ACTU to develop their policy areas free of interference from him as president, his ministers were expected to do likewise. He gave his imprimatur to those proposals that fitted with his view of what was needed for the economic and social transformation of Australia without threatening the survival of the government. He was determined to avoid the fate of the Whitlam government.[6] And he mostly did, remaining as prime minister for nearly three times longer than Whitlam, before being besieged by the economic challenges that had helped overwhelm his predecessor.

Yet Whitlam's achievements during his three years as prime minister had left a legacy that overshadowed much of what Hawke managed to do during his much longer occupation of the Lodge. Many of the Hawke government policies were improvements to ones that the Whitlam government had initiated but that had been wound back by Fraser, in healthcare, multiculturalism, the environment and foreign affairs. And several of the ministers who had served under Whitlam also served under Hawke, notably Bill Hayden, Paul Keating, Lionel Bowen and Tom Uren, providing some continuity between the two governments. But there was also continuity with the Fraser government when Hawke introduced economic policies from which Fraser had shrunk. They made the economy less protectionist, more focused on the opportunities in Asia and more open to international capital. Along with micro-reforms in a range of sectors, these changes helped to underpin the subsequent decades of economic growth.

Of equal moment was Hawke's passionate opposition to racism at a time when the Queensland premier, Joh Bjelke-Petersen, and Liberal leader, John Howard, had no compunctions about shoring up their political positions with appeals to Australian racism. Hawke stared them down, as he did Margaret Thatcher on South African apartheid, and the leaders of China when he allowed tens of thousands of Chinese students to remain in Australia after the Tiananmen Square massacre. But his courage deserted him on the issue of Aboriginal land rights, and he failed to carry forward the initiatives begun by Whitlam for fear of losing votes and being denied campaign funds in Western Australia. In his last minutes as prime minister, a tearful Hawke presided over the unveiling in parliament of the Barunga Statement, which had been presented to him by Aboriginal leader Yunupingu during the Barunga cultural festival in the Northern Territory in June 1988. The statement had called for 'a Treaty recognising our prior ownership, continued occupation and sovereignty, and affirming our human rights and freedom'. In response, Hawke promised them a treaty by 1990. It never eventuated. A treaty would have been a great and enduring legacy of his prime ministership. Instead, wiping away tears, he walked away from the ceremony and left parliament for the last time as prime minister, leaving the task of righting Australia's historic wrongs to his successors.[7]

He was also troubled by the rightward drift in Israel's politics. Few had been stauncher than Hawke in their support for Israel in the 1970s, only to become concerned by the implications of the continuing Israeli occupation of Gaza and the West Bank, and the oppression of the Palestinian people. The notion of Jewish and Palestinian nations living peacefully alongside each other had been the bipartisan cornerstone of Australian policy in the Middle East and naturally appealed to his political outlook. Such an outcome became much harder to envisage after the election in June 1996 of the right-wing leader of the Likud party, Benjamin Netanyahu, who replaced the Labour Party's Shimon Peres, the interim prime minister installed after the assassination by an extremist Israeli settler of Yitzhak Rabin. Any hopes of peace with the Palestinians died with the election of Netanyahu, who also dismantled parts of the social democratic society that Hawke had found so attractive about Israel.

It was in the wake of these developments that Hawke established a foundation in October 1996 to raise money for a technical school in Gaza. It came after a meeting between Hawke and the Palestinian representative in Australia, and was designed to assist the peace process by 'helping the Palestinian people to rebuild their economic infrastructure'. The estimated $3 million cost of the project was meant to come from donations by businesses and community groups, both Palestinian and Jewish. With the foundation being headquartered in his office, Hawke realised that success would depend on getting tax deductibility for the donations, which meant appealing to the newly elected prime minister, John Howard. Although support for the project came from the National Party leader and deputy prime minister, Tim Fischer, and the young Liberal backbencher Joe Hockey agreed to join the board, tax deductibility was never granted. Which meant that sufficient funds were never forthcoming and the foundation was eventually wound up. Hawke nonetheless continued his quest for a solution, supporting recognition for a Palestinian state.[8]

Questions about his political legacy were often twinned with questions about his feelings about death. Whenever asked, Hawke claimed not to fear the prospect of his inevitable demise. It seems that he feared the possibility of dementia much more, after seeing Hazel's sad decline and eventual death. By the late 1990s, it was clear to Sue Hawke that Hazel was beginning to struggle mentally, although she still maintained a heavy round of public engagements and speeches. It wasn't until 2001 that she was diagnosed with Alzheimer's disease. Hawke was distressed by the news and offered what help he could. But there was nothing to be done, and he seldom saw her thereafter: it was too unsettling.

At Ros's urging, when Hazel was dying in 2013, Hawke agreed to visit her aged-care home in Western Sydney. According to close friend Wendy McCarthy, their meeting was a poignant moment that 'made the end so much better' for Hazel. Kneeling beside her bed and holding her hand, he softly sang 'Danny Boy', causing Hazel 'to open her eyes and smile'. According to Ros, she murmured, 'I love you,' as he left. Upon her death soon after, there was a private service for family and friends at a crematorium, while a state memorial service was held on 25 June 2013 in the concert hall of the Opera House, where 1600 mourners listened to eulogies interspersed with music from the Sydney Symphony Orchestra. Accompanied by his children and grandchildren, Hawke was there alongside three other former prime ministers – Keating, Howard and Kevin Rudd – as well as the sitting prime minister, Julia Gillard, who would be replaced just three days later by Rudd. Although Hawke had released a statement noting how Hazel had been 'a constant support', it was considered inappropriate for him to speak at the service, or for D'Alpuget to be present. Instead, he spoke informally at a subsequent gathering of close friends and family.[9]

Troubled by the thought of developing Alzheimer's himself, Hawke sought to ward off the possibility by staying mentally active with cryptic crosswords and sudokus. His work also kept him busy. His mind was also kept active by his continuing interest in horseracing, as he calculated the odds, laid his bets and hobnobbed, beer in hand, with the characters who frequented the racetrack. He was a part-owner of several horses, one of which he shared with John Singleton, who'd given him a quarter share in a young filly called Belle du Jour as a present on his seventieth birthday. The party was held at Hawke's Northbridge home, where ice sculptures of a nude man and woman spouted wine from their penis and breasts, respectively. At the running of the Golden Slipper race at Sydney's Rosehill in 2000, Singleton laid a $100,000 bet on behalf of Hawke on their jointly owned horse, at odds of 10 to 1. Both men watched, Hawke more anxiously than Singleton, as their horse jumped at the start, leaving it last, only to see it run through the field and score a 'freakish' win that amazed and enriched its owners by some $2.5 million. Singleton was so excited that he shouted the public bar for the rest of the day.[10]

The new century saw a plethora of books and television programs about Hawke. In 2010, D'Alpuget published a second volume to her landmark biography that had helped usher in the Hawke prime ministership. The new book covered his time as prime minister, and prompted Keating to mount a strenuous objection to the 'rewriting' of history. In a blistering three-page letter to Hawke, he wrote: 'It is as if, Narcissus-like, you cannot find enough praise to heap upon yourself.' The book's portrayal of Hazel led to a heated altercation between D'Alpuget and Sue Pieters-Hawke in a Brisbane airport lounge.[11]

That relationship was repaired after Hazel's death, when Hawke became closer once again to his children and grandchildren. He also reinforced his links with the Australian public, through appearances at public events such as the Woodford Folk Festival or the races or the cricket. Just walking along the street could see him mobbed by admirers. In 2010, a raunchy telemovie starring Richard Roxburgh portrayed the different sides of Hawke, complete with an unflattering and unfair depiction of Hazel, while in November 2014 his life was explored in a two-part edition of the ABC's *Australian Story*. A million Australians tuned in to watch. And there were the regular spreads in newspapers and magazines, and a small book by D'Alpuget called *On Longing*, which told the story of her affair with Hawke. He seemed determined not to go quietly into the night. It was partly because of Keating's sporadic attacks on Hawke's record, even suggesting in 2014 that Hawke had been effectively absent as prime minister for five years following Ros's heroin crisis and the setback of the 1984 election.[12]

Although Hawke had lost the love of some in the party and the trade unions, he didn't abandon his attachment to the labour movement, which he would express at union or party functions with an emotional rendition of the union anthem 'Solidarity Forever'. He tried to remain a player in Labor leadership battles by supporting one candidate or another. He'd talked of Kim Beazley being his possible successor, and might have made him so if he'd been willing to step down as prime minister in the late 1980s. But he'd never been willing to stand aside for anyone. After Keating lost the 1996 election, Hawke threw his support behind Beazley, who came agonisingly close to defeating John Howard at the subsequent election, winning a majority of votes but not in the seats that mattered. When Beazley stood down after being hammered at the so-called '*Tampa* election' in 2001, Hawke spoke at a tribute dinner. The future Labor leader Mark Latham was there and recorded hearing Hawke give 'a long, ranting speech, talking about Kim as if he were dead' and call him 'the most "decent loser" in the history of Australian politics'. According to Latham, 'the speech wasn't really about Kim; it was, as ever, all about Bob'.[13] When Beazley's successor, the hapless Simon Crean, failed to get traction in the opinion polls, he was quickly pressured to resign in 2003, without being given the chance to contest a federal election. Beazley and Latham both sought to succeed him, with Latham narrowly winning the contest.

Although he was a staunch supporter of Beazley, Hawke tried to develop a close relationship with Latham, who was not impressed – at least initially. When Hawke spoke at a dinner in 2001 to celebrate the centenary of caucus, Latham described how the former prime minister had tried 'to reinvent himself as the father of multiculturalism, with no mention of his greatest achievement: opening up the economy', which Latham found curious. He was 'a tub-thumper who [had now] degenerated into a clown', wrote Latham. That impression was confirmed for Latham when Hawke, having been appointed to report on Beazley's election loss, attended the Flemington races with John Singleton, where a 'shit-faced Hawkie' was photographed 'leering and lurching at some young sheilas'. It was now the age of the internet, and Hawke was reportedly 'shitting himself' when the photos were widely circulated.[14]

It was only after Latham became Labor leader in 2003, with opinion polls suggesting he might defeat John Howard at the 2005 election, that Hawke made an effort to develop friendly relations with him. As a Labor loyalist and pedlar of political influence, Hawke could do no less. His first attempt fell flat when he invited Latham and his wife to lunch with him and D'Alpuget at their Northbridge home in March 2004. It was 'an amiable enough lunch and conversation, more workman-like than warm', noted Latham, who declined an invitation from Hawke to make use of the home's detached unit on the shoreline;

Hawke suggested that he could arrive surreptitiously by water taxi for any meetings that he wanted to keep private. 'He must think I'm James Bond,' wrote an amused Latham, who left with his wife just as 'the masseur was arriving for their afternoon session'.[15]

He was more impressed by Hawke later that year, when the pair met in Latham's office and Hawke made several useful suggestions regarding how Latham could fight the upcoming election. 'Maybe I've been wrong about the guy,' wrote Latham. After all, he was 'putting his shoulder to the wheel when I need it'. It wasn't enough for Latham, though, who was trounced at the election by the wily Howard.[16] Beazley then returned as Labor leader for two more years, before being toppled by an uneasy alliance between Kevin Rudd and Julia Gillard, which allowed Rudd to storm to victory in 2007.

Hawke was no longer a powerbroker but he had become a Labor icon who was wheeled out at campaign launches, dutifully toured electorates around the country and was featured at various anniversary events. Other times, he was content to sit among the audience when D'Alpuget was on stage publicising one of her books, or to act as a paid celebrity speaker, who would become inebriated and digress into bawdy jokes. He remained an unashamed 'bloke's bloke' who revelled in his love of women, of drinking, and of Australia and Australians. He would say that he wanted to be remembered as a 'dinky-di' Australian, and played to that image as he aged. Along with singing 'Solidarity Forever' at union and party events, he was fond of singing the unofficial national anthem 'Waltzing Matilda' and getting audiences to sing the chorus. He did so when he and D'Alpuget went to Bordertown for the unveiling of a bust of him, flying in a small plane rather than miss the event after the scheduled airline service was cancelled. At the age of eighty-eight, he delighted a crowd at the Sydney Cricket Ground, as well as the audience watching on television, when commentator Shane Warne noticed him in the crowd and urged him to down a pint of beer offered to him by a bystander. Unsurprisingly, he couldn't do it in the record time he'd achieved in Oxford, with the broadcast having to switch to the on-field action while Hawke doggedly completed the challenge.[17]

A few months later, Hawke was admitted to hospital in Sydney after returning by plane from Perth, where he'd attended Beazley's investiture as state governor. It was a mark of his determination and his loyalty to

Beazley that he made the trip. He was still suffering the lingering effects of a bacterial infection that he'd picked up in the Middle East in 2015, which had put him in hospital for an intensive course of antibiotics. D'Alpuget said she was so concerned by his condition that she paid a deposit on an apartment in Sydney's CBD. She'd already bought graves for them both, which were side by side in Macquarie Park cemetery. Hawke was also suffering from peripheral neuropathy, which had affected his balance and left him with 'nerve pain in his feet'. He took to walking with a stick or using a wheelchair. But he ditched the stick and wheelchair when he took to a yacht, captained by the America's Cup skipper John Bertrand on Sydney Harbour in early 2018. It was part of a program by *60 Minutes* to mark the twenty-fifth anniversary of his first prime ministership and to celebrate his love of Blanche. The walking stick didn't prevent him from falling and being hospitalised in May 2018. A mini-stroke and his growing deafness continued the deterioration in his health.[18]

As death closed in on him, Hawke was sanguine about his end. He told Craig Emerson, whom D'Alpuget dubbed his 'honorary son': 'It's time to go. I've achieved everything I wanted to.' He still managed to attend the Woodford Folk Festival in December 2018 but was too frail to appear on stage for his usual session, telling journalists that it would be his last time there and he doubted whether he'd live to see the next election.[19]

But he held on. Emerson arranged for Paul Keating to visit Hawke shortly before the election to be held on 18 May 2019, when they put aside their differences to issue a joint statement of support for Labor leader Bill Shorten, posing for photographers on the balcony of the Northbridge home, which was awaiting settlement after being sold for $9.2 million. In their statement Hawke and Keating reminded Australians that it was the Labor government that had transformed Australia in the 1980s and set the economy up for the decades of prosperity that followed. They were confident that Shorten would build on that proud record of progressive reform.[20]

For a couple of months, Blanche had had Emerson and other friends rostered to help with the physical effort of lifting her failing husband. On the day before his death, he and Blanche had watched the ABC news over dinner when he suddenly rose from the table and stumbled into the sitting room, where he crouched on the floor vomiting and complaining of terrible pain. His doctor was called and arrived within minutes to provide morphine. Carried to bed, Hawke died the next day, with Blanche holding his hand. The room seemed 'full of angels', said Blanche, and his face was 'extraordinarily peaceful'.[21]

It was two days before the election, which Shorten was widely predicted to win. Some thought Hawke's death at eighty-nine might boost Labor's chances. But it didn't. Despite his confident prediction of a Labor victory, the party was soundly defeated by Scott Morrison.

After a private service for family and friends, Hawke's ashes were interred in the Macquarie Park cemetery. A state funeral was held at the Opera House on 14 June, which had been planned by Hawke and his family several years before. It began with the singing of the national anthem, as thousands sat on the steps in the chilly air to watch the service on a big screen. There would be no religious participation, other than a performance of Handel's Hallelujah Chorus, which Hawke had conducted in 2009 as part of his eightieth birthday celebrations. Film of that event was played while the Sydney Symphony Orchestra and the Sydney Philharmonia Choirs reprised their performance. The series of heartfelt eulogies included speeches by Sue Pieters-Hawke and Blanche d'Alpuget, while Keating did Hawke proud with praise for his prime ministership and the achievements of their government.[22]

Hawke's will in 2016 had left his estate to D'Alpuget, while a separate agreement granted $750,000 to each of his three children and his stepson, artist Louis Pratt, from the sale of the Northbridge home. The amount was deemed insufficient by 59-year-old Ros, who was living on social welfare in a small rented flat, and she launched legal action to get a larger slice. The action was settled out of court and resulted in only a token increase.[23] It seemed that he could not escape the headlines, even in death.

In March 2023, the fortieth anniversary of his election as prime minister, part of his ashes were interred in the prime ministers' garden at the Melbourne General Cemetery, where several other prime ministers are buried. Prime Minister Anthony Albanese was there for the interment, along with the Victorian premier, Daniel Andrews, Craig Emerson and Blanche d'Alpuget. On the small headstone, the epitaph said simply: 'He loved Australians and they loved him back.'[24] Which was how he wanted, and deserved, to be remembered.

# Endnotes

**CHAPTER ONE: 1979–1980**

1. Laurie Oakes, *Labor's 1979 Conference, Adelaide*, Objective Publications, Canberra, 1979, pp. 3–4.
2. John Hurst, *Hawke: The Definitive Biography*, Angus & Robertson, Sydney, 1979, pp. 167–69; Whitlam was also prone to using sexual innuendo, albeit delivered in a wittier and less offensive fashion than Hawke. See Peter Blazey and Andrew Campbell, *The Political Dice Men*, Outback Press, Melbourne, 1974, pp. 118–19.
3. Hazel Hawke, *My Own Life*, Text, Melbourne, 1992, pp. 150–51; Blanche d'Alpuget, *Robert J. Hawke*, Penguin, Melbourne, 1984, pp. 388, 390–91; R.J.L. Hawke, *1979 Boyer Lectures: The Resolution of Conflict*, Australian Broadcasting Commission, Sydney, 1979.
4. Hawke, *1979 Boyer Lectures*, pp. 33–55.
5. G.S. Reid, 'Hawke's Boyer Lectures', *Quadrant*, May 1980.
6. D'Alpuget, *Robert J. Hawke*, p. 392; Hawke, *1979 Boyer Lectures*, pp. 56–67; *Quadrant*, May 1980; Author interview with Bob Carr.
7. Letters, Blandy to Hawke, 12 June 1980, Renouf to Hawke, 10 June 1980, and Shann to Hawke, c. June 1980, RH101, BHPML.
8. See Letter, Blainey to Hawke, 25 June 1980, and other documents in 'Records relating to the Hawke Advisory Team – R.J.L. Hawke', RH101, BHPML.
9. Bob Carr, 'Australian Trade Unionism in 1979', *Journal of Industrial Relations*, Vol. 22, No. 1, March 1980, pp. 98–102; 'Australian Political Chronicle, July-December 1979', *Australian Journal of Politics and History*, Vol. 26, No. 1, 1980, p. 97; *National Times*, 21 July, 28 July and 27 October 1979; *Sun-Herald*, 12 August 1979; *Australian Financial Review*, 29 October 1979.
10. Paul Kelly, *The Hawke Ascendancy*, Angus & Robertson, Sydney, 1984, p. 84; John Stubbs, *Hayden*, Mandarin, Melbourne, 1990, p. 201.
11. 'Australian Political Chronicle, July-December 1979', pp. 122–23; Ross McMullin, *The Light on the Hill*, Oxford University Press, Melbourne, 1991, pp. 332, 354, 398–99; Barry Jones, *A Thinking Reed*, Allen & Unwin, Sydney, 2006, p. 173; Marian Simms and Geoffrey Browne, 'Jean Isobel Melzer', *Biographical Dictionary of the Australian Senate*, Vol. 3, UNSW Press, Sydney, 2010, pp. 90–95; *Tharunka*, 25 April 1977; *Tribune*, 4 April and 1 August 1979; *Education*, 24 September 1979.
12. Kelly, *The Hawke Ascendancy*, pp. 116–17.
13. Kelly, *The Hawke Ascendancy*, pp. 116–17; Bob Hawke, *The Hawke Memoirs*, William Heinemann, Melbourne, 1994, p. 487; *Canberra Times*, 19 November 1979; *National Times*, 1 December 1979.
14. Author interview with Barry Donovan.
15. Letter, Hawke to Ryder, 22 August 1977, N68/1062-1065, ACTU Papers, NBAC; Author interview with Barry Donovan; Barry Donovan, *Steve Bracks and Jeff Kennett: My Part in their Rise and Fall – An Insider Tells*, Information Australia, Melbourne, 2000, pp. 72–76; for a synopsis of the proposed book, see Letter and

16     attachment, Donovan to D'Alpuget, 15 August 1980, MS 7348/3/18, D'Alpuget Papers, NLA.
16     Interview with Peter Redlich by D'Alpuget, 30 March 1981, MS 7348/2/12, and Letters, D'Alpuget to Hurst, 1 August 1979, and D'Alpuget to Hawke, 2 November [1979], MS 7348/3/17, D'Alpuget Papers, NLA; *Canberra Times*, 11 December 1979; *National Times*, 22 December 1979.
17     Robert Pullan, *Bob Hawke: A Portrait*, Methuen, Sydney, 1980, p. 9; Author interview with Robert Pullan.
18     Letters, D'Alpuget to Hurst, and D'Alpuget to Hawke, both 1 August 1979, MS 7348/3/17, D'Alpuget Papers, NLA
19     *Canberra Times*, 4 November 1977, 7 January and 18 November 1978; Letter, Hawke to D'Alpuget, 30 April 1977, MS 7348/3/19, D'Alpuget Papers, NLA.
20     *Canberra Times*, 4 November 1977, 7 January and 18 November 1978; *Bulletin*, 9 October 1979.
21     Author interview with Bob Carr.
22     *National Times*, 29 September 1979; *Bulletin*, 9 January 1980; Author interview with Bob Carr.
23     'Hawke Notes after 3–10 January Interviews', by D'Alpuget, MS 7348/2/11, D'Alpuget Papers, NLA.
24     *Bulletin*, 9 October 1979.
25     Letter, Peter Nolan to Hawke, 9 October 1980, and other documents in RH73, Personal Correspondence [August–October 1980], BHPML.
26     Interview with Bob Hawke by Paula Hamilton, 27 April 2000, 00523, JCPML.
27     Notes of an interview with Sam Stoljar, with added comments by D'Alpuget, and 'Hawke Notes after 3–10 January Interviews', by D'Alpuget, MS 7348/2/11, D'Alpuget Papers, NLA.
28     *Bulletin*, 9 January 1980.
29     Hazel Hawke 1980 Diary, JCPML 1271/9-12/10, Hazel Hawke Papers, JCPML; Hazel Hawke, *My Own Life*, pp. 118–19; *Bulletin*, 9 January and 15 April 1980.
30     *Woman's Day*, January 1980.
31     Hazel Hawke, *My Own Life*, pp. 130–35.
32     Hazel Hawke 1980 Diary, 3, 24, 25 and 26 March, JCPML 1271/9-12/10, Hazel Hawke Papers, JCPML.
33     D'Alpuget, *Robert J. Hawke*, p. 395; Undated newspaper cutting, c. March 1980, MS 7348/Folio Box 5, D'Alpuget Papers, NLA.
34     Hawke, *The Hawke Memoirs*, pp. 103–104; Hazel Hawke, *My Own Life*, p. 134; Interview with Bob Hawke by Andrew Denton, *Enough Rope*, ABC Television, 14 July 2008.
35     D'Alpuget, *Robert J. Hawke*, pp. 395–97.
36     Letter, Varghese to Hawke, 29 June 1981, RH73, Personal Correspondence [April–June 1981], BHPML; Memorandum of Fees by D.J. Killen, 27 August 1981, RH73, Personal Correspondence [July–September 1981], BHPML; Qantas Itinerary, 4 June 1981, and other documents in RH248, BHPML; See Hawke's racing photos in RH148/F2/1, BHPML.
37     Letter, Leibler to Hayden, 16 September 1980, and other documents in RH172/F5, BHPML; For documents related to 1980 election donations to Hawke's trust account, see RH172/F6, BHPML.
38     Hawke, *The Hawke Memoirs*, p. 105; Stubbs, *Hayden*, pp. 199–201; McMullin, *The Light on the Hill*, pp. 397–98.
39     Kelly, *The Hawke Ascendancy*, pp. 87–88; For details of Hawke's activities during the election campaign, see documents in RH172, BHPML.
40     Program for Hawke, 30 September 1980, RH172, BHPML.
41     D'Alpuget, *Robert J. Hawke*, p. 398; Blanche d'Alpuget, *Bob Hawke: The Complete Biography*, Simon & Schuster, Sydney, 2019, pp. 552–54; McMullin, *The Light on the Hill*, p. 398; Kelly, *The Hawke Ascendancy*, pp. 87–88; Bill Hayden, *Hayden: An Autobiography*, Angus & Robertson, Melbourne, 1996, pp. 331–32; Telegram, Hayden to Hawke, 7 October 1980, and other documents in RH172, Folder 5, BHPML

42  Hawke, *The Hawke Memoirs*, pp. 105–106; Hayden, *Hayden*, pp. 331–32; Kelly, *The Hawke Ascendancy*, pp. 86–88.

**CHAPTER TWO: 1981–1982**

1   McMullin, *The Light on the Hill*, p. 398; Gavin Souter, *Acts of Parliament*, Melbourne University Press, Melbourne, 1988, pp. 575–76; Hayden, *Hayden*, pp. 331–32; Kelly, *The Hawke Ascendancy*, pp. 86–88, 94–95; *Canberra Times*, 19 and 20 October 1980; *Bulletin*, 21 and 28 October 1980.
2   *Canberra Times*, 20 October 1980; *Bulletin*, 18 November 1980.
3   Telegram, Hayden to Hawke, 20 October 1980, RH75/3, BHPML.
4   Rob Chalmers, *Inside the Canberra Press Gallery: Life in the Wedding Cake of Old Parliament House*, ANU Press, Canberra, 2011.pp. 207–208.
5   Hansard, 25, 26 and 27 November 1980.
6   Letter, Kerin to Hawke, 21 January 1980, RH101/2, BHPML.
7   See note by D'Alpuget in MS 7348/1/5, NLA; *Bulletin*, 18 December 1979.
8   Hawke, *The Hawke Memoirs*, pp. 106–107; Hazel Hawke, *My Own Life*, p. 171; 'Hawke and Sir Peter Abeles', note by D'Alpuget, 2 September 1982, MS 7348/2/12, D'Alpuget Papers, NLA; Notes by D'Alpuget of talk with Gil Appleton, undated, MS 7348/2/12, D'Alpuget Papers, NLA; For details of the flat in Kingston, see documents in RH14, F27–F37 (M3826/1), BHPML.
9   Author interview with Barry Donovan; Blanche d'Alpuget, *On Longing*, Melbourne University Press, Melbourne, 2008, pp. 46–48; 'Hawke and Sir Peter Abeles', note by D'Alpuget, 2 September 1982, MS 7348/2/12, D'Alpuget Papers, NLA.
10  Communication to the author from Yolanda Benn Hellier; Interview with Chris Crellin by D'Alpuget, 9 April 1981, MS 7348/2/12, D'Alpuget Papers, NLA.
11  D'Alpuget, *Bob Hawke: The Complete Biography*, p. 649; Hazel Hawke, *My Own Life*, pp. 135–36, 144–45, 151; Undated newspaper cutting, c. September 1983, Newspaper cutting book, Hazel Hawke Papers, JCPML; Hazel Hawke, *My Own Life*, pp. 157, 163; see also Vera Wasowski, *Vera: My Story*, Black Inc., Melbourne, 2015.
12  Interview with Hawke by Michael Parkinson, 16 May 1981, *Parkinson in Australia*, www.youtube.com/watch?v=R0r_LXhYM58.
13  Conversation with Hawke by the author at the National Library; Hawke, *The Hawke Memoirs*, pp. 103–104; D'Alpuget, *Robert J. Hawke*, pp. 395–97; Hazel Hawke, *My Own Life*, p. 114; Interview with Peter Abeles by D'Alpuget, 24 August 1981, MS 7348/2/12, D'Alpuget Papers, NLA.
14  Hazel Hawke, *My Own Life*, pp. 163–69, 170–71.
15  Hazel Hawke, *My Own Life*, p. 134; *Age*, 20 March 1982; Letter, D'Alpuget to Hazel Hawke, 29 February 1980, MS 7348/3/17, D'Alpuget Papers, NLA.
16  Letter, D'Alpuget to Donovan, 24 July 1980, MS 7348/3/18, D'Alpuget Papers, NLA.
17  Letters (copies), D'Alpuget to Hazel Hawke, 30 April, 16 May and 24 July 1980, D'Alpuget to Ross Martin, 10 June 1980, and D'Alpuget to Colin Hayes, 3 March 1981, MS 7348/3/18, D'Alpuget Papers, NLA.
18  Ibid.
19  Letters, Hawke to Shimon Peres, and Hawke to Jim Shea, 4 September 1981, RH73, Personal Correspondence [July–September 1981], BHPML.
20  Letters, D'Alpuget to Hazel Hawke, 10 January 1982, and Hazel Hawke to D'Alpuget, 24 February 1982, MS 7348/3/19, D'Alpuget Papers, NLA; *Age*, 20 March 1982; *Canberra Times*, 28 July, 23 September and 5, 6 October 1982.
21  Ibid.
22  Undated note by D'Alpuget, MS 7348/3/14, D'Alpuget Papers, NLA.
23  Letter, Hawke to Graham Evans, c. September 1981, RH73, Personal Correspondence [April–June 1981], BHPML.
24  Barrie Cassidy, 'Politicians and Fruit Cakes: A Tawdry Tale', 19 October 2012, www.abc.net.au/news/2012-10-19/cassidy-politicians-and-fruit-cakes/4321228; Letter, T.J. Rao to Hawke, 10 September 1981, RH73, Personal Correspondence [July–September 1981], BHPML.
25  'Hawke and Hayden as ALP Leaders – Polls Easily Back Hawke', Undated paper, RH73, Personal Correspondence [October–December 1981], BHPML.

26  Hayden, *Hayden*, pp. 332–33; Stubbs, *Hayden*, pp. 212–14; Kelly, *The Hawke Ascendancy*, pp. 153–54.
27  Kelly, *The Hawke Ascendancy*, pp. 153–54; Author interview with Barry Jones.
28  Mullins, *Tiberius with a Telephone*, pp. 623–28; Kelly, *The Hawke Ascendancy*, p. 154; Stubbs, *Hayden*, p. 213; Graham Richardson, *Whatever It Takes*, Bantam Books, Sydney, 1994, pp. 91–93; *Bulletin*, 19 January 1982.
29  *The Age*, 4 May 1982.
30  Kelly, *The Hawke Ascendancy*, pp. 171–75; Richardson, *Whatever It Takes*, p. 117.
31  Hawke, *My Own Life*, p. 172–73; Hazel Hawke 1982 Diary, JCPML 1271/9-12/10, Hazel Hawke Papers, JCPML; Undated newspaper cutting, c. September 1983, Newspaper cutting book, Hazel Hawke Papers, JCPML.
32  Hazel Hawke 1982 Diary, JCPML 1271/9-12/10, Hazel Hawke Papers, JCPML.
33  Hawke, *My Own Life*, p. 172–73; Hazel Hawke 1982 Diary, JCPML 1271/9-12/10, Hazel Hawke Papers, JCPML.
34  Stubbs, *Hayden*, pp. 216–18; Kelly, *The Hawke Ascendancy*, pp. 176–89; Hayden, *Hayden*, pp. 339–41; Richardson, *Whatever It Takes*, pp. 93–94.
35  Ibid.
36  Stubbs, *Hayden*, pp. 216–18; Kelly, *The Hawke Ascendancy*, pp. 176–89; David McKnight, *Australia's Spies and Their Secrets*, Allen & Unwin, Sydney, 1994, pp. 291–94; Letter, Summers to Hawke, c. 25 June 1982, and undated article by Peter Bowers, RH73, Personal Correspondence, [June 1982], and 'Voters' Perceptions of Political Leaders', Survey by Quantum Market Research, April 1982, RH103, ALP National Executive Meeting, 1 and 2 July 1982, BHPML; *Bulletin*, 12 January 1982.
37  Kelly, *The Hawke Ascendancy*, pp. 192–95.
38  Mike Steketee and Milton Cockburn, *Wran: An Unauthorised Biography*, Allen & Unwin, Sydney, 1986, pp. 254–55; Richardson, *Whatever It Takes*, pp. 94–95.
39  Stubbs, *Hayden*, pp. 218–19; Kelly, *The Hawke Ascendancy*, pp. 192–95; Richardson, *Whatever It Takes*, pp. 94–95; Steketee and Cockburn, *Wran*, pp. 254–55.
40  Kelly, *The Hawke Ascendancy*, pp. 196–211; *Bulletin*, 23 December 1980.
41  Kelly, *The Hawke Ascendancy*, pp. 196–211; D'Alpuget, *Robert J. Hawke*, pp. 402–03; Richardson, *Whatever It Takes*, pp. 97–102.
42  Kelly, *The Hawke Ascendancy*, pp. 206–11; Stubbs, *Hayden*, pp. 222–24; D'Alpuget, *Robert J. Hawke*, pp. 402–03; Address by Hayden at ALP National Conference, Canberra, 6 July 1982, MSS 5095/117/2014, ML.
43  Ibid.
44  Telegram, Jenkins to Hawke, 8 July 1982, and Handwritten, undated notes listing supporters and those who whose support was unknown. RH75, BHPML.
45  Kerry O'Brien, *Keating*, Allen & Unwin, Sydney, 2015, pp. 119–21; Stubbs, *Hayden*, pp. 224–27; Author interview with Gareth Evans.
46  Ibid.
47  Stubbs, *Hayden*, pp. 224–26; Kelly, *The Hawke Ascendancy*, pp. 230–34; Statement by Hawke, 13 July 1982 and other documents in RH75, BHPML.

**CHAPTER THREE: 1982–1983**

1  Kelly, *The Hawke Ascendancy*, pp. 231–39; See documents in RH75, BHPML.
2  Telex message to Hawke from *National Times* editor Brian Toohey, 7 July 1982 and Note to Hawke from Toohey, 15 July 1982, RH73, Personal Correspondence [July 1982], BHPML; *Canberra Times*, 17 July 1982.
3  Hayden, *Hayden*, pp. 348–49; *Canberra Times*, 17 July 1982.
4  D'Alpuget, *Robert J. Hawke*, pp. 403–04; Stubbs, *Hayden*, pp. 224–27; Philip Chubb and Barry Donovan, *Chance Is Worth a Thousand Plans: Peter Redlich & the Creation of a National Law Firm*, Holding, Redlich & Co., Melbourne, 2013, pp. 66–7.
5  Letter, Blair to Hawke, 10 September 1982, RH73, BHPML.
6  Hazel Hawke 1982 Diary, JCPML 1271/9-12/10, Hazel Hawke Papers, JCPML.
7  Ibid.
8  *Sydney Morning Herald*, 7 December 2019; *Daily Mail*, 16 July and 8 December 2019; *New Daily*, 16 July 2019; *Herald Sun*, 15 December 2019; D'Alpuget, *Bob Hawke*, p. 650.
9  *Bulletin*, 21 September 1982.

10  Ibid.
11  *Canberra Times*, 28 July and 23 September 1982.
12  Hazel Hawke 1982 Diary, 11 and 12 September 1982, JCPML 1271/9-12/10, Hazel Hawke Papers, JCPML.
13  *Canberra Times*, 6 October 1982.
14  Guest List, Launch, 5 October 1982, RH73, Personal Correspondence [August 1982–September 1982], BHPML.
15  *Canberra Times*, 5 October, 6 October and 29 December 1982; *Australian Women's Weekly*, 20 October 1982; *Australian Jewish News*, 17 September, 15 October and 12 November 1982; *Australian Jewish Times*, 28 October 1982; *Bulletin*, 21 September 1982; *Age*, 15 March 1983.
16  Kelly, *The Hawke Ascendancy*, chapter 15.
17  Kelly, *The Hawke Ascendancy*, chapter 15; For Hayden's reaction, see documents in RH103, ALP Special National Executive, September 1982, BHPML.
18  Malcolm Fraser and Margaret Simons, *Malcolm Fraser: The Political Memoirs*, Miegunyah Press, Melbourne, 2010, pp. 603–604; Patrick Weller, *Malcolm Fraser PM*, Penguin, Melbourne, 1989, p. 205; Kelly, *The Hawke Ascendancy*, chapters 14–16; Hayden, *Hayden*, pp. 354–55; D'Alpuget, *Robert J. Hawke*, p. 405; *Bulletin*, 19 October and 9 November 1982.
19  Letter, Schildberger to Hawke, 14 December 1982, RH73, Personal Correspondence [October–December 1982], BHPML.
20  Kelly, *The Hawke Ascendancy*, pp. 308–309; Hayden, *Hayden*, pp. 351–52; Letter, Hawke to all members of caucus, 8 November 1982, RH73, Personal Correspondence [October–December 1982], BHPML; *Herald*, 8 November 1982; *Australian*, 7 and 9 November 1982; *Bulletin*, 23 November 1982.
21  John Button, *As It Happened*, Text, Melbourne, 1998, p. 189; Stubbs, *Hayden*, p. 233; Kelly, *The Hawke Ascendancy*, pp. 306–307; Author interview with Gareth Evans; *Herald*, 4 November 1982; *Bulletin*, 23 November 1982.
22  Hayden, *Hayden*, pp. 333–39; *Standard-Post*, 17 and 24 November 1982; *Sun*, 15 November 1982.
23  *Herald*, 20 November, 3, 4 and 6 December 1982; *Australian*, 2, 3, 5 and 6 December 1982; *Weekend Australian*, 20–21 November 1982; *Age*, 1, 2, 4 and 6 December 1982; *Standard-Post*, 1 December 1982; *Bulletin*, 23 November and 7 December 1982.
24  Ibid.
25  Button, *As It Happened*, pp. 189–93; Stubbs, *Hayden*, pp. 235–40; Patrick Weller, *Dodging Raindrops – John Button: A Labor Life*, Allen & Unwin, Sydney, 1999, pp. 140–45; *Bulletin*, 21, 28 December 1982 and 8 February 1983.
26  Ibid.
27  Richardson, *Whatever It Takes*, pp. 112–15; Author interview with Graham Freudenberg.
28  Stubbs, *Hayden*, pp. 240–41; O'Brien, *Keating*, p. 122; Richardson, *Whatever It Takes*, pp. 112–15; Button, *As It Happened*, pp. 190–98; Kelly, *The Hawke Ascendancy*, pp. 348–73.
29  Weller, *Dodging Raindrops*, pp. 146–47.

**CHAPTER FOUR: 1983**
1  Weller, *Dodging Raindrops*, pp. 144–47; Hayden, *Hayden*, pp. 356–62; Kelly, *The Hawke Ascendancy*, pp. 373–74; Hawke, *The Hawke Memoirs*, pp. 122–23; Author interview with Gareth Evans.
2  Ibid.
3  Hayden, *Hayden*, pp. 359–64; Kelly, *The Hawke Ascendancy*, pp. 375–77; Stubbs, *Hayden*, pp. 244–47; D'Alpuget, *Bob Hawke*, pp. 566–69; *Bulletin*, 8 and 15 February 1983.
4  D'Alpuget, *Bob Hawke*, pp. 568–69; Stubbs, *Hayden*, pp. 246–47; Kelly, *The Hawke Ascendancy*, pp. 348–84; Fraser and Simons, *Malcolm Fraser*, pp. 603–04; Author interview with Laurie Oakes.
5  Weller, *Dodging Raindrops*, pp. 147–48; Kelly, *The Hawke Ascendancy*, p. 386; Stubbs, *Hayden*, pp. 249–52; Hayden, *Hayden*, pp. 360–64.

6   Hawke, *The Hawke Memoirs*, pp. 122–27; Kelly, *The Hawke Ascendancy*, p. 386.
7   Hawke, *The Hawke Memoirs*, pp. 124–27.
8   Kelly, *The Hawke Ascendancy*, p. 386; O'Brien, *Keating*, p. 123.
9   Hawke, *The Hawke Memoirs*, pp. 124–29.
10  Fraser and Simons, *Malcolm Fraser*, pp. 604–05; *Sydney Morning Herald*, 4 February 1983.
11  Bramston, *Bob Hawke: Demons and Destiny*, Viking, Sydney, 2022, p. 258.
12  D'Alpuget, *Bob Hawke*, pp. 568–69; Author interview with Neal Blewett; *Sydney Morning Herald*, 4 February 1983; 'Just Call Me Bob', *Australian Story*, ABC Television, 17 November 2014.
13  Fraser and Simons, *Malcolm Fraser*, pp. 604–605; Kelly, *The Hawke Ascendancy*, pp. 387–94.
14  Hawke, *The Hawke Memoirs*, pp. 127–29; 'Just Call Me Bob', *Australian Story*, ABC Television, 10 November 2014.
15  Wasowski, *Vera*, pp. 207–08; Pieters-Hawke, *Hazel*, pp. 196–98.
16  Hazel Hawke, *My Own Life*, pp. 143–44; Pieters-Hawke, *Hazel*, pp. 196–98; 'Just Call Me Bob', *Australian Story*, ABC Television, 10 November 2014; Wasowski, *Vera*, pp. 207–08.
17  Hazel Hawke, *My Own Life*, p. 143; Pieters-Hawke, *Hazel*, pp. 197–98; Waskowski, *Vera*, pp. 204–07.
18  Ibid.
19  Hawke, *The Hawke Memoirs*, pp. 132–33.
20  Ibid.

**CHAPTER FIVE: 1983**
1   *Nationwide*, ABC Television, interview by Richard Carleton with Hawke, 3 February 1983.
2   Ibid; Richardson, *Whatever It Takes*, pp. 116–17, 123–24; Stubbs, *Hayden*, p. 251; Kelly, *The Hawke Ascendancy*, p. 399; D'Alpuget, *Bob Hawke*, pp. 576–78.
3   Richardson, *Whatever It Takes*, pp. 116–17, 123–24; Kelly, *The Hawke Ascendancy*, pp. 399–400; Interview with Hawke by Michael Parkinson, *Parkinson in Australia*, 16 May 1981, www.youtube.com/watch?v=R0r_LXhYM58; Author interview with Geoff Walsh.
4   Ibid; *Bulletin*, 15 and 22 February 1983.
5   Ibid; *Bulletin*, 15 and 22 February 1983.
6   Ibid.
7   Hawke, *The Hawke Memoirs*, pp. 129–33; Richardson, *Whatever It Takes*, pp. 121–30; McMullin, *The Light on the Hill*, p. 409; Laurie Oakes, *On the Record: Politics, Politicians and Power*, Hachette, Sydney, 2010, pp. 144–46.
8   David Day, *The Weather Watchers*, Melbourne University Publishing, Melbourne, 2007, pp. 400, 415–16; Frank Bongiorno, *The Eighties*, Black Inc., Melbourne, 2015, pp. 4–5.
9   Keith Scott, *Gareth Evans*, Allen & Unwin, Sydney, 1999, pp. 117–19; Kelly, *The Hawke Ascendancy*, p. 401.
10  Hawke, *The Hawke Memoirs*, pp. 134–35; Kelly, *The Hawke Ascendancy*, pp. 404–06.
11  Ibid.
12  Author interview with Gareth Evans.
13  Kelly, *The Hawke Ascendancy*, pp. 404–06; Hazel Hawke, *My Own Life*, pp. 144–6; Pieters-Hawke, *Hazel*, pp. 198–202.
14  Hawke's Election Campaign Speech, 16 February 1983, Museum of Australian Democracy, electionspeeches.moadoph.gov.au/speeches/1983-bob-hawke; Kelly, *The Hawke Ascendancy*, pp. 401–06; Author interview with Graham Freudenberg.
15  Hawke's Election Campaign Speech, 16 February 1983, Museum of Australian Democracy, electionspeeches.moadoph.gov.au/speeches/1983-bob-hawke.
16  Hawke, *The Hawke Memoirs*, pp. 136–37; Richardson, *Whatever It Takes*, p. 123.
17  Kelly, *The Hawke Ascendancy*, p. 406; Richardson, *Whatever It Takes*, p. 129.
18  Kelly, *The Hawke Ascendancy*, pp. 406–08; Hawke, *The Hawke Memoirs*, p. 135; Richardson, *Whatever It Takes*, p. 128; Weller, *Malcolm Fraser PM*, pp. 210–13.

19 Ibid.
20 Ibid.
21 Hazel Hawke, *My Own Life*, pp. 144–45; Pieters-Hawke, *Hazel*, pp. 199–200; Hawke, *The Hawke Memoirs*, pp. 139–42.
22 *Canberra Times*, 6 March 1983.
23 Kelly, *The Hawke Ascendancy*, pp. 412–18; Hazel Hawke, *My Own Life*, p. 145; *Canberra Times*, 6 March 1983.

## CHAPTER SIX: 1983

1 Graham Freudenberg, *A Figure of Speech*, Wiley, Brisbane, 2005, p. 213; Hawke, *The Hawke Memoirs*, pp. 150–52; Hazel Hawke, *My Own Life*, p. 146.
2 See 'Report of Task Force on Govt. Administration, Federal Parliamentary Labor Party', September 1982, and 'Labor and Quality of Government' by Hawke and Evans, February 1983. I am grateful to Gareth Evans for providing copies of these documents.
3 *Canberra Times*, 4 March 1983; David Marr, *Patrick White: A Life*, Random House, Sydney, 1991, p. 615.
4 Susan Ryan, *Catching the Waves*, HarperCollins, Sydney, 1999, pp. 247–51; Kelly, *The End of Certainty*, pp. 34–36, 97.
5 Kelly, *The Hawke Ascendancy*, pp. 410–12; Hawke, *The Hawke Memoirs*, pp. 145–47; O'Brien, *Keating*, pp. 128–34; John Edwards, *Keating: The Inside Story*, Penguin, Melbourne, 1996, pp. 171–72; Author interview with John Stone.
6 Author interview with John Stone.
7 Kelly, *The Hawke Ascendancy*, pp. 410–12; Hawke, *The Hawke Memoirs*, pp. 145–47; O'Brien, *Keating*, pp. 128–34; Edwards, *Keating*, pp. 171–72; Author interview with John Stone.
8 Hawke, *The Hawke Memoirs*, pp. 153–54; Kelly, *The End of Certainty*, pp. 56–57; O'Brien, *Keating*, pp. 136–37; Edwards, *Keating*, pp. 194–97.
9 O'Brien, *Keating*, p. 132; Hawke, *The Hawke Memoirs*, pp. 134–35, 157–59, 165–67, 174–75; David Day, *Paul Keating*, HarperCollins, Sydney, 2015, pp. 223–25; Richardson, *Whatever It Takes*, pp. 137–38; D'Alpuget, *Bob Hawke*, p. 596; Author interview with Ralph Willis; Author interview with Bob Hawke.
10 Ibid.
11 Hawke, *The Hawke Memoirs*, pp. 145–50; Edwards, *Keating*, pp. 171–72.
12 D'Alpuget, *Robert J. Hawke*, p. 192; C.J. Coventry, 'The "Eloquence" of Robert J. Hawke: United States Informer, 1973–79', *Australian Journal of Politics and History*, Vol. 67, No. 1, 2021.
13 McMullin, *The Light on the Hill*, pp. 343–44, 422–24; Scott, *Gareth Evans*, p. 112; Clyde Cameron, *The Cameron Diaries*, Allen & Unwin, Sydney, 1990, p. 314; Gareth Evans, *Incorrigible Optimist*, Melbourne University Press, Melbourne, 2017, p. 22.
14 McMullin, *The Light on the Hill*, pp. 422–24; Bongiorno, *The Eighties*, pp. 11–14; David Marr, *The Ivanov Trail*, Thomas Nelson, Melbourne, 1984, pp. 2–27; Brian Toohey, *Secret: The Making of Australia's Security State*, Melbourne University Press, Melbourne, 2019, p. 13; D'Alpuget, *Bob Hawke*, pp. 601–21; *Canberra Times*, 16 May 1983.
15 Transcript of an interview with Bob Hawke by Paula Hamilton, 27 April 2000, 00523, JCPML
16 Bramston, *Bob Hawke: Demons and Destiny*, Viking, Sydney, 2022, pp. 410–12; Author interview with Graham Evans; Author interview with Ross Garnaut; Author interview with Blanche d'Alpuget.
17 *New Idea*, 26 March 1983; *Age*, 15 March 1983.
18 Hazel Hawke, *My Own Life*, pp. 149–54; Diane Langmore, *Prime Minister's Wives*, McPhee Gribble, Melbourne, 1992, pp. 293–96; Letters, Margaret Kelly to RSPCA, 30 March 1983, Hazel Hawke to Kirsty Bentham, 14 April 1983, and Sharon Massey to Mr Brown, 20 May 1983, JCPML 00351[1], Hazel Hawke Papers, JCPM.
19 Ibid.
20 Ibid.

21  Transcript of National Press Club Speech by Hazel Hawke, 26 January 1984, JCPML00350/2, Hazel Hawke Papers, JCPML; Anne Summers, *Unfettered and Alive: A Memoir*, Allen & Unwin, Sydney, 2018, p. 152.
22  Author interview with Blanche d'Alpuget; *Uniken*, 22 July 1983.
23  Blanche d'Alpuget, *Winter in Jerusalem*, Secker & Warburg, London, 1986, pp. 12, 52–3; D'Alpuget, *On Longing*, pp. 21, 51–53.
24  Hawke, *The Hawke Memoirs*, p. 168; Weller, *Dodging Raindrops*, pp. 150–51; Peter Walsh, *Confessions of a Failed Finance Minister*, Random House, Sydney, 1995, pp. 76–78, 101–02; Neal Blewett, 'The Hawke Cabinets', in Susan Ryan and Troy Bramston (eds), *The Hawke Government*, Pluto Press, Sydney, 2003, pp. 73–87; Author interview with Graham Freudenberg.
25  Author interview with Graham Evans.
26  Kelly, *The End of Certainty*, pp. 57–58; Hawke, *The Hawke Memoirs*, pp. 162–67; Author interview with Graham Freudenberg; Author interview with Graham Evans; Author interview with Ross Garnaut; Author interview with Geoff Walsh; Ross Garnaut, 'Real Australians in Economics', in Brij Lal and Allison Ley (eds), *The Coombs: A House of Memories* (second edition), Australian National University Press, Canberra, 2014, p. 134.
27  The layout and décor of the prime ministerial suite can be viewed in Old Parliament House and remains much as it was in Hawke's day. Author interview with Graham Evans; Author interview with Geoff Walsh.
28  *Bulletin*, 2 August 1983; Hawke, *The Hawke Memoirs*, pp. 124–26.

**CHAPTER SEVEN: 1983**

1  Author interview with Ross Garnaut; Author interview with Barry Jones.
2  Hawke, *The Hawke Memoirs*, pp. 178–86; Bongiorno, *The Eighties*, pp. 16–20; Barry Jones, *A Thinking Reed*, Allen & Unwin, Sydney, 2006, pp. 337–38; Bramston, *Bob Hawke*, pp. 301–03; *Canberra Times*, 19 March 1983.
3  Freudenberg, *A Figure of Speech*, pp. 213–14; Hawke, *The Hawke Memoirs*, pp. 178–86; O'Brien, *Keating*, pp. 137–38; Kelly, *The End of Certainty*, pp. 65–68; Doug McEachern, 'Corporatism and Business Responses to the Hawke Government', *Australian Journal of Political Science*, Vol. 21, No. 1, September 2007; Address by Hawke to the National Economic Summit, 11 April 1983, pmtranscripts.pmc.gov.au/release/transcript-6083
4  Address by Hawke to the National Economic Summit, 11 April 1983, pmtranscripts.pmc.gov.au/release/transcript-6083
5  Hawke, *The Hawke Memoirs*, pp. 179–86; Jones, *A Thinking Reed*, pp. 337–39; *Canberra Times*, 15 April 1983.
6  Bramston, *Bob Hawke*, p. 302.
7  Scott, *Gareth Evans*, pp. 120–203; Author interview with Gareth Evans; *Canberra Times*, 11 April 1983.

**CHAPTER EIGHT: 1983**

1  John Blaxland, 'Tudor Harvey Barnett', *ADB*, Vol. 19, 2021.
2  For a comprehensive account of the Ivanov affair, see Marr, *The Ivanov Trail*; John Blaxland and Rhys Crawley, *The Official History of ASIO, 1975–1989*, Vol. III, Allen & Unwin, Sydney, 2016, pp. 213–16, 247–71; Hawke, *The Hawke Memoirs*, pp. 187–202; Scott, *Gareth Evans*, pp. 123–31; Evans, *Incorrigible Optimist*, p. 29.
3  Hawke, *The Hawke Memoirs*, p. 191.
4  Hawke, *The Hawke Memoirs*, pp. 187–202; Scott, *Gareth Evans*, pp. 123–31; Evans, *Incorrigible Optimist*, p. 29; Weller, *Dodging Raindrops*, pp. 167–68; Marr, *The Ivanov Trail*, pp. 5–15, 88; Brian Toohey and William Pinwill, *Oyster: The Story of the Australian Secret Intelligence Service*, William Heinemann, Melbourne, 1989, chapter 12.
5  Ibid.
6  Ibid.

7   Hawke, *The Hawke Memoirs*, pp. 187–202; Scott, *Gareth Evans*, pp. 123–31; Bongiorno, *The Eighties*, pp. 21–8; Evans, *Incorrigible Optimist*, pp. 28–29; Toohey and Pinwill, *Oyster*, p. 245; Author interview with Gareth Evans.
8   Richardson, *Whatever It Takes*, pp. 139–43; Marr, *The Ivanov Trail*, pp. 234–40, 255–56; Transcript of an interview with Evans by Max Walsh and Sam Lipski, *Sunday* program, 15 May 1983, Parliamentary Library, Canberra.
9   Richardson, *Whatever It Takes*, p. 141.
10  Richardson, *Whatever It Takes*, pp. 139–43; Hawke, *The Hawke Memoirs*, pp. 196–97; Marr, *The Ivanov Trail*, pp. 234–40, 255–56; Transcript of an interview with Evans by Max Walsh and Sam Lipski, *Sunday* program, 15 May 1983, Parliamentary Library, Canberra.
11  *Canberra Times*, 9, 16.
12  *Canberra Times*, 9, 16, 22, 24, 26, 28, 29 and 30 May 1983.
13  *Canberra Times*, 29 and 30 May 1983.
14  Hawke, *The Hawke Memoirs*, pp. 199–202; D'Alpuget, *Bob Hawke*, pp. 601–21; Richardson, *Whatever It Takes*, pp. 142–43; Peter Edwards, *Law, Politics and Intelligence: A Life of Robert Hope*, UNSW Press, Sydney, 2020, chapter 15.
15  Hawke, *The Hawke Memoirs*, pp. 199–202; D'Alpuget, *Bob Hawke*, pp. 601–21; Richardson, *Whatever It Takes*, p. 143; A.J. Brown, *Michael Kirby: Paradoxes and Principles*, Federation Press, Sydney, 2011, p. 176; Meena Blesing, 'Was Your Dad a Russian Spy?', Macmillan, Melbourne, 1986; *Canberra Times*, 13, 14, 16 May 1983; *National Times*, 17–23 August 1984.
16  An account of the visit to San Francisco by Hawke and Combe can be found in David Day, *Young Hawke*, HarperCollins, Sydney, 2024, pp. 336–37; D'Alpuget, *Bob Hawke*, pp. 613–21; Marr, *The Ivanov Trail*, pp. 294–303.
17  Marr, *The Ivanov Trail*, pp. 294–303; Hawke, *The Hawke Memoirs*, pp. 199–202; D'Alpuget, *Bob Hawke*, pp. 601–21; Stephen Charles, 'Spies Like Us? The David Combe Affair', *Victorian Bar News*, June 2017; *Canberra Times*, 15, 16 and 19 July, 17 November 1983; *Australian*, 12 July 2010; *National Times*, 1–7, 8–14, 15–21, 22–28 July, 5–11 August and 9–15 December 1983; Transcript of Prime Minister's Press Conference, 17 November 1983, pmtranscripts.pmc.gov.au/sites/default/files/original/00006267.pdf; Hansard, 17 November 1983.
18  Bramston, *Bob Hawke*, pp. 311, 319; D'Alpuget, *Bob Hawke*, pp. 619–21; McMullin, *The Light on the Hill*, p. 424; see also Marr, *The Ivanov Trail*.
19  Ibid.

**CHAPTER NINE: 1983**

1   As a narcissist, Hawke was sensitive about his height, even though it was about average for an Australian male of his age. He was apt to claim himself to be taller than he was. His passport to Oxford in 1952 had him as five foot ten inches, about three inches taller than his real height. Twenty years later, as president of the ACTU, a new passport had him half an inch taller at five foot ten and a half inches. When metric measurements were introduced, he said that he was 179 centimetres, which was six centimetres taller than his real height. Day, *Young Hawke*, p. 125; Hawke's passports are held in RH44, BHPML.
2   Hawke, *The Hawke Memoirs*, pp. 209–10; Transcript of a press conference by Hawke in Geneva, 10 June 1983, BHPML.
3   Hawke, *The Hawke Memoirs*, p. 205.
4   Hawke, *The Hawke Memoirs*, pp. 208–12; Transcript of Hawke's address to the Washington Press Club, 15 June 1983, pmtranscripts.pmc.gov.au/release/transcript-6136.
5   Transcript of Hawke's address to the Washington Press Club, 15 June 1983, pmtranscripts.pmc.gov.au/release/transcript-6136; *Age*, 20 June 1983; Hawke, *The Hawke Memoirs*, pp. 203–205; Kelly, *The End of Certainty*, p. 71.
6   David Day, 'Dr H.V. Evatt and the Search for a Sub-empire in the Southwest Pacific', in David Day (ed.), *Brave New World: Dr H.V. Evatt and Australian Foreign Policy*, University of Queensland Press, Brisbane, 1996, pp. 47–61.

7   Hawke, *The Hawke Memoirs*, pp. 339–44; Speech by Hawke at lunch for Zhao Ziyang, 18 April 1983, pmtranscripts.pmc.gov.au/sites/default/files/original/00006089.pdf; *Bulletin*, 26 April 1983; Author interview with Ross Garnaut.
8   Address by Hawke at the National Press Club, 27 June 1983, MSS 5095/117/2014, ML.
9   Walsh, *Confessions of a Failed Finance Minister*, chapter 7; Ryan, *Catching the Wave*, p. 216.
10  Author interview with John Dawkins; Author interview with Ralph Willis; Author interview with Neal Blewett; Author interview with Kim Beazley; Ryan, *Catching the Waves*, p. 216; Evans, *Incorrigible Optimist*, pp. 332–33.
11  Neal Blewett, 'The Hawke Cabinets' in Ryan and Bramston (eds), *The Hawke Government*, pp. 73–87.
12  Kelly, *The End of Certainty*, pp. 76–87; Hawke, *The Hawke Memoirs*, pp. 234–51; Edwards, *Keating*, pp. 216–24; Author interview with Bob Hawke; Author interview with Ross Garnaut; Author interview with John Dawkins.
13  Edwards, *Keating*, chapter 7; O'Brien, *Keating*, pp. 145–55; Walsh, *Confessions of a Failed Finance Minister*, pp. 98–99; Hawke, *The Hawke Memoirs*, pp. 238–49; Kelly, *The End of Certainty*, chapter 4.
14  Ibid.

**CHAPTER TEN: 1984**

1   Paul Barry, *The Rise and Fall of Alan Bond*, Bantam Books, Sydney, 1990, pp. 62–64, 118, 126–39; Bongiorno, *The Eighties*, pp. 33–40; D'Alpuget, *Bob Hawke*, pp. 622–23; Bramston, *Bob Hawke*, pp. 316–18; Peter Walsh, *Errors and Achievements: Economic Policy in the 1980s*, Shann Memorial Lecture, University of Western Australia, October 1991.
2   Bongiorno, *The Eighties*, pp. 33–40; D'Alpuget, *Bob Hawke*, pp. 622–23; Bramston, *Bob Hawke*, pp. 316–18; *Canberra Times*, 28 September 1983.
3   *Canberra Times*, 5 and 9 November 1983.
4   Hawke, *The Hawke Memoirs*, pp. 440–41; Di Yerbury, 'Arts Policy and Cultural Identity', in Ryan and Bramston, *The Hawke Government*, p. 255; Speech by Hawke to the Sports Writers' Annual Dinner, 29 July 1983, pmtranscripts.pmc.gov.au/sites/default/files/original/00006164.pdf; *Canberra Times*, 11 and 12 December 1983.
5   *Bulletin*, 2 August 1983.
6   *Canberra Times*, 20 October, 17 November 1983; *Bulletin*, 2 August 1983; Hansard, 10, 16 and 17 November 1983.
7   Weller, *Dodging Raindrops*, pp. 155–62, 169–71; John Button, 'Employment and Industry', in Ryan and Bramston, *The Hawke Government*, pp. 158–69; Hawke, *The Hawke Memoirs*, p. 166; Author interview with Barry Jones.
8   Tom Uren, *Straight Left*, Random House, Sydney, 1994, pp. 359–61; O'Brien, *Keating*, pp. 170–81.
9   Edwards, *Keating*, pp. 231–32, 250–51; O'Brien, *Keating*, pp. 177–78.
10  Curiously, Hawke made scant reference to Medicare in his otherwise voluminous memoirs. See Hawke, *The Hawke Memoirs*, pp. 176, 475; Stephen Duckett, 'Making a Difference in Health Care', in Ryan & Bramston (eds), *The Hawke Government*, pp. 215–24; Bramston, *Bob Hawke*, pp. 320–21.
11  Ryan, *Catching the Waves*, pp. 200–01, 211–13, 242–43; Hawke, *The Hawke Memoirs*, p. 409; Anne Summers, *Damned Whores and God's Police* (revised edition), Penguin, Melbourne, 2002, p. 9; For Summers' experience as head of the OSW, see Summers, *Unfettered and Alive*, chapter 5.
12  Ibid.
13  Ibid.
14  Hawke, *The Hawke Memoirs*, p. 409; Summers, *Damned Whores and God's Police*, p. 7; Summers, *Unfettered and Alive*, pp. 152, 158; Ryan, *Catching the Waves*, pp. 211–13; Pieters-Hawke, *Hazel*, p. 102; D'Alpuget, *Robert J. Hawke*, p. 198; *National Times*, 8–14 July 1983.
15  Scott, *Gareth Evans*, pp. 148–69; Evans, *Incorrigible Optimist*, pp. 32–33; Uren, *Straight Left*, pp. 366–67; *National Times*, 29 March–4 April 1985.

16    O'Brien, *Keating*, pp. 168–69; Richardson, *Whatever It Takes*, pp. 163–67; Hawke, *The Hawke Memoirs*, pp. 260–63; *Canberra Times*, 6 March 1983.

**CHAPTER ELEVEN: 1984**
1     Hawke, *The Hawke Memoirs*, pp. 260–61.
2     *Guardian*, 14 and 15 September 2017; *Age*, 2 February 1984 and 2 February 2024.
3     Jenny Hocking, *Lionel Murphy: A Political Biography*, Cambridge University Press, Melbourne, chapter 19; Bongiorno, *The Eighties*, pp. 100–04; McMullin, *The Light on the Hill*, pp. 429–30; Hawke, *The Hawke Memoirs*, pp. 266–8; John Howard, *Lazarus Rising: A Personal and Political Autobiography*, HarperCollins, Sydney, 2010, p. 154; Marian Wilkinson, *The Fixer: The Untold Story of Graham Richardson*, William Heinemann, Melbourne, 1996, pp. 240–41; Evans, *Incorrigible Optimist*, pp. 29–32; *Sydney Morning Herald*, 23 July 2017; David Wilson and Lindsay Murdoch, *Big Shots: A Who's Who in Australian Crime*, Sun Books, Melbourne, 1985, chapters 11 and 12; Bob Bottom, *Bugged!*, Macmillan, Melbourne, 1989, chapter 4; *Sydney Morning Herald*, 17 June 1989; *Guardian*, 15 September 2017; *National Times*, 25 November–1 December 1983, 27 July–2 August and 31 August–6 September 1984; see also Stephen Walmsley, *The Trials of Justice Murphy*, LexusNexus, Sydney, 2017.
4     Wilkinson, *The Fixer*, pp. 234–40; Steketee and Cockburn, *Wran*, chapter 14; Bob Bottom, *The Godfather in Australia*, Magistra Publishing, Melbourne, 1979, pp. 33, 163–79; Bob Bottom, *Without Fear or Favour*, Sun Books, Melbourne, 1984, chapter 10, pp. 150–52; Bob Bottom, *Connections II: Crime Rackets and Networks of Influence in Australia*, Macmillan, Melbourne, 1987, pp. 112–13; David Wilson, *Big Shots II*, Macmillan, Melbourne, 1987, pp. 46–59; K.S. Inglis, *Whose ABC?: The Australian Broadcasting Corporation, 1983–2006*, Black Inc., Melbourne, 2006, pp. 18–28; *National Times*, 1–7 July, 7–13 October 1983 and 3–9 August 1984.
5     Author interview with Phillip Adams.
6     Rodney Tiffen, 'Was Neville Wran Corrupt?', *Inside Story*, 31 August 2021. Several defences of Wran have been made, the most recent being by a former staffer, Milton Cockburn in *The Assassination of Neville Wran*, Connor Court Publishing, Brisbane, 2024.
7     Steketee and Cockburn, *Wran*, chapter 14; *National Times*, 1–7 July and 7–13 October 1983.
8     *National Times*, 9–15 March.
9     Bottom, *The Godfather in Australia*, pp. 77–81; *Age*, 17 and 18 November 1983; File on Salvatore Amarena, Released under the US John F. Kennedy Assassination Records Collection Act, /upload.wikimedia.org; *Canberra Times*, 18 November 1983; *National Times*, 18–24 November 1983, 17–23 February, 7–13 September 1984 and 20–26 September 1985; *Eye*, August 1987.
10    *National Times*, 18–24 November 1983, 17–23 February, 7–13 September 1984 and 20–26 September 1985; *Eye*, August 1987.
11    Bongiorno, *The Eighties*, pp. 95–105; Alfred W. McCoy, *Drug Traffic: Narcotics and Organised Crime in Australia*, Harper & Row, Sydney, 1980; Bottom, *The Godfather in Australia*, p. 11; Bob Bottom, *Shadow of Shame: How the Mafia Got Away with the Murder of Donald Mackay*, Sun Books, Melbourne, 1988; Bob Bottom, *Fighting Organised Crime: Triumph and Betrayal in a Lifelong Campaign*, BBP, Nelson Bay, 2009, pp. 5–17, 163–64; Bob Bottom, *Without Fear or Favour*, Sun Books, Melbourne, 1984, pp. 163–64; Wilson and Murdoch, *Big Shots*, p. 5; Bramston, *Bob Hawke*, pp. 329–30; Alan Saffron, *Gentle Satan: My Father*, Abe Saffron, Penguin, Melbourne, 2008, p. 99; Paul Barry, *The Rise and Rise of Kerry Packer*, ABC Books, Sydney, 1993, chapters. 12–15; *National Times*, 3–9 August, 21–27 September 1984.
12    Ibid.
13    Ibid.
14    Bottom, *The Godfather in Australia*, p. 11.
15    *Canberra Times*, 28 September 1984.
16    Hansard, 13 September 1984.

17  Hansard, 17 November 1983; 'Hawke and Sir Peter Abeles', note by D'Alpuget, 2 September 1982, MS 7348/2/12, D'Alpuget Papers, NLA.
18  Hawke, *The Hawke Memoirs*, pp. 268–70; Bramston, *Bob Hawke*, pp. 329–30; Hansard, 13 September and 2 October 1984; Author interview with Geoff Walsh.
19  *National Times*, 31 August–6 September, 26 October–1 November 1984 and 26 April–2 May 1985; *Canberra Times*, 1 May and 2 October 1985.
20  Hazel Hawke, *My Own Life*, p. 166; Pieters-Hawke, *Hazel*, pp. 242–43; Bramston, *Bob Hawke*, p. 328; Hawke, *The Hawke Memoirs*, pp. 263–65.
21  O'Brien, *Keating*, pp. 202–03; Day, *Keating*, pp. 245–46; Hawke, *The Hawke Memoirs*, pp. 277–78; Hazel Hawke, *My Own Life*, p. 170; Pieters-Hawke, *Hazel*, pp. 242–45; D'Alpuget, *Bob Hawke*, p. 657; Claire Dan, *Ups and Downs*, Books and Writers, Sydney, 2008, p. 200; Author interview with Kim Beazley; Author interview with Gareth Evans; Author interview with Ross Garnaut.
22  Jill Margo, *Frank Lowy*, HarperCollins, Sydney, 2000, p. 199.
23  Hawke, *The Hawke Memoirs*, p. 272.
24  Hawke, *The Hawke Memoirs*, pp. 270–73; Pieters-Hawke, *Hazel*, pp. 242–43; Hazel Hawke, *My Own Life*, pp. 166–67; Kelly, *The End of Certainty*, pp. 140–41; D'Alpuget, *Bob Hawke*, pp. 650–57; *Weekend Australian*, 19–20 March 2022.
25  Hawke, *The Hawke Memoirs*, pp. 270–73; Pieters-Hawke, *Hazel*, pp. 242–43; Hazel Hawke, *My Own Life*, pp. 166–67; Author interview with Geoff Walsh.
26  Hawke, *The Hawke Memoirs*, p. 274.
27  Richardson, *Whatever It Takes*, pp. 163, 167; Hawke, *The Hawke Memoirs*, p. 274; D'Alpuget, *Bob Hawke*, pp. 656–57.
28  Hawke, *The Hawke Memoirs*, pp. 274–75; D'Alpuget, *Bob Hawke*, pp. 659–60; Author interview with Graham Evans.
29  Howard, *Lazarus Rising*, p. 146; Richardson, *Whatever It Takes*, pp. 164–67; D'Alpuget, *Bob Hawke*, pp. 659–62.
30  Richardson, *Whatever It Takes*, pp. 168–69; Hawke, *The Hawke Memoirs*, pp. 298–99; D'Alpuget, *Bob Hawke*, pp. 658–59.
31  O'Brien, *Keating*, pp. 201–06; Walsh, *Confessions of a Failed Finance Minister*, p. 126.
32  Campaign speech by Hawke, 13 November 1984, electionspeeches.moadoph.gov.au/speeches/1984-bob-hawke; Kelly, *The End of Certainty*, pp. 140–48.
33  Hawke's campaign speech, 13 November 1984, and Peacock's campaign speech, 15 November 1984, electionspeeches.moadoph.gov.au/speeches/1984-andrew-peacock; Stan Anson, 'The Rhetorical Uses of John Curtin', *Journal of Australian Studies*, Vol. 10, No. 19.
34  Richardson, *Whatever It Takes*, p. 168.
35  O'Brien, *Keating*, pp. 204–05.
36  Hawke, *The Hawke Memoirs*, pp. 276–77.
37  Great Debate between Bob Hawke and Andrew Peacock at the National Press Club on 26 November 1984, ORAL TRC 1709, NLA; Rodney Smith, 'David Paul Landa', *ADB*, Vol. 18, 2012.
38  Ibid.
39  Great Debate between Bob Hawke and Andrew Peacock at the National Press Club on 26 November 1984, ORAL TRC 1709, NLA.
40  Ibid.
41  Letter, Hawke to H.A.Caplan, manager of the Boulevard Hotel, 23 February 1982, RH73, Personal Correspondence [October–December 1981], BHPML; Great Debate between Bob Hawke and Andrew Peacock at the National Press Club on 26 November 1984, ORAL TRC 1709, NLA.
42  Great Debate between Bob Hawke and Andrew Peacock at the National Press Club on 26 November 1984, ORAL TRC 1709, NLA; Wilson and Murdoch, *Big Shots*, chapters 15–16; Bottom, *Without Fear or Favour*, pp. 163–64; Bob Bottom, *Inside Victoria: A Chronicle of Scandal*, Pan Macmillan, Sydney, 1991, p. 61; Kevin Perkins, *Bristow: Last of the Hard Men*, Bonmoat, Sydney, 2003, p. 216; *National Times*, 11–17 November 1983; Hawke had first met Bristow in 1979, when he and journalist George Negus had gone with Bristow on a drinking spree. See *National Times*, 22–28 March 1985.

| | |
|---|---|
| 43 | Hansard, 3 April 1984; *National Times*, 23–29 September 1984; *Canberra Times*, 6 and 10 October 1984; *Age*, 10 October and 28 November 1984. I am grateful to Paul Wray-McCann for bringing some of these details to my attention. |
| 44 | Ibid. |
| 45 | *Canberra Times*, 27 November 1984; *Sydney Morning Herald*, 27 November 1984. |
| 46 | '1984 Federal Election Count', www.youtube.com/watch?v=l4ONodM7Lgc, www.youtube.com/watch?v=G-Jph0M3_9o; Andrew Peacock's Concession Speech, 1 December 1984, www.youtube.com/watch?v=G-Jph0M3_9o; Hawke, *The Hawke Memoirs*, pp. 275–76; Howard, *Lazarus Rising*, pp. 145–46; D'Alpuget, *Bob Hawke*, p. 662; Author interview with Graham Freudenberg. |
| 47 | Ibid. |

## CHAPTER TWELVE: 1984–1985

| | |
|---|---|
| 1 | Uren, *Straight Left*, p. 367; Hawke, *The Hawke Memoirs*, pp. 275–76; Kelly, *The End of Certainty*, pp. 149–52. |
| 2 | Ibid. |
| 3 | Richardson, *Whatever It Takes*, p. 170; Hawke, *The Hawke Memoirs*, pp. 275–76; Howard, *Lazarus Rising*, pp. 147–48; McMullin, *The Light on the Hill*, p. 425; D'Alpuget, *Bob Hawke*, pp. 666–67; Gareth Evans, *Inside the Hawke Keating Government: A Cabinet Diary*, Melbourne University Press, Melbourne, 2014, pp. 48–50; Kelly, *The End of Certainty*, p. 159; Hayden, *Hayden*, pp. 413–15; *National Times*, 1–7 and 8–14 February 1985. |
| 4 | Richardson, *Whatever It Takes*, chapter 8. |
| 5 | Richardson, *Whatever It Takes*, chapter 8; Hawke, *The Hawke Memoirs*, pp. 286–92; D'Alpuget, *Bob Hawke*, pp. 663–77; Evans, *Inside the Hawke Keating Government*, pp. 54–55; Edwards, *Keating*, p. 259; Weller, *Dodging Raindrops*, pp. 188–89; Hayden, *Hayden*, pp. 412–16. |
| 6 | Hawke, *The Hawke Memoirs*, pp. 286–92; Evans, *Inside the Hawke Keating Government*, pp. 54–55. |
| 7 | Hawke, *The Hawke Memoirs*, pp. 288–91; Evans, *Inside the Hawke Keating Government*, pp. 58–60: D'Alpuget, *Bob Hawke*, p. 671; Bramston, *Bob Hawke*, pp. 342–43. |
| 8 | Ibid. |
| 9 | Ibid. |
| 10 | Evans, *Inside the Hawke Keating Government*, pp. 99–100. |
| 11 | Bramston, *Bob Hawke*, pp. 346–49; Hawke, *The Hawke Memoirs*, pp. 340–47; D'Alpuget, *Bob Hawke*, pp. 684–97. |
| 12 | Hawke, *The Hawke Memoirs*, chapter 19; O'Brien, *Keating*, pp. 206–209; Edwards, *Keating*, pp. 265–70; Kelly, *The End of Certainty*, chapter 9. |
| 13 | O'Brien, *Keating*, pp. 211–19; Uren, *Straight Left*, pp. 374–75; Kelly, *The End of Certainty*, chapter 9; Bramston, *Bob Hawke*, pp. 360–65; Edwards, *Keating*, pp. 265–75: *The Age*, 29 May 2010. |
| 14 | Ibid. |
| 15 | Ibid. |
| 16 | Ibid. |
| 17 | Walsh, *Confessions of a Failed Finance Minister*, pp. 145–46; Kelly, *The End of Certainty*, chapter 9. |
| 18 | Evans, *Inside the Hawke Keating Government*, pp. 112–13; Kelly, *The End of Certainty*, chapter 9. |
| 19 | Richardson, *Whatever It Takes*, p. 176; Edwards, *Keating*, pp. 274–75; Hawke, *The Hawke Memoirs*, p. 305; Evans, *Inside the Hawke Keating Government*, pp. 112–13; Author interview with Graham Freudenberg. |
| 20 | Edwards, *Keating*, pp. 270–71; Hawke, *The Hawke Memoirs*, pp. 307–14; Walsh, *Confessions of a Failed Finance Minister*, pp. 145–46; Bramston, *Bob Hawke*, pp. 362–64; Kelly, *The End of Certainty*, chapter 9; '1985 Tax Summit', *Sunday*, Channel Nine, NFSA. |
| 21 | Hawke, *The Hawke Memoirs*, pp. 306–14; Kelly, *The End of Certainty*, chapter 9. |

22  O'Brien, *Keating*, pp. 218–21; Hawke, *The Hawke Memoirs*, pp. 306–14; Kelly, *The End of Certainty*, pp. 168–73; Richardson, *Whatever It Takes*, pp. 180–82; Weller, *Dodging Raindrops*, p. 189; Author interview with Phillip Adams.
23  'Closing Remarks – National Taxation Summit – 4 July 1985'; Evans, *Inside the Hawke Keating Government*, pp. 142–43, 155; Richardson, *Whatever It Takes*, p. 182; O'Brien, *Keating*, pp. 215–22; Bramston, *Bob Hawke*, pp. 363–64; Kelly, *The End of Certainty*, pp. 172–73.
24  'Closing Remarks – National Taxation Summit – 4 July 1985'; Evans, *Inside the Hawke-Keating Government*, pp. 142–43, 155.
25  Richardson, *Whatever It Takes*, p. 182; O'Brien, *Keating*, pp. 215–22; Bramston, *Bob Hawke*, pp. 363–64; Kelly, *The End of Certainty*, pp. 172–73.
26  Evans, *Inside the Hawke Keating Government*, pp. 152–53; 223–24; Liz Ross, *Dare to Struggle, Dare to Win!*, Vulgar Press, Melbourne, 2004.
27  Ibid; For details about Saffron's corruption of political and police officials, see Tony Reeves, *Mr Sin: [The Abe Saffron Dossier]*, Allen & Unwin, Sydney, 2007; Saffron, *Gentle Satan*; and Bottom, *Connections II*.
28  Evans, *Inside the Hawke Keating Government*, pp. 152–56; Saffron, *Gentle Satan*, pp. 110–11, 214–20; Don Stewart, *Recollections of an Unreasonable Man*, ABC Books, Sydney, 2007, pp. 194–95; Bottom, *Bugged!*, p. 116; Roberta Sykes, *Snake Dancing*, Allen & Unwin, Sydney, 1998, pp. 53–55; Author interview with Ralph Willis.
29  Evans, *Inside the Hawke Keating Government*, pp. 152–56; Saffron, *Gentle Satan*, pp. 110–11, 214–20; Stewart, *Recollections of an Unreasonable Man*, pp. 194–95; Bottom, *Bugged!*, p. 116.
30  Evans, *Inside the Hawke Keating Government*, pp. 223–24.

**CHAPTER THIRTEEN: 1986**

1  In January 1986, Evans was told by businessman Robert Holmes à Court, who'd been defeated by Abeles in his bid for Ansett Transport Industries, that 'Kerry Packer and Peter Abeles were just plain crooks, although not necessarily the "Mr Bigs" they were sometimes alleged to be'. Diary entry, 6 January 1986, Evans, *Inside the Hawke Keating Government*, pp. 248–49; Walsh, *Confessions of a Failed Finance Minister*, pp. 165–66.
2  Diary entry, 20 August 1985, Evans, *Inside the Hawke Keating Government*, pp. 172–73.
3  Evans, *Inside the Hawke Keating Government*, pp. 172–73; Walsh, *Confessions of a Failed Finance Minister*, pp. 165–66.
4  Howard, *Lazarus Rising*, pp. 149–52; Kelly, *The End of Certainty*, chapter 10.
5  Hawke, *The Hawke Memoirs*, pp. 367–69; Day, *Keating*, pp. 282–83; Kelly, *The End of Certainty*, chapter 11.
6  Ibid.
7  O'Brien, *Keating*, pp. 233–50; Hawke, *The Hawke Memoirs*, pp. 369–75; Richardson, *Whatever It Takes*, pp. 199–200.
8  Ibid.
9  Ibid; Author interview with Ross Garnaut.
10  Craig Emerson, *The Boy from Baradine*, Scribe, Melbourne, 2018, pp. 113–18; Kelly, *The End of Certainty*, chapter 11; Bramston, *Bob Hawke*, pp. 367–71.
11  Howard, *Lazarus Rising*, p. 153.
12  Emerson, *The Boy from Baradine*, pp. 113–18; Kelly, *The End of Certainty*, chapter 11; Bramston, *Bob Hawke*, pp. 367–71.
13  Emerson, *The Boy from Baradine*, pp. 114–15; Hawke, *The Hawke Memoirs*, pp. 375–85; Peter Walsh, 'Errors and Achievements: Economic Policy in the 1980s', Shann Memorial Lecture, University of Western Australia, October 1991, pp. 7–10; Kelly, *The End of Certainty*, pp. 211–27; Bramston, *Bob Hawke*, pp. 369–70.
14  Ibid.
15  Barry, *The Rise and Fall of Alan Bond*, pp. 142–58; Walsh, *Confessions of a Failed Finance Minister*, p. 89.
16  Ibid; Kelly, *The End of Certainty*, p. 344.

17 Ibid.
18 Evans, *Inside the Hawke Keating Government*, pp. 378–79; John Pilger, *A Secret Country*, Jonathon Cape, London, 1989, chapter 6; Margo, *Frank Lowy*, pp. 197–99; Barry, *The Rise and Fall of Alan Bond*, pp. 142–58; *Eye*, July 1987.
19 Ibid.
20 Weller, *Dodging Raindrops*, p. 189; see also Paul Chadwick, *Media Mates: Carving Up Australia's Media*, Sun Books, Melbourne, 1989.
21 O'Brien, *Keating*, pp. 266–86; Weller, *Dodging Raindrops*, p. 189; William Shawcross, *Rupert Murdoch*, Random House, Sydney, 1992, pp. 360–70; Barry, *The Rise and Rise of Kerry Packer*, chapter 16; see also Chadwick, *Media Mates*.
22 O'Brien, *Keating*, pp. 266–86; Weller, *Dodging Raindrops*, p. 189; Shawcross, *Rupert Murdoch*, pp. 360–70; Barry, *The Rise and Rise of Kerry Packer*, chapter 16; see also Chadwick, *Media Mates*.
23 Shawcross, *Rupert Murdoch*, pp. 360–70; Colleen Ryan, *Fairfax: The Rise and Fall*, Miegunyah Press, Melbourne, 2013, pp. 51–55; Pilger, *A Secret Country*, pp. 206–13; John Menadue, *Things You Learn Along the Way*, David Lovell Publishing, Melbourne, 1999, pp. 116–19; Margo, *Frank Lowy*, pp. 209–10; *Australian Financial Review*, 31 July 1992.
24 Alan Ramsey, *The Way They Were*, NewSouth, Sydney, 2011, pp. 53–54, 72–76; Barry, *The Rise and Rise of Kerry Packer*, pp. 367–68, 412–14; Pilger, *A Secret Country*, pp. 213–17.
25 Ibid.
26 *Sydney Morning Herald*, 23 July 2017.
27 Hocking, *Lionel Murphy*, chapter 20.
28 Ibid.
29 Evans, *Inside the Hawke Keating Government*, pp. 356–68; Hocking, *Lionel Murphy*, chapter 20; Stephen Charles, 'The Murphy Papers: The Parliamentary Commission of Inquiry', Samuel Griffith Society Proceedings, 2018; *Sydney Morning Herald*, 6 March 2021.
30 Ibid.
31 After his death, Murphy had many defenders who questioned the legality and veracity of the *Age* tapes and extolled his work as a senator and judge. See Jocelynne Scutt (ed.), *Lionel Murphy: A Radical Judge*, McCulloch Publishing, Melbourne, 1987. For a detailed analysis of the corruption linking Murphy, Wran, Ryan, Farquhar, Foord, Saffron, Murray Wood and others, see Clarrie Briese, *Corruption in High Places*, Noble Books, Sydney, 2021; Kevin Perkins, *The Gambling Man*, Polynesian Press, Nuku'alofa, Tonga, 1990, pp. 338–39; *Sydney Morning Herald*, 23 July 2017; *National Times*, 8–14 June, 27 July–2 August, 3–9 August and 17–23 August 1984; *Canberra Times*, 13 March 1987.
32 The allegations and the supporting documentation considered by the parliamentary inquiry have now been released and can be viewed on the federal parliamentary website. George Negus, 4th Lionel Murphy Memorial Lecture, 13 November 1990; Hawke, *The Hawke Memoirs*, pp. 266–68; *National Times*, 20–26 September 1985.
33 Ibid.
34 The forty-one allegations that were partially investigated by the commission were revealed in 2017. *Guardian*, 14 September 2017; *Sydney Morning Herald*, 14 September 2017.
35 When the commission's allegations concerning Packer were published in *The National Times*, Packer rejected all of them and claimed there was a conspiracy between Costigan and the Fairfax press. He dismissed *The National Times* as 'a disgusting publication'. In response, Costigan rejected all of Packer's objections. See Evan Whitton, *Can of Worms: A Citizen's Reference Book to Crime and the Administration of Justice*, Fairfax Library, Sydney, 1986, pp. 194–95; Reeves, *Mr Sin: [The Abe Saffron Dossier]*, Allen & Unwin, Sydney, 2007, pp. 157–58; Bottom, *Fighting Organised Crime*, pp. 20–28, 41–44; *Sydney Morning Herald*, 22 October 1986 and 6 March 2021; *Age*, 20 May 2023; *National Times*, 8–14 June, 14–20 and 21–27 September, 5–11 October, 2–8 November and 9–15 November 1984.
36 Ibid.

37  Wilson, *Big Shots II*, pp. 38, 146–47; Bob Bottom, *Bugged!*, pp. 147–50; Wilkinson, *The Fixer*, chapter 15; Reeves, *Mr Sin*, pp. 210–11. Books on organised crime and corruption in the mid-1980s include Bob Bottom, *Without Fear or Favour*; Richard Hall, *Disorganised Crime*, University of Queensland Press, Brisbane, 1986; David Hickie, *The Prince and the Premier*, Angus & Robertson, Sydney, 1985; Jonathan Kwitny, *The Crimes of Patriots: A True Tale of Dope, Dirty Money, and the CIA*, Simon & Schuster, New York, 1987; Whitton, *Can of Worms*; Evan Whitton, *Can of Worms II: A Citizen's Reference Book to Crime and the Administration of Justice*, Fairfax Library, Sydney, 1987; Wilson and Murdoch, *Big Shots. National Times*, 19–25 October 1984.
38  Whitton, *Can of Worms II*, pp. 142–43; Steketee and Cockburn, *Wran*, pp. 254, 289–91; Gavin Souter, *Heralds and Angels: The House of Fairfax, 1841–1990*, Melbourne University Press, Melbourne, 1991, pp. 148–49; Perkins, *The Gambling Man*, pp. 338–39; Bob Bottom, *Connections II*, pp. 112–13; Bottom, *Fighting Organised Crime*, pp. 29–38; *National Times*, 11–17 July 1982, 9–15 March, 13–19 April, 20–26 July and 24–30 August 1984, 29 March–4 April 1985; *Tharunka*, 2 October 1990.
39  Ibid.
40  Ibid.; Dan, *Ups and Downs*, p. 249.
41  *Canberra Times*, 24 February and 18 May 1988.
42  *National Times*, 6–12 July 1984.
43  The interview with Carleton can be seen at www.youtube.com/watch?v=L1aDvcP7-dw.
44  Inglis, *Whose ABC?*, pp. 16–38.
45  A detailed account of the Humphreys case can be found in Whitton, *Can of Worms II*; Inglis, *Whose ABC?*, pp. 16–38; *National Times*, 4–10 May 1984, 15–21 March, 29 March–4 April and 14–20 June 1985; *Sydney Morning Herald*, 24 April 2014 and 28 January 2021.
46  Whitton, *Can of Worms*, pp. 13, 38–39, 87–88, 165–99, 245; Whitton, *Can of Worms II*, p. 139; Inglis, *Whose ABC?*, pp. 124–29; Gillian Appleton, *Diamond Cuts*, Macmillan, Sydney, 2000, pp. 211–31; Evans, *Inside the Hawke Keating Government*, pp. 69–71; *National Times*, 10–16 August and 21–27 September 1984; *Sydney Morning Herald*, 22 May 2015; *Australian Financial Review*, 18 July 2024.
47  Ibid.
48  Inglis, *Whose ABC?*, pp. 126–29, 155; *National Times*, 4–10 May 1984.
49  Ibid.
50  Ibid.
51  Wendy McCarthy, *Don't Be Too Polite, Girls*, Allen & Unwin, Sydney, 2022, pp. 221–26; Geoffrey Whitehead, *Inside the ABC*, Penguin, Melbourne, 1988, chapter 13; Inglis, *Whose ABC?*, pp. 132–49; Clement Semmler, 'The Wasting of Whitehead: Inside the ABC', *Quadrant*, 1 March 1989; *Australian Financial Review*, 6 November 1986.
52  Ibid.

**CHAPTER FOURTEEN: 1987**

1  *Times on Sunday*, 18 January 1987.
2  Hawke, *The Hawke Memoirs*, pp. 437–38; Hazel Hawke, *My Own Life*, p. 183.
3  *New Idea*, 24 January 1987.
4  Stephen Mills, *The Hawke Years: The Story from Inside*, Viking, Melbourne, 1993, pp. 97–98; Hawke, *The Hawke Memoirs*, pp. 437–43; D'Alpuget, *Bob Hawke*, p. 701; Emerson, *The Boy from Baradine*, pp. 139–43.
5  O'Brien, *Keating*, pp. 305–06; Mills, *The Hawke Years*, pp. 97–98; Howard, *Lazarus Rising*, chapter 16; Richardson, *Whatever It Takes*, pp. 200–03; Hawke, *The Hawke Memoirs*, pp. 437–43; D'Alpuget, *Bob Hawke*, p. 701; Emerson, *The Boy from Baradine*, pp. 139–43; Phil Dickie, *The Road to Fitzgerald: Revelations of Corruption Spanning Four Decades*, University of Queensland Press, Brisbane, 1988, pp. 131–32.
6  Howard, *Lazarus Rising*, chapter 16; Kelly, *The End of Certainty*, chapters 15–16.
7  Ibid.
8  Howard, *Lazarus Rising*, chapter 16; D'Alpuget, *Bob Hawke*, chapter 24; Kelly, *The End of Certainty*, chapters 15–16; O'Brien, *Keating*, p. 186.

| | |
|---|---|
| 9 | Richardson, *Whatever It Takes*, pp. 200–03; Hawke, *The Hawke Memoirs*, pp. 387–89; Blanche D'Alpuget, *Bob Hawke*, chapter 24; Howard, *Lazarus Rising*, chapter 16; O'Brien, *Keating*, pp. 186–87, 289–90. |
| 10 | Inglis, *Whose ABC?*, pp. 213–16; John Pilger, *A Secret Country*, Jonathan Cape, London, 1989, pp. 218–25; *Australian Financial Review*, 3 November 1989; *Canberra Times*, 9 March and 13 April 1987; *The Journalist*, June/July 1987. |
| 11 | Ibid. |
| 12 | Ibid. |
| 13 | Mills, *The Hawke Years*, pp. 99–102. |
| 14 | Ibid. |
| 15 | Ibid. |
| 16 | Neil Chenoweth, *Rupert Murdoch: The Untold Story of the World's Greatest Media Wizard*, Random House, New York, 2001, p. 88; Author interview with Graham Freudenberg. |
| 17 | Hawke, *The Hawke Memoirs*, pp. 387–88; D'Alpuget, *Bob Hawke*, p. 714; O'Brien, *Keating*, pp. 290–92, 298–300; Bramston, *Bob Hawke*, pp. 378–79. |
| 18 | Richardson, *Whatever It Takes*, p. 203; Hawke, *The Hawke Memoirs*, pp. 388–92; Author interview with Graham Freudenberg. |
| 19 | Howard, *Lazarus Rising*, p. 164; Hawke, *The Hawke Memoirs*, pp. 388–92; Emerson, *The Boy from Baradine*, pp. 148–49; O'Brien, *Keating*, pp. 298–301. |
| 20 | For details of the corruption among leading police, business and political figures, see Matthew Condon's trilogy: *Three Crooked Kings*, University of Queensland Press, Brisbane, 2013; *Jacks and Jokers*, University of Queensland Press, Brisbane, 2014; *All Fall Down*, University of Queensland Press, Brisbane, 2015. See also Phil Dickie, *The Road to Fitzgerald and Beyond*, University of Queensland Press, Brisbane, 1989, and Whitton, *Can of Worms II*. The *Four Corners* program 'The Moonlight State' can be found at www.abc.net.au/news/2011-08-08/the-moonlight-state---1987/2832198; Author interview with Chris Masters; Author interview with Nigel Powell; *Guardian*, 31 December 2017. |
| 21 | Kelly, *The End of Certainty*, chapter 17; Hawke, *The Hawke Memoirs*, pp. 192–93; Bramston, *Bob Hawke*, pp. 379–81; Frank Bongiorno, '1987: Labor Makes It Three', in Benjamin Jones, Frank Bongiorno and John Uhr (eds), *Elections Matters: Ten Federal Elections that Shaped Australia*, Monash University Publishing, Melbourne, 2018. |
| 22 | Richardson, *Whatever It Takes*, pp. 202–208; Howard, *Lazarus Rising*, pp. 165–69; Hawke, *The Hawke Memoirs*, chapter 23; Bongiorno, *The Eighties*, pp. 178–88. |
| 23 | Ibid. |
| 24 | Hawke, *The Hawke Memoirs*, pp. 398–402; Kelly, *The End of Certainty*, chapter 18; Richardson, *Whatever It Takes*, pp. 206–208; Emerson, *The Boy from Baradine*, pp. 150–51; Bongiorno, *The Eighties*, p. 188; *Lateline*, ABC Television, 6 June 2016. |
| 25 | Ibid. |
| 26 | Emerson, *The Boy from Baradine*, pp. 154–55; Bramston, *Bob Hawke*, pp. 383–84. |
| 27 | Bramston, *Bob Hawke*, pp. 383–84; Richardson, *Whatever It Takes*, p. 209; Hawke, *The Hawke Memoirs*, pp. 403–404; Emerson, *The Boy from Baradine*, pp. 154–55; Bob Hawke Election Speech, 23 June 1987, electionspeeches.moadoph.gov.au/speeches/1987-bob-hawke; *Sydney Morning Herald*, 23 and 24 June 1987; *Canberra Times*, 8 July 1987. |
| 28 | Hawke, *The Hawke Memoirs*, pp. 403–404; Speech by Hawke, 23 August 1987, pmtranscripts.pmc.gov.au/release/transcript-7207. |
| 29 | Mills, *The Hawke Years*, pp. 74–75; Hawke, *The Hawke Memoirs*, p. 496; Bongiorno, *The Eighties*, pp. 10–11, 146, 187; Kelly, *The End of Certainty*, p. 344; Bramston, *Bob Hawke*, pp. 709–10; Paul Barry, *The Rise and Rise of Kerry Packer*, pp. 479–80. |
| 30 | Ibid. |
| 31 | Richardson, *Whatever It Takes*, pp. 213–15 |
| 32 | Richardson, *Whatever It Takes*, chapter 13; Emerson, *The Boy from Baradine*, pp. 147–48; Hawke, *The Hawke Memoirs*, pp. 393–97; Mills, *The Hawke Years*, pp. 74–75; Kelly, *The End of Certainty*, pp. 353–54. |
| 33 | Ibid. |

34 Richardson, *Whatever It Takes*, pp. 209–10; Bongiorno, *The Eighties*, p. 187; Hawke, *The Hawke Memoirs*, pp. 401–04, 410–13; Bramston, *Bob Hawke*, pp. 383–86; Kelly, *The End of Certainty*, chapter 18.
35 *Eye*, July 1987; Author interview with Brian Toohey.
36 Richardson, *Whatever It Takes*, pp. 209–10; Bongiorno, *The Eighties*, p. 187; *Eye*, July 1987; Author interview with Brian Toohey.
37 Howard, *Lazarus Rising*, pp. 169–70; Hawke, *The Hawke Memoirs*, pp. 411–13; Emerson, *The Boy from Baradine*, pp. 160–61; Frank Bongiorno, '1987: Labor Makes It Three', in Jones, Bongiorno and Uhr (eds), *Elections Matters*; Ramsey, *The Way They Were*, p. 150; Hazel Hawke, *My Own Life*, pp. 188–99; *Times on Sunday*, 5 and 12 July 1987.
38 Ibid.
39 Hazel Hawke, *My Own Life*, pp. 188–99; *Times on Sunday*, 5 and 12 July 1987; *Canberra Times*, 15 July 1987; *Woman's Day*, 24 January 1987; Hawke's three-day Queensland sojourn on Lowy's yacht is listed in his statement of pecuniary interests for 1987. See documents in RH211, F9, BHPML.
40 Howard, *Lazarus Rising*, pp. 169–70; Hawke, *The Hawke Memoirs*, pp. 411–13; Bongiorno, '1987: Labor Makes It Three'; *Times on Sunday*, 5 and 12 July 1987; *Canberra Times*, 15 July 1987.
41 Hawke, *The Hawke Memoirs*, pp. 412–21; Weller, *Dodging Raindrops*, p. 207; O'Brien, *Keating*, pp. 321–25; Evans, *Incorrigible Optimist*, pp. 84–91.
42 Weller, *Dodging Raindrops*, p. 207.
43 Michelle Grattan (ed.), *Australian Prime Ministers*, New Holland, Sydney, 2000, p. 466; Hawke, *The Hawke Memoirs*, pp. 412–21; O'Brien, *Keating*, pp. 321–25; Evans, *Incorrigible Optimist*, pp. 84–91; *Times on Sunday*, 20 and 27 September 1987.
44 Ryan, *Catching the Waves*, pp. 226–27, 230–39, 256–60; Walsh, *Confessions of a Failed Finance Minister*, pp. 169–72; Bramston, *Bob Hawke*, p. 391; Evans, *Inside the Hawke Keating Government*, pp. 115, 118–20; Jim McMorrow, 'Education Policy', in Ryan and Bramston (eds), *The Hawke Government*, pp. 184–201.
45 Ibid.
46 Speech by Hawke at Victorian ALP Conference, 23 August 1987, pmtranscripts.pmc.gov.au/sites/default/files/original/00007207.pdf; Mills, *The Hawke Years*, pp. 70–74.
47 *Canberra Times*, 12 September 1987.
48 Ibid.
49 Evans, *Incorrigible Optimist*, pp. 85–86; Kelly, *The End of Certainty*, pp. 387–89; Anne Davies, 'Mates and Micro-Economic Reform', in Ryan and Bramston (eds), *The Hawke Government*, pp. 291–93.
50 John Williams, *The Fortunate Life of a Vindicatrix Boy*, self-published, 2005, pp. 136–38; Mills, *The Hawke Years*, pp. 106–07; Evans, *Incorrigible Optimist*, pp. 85–86; Chalmers, *Inside the Canberra Press Gallery*, p. 209; *Times on Sunday*, 30 August 1987.
51 Clement Semmler, *Pictures on the Margin: Memoirs*, University of Queensland Press, Brisbane, 1991, pp. 95–96, 119
52 Ken Inglis, *This Is the ABC*, Melbourne University Press, Melbourne, 1983, pp. 216–22; Inglis, *Whose ABC?*, pp. 128, 153–71; Evans, *Incorrigible Optimist*, pp. 91–93; 155, 387; Author interview with Marian Wilkinson; *Sydney Morning Herald*, 5 August 2006.
53 Ramsey, *The Way They Were*, pp. 99–103; Ken Inglis, *This Is the ABC*, Melbourne University Press, Melbourne, 1983, pp. 216–22; *Sydney Morning Herald*, 5 August 2006.
54 See Whitton, *Can of Worms II*; Jonathan Kwitny, *The Crimes of Patriots*.
55 Keith Jackson, '"No, I Won't Sell the ABC" – My Fondest Memory of Bob Hawke', www.pngattitude.com/2019/05/no-i-wont-sell-the-abc-my-fondest-memory-of-bob-hawke.html; 'Flying High', *Four Corners*, ABC Television, 2 November 1987; Author interview with Marian Wilkinson.

56 Ibid.
57 Souter, *Heralds and Angels*, pp. 163–64, 173–77; Evans, *Incorrigible Optimist*, pp. 92–93; Bongiorno, *The Eighties*, pp. 123–25; *Times on Sunday*, 20 December 1987 and 3 January 1988.
58 Ibid.
59 Ibid.
60 Kelly, *The End of Certainty*, pp. 363–67.
61 Emerson, *The Boy from Baradine*, pp. 163–64; Hawke, *The Hawke Memoirs*, p. 365; Walsh, *Confessions of a Failed Finance Minister*, pp. 183–84; Author interview with Laurie Oakes; *Times on Sunday*, 20 September 1987.
62 Barry, *The Rise and Fall of Alan Bond*, p. 289; Wilkinson, *The Fixer*, pp. 275–79; Walsh, *Confessions of a Failed Finance Minister*, p. 154; Bongiorno, *The Eighties*, chapter 9; O'Brien, *Keating*, pp. 341–47; Edwards, *Keating*, pp. 315–17; *Times on Sunday*, 9 August and 25 October 1987.
63 Hawke, *The Hawke Memoirs*, pp. 354–65; Rutland, *Lone Voice*, pp. 429–31; Emerson, *The Boy From Baradine*, pp. 165–67; *Times on Sunday*, 29 November and 1 December 1987.
64 Ibid.
65 Hawke, *The Hawke Memoirs*, pp. 357–65.
66 Kelly, *The End of Certainty*, p. 447.

**CHAPTER FIFTEEN: 1988**

1 McCarthy, *Don't Be Too Polite, Girls*, pp. 246–51; Hawke, *The Hawke Memoirs*, pp. 443–45; Hazel Hawke, *My Own Life*, pp. 192–93; *Border Mail*, 17 May 2019.
2 Ibid.
3 McKenna, *An Eye for Eternity*, pp. 618—20.
4 Barry, *The Rise and Fall of Alan Bond*, p. 289.
5 Hazel Hawke, *My Own Life*, pp. 194–95; Barry, *The Rise and Fall of Alan Bond*, p. 289.
6 Letter, Prince Charles to Hawke, 6 February 1988, RH211, F13, BHPML.
7 Bramston, *Bob Hawke*, pp. 468–71; Bongiorno, *The Eighties*, pp. 247–50.
8 McCarthy, *Don't Be Too Polite, Girls*, pp. 252–54; Hawke, *The Hawke Memoirs*, pp. 443–45; Bongiorno, *The Eighties*, pp. 240–47; Emerson, *The Boy from Baradine*, pp. 162–63; *Times on Sunday*, 17 and 24 January 1988.
9 Patrick Dodson, Martin Morbray and Warren Snowden, 'Promise, Confrontation and Compromise in Indigenous Affairs', in Ryan and Bramston (eds), *The Hawke Government*, pp. 296–310; Bramston, *Bob Hawke*, pp. 468–71.
10 Speech by Hawke, 9 May 1988, pmtranscripts.pmc.gov.au/release/transcript-7319; Mark McKenna, *An Eye for Eternity: The Life of Manning Clark*, Melbourne University Press, Melbourne, 2011, pp. 617–18; Dodson, Morbray and Snowden, 'Promise, Confrontation and Compromise in Indigenous Affairs', in Ryan and Bramston (eds), *The Hawke Government*, pp. 296–310.
11 Ibid.
12 Summers, *The End of Equality*, pp. 195, 206–207; Summers, *Unfettered and Alive*, pp. 155–59; Susan Ryan, 'Women's Policy', in Ryan and Bramston (eds), *The Hawke Government*, pp. 202–14; Hawke, *The Hawke Memoirs*, pp. 409–10.
13 Ibid.
14 Ryan, *Catching the Waves*, pp. 244–45; Summers, *The End of Equality*, pp. 206–207; Summers, *Unfettered and Alive*, pp. 155–59; Susan Ryan, 'Women's Policy', in Ryan and Bramston (eds), *The Hawke Government*, pp. 202–14; Anne Summers, *The Misogyny Factor*, NewSouth, Sydney, 2013, p. 37.
15 Ibid.
16 Ibid.
17 Ibid.
18 Dickie, *The Road to Fitzgerald and Beyond*, pp. 269–71; Bramston, *Bob Hawke*, p. 221; *Canberra Times*, 30 April, 8 May, 22 June and 12 August 1991.
19 Ibid.; David Day, *Young Hawke*, pp. 250–51; Bramston, *Bob Hawke*, p. 221; D'Alpuget, *Bob Hawke*, pp. 370–71.

20  Reeves, *Mr Sin*, pp. 205–07; Dickie, *The Road to Fitzgerald and Beyond*, pp. 269–71; Fitzgerald Report, www.cccinquiry.qld.gov.au, pp. 103–06; Brian Stevenson, 'Russell James (Russ) Hinze', ADB, Vol. 19, 2021; *Times on Sunday*, 6 and 13 March 1988; *Courier-Mail*, 12 February 2017; *Sydney Morning Herald*, 28 October 1988; *Age*, 4 March 1988; *Canberra Times*, 22 and 29 November 1988; *Australian Financial Review*, 29 November 1988; Hansard, 10 December 1987.
21  Kelly, *The End of Certainty*, pp. 437–48; Hawke, *The Hawke Memoirs*, pp. 445–50; Emerson, *The Boy From Baradine*, pp. 168–69; *Times on Sunday*, 14 and 28 February, 6 March 1988.
22  Ibid.
23  Ibid.
24  Lipski and Rutland, *Let My People Go*, pp. 1–2, 7–14; Rutland, *Lone Voice*, pp. 433–35, 439–40; Hawke, *The Hawke Memoirs*, pp. 354–66; Bramston, *Bob Hawke*, pp. 424–27; 'Celebration for Former Refuseniks, Melbourne, 17 May 1988', Speech by Hawke, pmtranscripts.pmc.gov.au/sites/default/files/original/00007322.pdf; David Day, *Conquest: How Societies Overwhelm Others*, Oxford University Press, Oxford, 2008, p. 233.
25  Ibid.
26  Ibid.
27  Ibid.
28  Hayden, *Hayden*, p. 499; *Times on Sunday*, 18 October 1987; Malcolm Farr, 'Bob Hawke's nude Prime Ministerial meetings', news.com.au, 27 August 2014.
29  Bramston, *Bob Hawke*, pp. 401–402.
30  Evans, *Incorrigible Optimist*, pp. 85–86.
31  Menadue, *Things You Learn Along the Way*, pp. 267–70
32  Kelly, *The End of Certainty*, pp. 391–3; Ramsey, *The Way They Were*, pp. 261–64; Menadue, *Things You Learn Along the Way*, pp. 267–70; Evans, *Incorrigible Optimist*, pp. 85–86.
33  Stephen Holt, 'Alan Douglas Reid', *ADB*, Vol. 18, 2012.
34  Kelly, *The End of Certainty*, chapter 23; *Times on Sunday*, 13 September 1987.
35  Walsh, *Confessions of a Failed Finance Minister*, pp. 193–95.
36  Day, *Keating*, pp. 305–09.
37  Interview with Stephen Mills by Edward Helgeby, OPH OHI 306, Museum of Australian Democracy; Richardson, *Whatever It Takes*, pp. 245–50.
38  Weller, *Dodging Raindrops*, pp. 213–14; Kelly, *The End of Certainty*, pp. 438–51; O'Brien, *Keating*, pp. 347–61; Walsh, *Confessions of a Failed Finance Minister*, pp. 193–95; Richardson, *Whatever It Takes*, pp. 245–50; *Times on Sunday*, 22 November 1987.
39  Hawke, *The Hawke Memoirs*, pp. 447–49; Kelly, *The End of Certainty*, pp. 446–47.
40  Ibid.; Weller, *Dodging Raindrops*, pp. 213–14.
41  'Unmasking Max', *Australian Story*, ABC Television, 18 October 2021; *Sydney Morning Herald*, 13 March 2015 and 17 May 2019; Author interview with Don Watson; Author interview with Max Gillies.
42  Hayden, *Hayden*, pp. 496–97; Hawke, *The Hawke Memoirs*, pp. 125, 404–08; Emerson, *The Boy From Baradine*, p. 168
43  Ibid.; *Canberra Times*, 9 October 1988.
44  Kelly, *The End of Certainty*, pp. 451–56; Hawke, *The Hawke Memoirs*, pp. 450–53; Richardson, *Whatever It Takes*, chapter 14.
45  Ibid.
46  Hawke, *The Hawke Memoirs*, pp. 452–53; Day, *Keating*, pp. 310–11; Richardson, *Whatever It Takes*, pp. 295–96.
47  Ibid.; O'Brien, *Keating*, pp. 360–64.

**CHAPTER SIXTEEN: 1989**

1  Hawke, *The Hawke Memoirs*, pp. 443–44; Bramston, *Bob Hawke*, pp. 414–15; D'Alpuget, *On Longing*, pp. 59–60; Langmore, *Prime Ministers' Wives*, pp. 302–305; Author interview with Don Watson; Author interview with Blanche d'Alpuget.
2  Kelly, *The End of Certainty*, chapters 21, 24; Howard, *Lazarus Rising*, pp. 172–73, 176.

3   Ibid.
4   Bongiorno, *The Eighties*, pp. 59–71, 253–58; Andrew Markus and M.C. Ricklefs (eds), *Surrender Australia: Essays in the Study and Uses of History*, Allen & Unwin, Sydney, 1985, pp. 1–9; Kelly, *The End of Certainty*, chapters 7 and 22; Robert Manne and David Corlett, 'Sending Them Home: Refugees and the New Politics of Indifference', *Quarterly Essay* 13; *Sydney Morning Herald*, 18 April 2006; *Guardian*, 5 June 2015.
5   Ibid.
6   *Canberra Times*, 29 November 1988; *Australian Financial Review*, 29 November 1988 and 6 April 1990.
7   Johannah Bevis, 'No More Labour for the Knight: An Overview of Sir Jack Egerton's Leadership', *Queensland Journal of Labour History*, September 2015; *Canberra Times*, 29 November 1988; *Australian Financial Review*, 29 November 1988 and 6 April 1990.
8   Report of the Fitzgerald Inquiry, 3 July 1989, pp. 104–106; Transcript of Interview with Jana Wendt, 4 March 1988, RH215, BHPML; *Australian Financial Review*, 4 March 1988.
9   *Sunday Mail*, 27 November 1988; Hansard, 28 and 29 November 1988; Transcript of News Conference by Hawke, 30 November 1988, and other documents relating to the defamation action taken against Queensland Newspapers, see RH215, BHPML.
10  *Australian Financial Review*, 29 November 1988; *Canberra Times*, 29, 30 November and 1 December 1988.
11  Ibid.
12  *Australian Jewish News*, 2 December 1988; *Canberra Times*, 1 and 22 December 1988, 24 February 1989; *Age*, 22 December 1988; see also documents in RH215, BHPML.
13  Ibid.
14  Ibid.
15  Ibid.
16  O'Brien, *Keating*, pp. 373–89; Walsh, *Confessions of a Failed Finance Minister*, p. 154; Kelly, *The End of Certainty*, chapter 26.
17  See Barry, *The Rise and Fall of Alan Bond*; Inglis, *Whose ABC?*, p. 184; *Australian Financial Review*, 25 June 1993.
18  Ibid.
19  Bramston, *Bob Hawke*, pp. 221–22.
20  Shawcross, *Rupert Murdoch*, pp. 360–70; Pilger, *A Secret Country*, pp. 206–13; Menadue, *Things You Learn Along The Way*, pp. 116–19; *Australian Financial Review*, 6 April 1990 and 31 July 1992; *Age*, 15 September 2001.
21  Mark Hearn, *Organising Union: Transport Workers Face the Challenge of Change, 1989–2013*, Melbourne University Publishing, Melbourne, 2017, p. 112; *Australian Financial Review*, 31 July 1992; *Age*, 15 September 2001.
22  Chenoweth, *Rupert Murdoch*, pp. 63–66; Norm Lipson and Adam Walters, *The Accidental Gangster: The Life and Times of Bela Csidei*, Park Street Press, Sydney, 2006, p. 128; Hawke, *The Hawke Memoirs*, chapter 26; Colleen Ryan and Glenn Burge, *Corporate Cannibals: The Taking of Fairfax*, Reed Books, Melbourne, 1992, pp. 152–43; *Washington Times*, 5 August 2021.
23  Ibid.
24  Hawke, *The Hawke Memoirs*, chapter 26; O'Brien, *Keating*, pp. 565–67; Evans, *Incorrigible Optimist*, pp. 87–88; Mary Sheehan and Sonia Jennings, *A Federation of Pilots: The Story of an Australian Air Pilots' Union*, Melbourne University Publishing, Melbourne, 2010, chapter 5; Paul Edgley, *Into the Wind*, Boolarong Press, Brisbane, 2021, pp. 176–77; Lipson and Walters, *The Accidental Gangster*, p. 128; Williams, *The Fortunate Life of a Vindicatrix Boy*, pp. 136–38; *Canberra Times*, 4 August 1987.
25  Sheehan and Jennings, *A Federation of Pilots*, chapter 5; Hawke, *The Hawke Memoirs*, pp. 457–58; Edgley, *Into the Wind*, chapters 18–21.
26  Sheehan and Jennings, *A Federation of Pilots*, chapter 5; Edgley, *Into the Wind*, chapters 18–21.

27  Sheehan and Jennings, *A Federation of Pilots*, chapter 5; Hawke, *The Hawke Memoirs*, pp. 457–58; Edgley, *Into the Wind*, chapters 18–21; Bradley Bowden, *Driving Force: The History of the Transport Workers' Union of Australia 1883–1992*, Allen & Unwin, Sydney, 1993, pp. 145–46, p. 178.
28  Edgley, *Into the Wind*, pp. 194–99.
29  Sheehan and Jennings, *A Federation of Pilots*, chapter 5; Edgley, *Into the Wind*, pp. 206–08.
30  Ibid.
31  Ibid.; Transcript of interview with Hawke by Richard Carleton, 12 November 1989, pmtranscripts.pmc.gov.au/release/transcript-7805.
32  Edgley, *Into the Wind*, pp. 226–29; Sheehan and Jennings, *A Federation of Pilots*, chapter 5; *Australian*, 25 August 1989.
33  Edgley, *Into the Wind*, pp. 226–29; Sheehan and Jennings, *A Federation of Pilots*, chapter 5; Christine Jennett, 'Political Review: August–October 1989', *Australian Quarterly*, Summer 1989, pp. 500–05; Letter, Hawke to Paul Edgley, 14 September 1989, a copy of which was kindly provided to the author by Paul Edgley.
34  Ibid.
35  Richardson, *Whatever It Takes*, pp. 166–67.
36  Sheehan & Jennings, *A Federation of Pilots*, chapter 5; Hawke, *The Hawke Memoirs*, pp. 457–64; Kelly, *The End of Certainty*, pp. 544, 548; *Australian Financial Review*, 28 September 1989; *Sydney Morning Herald*, 24 August 1989; *Age*, 25 August 1989.
37  Hawke, *The Hawke Memoirs*, pp. 457–64; Transcript of interview with Hawke by Richard Carleton, 12 November 1989, pmtranscripts.pmc.gov.au/release/transcript-7805; Speech by Hawke at the National Press Club, 7 December 1989, pmtranscripts.pmc.gov.au/release/transcript-7849.
38  Sheehan and Jennings, *A Federation of Pilots*, chapter 5; Hawke, *The Hawke Memoirs*, pp. 457–64; *Sun-Herald*, 4 November 1990.

**CHAPTER SEVENTEEN: 1989**

1  Speech by Hawke at the National Press Club, 7 December 1989, pmtranscripts.pmc.gov.au/release/transcript-7849.
2  Kelly, *The End of Certainty*, chapters 24, 25; Howard, *Lazarus Rising*, pp. 174–81; Walsh, *Confessions of a Failed Finance Minister*, pp. 169–72.
3  Ibid.
4  Weller, *Dodging Raindrops*, pp. 219–20.
5  Walsh, *Confessions of a Failed Finance Minister*, pp. 199–200.
6  Richardson, *Whatever It Takes*, pp. 256–63; Weller, *Dodging Raindrops*, pp. 216–17; Hawke, *The Hawke Memoirs*, pp. 394–96, 464–66: Kelly, *The End of Certainty*, pp. 536–42.
7  Kelly, *The End of Certainty*, pp. 536–40; Richardson, *Whatever It Takes*, pp. 256–61; Walsh, *Confessions of a Failed Finance Minister*, pp. 212–13; Emerson, *The Boy from Baradine*, pp. 184–86.
8  Hawke, *The Hawke Memoirs*, pp. 467–72; Day, *Antarctica*, pp. 515–18.
9  Transcript of Joint Press Conference with Hawke, Evans and Richardson, 22 May 1989, and other documents in RH92, BHPML; Author interview with Bob Hawke.
10  Emerson, *The Boy from Baradine*, pp. 182–90, 196–97; Day, *Paul Keating*, pp. 321–23; Evans, *Incorrigible Optimist*, pp. 130–31; Hawke, *The Hawke Memoirs*, pp. 467–72; D'Alpuget, *Bob Hawke*, pp. 802–06; Bob Hawke and Derek Rielly, *Wednesdays with Bob*, Pan Macmillan, Sydney, 2017, p. 48; Author interview with Bob Hawke.
11  Emerson, *The Boy from Baradine*, p. 184.
12  Hawke, *The Hawke Memoirs*, pp. 339–54, 429–34; Bramston, *Bob Hawke*, pp. 444–47; *Australian Financial Review*, 12 May 2023; Author interview with Ross Garnaut.
13  Hazel Hawke, *My Own Life*, pp. 189–90; Interview with Pandora Livanes, 2014, oralhistories.moadoph.gov.au/pandora-livanes.html; *Weekend Australian*, 2–3 December 1989.
14  Kelly, *The End of Certainty*, pp. 544–53.
15  Ibid.

16   Alan Ramsey, *The Way They Were*, NewSouth, Sydney, 2011, pp. 72–76; Kelly, *The End of Certainty*, pp. 544–53; Transcript of interview with Doug Aiton, 10 March 1989, pmtranscripts.pmc.gov.au/sites/default/files/original/00007523.pdf; *Age*, 17 March 1986.

## CHAPTER EIGHTEEN: 1990

1   Regarding the confusion about Clem's date of birth, see David Day, *Young Hawke*, p. 357. That confusion persisted at his death, when Bob Hawke suggested he was ninety-one, while other sources claimed he was ninety-two. See Hazel Hawke, *My Own Life*, p. 179; Pieters-Hawke, *Hazel*, pp. 291–93; Bramston, *Bob Hawke*, p. 454; D'Alpuget, *Bob Hawke*, pp. 847–48; Hawke, *The Hawke Memoirs*, pp. 16, 136; Interview with Bob Hawke by Andrew Denton, *Enough Rope*, ABC Television, 14 July 2008; *Canberra Times*, 24 and 28 December 1989.
2   Ibid.
3   Howard, *Lazarus Rising*, pp. 171–79; Kelly, *The End of Certainty*, pp. 419–33.
4   Richardson, *Whatever It Takes*, pp. 255–64; Mills, *The Hawke Years*, pp. 116–22; Emerson, *The Boy From Baradine*, pp. 184–86, 199–201; Hawke, *The Hawke Memoirs*, pp. 476–78; Kelly, *The End of Certainty*, chapter 28; *Australian*, 16 January 2022.
5   Ibid.
6   Mills, *The Hawke Years*, pp. 123–31.
7   Ibid.
8   Weller, *Dodging Raindrops*, p. 221.
9   Ibid.
10  Mills, *The Hawke Years*, pp. 130–34; Emerson, *The Boy from Baradine*, p. 206; Richardson, *Whatever It Takes*, pp. 265–77; Hawke, *The Hawke Memoirs*, pp. 479–85.
11  Ibid.
12  Ibid.
13  Hawke, *The Hawke Memoirs*, pp. 479–85; Transcript of Debate with Andrew Peacock, 25 February 1990, pmtranscripts.pmc.gov.au/sites/default/files/original/00007924.pdf; Mills, *The Hawke Years*, pp. 130–34; Richardson, *Whatever It Takes*, pp. 267–68; *Canberra Times*, 26 February 1990.
14  Ibid.
15  Richardson, *Whatever It Takes*, pp. 269–74.
16  Kelly, *The End of Certainty*, chapter 30; Policy Launch by Hawke, 8 March 1990, pmtranscripts.pmc.gov.au/sites/default/files/original/00007944.pdf.
17  Mills, *The Hawke Years*, pp. 130–37; Bramston, *Bob Hawke*, p. 481.
18  Walsh, *Confessions of a Failed Finance Minister*, p. 228.
19  For details of the time that Braddon spent with a young Hawke in London, see Day, *Young Hawke*, pp. 101–102; Letter, Braddon to James Whitehead, 23 March 1990, ACC 04/162, Box 2A, Russell Braddon Papers, NLA.
20  Richardson, *Whatever It Takes*, p. 274; Kelly, *The End of Certainty*, p. 578; Letter, Braddon to James Whitehead, 23 March 1990, ACC 04/162, Box 2A, Russell Braddon Papers, NLA.
21  Bongiorno, *The Eighties*, p. 297; Hawke, *The Hawke Memoirs*, pp. 484–85; Kelly, *The End of Certainty*, pp. 586–87.
22  Ibid.
23  Freudenberg, *A Figure of Speech*, p. 249; Letter, Braddon to James Whitehead, 29 March 1990, ACC 04/162, Box 2A, Russell Braddon Papers, NLA.
24  Ramsay, *The Way They Were*, p. 153; Weller, *Dodging Raindrops*, p. 222.
25  Walsh, *Confessions of a Failed Finance Minister*, pp. 229–32.
26  Ibid.
27  Richardson, *Whatever It Takes*, pp. 278–84.
28  Bramston, *Bob Hawke*, pp. 461–62; D'Alpuget, *Bob Hawke*, pp. 822–30.
29  Richardson, *Whatever It Takes*, pp. 278–84; Hawke, *The Hawke Memoirs*, pp. 486–88; Bramston, *Bob Hawke*, pp. 461–2; Neal Blewett, *A Cabinet Diary: A Personal Record of the First Keating Government*, Wakefield Press, Adelaide, 1999, p. 216; Author interview with Bob Hawke; *Age*, 24 October 2009.

## CHAPTER NINETEEN: 1990

1. The inscription on their graves can be found at www.findagrave.com/memorial/151300384/arthur-clarence-hawke and www.findagrave.com/memorial/151300383/edith_emily-hawke.
2. Inglis, *Whose ABC?*, pp. 191–92; Bongiorno, *The Eighties*, pp. 258–62; Freudenberg, *A Figure of Speech*, pp. 249–50; Hawke, *The Hawke Memoirs*, pp. 526–27; *Guardian*, 8 October 2018.
3. Freudenberg, *A Figure of Speech*, pp. 249–50; Joan Beaumont (ed.), *Australia's War 1914–18*, Allen & Unwin, Sydney, 1995, pp. 174–76; Transcript of Interview with Hawke by John Brown on 2UE, 17 December 1990, pmtranscripts.pmc.gov.au/release/transcript-8236; *The 7.30 Report*, ABC Television, 25 April 1990.
4. Emerson, *The Boy from Baradine*, pp. 220–21.
5. Ibid.; O'Brien, *Keating*, pp. 395–96, 402–04; Mills, *The Hawke Years*, chapter 9.
6. Bramston, *Bob Hawke*, p. 466.
7. Bramston, *Bob Hawke*, pp. 466–67; Evans, *Incorrigible Optimist*, pp. 87–88; Hawke, *The Hawke Memoirs*, pp. 489–96.
8. Ramsay, *The Way They Were*, pp. 261–64; Richardson, *Whatever It Takes*, pp. 305–07; Michael Easson, 'Privatising Qantas and Australian Airlines', *Labor Forum*, Vol. 1, No. 1, May–July 1991; Transcript of News Conference by Hawke, 6 September 1990, pmtranscripts.pmc.gov.au/sites/default/files/original/00008116.pdf; Transcript of Joint News Conference with Beazley, 24 September 1990, pmtranscripts.pmc.gov.au/release/transcript-8143; *Canberra Times*, 17, 25, 27 and 28 August and 8 September 1990.
9. Ibid.
10. *Canberra Times*, 4 August 1990.
11. Hawke, *The Hawke Memoirs*, pp. 511–14; Bramston, *Bob Hawke*, pp. 487–91.
12. Mills, *The Hawke Years*, pp. 141–52; Hawke, *The Hawke Memoirs*, pp. 514–20; Bramston, *Bob Hawke*, pp. 491–92.
13. Margo, *Frank Lowy*, p. 283.
14. Transcript of Interview with Hawke by John Brown on 2UE, 17 December 1990, pmtranscripts.pmc.gov.au/release/transcript-8236.
15. Hawke, *The Hawke Memoirs*, pp. 497–98; Kelly, *The End of Certainty*, pp. 618–69; Bramston, *Bob Hawke*, p. 498; *Age*, 26 October 1990; *Sydney Morning Herald*, 24 October 1990; *Weekend Australian*, 2–3 December 1989.
16. Ibid.
17. Ibid.
18. Day, *Keating*, pp. 330–31; Walsh, *Confessions of a Failed Finance Minister*, p. 154; Richardson, *Whatever It Takes*, pp. 293–95; Kelly, *The End of Certainty*, pp. 617–18; O'Brien, *Keating*, pp. 397–99.
19. Bramston, *Bob Hawke*, pp. 499–500; Kelly, *The End of Certainty*, pp. 621–23; O'Brien, *Keating*, pp. 406–14; Transcript of interview by Hawke with Howard Sattler, 29 November 1990, pmtranscripts.pmc.gov.au/sites/default/files/original/00008216.pdf; *Guardian*, 31 December 2015.
20. O'Brien, *Keating*, pp. 411–18; Day, *Keating*, pp. 336–7; Bramston, *Bob Hawke*, pp. 500–01; Hawke, *The Hawke Memoirs*, pp. 498–501; Richardson, *Whatever It Takes*, pp. 298–303; Kelly, *The End of Certainty*, pp. 623–25.
21. Richardson, *Whatever It Takes*, pp. 298–300; Bramston, *Bob Hawke*, pp. 500–01; Transcript of Hawke's press conference, 11 December 1990, pmtranscripts.pmc.gov.au/sites/default/files/original/00008231.pdf.
22. Ibid.

## CHAPTER TWENTY: January–June 1991

1. Richardson, *Whatever It Takes*, pp. 295–99.
2. Hawke, *The Hawke Memoirs*, pp. 498–501.
3. Richardson, *Whatever It Takes*, pp. 295–99; Mills, *The Hawke Years*, pp. 213–21; Hawke, *The Hawke Memoirs*, pp. 498–500; O'Brien, *Keating*, pp. 418–20; Kelly, *The End of Certainty*, pp. 621–26.

4   Mills, *The Hawke Years*, chapter 6; Richardson, *Whatever It Takes*, pp. 307–308; Jones, *A Thinking Reed*, pp. 504–506; Statement by the Prime Minister, 17 January 1991, pmtranscripts.pmc.gov.au/release/transcript-8245; Speech by Hawke, 22 January 1991, pmtranscripts.pmc.gov.au/sites/default/files/original/00008247.pdf.
5   Mills, *The Hawke Years*, pp. 145–47; Bramston, *Bob Hawke*, pp. 486–97.
6   Ibid.
7   Kelly, *The End of Certainty*, pp. 625–27; Hawke, *The Hawke Memoirs*, pp. 500–502.
8   Ibid.
9   Ibid.
10  Bramston, *Bob Hawke*, pp. 501–503; Hawke, *The Hawke Memoirs*, pp. 511–26; Kelly, *The End of Certainty*, pp. 625–27.
11  Ibid.
12  Wilkinson, *The Fixer*, pp. 334–36; Hawke, *The Hawke Memoirs*, pp. 496–97; D'Alpuget, *Bob Hawke*, pp. 869–72; *Canberra Times*, 11 April 1991 ; Quentin Beresford, *The Godfather: The Life of Brian Burke*, Allen & Unwin, Sydney, 2008, Chap. 5.
13  Ibid.
14  *Canberra Times*, 11 April 1991.
15  Richardson, *Whatever It Takes*, p. 309; Hawke, *The Hawke Memoirs*, p. 486; Wilkinson, *The Fixer*, pp. 334–36; Kelly, *The End of Certainty*, pp. 627–28; *Canberra Times*, 5, 11, 12, 13, 14, 16 and 17 April and 22 May 1991.
16  Ibid.
17  *Canberra Times*, 4 May 1991.
18  Richardson, *Whatever It Takes*, pp. 309–14.
19  Kelly, *The End of Certainty*, p. 631; *Canberra Times*, 11 and 14 May 1991.
20  Hazel Hawke, *My Own Life*, p. 218; Kelly, *The End of Certainty*, p. 631.
21  *Canberra Times*, 15 May 1991.
22  Mills, *The Hawke Years*, p. 217; Kelly, *The End of Certainty*, pp. 629–31.
23  O'Brien, *Keating*, pp. 424–25; Kelly, *The End of Certainty*, pp. 628–32; Weller, *Dodging Raindrops*, pp. 228–31.
24  Ibid.
25  Ibid.
26  Richardson, *Whatever It Takes*, pp. 314–21; Kelly, *The End of Certainty*, pp. 628–34.
27  Ibid.
28  Ibid.
29  Hawke, *The Hawke Memoirs*, pp. 503–505; Kelly, *The End of Certainty*, pp. 628–36; Mills, *The Hawke Years*, chapter 10; Bramston, *Bob Hawke*, pp. 504–14.
30  Ibid.
31  Ibid.
32  Ibid.
33  Richardson, *Whatever It Takes*, p. 310; O'Brien, *Keating*, p. 426; Hawke, *The Hawke Memoirs*, pp. 537–44; Mills, *The Hawke Years*, pp. 244–46; Bramston, *Bob Hawke*, p. 514.

**CHAPTER TWENTY-ONE: June–December 1991**

1   Ibid.
2   Mills, *The Hawke Years*, pp. 67–68, 246–47, 251–53.
3   Diane Langmore, 'Jean Dorothy Sinclair', *ADB*, Vol. 19, 2021; Speech by Hawke, 26 June 1991, pmtranscripts.pmc.gov.au/release/transcript-8312.
4   Mills, *The Hawke Years*, pp. 67–68, 246–47, 251–53; D'Alpuget, *On Longing*, p. 62; Speech by Hawke, 26 June 1991, pmtranscripts.pmc.gov.au/release/transcript-8312; Author interview with Niel Gunson.
5   *Canberra Times*, 25, 26, 27, 28 and 29 June and 1 July 1991.
6   Ibid.
7   *Canberra Times*, 20 and 22 June 1991.
8   Hawke, *The Hawke Memoirs*, pp. 505–10; Richardson, *Whatever It Takes*, pp. 322–24; Author interview with Bob Hawke.
9   Hayden, *Hayden*, p. 484; Richardson, *Whatever It Takes*, p. 327.

10  Ibid.
11  Richardson, *Whatever It Takes*, pp. 327–31; Bramston, *Bob Hawke*, pp. 433–37; Hawke, *The Hawke Memoirs*, chapter 20, pp. 497–98; Mills, *The Hawke Years*, p. 257; *Age*, 26 August 2023.
12  Mills, *The Hawke Years*, pp. 263–65; Richardson, *Whatever It Takes*, pp. 331–32.
13  Ibid.
14  O'Brien, *Keating*, pp. 427–33; *Canberra Times*, 2 and 7 December 1991.
15  Ibid.
16  Ibid.
17  Ibid.
18  Mills, *The Hawke Years*, pp. 266–67; Bramston, *Bob Hawke*, pp. 522–23; *Canberra Times*, 29 November and 1, 4 and 5 December 1991.
19  Ibid.
20  Mills, *The Hawke Years*, pp. 266–82; Hawke, *The Hawke Memoirs*, pp. 551–56.
21  *Canberra Times*, 7, 9, 10 and 14 December 1991.
22  Mills, *The Hawke Years*, pp. 266–82; Hawke, *The Hawke Memoirs*, pp. 551–56.
23  Blewett, *A Cabinet Diary*, pp. 9–14; Mills, *The Hawke Years*, pp. 283–89; Bramston, *Bob Hawke*, p. 526.
24  Ibid.
25  Ibid.
26  Richardson, *Whatever It Takes*, pp. 336–39; Mills, *The Hawke Years*, pp. 283–89; Langmore, *Prime Ministers' Wives*, p. 306; Blewett, *A Cabinet Diary*, pp. 9–14; Hawke, *The Hawke Memoirs*, pp. 557–59; *Canberra Times*, 19, 20 and 21 December 1991.
27  Ibid.
28  Ibid.
29  Hawke, *The Hawke Memoirs*, pp. 559–61; Pieters-Hawke, *Hazel*, pp. 308–11; O'Brien, *Keating*, pp. 434–35; Bramston, *Bob Hawke*, 530–35; Transcript of Keating's Press Conference, 19 December 1991, pmtranscripts.pmc.gov.au/release/transcript-8367.
30  Ibid.
31  Ibid.

**CHAPTER TWENTY-TWO: 1992–1994**

1  Mills, *The Hawke Years*, p. 251; Pieters-Hawke, *Hazel*, p. 310.
2  Hazel Hawke, *My Own Life*, pp. 227–31; Pieters-Hawke, *Hazel*, pp. 312–20.
3  Ibid.
4  Ibid.; Diary entry, 26 January 1992, Blewett, *A Cabinet Diary*, p. 29.
5  Hazel Hawke, *My Own Life*, pp. 227–31; Pieters-Hawke, *Hazel*, p. 312; Bramston, *Bob Hawke*, pp. 543–49.
6  For Hawke's annual declarations of pecuniary interests, see the documents in RH211, BHPML.
7  Pieters-Hawke, *Hazel*, pp. 315–16; *Sydney Morning Herald*, 6 February 1992, *Canberra Times*, 21 February 1992.
8  Diary entry, 20 February 1992, Blewett, *A Cabinet Diary*, pp. 52–53; *Canberra Times*, 22 February 1992.
9  Hazel Hawke, *My Own Life*, pp. 231–2; Pieters-Hawke, *Hazel*, pp. 324–31.
10  Ibid.
11  Pieters-Hawke, *Hazel*, pp. 321–40, 343–9.
12  Ibid.; Langmore, *Prime Ministers' Wives*, p. 306; Transcript of interview with Mike Carlton, 22 February 1990, pmtranscripts.pmc.gov.au/sites/default/files/original/00007920.pdf; *Australian Financial Review*, 30 March 1994.
13  Bramston, *Bob Hawke*, pp. 544–54.
14  Bramston, *Bob Hawke*, pp. 544–55; Robert Penfold, '"Everyman" Bob Hawke's surprise post-PM career on 60 Minutes', www.9news.com.au/national/bob-hawke-60-minutes-reporter-robert-penfold-memory/26d66c4a-096f-4b60-999e-8b02fb31ba88; Email to the author from Keith Rayner, 19 December 2019; Author interview with Phillip Adams; Author interview with Blanche d'Alpuget.

15    Speech by Hawke at Premier Zhao's Welcoming Banquet, 19 May 1986, pmtranscripts.pmc.gov.au/sites/default/files/original/00006915.pdf; Speech by Hawke launching the Garnaut Report, 'Australia and the Northeast Asian Ascendancy', 22 November 1989, pmtranscripts.pmc.gov.au/release/transcript-7826; James Curran, 'Inside the Tent: Bob Hawke's Ringside Seat to China's Reforms, Beijing 1986', Australia-China Relations Institute, University of Technology Sydney, May 2023; *Australian Financial Review*, 12 May 2023.
16    Diary entry, 17 July 1992, Blewett, *A Cabinet Diary*, pp. 182–83; Bramston, *Bob Hawke*, pp. 544–48, 553–54; *Australian Financial Review*, 30 March 1994, 5 June 1997 and 24 October 2021.
17    Don Watson, *Recollections of a Bleeding Heart*, Random House, Sydney, 2002, pp. 309–11; Richardson, *Whatever It Takes*, pp. 348–56; Edwards, *Keating*, p. 507; Bramston, *Bob Hawke*, pp. 548–49; *Canberra Times*, 25 March 1993.
18    Ibid. The author was one of those who secured a ticket to the dinner.
19    O'Brien, *Keating*, pp. 420–21, 680–84; Hawke, *The Hawke Memoirs*, pp. ix–xi; Bramston, *Bob Hawke*, pp. 550–51; Pieters-Hawke, *Hazel*, p. 337; Watson, *Recollections of a Bleeding Heart*, pp. 364–65, 500–501, 507–508; Joshua Black, 'Secrets and Scandals', The Conversation, 22 April 2020; *Age*, 20 September 2005; *Canberra Times*, 17 and 29 August and 6 December 1994.
20    Ibid.; Joshua Black, 'A Life Triumphantly Well Written: Producing the Hawke Legacy, 1979–2019', *ANU Historical Journal*, No. 2, October 2020.
21    Ibid.

**CHAPTER TWENTY-THREE: 1995**

1    D'Alpuget, *On Longing*, pp. 62, 67–76; Pieters-Hawke, *Hazel*, pp. 347–48; Bramston, *Bob Hawke*, pp. 551–52; *West Australian*, 30 November 1994; 'Hawke: The Interview', Bob Hawke interview with Hugh Riminton, 28 June 2013, Channel Ten, www.youtube.com/watch?v=7p9eCfpetik.
2    Ibid.
3    Author interview with Blanche d'Alpuget.
4    Ibid.
5    Ibid.
6    *Canberra Times*, 3 January and 6 February 1995.
7    For correspondence related to the wedding and the photo shoot, see documents in RH201, F2, BHPML.
8    Details about the marriage celebrant can be found on his website, www.marioschoenmaker.com; Bramston, *Bob Hawke*, pp. 552–53; *Age*, 24 July 1995; *Canberra Times*, 13 February 1995.
9    Pieters-Hawke, *Hazel*, pp. 347–56; Sue Pieters-Hawke, *Hazel's Journey*, Macmillan, Sydney, 2004, p. 179.
10    Wasowski, *Vera*, p. 204.
11    Bramston, *Bob Hawke*, pp. 552–53; Pieters-Hawke, *Hazel*, pp. 347–56; Pieters-Hawke, *Hazel's Journey*, p. 179; *Daily Mail*, 1 September 2024.
12    Author interview with Blanche d'Alpuget.
13    Bramston, *Bob Hawke*, pp. 553–54.
14    Ibid; *Sydney Morning Herald*, 8 April 2009, 11 November 2012; *Daily Mail*, 12 April 2020; *Daily Telegraph*, 8 April 2019.
15    Author interview with Blanche d'Alpuget.
16    Watson, *Recollections of a Bleeding Heart*, p. 652; *Australian Financial Review*, 21 May 1993, 3 October 1996, 29 June and 3 July 1999.
17    Dan, *Ups and Downs*, chapter 28; Transcript of Interview with Mike Carlton, 22 February 1990, pmtranscripts.pmc.gov.au/sites/default/files/original/00007920.pdf; *PM*, ABC Radio National, 25 June 1999; *Australian Financial Review*, 21 May 1993, 29 June and 3 July 1999; *Weekend Australian*, 29 June 1999; *Sydney Morning Herald*, 15 January 2001.
18    Bramston, *Bob Hawke*, pp. 554–55; Watson, *Recollections of a Bleeding Heart*, pp. 655–65; Greg Combet, *The Fights of My Life*, Melbourne University Press, Melbourne, 2014, pp. 67–70; O'Brien, *Keating*, pp. 735–36; Transcript of Paul

Keating's press conference, 19 November 1995, pmtranscripts.pmc.gov.au/release/transcript-9849; *Australian Financial Review*, 27 November 1995.

**CHAPTER TWENTY-FOUR: 1996–2019**

1. Day, *Keating*, pp. 355–60, 401–04.
2. Ibid.
3. Ibid.
4. Bongiorno, *The Eighties*, p. 287; *Guardian*, 31 December 2015.
5. Author interview with Bob Hawke; MSN News, 1 January 2016; see documents in RH92, 'Records Relating to Antarctica – R.J.L. Hawke', BHPML; Bob Hawke, 'A Confident Australia', inaugural Hawke Lecture, 12 May 1998, BHPML; *Australian*, 5 October 2017.
6. Ryan, *Catching the Waves*, pp. 234–35; Summers, *Unfettered and Alive*, pp. 155–59; Susan Ryan, 'Women's Policy' and Troy Bramston, 'The Hawke Leadership Model', in Ryan and Bramston (eds), *The Hawke Government*, pp. 67–68, 202–14.
7. Mills, *The Hawke Years*, pp. 295–98; Dodson, Morbray and Snowden, 'Promise, Confrontation and Compromise in Indigenous Affairs', in Ryan and Bramston (eds), *The Hawke Government*, pp. 305–07; *The Age*, 2 November 2019 and 3 April 2023.
8. Bramston, *Bob Hawke*, p. 427; Alex Burtson-Chorowicz, 'When Israel turned Right, Hawke made a U-turn', *Jewish Independent*, 21 May 2019; Letters, Hawke to John Howard, 24 December 1996 and Hawke to Alexander Downer, 9 May 1997 and other documents in RH210, BHPML; *Australian*, 24 February 2016.
9. Pieters-Hawke, *Hazel's Journey*, pp. 65–66, 79, 201; McCarthy, *Don't Be Too Polite, Girls*, pp. 456–61; Pieters-Hawke, *Hazel*, pp. 367–417; *Guardian*, 25 June 2013; *Age*, 26 June 2013.
10. Bramston, *Bob Hawke*, p. 561; Hawke and Rielly, *Wednesdays with Bob*, p. 191; Edward Sadler, 'Singo Recalls $1m Collect with PM', www.racing.com/news/2022-12-18/news-feature-the-day-singo-hawke-won-$1m, 18 December 2022; *Guardian*, 23 December 2017; 'Belle du Jour', www.racerate.com/Belle_Du_Jour.htm.
11. *Age*, 27 August 2014; *Herald Sun*, 27 June 2011..
12. Sue Pieters-Hawke (ed.), *Remembering Bob*, Allen & Unwin, Sydney, 2019, p. xvi; *Weekend Australian*, 10–11 July 2010; *Australian*, 25 August 2010 and 16 July 2019; *Weekly Review*, 28 August 2013; *Age*, 17 January, 21 and 31 July 2010; *Woman's Day*, 17 October 2011; Letter, Keating to Hawke, 12 July 2010, BHPML.
13. Mark Latham, *The Latham Diaries*, Melbourne University Press, Melbourne, 2005, p. 186; Bramston, *Bob Hawke*, p. 557.
14. Latham, *The Latham Diaries*, pp. 181, 329–30.
15. Ibid.
16. Ibid.
17. *Sydney Morning Herald*, 5 January and 7 May 2018; *Weekend Australian*, 30/31 December 2017; *Herald Sun*, 3 May 2016.
18. Dedication page in D'Alpuget, *Bob Hawke*; *Sydney Morning Herald*, 7 May 2018 and 17 July 2019; *Australian*, 18 November 2017 and 9 December 2019; 'Bob and Blanche Find Graves Together', 24 August 2013, www.news.com.au; *Age*, 24 August 2013; *Sunday Age*, 30 December 2018 Program about Hawke and D'Alpuget, *60 Minutes*, 2018.
19. Dedication page in D'Alpuget, *Bob Hawke*; *Sunday Age*, 30 December 2018.
20. Speech by Emerson at Hawke's Memorial Service, www.youtube.com/watch?v=6iYkg71z3Pk.
21. Author interview with Blanche d'Alpuget.
22. The author attended the service, watching with the large crowd on the steps of the Opera House.
23. Pieters-Hawke (ed.), *Remembering Bob*, p. xvi; *Daily Mail*, 22 August 2020; *Sydney Morning Herald*, 20 July 2019 and 5 March 2023.
24. Ibid.

# Bibliography

**PRIMARY DOCUMENTS**

**John Curtin Prime Ministerial Library**
Hazel Hawke, Papers

**Bob Hawke Prime Ministerial Library, University of South Australia**
Bob Hawke, Papers

**Mitchell Library, Sydney**
Clyde Cameron, Papers
Richard Klugman, Papers

**Museum of Australian Democracy, Canberra**
Interview with Pandora Livanes by Joan Armitage
Interview with Stephen Mills by Edward Helgeby

**National Archives, London**
Records of the Prime Minister's Office, Correspondence and Papers, 1979–97

**National Library of Australia**
Blanche d'Alpuget, Papers
Russell Braddon, Papers
John Button, Papers
Clyde Cameron, Papers
Manning Clark, Papers
Interview with Sir Peter Abeles by Daniel Connell, 1985
Interview with Russell Braddon by Vivienne Rae-Ellis, 1984
Interview with Gordon Scholes by Gary Sturgess, August 2010
Craig McGregor, Papers
Sir Billy Snedden, Papers

**Parliamentary Library, Canberra**
Newspaper cutting files relating to Bob Hawke and Paul Keating

**Author Interviews**
Phillip Adams
Blanche d'Alpuget
Kim Beazley
Neil Blewett

Bob Carr
Moss Cass
Barrie Cassidy
John Dawkins
Barry Donovan
John Edwards
Craig Emerson
Gareth Evans
Graham Evans
Graham Freudenberg
Ross Garnaut
Max Gillies
Gary Gray
Bob Hawke
John Howard
Barry Jones
Tom Keneally
Chris Masters
Neil Mitchell
Laurie Oakes
Colin Parkes
Nigel Powell
Robert Pullan
Susan Ryan
John Stone
Brian Toohey
Tom Uren
Geoff Walsh
Don Watson
Marian Wilkinson
Ralph Willis

**Media Interviews**
Interview with Blanche d'Alpuget by Mia Freeman, www.mamamia.com.au/blanche-dalpuget-interview, 2018
Interview with Bob Hawke by Richard Fidler, ABC Radio, 2015
Interview with Bob and Clem Hawke by Michael Parkinson, *Parkinson in Australia*, 1981

**Newspapers & Magazines**
*Australian Jewish News*, Melbourne
*Australian Women's Weekly*, Sydney
*Canberra Times*, Canberra
*Courier-Mail*, Brisbane
*Eye*, Glebe
*Financial Review*, Sydney
*Guardian*, London
*Honi Soit*, Sydney
*Independent*, London
*National Times*, Sydney
*Nation Review*, Sydney
*New Idea*, Sydney
*News*, Adelaide
*New Weekly*, Sydney
*New York Times*, New York
*Quadrant*, Sydney
*Sunday Times*, London
*Sunday Times*, Perth
*Sydney Morning Herald*, Sydney
*Tharunka*, Kensington, NSW
*Times*, London
*Tribune*, Sydney
*Uniken*, University of New South Wales
*Weekly Times*, Melbourne
*West Australian*, Perth

## Books

Blanche d'Alpuget, *Bob Hawke: The Complete Biography*, Simon & Schuster, Sydney, 2019
Blanche d'Alpuget, *Hawke: The Prime Minister*, Melbourne University Press, Melbourne, 2010
Blanche d'Alpuget, *On Longing*, Melbourne University Press, Melbourne, 2008
Blanche d'Alpuget, *Robert J. Hawke*, Penguin, Melbourne, 1984
Blanche d'Alpuget, *Winter in Jerusalem*, Secker & Warburg, London, 1986
Stan Anson, *Hawke: An Emotional Life*, (updated edition), McPhee Gribble, Melbourne, 1992
Gillian Appleton, *Diamond Cuts: An Affectionate Memoir of Jim McClelland*, Macmillan, Sydney, 2000
*Australian Dictionary of Biography*, various vols, Melbourne University Press, Melbourne
Philip Ayres, *Malcolm Fraser: A Biography*, William Heinemann, Melbourne, 1987
Paul Barry, *The Rise and Fall of Alan Bond*, Bantam Books, Sydney, 1990
Paul Barry, *The Rise and Rise of Kerry Packer*, ABC Books, Sydney 1993
Quentin Beresford, *The Godfather: The Life of Brian Burke*, Allen & Unwin, Sydney, 2008
John Blaxland and Rhys Crawley, *The Official History of ASIO, 1975–1989: The Secret Cold War*, Allen & Unwin, Sydney, 2016
Paul Bleakley, *The Australian Gamble: Organized Crime Down Under*, Rowman & Littlefield, Lanham, Maryland, 2023
Meena Blesing, *'Was Your Dad a Russian Spy?'*, Macmillan, Melbourne, 1986
Neal Blewett, *A Cabinet Diary: A Personal Record of the First Keating Government*, Wakefield Press, Adelaide, 1999
Frank Bongiorno, *Dreamers and Schemers: A Political History of Australia*, La Trobe University Press, Melbourne, 2022
Frank Bongiorno, *The Eighties: The Decade that Transformed Australia*, Black Inc., Melbourne, 2015
Frank Bongiorno, *The Sex Lives of Australians* (second edition), Black Inc., Melbourne, 2015
Bob Bottom, *Bugged!*, Macmillan, Melbourne, 1989
Bob Bottom, *Connections II: Crime Rackets and Networks of Influence in Australia*, Macmillan, Melbourne, 1987
Bob Bottom, *Fighting Organised Crime: Triumph and Betrayal in a Lifelong Campaign*, BBP, Nelson Bay, 2009
Bob Bottom, *The Godfather in Australia*, Magistra Publishing, Melbourne, 1979
Bob Bottom, *Shadow of Shame: How the Mafia Got Away with the Murder of Donald Mackay*, Sun Books, Melbourne, 1988
Bob Bottom, *Without Fear or Favour*, Sun Books, Melbourne, 1984
Bradley Bowden, *Driving Force: The History of the Transport Workers' Union of Australia 1883–1992*, Allen & Unwin, Sydney 1993
Chris Bowen, *The Money Men: Australia's 12 Most Notable Treasurers*, Melbourne University Press, Melbourne, 2015
Margaret Bowman and Michelle Grattan, *Reformers: Shaping Australian Society from the 60s to the 80s*, Collins Dove, Melbourne, 1989
Tom Bramble, *Trade Unionism in Australia: A History from Flood to Ebb Tide*, Cambridge University Press, Melbourne, 2008
Troy Bramston, *Bob Hawke: Demons and Destiny*, Viking, Sydney, 2022

Judith Brett (ed.), *Political Lives*, Allen & Unwin, Sydney, 1997
Clarrie Briese, *Corruption in High Places*, Noble Books, Sydney, 2021
Richard Broinowski, *Fact or Fission?: The Truth About Australia's Nuclear Ambitions*, Scribe, Melbourne, 2003
A.J. Brown, *Michael Kirby: Paradoxes and Principles*, Federation Press, Sydney, 2011
John Brown, *Brownie: The Minister for Good Times*, Good Times Press, Sydney, 2023
Brian Burke, *A Tumultuous Life*, self-published, Perth, 2017
Peter Butt, *Merchants of Menace*, Blackwattle Press, Sydney, 2015
John Button, *As It Happened*, Text, Melbourne, 1998
John Button, *Flying the Kite: Travels of an Australian Politician*, Random House, Sydney, 1994
John Button, *On the Loose*, Text, Melbourne, 1996
Frank Cain, *Terrorism and Intelligence in Australia: A History of ASIO and National Surveillance*, Australian Scholarly Publishing, Melbourne, 2008
Clyde Cameron (ed.), *The Cameron Diaries*, Allen & Unwin, Sydney, 1990
Moss Cass, Vivien Encel and Anthony O'Donnell, *Moss Cass and the Greening of the Australian Labor Party*, Australian Scholarly Publishing, Melbourne, 2017
Paul Chadwick, *Media Mates: Carving Up Australia's Media*, Sun Books, Melbourne, 1989
Rob Chalmers, *Inside the Canberra Press Gallery: Life in the Wedding Cake of Old Parliament House*, ANU Press, Canberra, 2011
Neil Chenoweth, *Packer's Lunch*, Allen & Unwin, Sydney, 2007
Neil Chenoweth, *Rupert Murdoch: The Untold Story of the World's Greatest Media Wizard*, Random House, New York, 2001
Philip Chubb and Barry Donovan, *Chance Is Worth a Thousand Plans: Peter Redlich and the Creation of a National Law Firm*, Holding, Redlich & Co., Melbourne, 2013
David Clune (with John Upton), *Inside the Wran Era: The Ron Mulock Memoirs*, Connor Court Publishing, Ballarat, 2015
Milton Cockburn, *The Assassination of Neville Wran*, Connor Court Publishing, Redland Bay, 2024
Greg Combet, *The Fights of My Life*, Melbourne University Press, Melbourne, 2014
James Curran, *Australia's China Odyssey: From Euphoria to Fear*, NewSouth, Sydney, 2022
James Curran, *The Power of Speech*, Melbourne University Press, Melbourne, 2004
Claire Dan, *Ups and Downs*, Wild & Woolley, Sydney, 2008
David Day, *Antarctica: A Biography*, Random House, Sydney, 2012
David Day, *Conquest: How Societies Overwhelm Others*, Oxford University Press, Oxford, 2008
David Day, *Paul Keating: The Biography*, HarperCollins, Sydney, 2015
David Day, *Young Hawke: The Making of a Larrikin*, HarperCollins, Sydney 2024
Phil Dickie, *The Road to Fitzgerald: Revelations of Corruption Spanning Four Decades*, University of Queensland Press, Brisbane, 1988
Phil Dickie, *The Road to Fitzgerald and Beyond*, University of Queensland Press, Brisbane, 1989

Barry Donovan, *Reconnecting Labor*, Scribe, Melbourne, 2006
Barry Donovan, *Steve Bracks and Jeff Kennett: My Part in their Rise and Fall – An Insider Tells*, Information Australia, Melbourne, 2000
Nick Dyrenfurth and Frank Bongiorno, *A Little History of the Australian Labor Party* (revised edition) NewSouth, Sydney, 2024
Barrie Dyster and David Meredith, *Australia in the International Economy in the Twentieth Century*, Cambridge University Press, Melbourne, 1990
Paul Edgley, *Into the Wind*, Boolarong Press, Brisbane, 2021
John Edwards, *Keating: The Inside Story*, Viking, Melbourne, 1996
Peter Edwards, *Law, Politics and Intelligence: A Life of Robert Hope*, UNSW Press, Sydney, 2020
Craig Emerson, *The Boy from Baradine*, Scribe, Melbourne, 2018
Gareth Evans, *Incorrigible Optimist: A Political Memoir*, Melbourne University Press, Melbourne, 2017
Gareth Evans, *Inside the Hawke Keating Government: A Cabinet Diary*, Melbourne University Press, Melbourne, 2014
Gareth Evans and Bruce Grant, *Australia's Foreign Relations: In the World of the 1990s*, Melbourne University Press, Melbourne, 1991
John Faulkner and Stuart Macintyre (eds), *True Believers: The Story of the Federal Parliamentary Labor Party*, Allen & Unwin, Sydney, 2001
Malcolm Fraser and Margaret Simons, *Malcolm Fraser: The Political Memoirs*, Miegunyah Press, Melbourne, 2010
George Freeman, *George Freeman: An Autobiography*, George Freeman, Sydney, 1988
Graham Freudenberg, *A Figure of Speech: A Political Memoir*, Wiley, Brisbane, 2005
David Goldsworthy (ed.), *Facing North: A Century of Australian Engagement with Asia*, Vol. 1, Melbourne University Press, Melbourne, 2001
Michelle Grattan (ed.), *Australian Prime Ministers*, New Holland, Sydney, 2000
Richard Hall, *Disorganised Crime*, University of Queensland Press, Brisbane, 1986
Bob Hawke, *The Hawke Memoirs*, William Heinemann, Melbourne, 1994
R.J.L. Hawke, *1979 Boyer Lectures: The Resolution of Conflict*, Australian Broadcasting Commission, Sydney, 1979
Hazel Hawke, *My Own Life: An Autobiography*, Text, Melbourne, 1992
Hazel Hawke (ed.), *Reflections on Marriage*, Text, Melbourne, 1996
Bill Hayden, *Hayden: An Autobiography*, Angus & Robertson, Sydney, 1996
Brian Head and Allan Patience (eds), *From Fraser to Hawke: Australian Public Policy in the 1980s*, Longman Cheshire, Melbourne, 1989
Roy Higgins (with Terry Vine), *The Professor*, Caribou Publications, Melbourne, 1984
Jenny Hocking, *Lionel Murphy: A Political Biography*, Cambridge University Press, Melbourne, 1997
Dino Hodge, *Don Dunstan: Intimacy and Liberty*, Wakefield Press, Adelaide, 2014
John Howard, *Lazarus Rising: A Personal and Political Autobiography*, HarperCollins, Sydney, 2010
K.S. Inglis, *Whose ABC?: The Australian Broadcasting Corporation, 1983–2006*, Black Inc., Melbourne, 2006
Christine Jennett and Randal Stewart (eds), *Hawke and Australian Public Policy: Consensus and Restructuring*, Macmillan Education, Melbourne, 1990

Barry Jones, *Sleepers, Wake!: Technology and the Future of Work*, Oxford University Press, Melbourne, 1982

Benjamin Jones, Frank Bongiorno and John Uhr (eds), *Elections Matter: Ten Federal Elections that Shaped Australia*, Monash University Publishing, Melbourne, 2018

Paul Keating, *Afterwords: The Post-Prime Ministerial Speeches*, Allen & Unwin, Sydney, 2011

Paul Kelly, *The Hawke Ascendancy*, Angus & Robertson, Sydney, 1984

Paul Kelly, *The March of Patriots: The Struggle for Modern Australia*, Melbourne University Press, Melbourne, 2009

Jonathan Kwitny, *The Crimes of Patriots: A True Tale of Dope, Dirty Money, and the CIA*, Simon & Schuster, New York, 1987

Terry Lane, *As the Twig Is Bent*, CollinsDove, Melbourne, 1979

Diane Langmore, *Prime Ministers' Wives*, McPhee Gribble, Melbourne, 1992

John Langmore and John Quiggin, *Work for All: Full Employment in the Nineties*, Melbourne University Press, Melbourne, 1994

Mark Latham, *The Latham Diaries*, Melbourne University Press, Melbourne, 2005

Sam Lipski and Suzanne Rutland, *Let My People Go: The Untold Story of Australia and the Soviet Jews 1959–89*, Hybrid, Melbourne, 2015

Norm Lipson and Adam Walters, *The Accidental Gangster: The Life and Times of Bela Csidei*, Park Street Press, Sydney, 2006

Graham Little, *Speaking for Myself: Interviews with Notable Australians*, McPhee Gribble Publishers, Melbourne, 1989

Wendy McCarthy, *Don't Be Too Polite, Girls: A Memoir*, Allen & Unwin, Sydney, 2022

James McClelland, *Stirring the Possum: A Political Autobiography*, Penguin, Melbourne, 1989

Alfred W. McCoy, *Drug Traffic: Narcotics and Organised Crime in Australia*, Harper & Row, Sydney, 1980

Alfred W. McCoy, *The Politics of Heroin: CIA Complicity in the Global Drug Trade*, Lawrence Hill Books, New York, 1991

Mark McKenna, *An Eye for Eternity: The Life of Manning Clark*, Melbourne University Press, Melbourne, 2011

David McKnight, *Australia's Spies and their Secrets*, Allen & Unwin, Sydney, 1994

David McKnight, *Rupert Murdoch: An Investigation of Political Power*, Allen & Unwin, 2012

David McKnight (ed.), *Moving Left: The Future of Socialism in Australia*, Pluto Press, Sydney, 1986

Ross McMullin, *The Light on the Hill: The Australian Labor Party 1891–1991*, Oxford University Press, Melbourne, 1991

Graham Maddox, *The Hawke Government and Labor Tradition*, Penguin, Melbourne, 1989

Terence Maher, *Alan Bond*, Mandarin, London, 1990

Desmond Manderson, *From Mr Sin to Mr Big: A History of Australian Drug Laws*, Oxford University Press, Melbourne, 1993

Bruce Mansfield, *Summer Is Almost Over: A Memoir*, Barton Books, Canberra, 2012

Jill Margo, *Frank Lowy: Pushing the Limits*, HarperCollins, Sydney, 2000

Andrew Markus and M.C. Ricklefs (eds), *Surrender Australia: Essays in the Study and Uses of History*, Allen & Unwin, Sydney, 1985
David Marr, *The Ivanov Trail*, Thomas Nelson, Melbourne, 1984
David Marr, *Patrick White: A Life*, Random House, Sydney, 1991
David Marr (ed.), *Patrick White: Letters*, Jonathan Cape, London, 1994
Chris Masters, *Not for Publication*, ABC Books, Sydney, 2002
Brian Matthews, *Manning Clark: A Life*, Allen & Unwin, Sydney, 2008
John Menadue, *Things You Learn Along The Way*, David Lovell Publishing, Melbourne, 1999
Alex Millmow, *The Gypsy Economist: The Life and Times of Colin Clark*, Palgrave Macmillan, Singapore, 2021
Stephen Mills, *The Hawke Years: The Story from the Inside*, Viking, Melbourne, 1993
George Munster, *A Paper Prince*, Viking, Melbourne, 1985
Brad Norington, *Sky Pirates: The Pilots' Strike that Grounded Australia*, ABC, Sydney, 1990
Laurie Oakes, *On the Record: Politics, Politicians and Power*, Hachette, Sydney, 2010
Laurie Oakes, *Power Plays: The Real Stories of Australian Politics*, Hachette, Sydney, 2008
Kerry O'Brien, *Keating*, Allen & Unwin, Sydney, 2015
Bobbie Oliver, *Unity Is Strength: A History of the Australian Labor Party and the Trades and Labor Council in Western Australia, 1899–1999*, API Network, Perth, 2003
Kevin Perkins, *Bristow: Last of the Hard Men*, Bonmoat, Sydney, 2003
Kevin Perkins, *The Gambling Man*, Polynesian Press, Nuku'alofa, Tonga, 1990
Sue Pieters-Hawke, *Hazel: My Mother's Story*, Macmillan, Sydney, 2011
John Pilger, *A Secret Country*, Jonathan Cape, London, 1989
Robert Pullan, *Bob Hawke: A Portrait*, Methuen, Sydney, 1980
Alan Ramsey, *A Matter of Opinion*, Allen & Unwin, Sydney, 2009
Alan Ramsey, *The Way They Were*, NewSouth, Sydney, 2011
Geoffrey Reading, *High Climbers: Askin and Others*, John Ferguson, Sydney, 1989
Tony Reeves, *Mr Sin: [The Abe Saffron Dossier]*, Allen & Unwin, Sydney, 2007
Tony Reeves, *The Real George Freeman*, Penguin, Melbourne, 2011
Graham Richardson, *Whatever It Takes*, Bantam Books, Sydney, 1994
Matthew Ricketson (ed.), *The Best Australian Profiles*, Black Inc., Melbourne, 2004
Liz Ross, *Dare to Struggle, Dare to Win!: Builders Labourers Fight Deregistration, 1981–1994*, Vulgar Press, Melbourne, 2004
Suzanne D. Rutland, *Lone Voice: The Wars of Isi Leibler*, Hybrid Publishers, Melbourne, 2021
Colleen Ryan, *Fairfax: The Rise and Fall*, Melbourne University Publishing, Melbourne, 2013
Colleen Ryan and Glenn Burge, *Corporate Cannibals: The Taking of Fairfax*, Reed Books, Melbourne, 1992
Susan Ryan, *Catching the Waves: Life in and out of Politics*, HarperCollins, Sydney, 1999
Susan Ryan and Troy Bramston (eds), *The Hawke Government: A Critical Retrospective*, Pluto Press, Melbourne, 2003

Alan Saffron, *Gentle Satan: My Father, Abe Saffron*, Penguin, Melbourne, 2008
Russell Schneider, *The Colt from Kooyong: Andrew Peacock, A Political Biography*, Angus & Robertson, Sydney, 1981
Keith Scott, *Gareth Evans*, Allen & Unwin, Sydney, 1999
Jocelynne Scutt (ed.), *Lionel Murphy: A Radical Judge*, McCulloch Publishing, Melbourne, 1987
Clement Semmler, *Pictures on the Margin: Memoirs*, University of Queensland Press, Brisbane, 1991
William Shawcross, *Rupert Murdoch*, Random House, Sydney, 1992
Mary Sheehan and Sonia Jennings, *A Federation of Pilots: The Story of an Australian Air Pilots' Union*, Melbourne University Publishing, Melbourne, 2010
Gavin Souter, *Acts of Parliament: A Narrative History of Australia's Federal Legislature*, Melbourne University Press, Melbourne, 1988
Gavin Souter, *Heralds and Angels: The House of Fairfax, 1841–1990*, Melbourne University Press, Melbourne, 1991
Don Stewart, *Recollections of an Unreasonable Man: From the Beat to the Bench*, ABC Books, Sydney, 2007
John Stubbs, *Hayden*, Mandarin, Melbourne, 1990
Anne Summers, *The Misogyny Factor*, NewSouth, Sydney, 2013
Anne Summers, *Unfettered and Alive: A Memoir*, Allen & Unwin, Sydney, 2018
Anne Summers, *The End of Equality: Work, Babies and Women's Choices in 21st Century Australia*, Random House, Sydney, 2003
Gwenda Tavan, *The Long, Slow Death of White Australia*, Scribe, Melbourne, 2005
Brian Toohey and Marian Wilkinson, *The Book of Leaks*, Angus & Robertson, Sydney, 1987
Brian Toohey and William Pinwill, *Oyster: The Story of the Australian Secret Intelligence Service*, William Heinemann, Melbourne, 1989
Brian Toohey, *Secret: The Making of Australia's Security State*, Melbourne University Press, Melbourne, 2019
Jerome Tuccille, *Murdoch: A Biography*, Piatkus, London, 1990
Chris Wallace, *Political Lives: Australian Prime Ministers and Their Biographers*, UNSW Press, Sydney, 2023
Chris Wallace (ed.), *Telling Lives: The Seymour Biography Lecture, 2005–2023*, National Library of Australia Publishing, Canberra, 2024
Stephen Walmsley, *The Trials of Justice Murphy*, LexisNexis, Sydney, 2017
Shane Warne (with Mark Nicholls), *No Spin*, Ebury Press, Sydney, 2018
Vera Wasowski, *Vera: My Story*, Black Inc., Melbourne, 2015
Bill Waterhouse, *What Are The Odds: The Bill Waterhouse Story*, Vintage, Sydney 2010
Don Watson, *Recollections of a Bleeding Heart: A Portrait of Paul Keating PM*, Random House, Sydney, 2002
Patrick Weller, *Dodging Raindrops – John Button: A Labor Life*, Allen & Unwin, Sydney, 1999
Geoffrey Whitehead, *Inside the ABC*, Penguin, Melbourne, 1988
Evan Whitton, *Can of Worms: A Citizen's Reference Book to Crime and the Administration of Justice*, Fairfax Library, Sydney, 1986
Evan Whitton, *Can of Worms II: A Citizen's Reference Book to Crime and the Administration of Justice*, Fairfax Library, Sydney, 1987

Marian Wilkinson, *The Fixer: The Untold Story of Graham Richardson*, William Heinemann, Melbourne, 1996
Mike Willesee, *Memoirs*, Macmillan, Sydney, 2017
John Williams, *The Fortunate Life of a Vindicatrix Boy*, self-published, 2005
David Wilson and Lindsay Murdoch, *Big Shots: A Who's Who in Australian Crime*, Sun Books, Melbourne, 1985
David Wilson, *Big Shots II*, Macmillan, Melbourne, 1987

**Journal Articles**

Stan Anson, 'The Rhetorical Uses of John Curtin', *Journal of Australian Studies*, Vol. 10, No. 19
'Australian Political Chronicle, July–December 1979', *Australian Journal of Politics and History*, April 1980
Joshua Black, 'A Life Triumphantly Well Written: Producing the Hawke Legacy, 1979–2019', *ANU Historical Journal*, No. 2, October 2020
Bradley Bowden, 'The Rise and Decline of Australian Unionism: A History of Industrial Labour from the 1820s to 2010', *Labour History*, May 2011
Nicholas Bromfield, 'Welcome Home: Reconciliation, Vietnam Veterans, and Anzac During the Hawke Government', *Australian Journal of Political Science*, Vol. 52, No. 2
John Button, 'Beyond Belief: What Future for Labor?', *Quarterly Essay*, Issue 6, 2002
Bob Carr, 'Australian Trade Unionism in 1979', *Journal of Industrial Relations*, March 1980
Stephen Charles, 'The Murphy Papers: The Parliamentary Commission of Inquiry', *Samuel Griffith Society Proceedings*, 2018
Stephen Charles, 'Spies Like Us?: The David Combe Affair', *Victorian Bar News*, June 2017
C.J. Coventry, 'The "Eloquence" of Robert J. Hawke: United States Informer, 1973–79', *Australian Journal of Politics and History*, Vol. 67, No. 1, 2021
David Halpin, 'Life with Lionel', *Matilda*, September 1985
G.C. Harcourt, 'The Systematic Downside of Flexible Labour Market Regimes: Salter Revisited', *Economic and Labour Relations Review*, Vol. 23, No. 2
Stephen Holt, 'Bob Hawke's Boon Companion', *Quadrant Online*, 17 May 2019
Christine Jennett, 'Political Review: August–October 1989', *Australian Quarterly*, Summer 1989
P.D. Jonson and G.R. Stevens, 'The 1930's and the 1980's: Some Facts', *Research Discussion Paper*, Reserve Bank of Australia, September 1983
Ben Kunkler, 'Hawke Hagiography: Getting over the Prime Larrikin', *Overland*, April 2018
Yacov Livne and Yossi Goldstein, '"Let My People Go": The Beginnings of Israel's Operation to Open Soviet Immigration Gates', *Soviet and Post-Soviet Review*, No. 47, 2020
Doug McEachern, 'Corporatism and Business Responses to the Hawke Government', *Australian Journal of Political Science*, Vol. 21, No. 1, September 2007
G.S. Reid, 'Hawke's Boyer Lectures', *Quadrant*, May 1980
Clement Semmler, 'The Wasting of Whitehead: Inside the ABC', *Quadrant*, 1 March 1989
Mike Steketee, 'Was Bob Askin Corrupt?', *Inside Story*, 9 April 2021

Glenn Stevens, 'Inflation and Disinflation in Australia: 1950–91', *Reserve Bank of Australia Conference Paper*, 1992
Tony Thomas, 'Bob Hawke's Sugar Daddies', *Quadrant*, September 2022
Rodney Tiffen, 'Was Neville Wran Corrupt?', *Inside Story*, 31 August 2021
Stephen Walmsley, 'Lessons from a High Court Scandal', *Law Society Journal*, 1 April 2017

**Reports, Booklets, Lectures, etc.**
Neal Blewett, *Getting It Right – Some Thoughts on the Politics of Consensus*, Australian National University, 1983
Justice Michael Kirby, *10th Lionel Murphy Memorial Lecture*, 21 October 1996
Peter Walsh, *Errors and Achievements: Economic Policy in the 1980s*, Shann Memorial Lecture, University of Western Australia, October 1991

**Theses**
Khaled Alnkhailan, 'The Theory of Successful Criminal Entrepreneurs', PhD Thesis, Queensland University of Technology, 2017
Jessica Amos, 'The National Times: Bastard of a Paper', MA Thesis, University of Wollongong, 2005
Jim Chalmers, 'Brawler Statesman: Paul Keating and Prime Ministerial Leadership in Australia', PhD Thesis, Australian National University, 2004
Liam Lander, 'Official Deviance Exposed: An Historical Examination of Political Scandals in Late Twentieth-Century Australia', BA (Hons), Charles Sturt University, 2023

# Acknowledgments

In the companion volume, *Young Hawke*, it was explained that these books do not comprise an authorised biography. Apart from a couple of interviews about Antarctica and about Paul Keating, it didn't have Bob Hawke's active assistance. But neither did it have his opposition, nor that of his family, for which I am most grateful as it made my research much easier.

Many of his colleagues, staff, friends and associates, who are listed under 'author interviews' in the bibliography, were generous with their time. I would like to particularly mention Phillip Adams, Kim Beazley, Neil Blewett, Bob Carr, Barrie Cassidy, John Dawkins, Barry Donovan, Gareth Evans, Graham Evans, Ross Garnaut, Max Gillies, Barry Jones, Laurie Oakes, Colin Parkes, John Stone, Brian Toohey, Geoff Walsh, Don Watson and Ralph Willis.

As with *Young Hawke*, this volume is beholden to those who'd trod this path before, which facilitated my own journey. There was the work of earlier biographers, Blanche d'Alpuget, John Hurst, Rob Pullen, Stan Anson and Troy Bramston, along with the authors of the many books listed in the bibliography and the contemporary journalists whose work is credited in the endnotes.

Also helpful were the staff of the libraries that were visited over more than a decade of research in Australia and Britain. At the Bob Hawke Prime Ministerial Library in Adelaide, Adam Kauschke was most helpful in providing access to Hawke's personal and official papers, while Sally Laming and Nathan Hobby were of great assistance with the papers of Hazel Hawke at the John Curtin Prime Ministerial

Library in Perth, while the Hawke family kindly provided permission to reproduce photographs from these collections.

A constant companion over the last ten years was the Trove website, which is run by the National Library of Australia and provides access to many Australian newspapers and magazines and information about the location of sometimes elusive books. The National Library also holds many collections of papers and some interviews relating to Hawke. I am particularly grateful to Blanche d'Alpuget for allowing access to her research papers and for kindly agreeing to an interview. La Trobe University has provided an academic home and the ever-helpful staff of the library have located sometimes hard-to-get books from other libraries around Australia.

At HarperCollins, I have been blessed with supportive publishers in Helen Littleton and Scott Forbes, while the text has been improved by the editing work of Neil Thomas, Julian Welch and Lachlan McLaine.

As always, Silvia has been a boon companion on yet another absorbing journey. It is to her that this volume is lovingly dedicated.

# Index

A Current Affair 300
'a little crook', description by Peacock 136, 138, 144
ABC
   'Eight Cents a Day' campaign 201
   legal action threat 200
   offer of employment to Bacon withdrawn 202
   Peacock and Hawke 'Great Debate' 254
   politics of senior appointments 179
Abeles, Sir Peter
   and airlines competition 199
   appointed to Reserve Bank board 176
   at biography launch 55
   at secret succession meeting 223
   author of strategy against pilots 236
   benefits from pilots' strike 240
   benefits from pliable ministers 260
   corrupts officials of TWU 201
   funds Hawke in Canberra 34
   gets away with currency manipulation 176
   Hawke's association with unwise 136
   helps with Ros' treatment 138
   lays trap for pilots with Hawke 234
   links with American mafia exposed in Kwitny book 201
   loses influence and dies 312
   pays off American mafia 201
   pays off corrupt Askin on retirement 201
   pays off Wran on retirement 201
   prevaricates on Kirribilli agreement 273
   sacks baggage handlers 235
   schmoozed Hawke since first meeting 311–312
   supported by Hawke 232–233
Aboriginal Deaths in Custody Royal Commission 209
Aboriginal land rights 129
Accord *see* Prices and Incomes Accord
Adams, Phillip, supports Hawke 46
Advisory Committee on Prices and Incomes 165
'Age' tapes 131, 134, 135
airline privatisation 217–218
alcoholism, early 3, 10
Aldred, Ken 108–109
Amarena, Salvatore 133

American alliance, scepticism by Hayden 45
America's Cup 120–121
Ansett 233
Antarctic environment, protection of 246, 315
Antarctic mining convention 247
Antarctica, as world park 246–247
anti-discrimination measures 212
Anzac legend 263
ANZUS alliance 45
Arbitration Commission 14–15
'armed action' in Kuwait 273–274
arrogance of Hawke 214
Ash Wednesday (Feb '83) 80
Asia-Pacific Economic Cooperation (APEC) 248
ASIO, involvement in Australian politics 91–92
Askin, Sir Robert 201
assets test on pensions 140–141
Australia Card 188
Australia Post, corporatising 197
Australian Airlines
   cabinet approves sale of 264, 265
   corporatising 197
   problems with 233
   sensitivity of sale 199–200
Australian Conservation Foundation 194
Australian Council of Trade Unions (ACTU) 3, 4, 313
Australian Democrats 73–74, 247
Australian Federation of Air Pilots (AFAP), detaches from Accord 234, 236
Australian Sports Commission 122
*Australian Story* 320
*Australian Women's Weekly* 310
Australians, living beyond their means 166
Ayers Rock (Uluru) 209–210

Bacon, Wendy 175–176
balance-of-payments deficit 243
'banana republic' 164–166
Bannon, John 57
Barker, Ian QC 109–110
Barnett, Harvey 105
Barron, Peter 75, 98
Barunga Statement 317
Bathurst, cabinet meeting in 185–186

Beazley, Kim
  challenge from 32
  and telecommunications market 264
  made defence minister 197
  made finance minister 290
  Hawke supports after 1996 election loss 321
  as preferred successor to Hawke 269
BHP, deal with 123
Bicentenary 207–209
Bicentenary celebrations, protests against 209
'Biggles' (Gareth Evans' nickname) 104
biographies
  by D'Alpuget 54, 320
  first by Hurst 10
  second by Pullan 18
Bjelke-Petersen, Joh 103, 182–183, 188
Blainey, Geoffrey 14, 227
Blair, Tony 52
Blandy, Dick 13
Blewett, Neal 32, 125, 300
Blunt, Charles 243
Bond, Alan 204, 208
  and America's Cup 120
  buys media networks 170
  declared bankrupt and jailed 232
Bottom, Bob, *The Godfather in Australia* (1979) 135
bottom-of-the-harbour tax avoidance schemes 56
Bourke's discount store 4
Bowen, Lionel 32, 46, 97
Bowers, Peter 144–146
Boyer Lectures (1979) 10–12
Braddon, Russell 257
Bramston, Troy 93–94, 311
briefing paper on polls (1981) 41
Brown, Bob, shows Richardson logging in Tas 193
Brown, Neil 229
Bruce electorate, won by Liberals (1983) 108
Bryant, Gordon 15
Bryce, Quentin 211
budget (1987) 203
*Bulletin* 20–21
Burke, Brian 81, 129, 167, 276–277
bushfires (Feb '83) 80
Button, John
  amused by Hawke's self-delusions 62
  conflicting loyalties to Hayden and Hawke 63–64
  member of inner cabinet 97
  negotiates with BHP, trade unions and governments 123
  opposes environmental concerns strategy 244
  predicts Hawke comeback 52
  refuses high commissionership in London 259
  suspects succession agreement reached 253
  tries to convince Hayden to step down 60–61
  urges further cuts to tariffs 243

cabinet
  decision-making in 100–101
  meet in Bathurst 185–186
  principle of solidarity to apply in 116
Cain, John 42–43, 45
Cairns, Jim 56
Cameron, Clyde 47
Cameron, Rod 43, 239–240, 247–248, 249
Cammell, Helga 21, 112–113
campaign song on TV ad 190–191
*Can of Worms*, Evan Whitton (1987) 201
Canberra 33–34
*The Canberra Times* 300
capital gains tax 141, 153
carbon taxes on emissions 316
Carleton, Richard 72, 143–144, 239
Carr, Bob 20–21, 54
caucus 12–13, 47, 150, 281, 282
caucus Christmas dinner (1991) 293
Centre Unity faction 16
'child poverty elimination by 1990' 191–192
China 115, 152
Chipp, Don 73
CIA, involvement in Australian politics 91–93
Cleary, Phil 300
Combe, David
  appeasement of 125
  at biography launch 55
  being recruited as Soviet agent 105
  Canadian appointment 111
  declares innocence 109
  gives corruption details to *National Times* 175
  as Hawke supporter and lobbyist 106–107
  involvement with Ivanov 92–93
  supported by MPs and union delegates 110–111
  to be placed under surveillance 107
Commonwealth Bank, government sells 30% of 264
Commonwealth Heads of State Government Meeting (CHOGM) 268
confidential think tank 13
Connell, Laurie
  abandoned by Hawke 232
  and corrupt politics in Qld and WA 193
  Hawke fishing with 167
  proposes tax on gold to Hawke 193
  Rothwells Bank collapse 204–205
consumer price index 126
consumption tax 153–155
Coronation Hill 244, 286–287
corruption, in Australia 187–188
Costigan, Frank 56
Crean, Simon 321
*The Crimes of Patriots: A True Tale of Dope, Dirty Money, and the CIA* by Jonathan Kwitny 201
cross-media rules on ownership 169
Csidei, Bela 133
currency devaluation 91
Curtin, John 36, 114–115

d'Alpuget, Blanche
    asks for Hazel's cooperation 36–37, 38
    biography of Sir Richard Kirby 19
    buys graves for herself and Hawke 323
    discusses biography with Hawke 55–56
    Hawke biography in shops (Oct '82) 54
    Hawke biography (vol 2) 320
    helps with *The Hawke Memoirs* 305
    as official biographer 18–20
    *On Longing* 320
    prepares to write biography 37–39
    publishes *Winter in Jerusalem* 96
    resumes relationship with Hawke 225
    speech at Hawke's funeral 324
    watches from a distance 95
Dawkins, John 198, 244
defamation actions, Hawke's threats of 230
defamation laws, Hawke's readiness to use 18
delegation, Hawke boasts of ability 116
deregulation of economy 125
developers, tactics used by 232
Diamond, Betty 228–229
dividend imputation 153
divisiveness in Australia 11–12
divorce announced in 1994 306
dodgy characters, Hawke's association with 122
Dolan, Cliff 21, 62, 102
dollar 117–118, 164
Donovan, Barry 17–18, 34
Doogue, Geraldine 54
double-dissolution election (1987) 188
drought in Eastern Australia (1982) 75
'drover's dog' statement by Hayden 68
Ducker, John 178
Duffy, Michael 168, 178, 179

early election in first term 126
East-West Airlines 199
economic direction 100–101
economic rationalisation 214
economy 189, 256
education funding 127
Egerton, Jack 228–229
'Eight Cents a Day' campaign by ABC 201
El Niño (1982) 75
election (1980) against Fraser 27–30
election (1984) 140–143, 146
election (1987) 181
election (1989) 244
election (1990), launch speech 255–256, 258
election campaign opening (1983) 78
elections, safe Labor seats lose most votes 196
Elliott, John 226
Emerson, Craig 166, 263
empty promises made by Hawke 141
environment protection 193
environmental concerns 244
environmental initiatives 315–316
equal opportunity, legislation 211
ethnic make-up changing 226–227
Evans, Gareth
    asks RAAF to photograph Gordon River dam site 104
    chairs party task force 87
    Hawke 'becoming more isolated from real-world concerns' 155
    on illegal phone tapping 175
    made transport and communications minister 197
    member of inner cabinet 97
    not at leadership vote 293
    as shadow attorney-general 76
    supports closer supervision of ASIO 92
    to provide airline privatisation proposals 217–218
Evans, Graham 94, 98
exchange controls, lifting 117
Expenditure Review Committee (ERC) 117, 187
export prices stay low 166
*The Eye* magazine 195

factional machinations 16–17
Fairfax newspapers 178, 202
Family Allowance Supplement 252–253
Farmer, Richard 75, 81
Farquhar, Murray 132, 177
Federated Ship Painters and Dockers Union 56
female MPs, four at opening of Parliament House 210–211
*Fightback!* package as Hawke's undoing 289, 290
First Fleet re-creation 208–209
Fitzgerald, Tony QC, corruption inquiry 188, 212–213
fixed-term parliaments 129
Flinders electorate 57–59, 82
Foord, John 137
foreign banks entry 315
*Four Corners*, exposes corruption 177, 178, 200
Fraser, Malcolm
    calls early election 65
    campaigning difficulties 81
    confident prior to election 68–69
    economic profligacy of his government 89–90
    makes error with industrial relations 69
    opposition from 14
    passes new industrial relations laws 14–15
    race to Governor-General 67–68
    and Royal Commission report on tax evasion 56
    wins 1980 election 31
Freeman, George 132
Freudenberg, Graham
    1983 winner's after-dinner speech 87
    presses for election 186–187
    speech for Gallipoli anniversary 262
    speech writer 77, 98
    wrote Whitlam's campaign speech (1972) 79
Friedman, Milton, monetarist economist 88
fringe benefits tax 153
fundraising lunch in WA (1987) 276

Gallipoli trip for 75th anniversary 261–263
Gandhi, Indira, Hawke tells crude joke about (1981) 41

Garnaut report on north-east Asia, Hawke launches 303
Garnaut, Ross
  appointed ambassador to China 248, 303
  as economics adviser 98
  report on north-east Asia 303
  supports dollar float 117–118
Gillies, Max, pokes fun at Hawke's narcissism 221
global warming not on Hawke's agenda 245
*The Godfather in Australia*, Bob Bottom (1979) 135
Gold Coast, Hawke and Kornhauser on 228–229
gold tax 276
goods and services tax (GST)
  Button urges Hawke to consider 243
  Hewson proposes 287–288
goodwill, enormous reservoir of 80
Gordon River dam site flyover by RAAF 104
Goss, Wayne 249
government railways, corporatising 197
government shipping line, corporatising 197
Grattan, Michelle 116
'Great Debate', Hawke wins 255
Grimes, Don 97

Halfpenny, John 50
Harris, Ted 234–235
Haupt, Robert 195
**Hawke, Bob**
  **family, character, and personal life**
    70th birthday party 319
    advised to reign in temper 73
    ageing 122, 322
    announces divorce 306
    arrogance of 214
    assets of 299
    attire, preferred 129
    at Australian Open with Hazel 298
    attempts to stop heavy drinking 24–25
    becoming more isolated from real-world concerns 155
    buys flat in Canberra 34
    childhood and young life 1–2
    death of 323–324
    deeply depressed 138
    dream home turning into nightmare 301–302
    drunkenness as repeated source of tension with d'Alpuget 310
    early drinking 3, 10
    eats healthy diet 249
    feels humiliated at Hazel's book launch 301
    financial affairs after retirement 299–300
    fondness for alcohol 3, 10
    given popular receptions 74
    gives *Woman's Day* fee to charity 308
    has arguments with Hazel 302
    has read *The Second Sex* 129
    helps 'refuseniks' 11, 205–206, 215
    home situation 4
    hurt by biography 55–56
    income in retirement 302, 304
    jealous of d'Alpuget 308
    lacks self-awareness 39
    last days at Lodge 297
    leads fast life 21–22
    lengthens legs of PM's chair 101–102
    life post-divorce 309–310
    liked for larrikinism 10
    loses temper with Carleton and aged pensioner 239
    messiah complex becoming God complex 285
    modus vivendi in marriage 22–23
    mother's death 5
    mother's plans for 2
    moves to Double Bay 298
    narcissism 3, 39
    opposes racism 317
    parents' burial 261
    part owner of racehorses 26
    passionate about sport 121–122
    payments from magazines and TV 310
    pleasing parents 2
    possible effects of divorce 34–35
    postpones prostate operation 252
    praises Hazel 300
    preferred attire 129
    proposes to d'Alpuget (1979) 307
    protesters at wedding with d'Alpuget 309
    readiness to use defamation laws 18
    renovation of Northbridge home 298
    resumes d'Alpuget relationship 225
    resumes drinking after leaving Parliament 302, 307–308
    Rhodes scholarship 2–3
    seeks applause of international audience 206
    sexual dalliances when PM 93–94
    sings to Hazel on her deathbed 319
    some business dealings less than reputable 310
    stops drinking 25
    in tears at press conference 139
    termination payment from ACTU 21
    thinks his leadership inevitable 39–40
    traumatised by first part of D'Alpuget biography 39
    used to forgiveness for transgressions 55, 74
    as womaniser 3–4, 10
    worries about being poorer 294, 297, 299
  **elections**
    1990 election pitch 254–255
    announces double-dissolution election date 188
    approval rating in 1980 poll 22–23
    claims victory (1983) 82–83
    hopes for electoral win 181
    performs poorly in 1984 election campaign 142–143
    personal approval rating slump 74
    polling shows lead over Fraser and Hayden 45–46
    in TV debate with Peacock 143

Index        369

**international activities**
    appears with Bishop Desmond Tutu on ABC 303
    attends ILO congress in Geneva 112–113
    as conduit for Western businesses in China 303
    covers 1992 UK election for *60 Minutes* 303
    defends expulsion of Ivanov in royal commission 110
    emphasises closeness with USA 113–114
    hosts visit by Chinese premier Zhao Ziyang 115
    involved in establishing Asia-Pacific Economic Cooperation (APEC) 248
    overseas when stock market crashes 204
    pressures South Africa on apartheid 248
    reports on famine in Somalia 303
    secretly agrees to secret MX missile tests 149
    talks with Gorbachev in Moscow 205
    talks with Suharto in Indonesia 112
    trip to Europe (1980) 25–26
    welcomes Chinese after Tiananmen Square massacre 248–249
**relations with Keating**
    at Keating's night of triumph 305
    at secret succession meeting 223
    attends Keating's campaign launch and predicts loss 304
    Keating's speech at business lunch better than Hawke's 143
    Kirribilli agreement with Keating 223
    misleading claims about Keating 289–290
    Ray warns that Keating has caucus majority 292
**rivalry with Keating 219–220**
    visits Washington with Keating 113
**relations with others**
    antipathy towards Fairfax 203
    befriends Shulz of Bechtel Corporation 113
    defends Wran and Ducker 178
    denials and aggression towards Carleton 72–73
    personal advisors 75, 97-98
    refuses to support Melzer in Senate 17
    tries to befriend Latham 321–322
**businessmen and corruption**
    association with dodgy characters 122
    believes Murdoch and Packer to be 'mates' of Labor party 202
    buys Melbourne office building on behalf of Asian investors 304
    Defends Wran and Ducker 178
    delivers eulogy at funeral of Abeles 312
    dodges Landa's corruption claim 144
    manipulates ABC and SBS appointments 179
    misuses Accord against pilots 234–235
    supports Kornhauser's development plans 228
    wins Golden Slipper with John Singleton 319–320
    worries about taint of corruption 133
**political actions and achievements**
    aims to destroy pilot's union 236–237
    applies assets and income tests on pensions 140–141
    boasts about ability to delegate 116
    calls for Hayden's resignation 41–42
    chairs cabinet 97
    as centre of government power 116–117
    claims control of resistance to pilot's claims 236
    convenes National Economic Summit 100–103
    creates inner cabinet 96–97
    dominates journalists and press gallery 176–177
    early involvement in politics 2
    establishes confidential think tank 13
    harks back to legacy of Curtin 79–80
    has plan for Middle East peace 206
    imaginings on winning 87–88
    increases number of MPs in lower house 140
    intends to complete 7 or 8 years as PM 181
    lays trap for pilots 234
    maiden speech (1980) 33
    mostly agrees to factional choices (1990) 259
    as peacemaker and consensus-builder 78–79
    promises in campaign speech (1983) 79
    outlines economic direction 100–101
    positive achievements 316–318
    reinforces links with public 320
    suggests republic 11
    supports expansion of fossil-fuel industries 245
    taxes lump sum superannuation payouts 140–141
    tries to recapture optimism of first term 152
**negative actions and outcomes**
    aghast at Whitlam's tariff cuts 123
    called 'a little crook' by Peacock 136, 138, 144
    cessation of influential positions 21
    challenges Hayden too early 48–49
    demeans himself over pilots' strike 239
    difficulty naming major achievements 315
    empty promises made 141
    hands resignation to Hayden 293–294
    informed of ballooning deficit by Stone 89
    loses leadership challenge 51
    loses senior advisers 184
    makes empty promises 141
    misreads history 114–115
    misunderstands Curtin 114–115

    raises questions about Hayden 57–59
    resigns from ACTU 5, 21, 28
    retires from Parliament 299
    told to resign 291
    walks out of *7.30 Report* interview 184
    warned of challenges in Canberra 33–34
Hawke, Clem (father) 250, 52
Hawke, Hazel
    completes memoirs 300
    cooperates with D'Alpuget 37, 38
    develops separate life 70–71
    effect of D'Alpuget biography on 55
    handles issues with children 24
    has Alzheimer's disease 319
    has brain tumour removed 298
    has surgery 44
    left out of leadership scheming 69–70
    life as PM's wife 94–95
    loneliness of 36
    manages household finances 22
    moves to Canberra 35–36
    personal development of 23–24
    in poor health 302
    praise from Hawke 196
    rapprochement with Hawke (1983) 78
    reluctant to divorce 35
    speaks at book launch 301
    supportive on European trip (1982) 44
    voted 'national living treasure' 309
*The Hawke Memoirs* (1994) 305
Hawke, Rosslyn (daughter)
    addicted to heroin 137–138
    dissuaded by father from going to police 53
    has baby at Sandringham home 94
    takes legal action to get larger share of estate 324
    tells of rape by Landeryou 53
Hawke, Stephen (son) 24
Hawke, Susan (daughter) 137
Hayden, Bill
    calls leadership meeting 48
    creates Medibank 9
    'drover's dog could lead to victory' 68
    effect of McMahon's resignation on 42
    election campaign (1980) 27–30
    Hawke calls for resignation 41–42
    Hawke campaigns strongly for 29
    Hawke hopes to challenge 15
    keeps leadership after Hawke challenge 51
    lacklustre in Flinders by-election 59
    on Medicare co-payment 287
    member of inner cabinet 97
    nervous about Hawke 43
    rattled by Hawke 42
    resigns Labor leadership 64–67
    seeks assurances from Hawke 62
    and 'social contract' 27
    tells Queen electoral disaster likely 251
    tells Queen of official corruption 256
    to deny access to US nuclear warships 45
    undermining of 43–44
health insurance and CPI 126
Herald and Weekly Times 169–170

Herscu, George 232
Hewson, John
    demands Hawke call election 291
    as new Liberal leader 258
    outpolling Hawke 265
    proposes 15% goods and services tax 287–288
    at Gallipoli with Hawke 262
Higgins, Chris 270
Higher Education Contribution Scheme (HECS) 212
Hill, David 179, 200
Hinze, Russ, investigated by Fitzgerald 212–213
history, Hawke misreads 114–115
*HMS Endeavour*, Bond to build replica 208
Hodgman, Michael 146
Hogg, Bob
    impresses Tony Blair 52
    as political adviser 98
    supports Hawke 43
    tells Hawke to resign 282
Holmes á Court, Janet 300–301
Holt, Fiona 23
Hope, Robert 109–110
Horne, Donald 120
House of Representatives, Hawke increases numbers in 140
Howard, John
    announces tax reduction policy 189
    attacks Hawke over corruption 227–228
    becomes Liberal leader 163
    ends Coalition 183
    fears immigration and multiculturalism 251
    huge mistake in tax cut figures 190
    'One Australia' campaign 227
    problems of 226
    proposed tax cuts get increased support 194
    sacks Peacock from deputy position 183
    secret campaign to bring down 243
Howe, Brian 187, 284
Human Rights and Equal Opportunity Commission 211
Hurford, Chris 213
Hurst, John 10, 18
Hussein, Saddam 266, 274

impartiality of Hawke questioned 202
'impertinence' by ABC presenters 177
income taxes, plan to reduce 153
incomes test on pensions 140–141
increasing inequality 316
Indigenous people
    dispossession of 208
    plans and fails to conclude treaty with 197, 287
    treaty promised before end of 1988 209
inefficient secondary industries 165
inflationary spiral broken 126
inner cabinet 96–97
interest rates 231, 243, 252
International Labour Organisation (ILO) 11, 25

investigative journalists 213
investment boom 231
Iraq blockade, Hawke offers navy ships for 266
*Irises*, van Gogh, bought by Bond in crooked deal 208
Israel, fearmongering about 215–216
Israeli cause, Hawke passionately committed to 267
Ivanov, Valery 92, 105, 107

Jackson, Rex 133
Jewish community
   Hawke's double message to 215
   support from 26
Johns, Brian 179
Johnston, Bob 91, 117–118
Jones, Barry 286

Kakadu National Park expansion 244–245
Keating, Annita, friend of Hazel 95
Keating, Paul
   and Aboriginal Land Rights 314
   ambitions of 20
   announces recession 269
   announces referendum on republic 314
   appointed by Hayden as shadow treasurer 61
   at secret succession meeting 223
   breaks Royal protocl 314
   conflicted about Hawke 49
   leadership challenge 162, 278, 280
   defends Hawke against Hewson 277
   and dollar float 118–119
   economic policy launch difficult for 76–77
   embraces Kokoda Track legend 314
   expects to be Treasurer and not Willis 90–91
   forces succession meeting with Hawke 279–280
   frustrated at delay in leadership transfer 219
   gains approval for consumption tax 154
   generous in win over Hawke 293
   has health problems 182
   hits back at Hawke at dinner 270–271
   keeps ambition in check (1990) 253
   member of inner cabinet 97
   mini-budget blamed for by-election losses 109
   mixed feelings about Hayden's resignation 67
   opinion of Hawke (1982) 47, 158
   opposes limiting $CO_2$ emissions 245
   presses Hawke for leadership 268
   proposes new taxes 153
   reaction to Tax Summit 156–157
   rivalry with Hawke 219–220, 315
   secures deputy prime ministership 260
   sixth budget delivered (1988) 219
   suggests Accord might not end wage-price spiral 77
   switches support to Hawke 50
   threatens to retire from parliament 275, 290
   visits Washington with Hawke 113

Kelly, Paul 281
Kelty, Bill
   at National Economic Summit 102
   at secret succession meeting 223, 312–313
   helps lay trap for pilots 234
   sides with Keating on Kirribilli agreement 273
   tells Hawke to resign 282
Kerin, John
   co-payment for Medicare patients 287
   dumped as treasurer 290–291
   opposes environmental concerns strategy 244
   as treasurer 284
   warns of challenges in Canberra 33–34
Keynesian inclinations of most ministers 90
Keynesian-type stimulus measures 76
Kirby, Sir Richard 19
Kirribilli agreement
   going back on 263
   Hawke breaks for the sake of the party 275
   Hawke has excuse to renounce 271
   ramifications of 267–268
   terms of 272–273
Kornhauser, Eddie
   called 'honourable man' by Hawke 213
   Hawke supports development plans 228
   Hawke's association with unwise 136
   investigated by Fitzgerald 212–213
   supported by Hawke 232–233
Kuwait, attempt to expel Iraqi forces from 273
Kwitny, Jonathon, *The Crimes of Patriots: A True Tale of Dope, Dirty Money, and the CIA* 201

Labor party
   centenary conference 284, 285
   small swing to in 1987 election 195
   swing to during Keating election 304–305
   swings against (1988) 214–215
   wins third election victory (1987) 195
Labor party national president vote ends in tie 286
Labor party task force on running government 87
Labor polling, high approval given 74
land rights legislation 210
Landa, Paul 143–144
Landeryou, Bill 52, 56
Latham, Mark 321
Lawrence, Carmen 255, 276
Laws, John 164–165
leadership
   Hawke reluctant to consider transition 218
   Hawke tries to make election about 255
   inevitability of 39–40
   Keating considers challenge 162
   Liberals divided between Howard and Peacock 162–163
   polling high for Hawke 74
   questions about succession 218
Leibler, Isi 55, 216
Lewis, Sir Terry 212, 228
Liberal MPs cross floor to vote on immigration policy 2515

Liberal party leadership struggle (1990) 251
Liberal scare campaign during 1983 election
    88–89
Loosley, Stephen 286
Lowy, Frank 167, 168, 170, 267
lump-sum superannuation payouts, tax on
    140–141
Lynch, Sir Philip 58

McCarthy, Brian 237
machinery of government, big changes
    planned 197
McHugh, Michael QC 109–110
Mackay, Donald 135, 174
Mackerras, Malcolm 60
McLachlan, Ian 183
McMahon, Billy 42
McMullan, Bob 43, 75
markets hoped to solve economic problems
    116
Masters, Chris 188
media, Hawke features in (1980-81) 34
media diversity a pretence 169
media exposure tightly controlled (1990) 252
Medibank Private 125
Medicare 125, 287
Melzer, Jean 16–17
Middle East peace plan 206
Middle Harbour, Hawke's buy house in 279
Mills, Stephen 252
mining in Antarctica opposed 245
monetarist inclinations of Hawke's colleagues
    90
Moscow, Hawke talks with Gorbachev in 205
Murdoch, Rupert
    becomes wealthier from concentration of
        media ownership 194–195
    Hawke tries to mollify 168
    sacks print workers 234
    sells media assets to Lowy 170
Murphy, Lionel
    acquitted on appeal of protecting Ryan
        171
    commission of inquiry ends in failure 172
    friendship with Morgan Ryan 131–132
    guilty of perverting course of justice 158
    has terminal cancer 172
    legal fees granted to 173
    phone calls with Saffron 131–132
    Senate inquiry finds against 171
Murray-Darling river system 245
MX missiles, secret tests 149

naked Hawke 216–217
narcissism 39, 77, 174, 221, 263
    at Oxford 3
    Hawke expects forgiveness for all
        transgressions 55, 74
National Agenda for Women launched 211
National Crime Authority (NCA) 135,
    173–174
National Economic Summit 100–103
National Identity Card 157
National Press Club, Hawke speaks at 242
National Tax Summit 141, 155–157

*The National Times*
    links Hawke with Abeles and Kornhauser
        175
    links Hawke and Abeles to mafia 175
    reports on links between crime and
        politicians 110
    stories about Abeles ignored by other
        media 199–200
    stories about largesse from Abeles 51
*Nationwide*, Hawke refuses to appear on 177
negative gearing allowed 203
new Parliament House opened 225
'no Australian child living in poverty' 191–192
NSW Right 46, 90

Oakes, Laurie 65, 280–282
Office for Status of Women (OSW) 128
oil spill off Antarctica 246
'One Australia' campaign, Howard's 227
opinion polls, swing to Hewson and Liberals
    292
Oxley by-election 221–222
    swing against Labor 221–222

Packer, Kerry
    becomes wealthier due to concentration of
        media ownership 194
    benefits from pliable ministers 260
    in Costigan royal commission 135
    Hawke tries to mollify 168
    protected by Hawke 170
parliament opened by Queen (1988) 210
Peacock, Andrew
    1990 election pitch 254–255
    on Bjelke-Petersen's crusade 183
    calls Hawke 'a little crook' 136, 138, 144
    as campaign threat 143
    car conversation with Kennett about
        Howard 183
    clear winner of TV debate 146
    moves censure motion for closure of
        Costigan royal commission 136
    not invited to National Economic Summit
        101
    personal traits of 122
    re-appointed deputy to Howard 226
    reinstalled as leader 243, 251
    tactics in leadership contest 163
    in TV debate with Hawke 143
pensions, assets and incomes tests on 140–141
Peres, Shimon, fears about Israel affect Hawke
    215
personal advisers, Hawke relies on 97–98
phone tapping, laws against unauthorised 173
Pieters-Hawke, Sue, speech at Hawke's funeral
    324
Pilger, John, Hawke interviewed by 184–185
pilots 234–238
pilot's strike 234–239
police integrity 159–160
political corruption, ABC and *National Times*
    pursue 174–175
press conference, Hawke in tears at 139
Prices and Incomes Accord
    benefits of 127

central to Hawke's success 125
idea of 102–103, 242
negative effect of 192
not producing desired economic outcomes 240–241
union movement accepts 123–124
Prince Charles admires Hawke's ability to spot cleavage 209
private phone conversations, police make tape recordings of 175
privatisation
denounced by Hawke in 1985 217
Labor party platform opposes 198–199
opposition to 216
privatisation of public enterprises
Hawke's support for 214
lack of party support for 198
pro-Americanism, Hawke's unthinking 150
protection lobby, power of 123
public enterprises, privatisation of lacks support 198
Pullan, Robert 18

Qantas 197, 264, 265

RAAF flyover of Gordon River dam site 104
Ray, Robert 16–17, 213–214
Reagan, Ronald
and Friedman economics 88
sacks air traffic controllers 233–234
reconciliation, theme of Labor's election campaign 71
referendum for four-year terms planned 197
'refuseniks' 11, 205–206, 215
Reith, Peter 58, 82
Remembrance Day vs America's Cup celebrations 121
Renouf, Alan 13
'The Resolution of Conflict', Boyer Lectures (1979) 11
retirement, questions about Hawke's 218
Richardson, Graham
appalled at Hawke losing his temper 239
approves second preferences strategy 244
assists Keating to unseat Hawke 268, 272
assures Keating of win 304
Bob Brown shows logging in Tas 193
confirms Keating's challenge 280
doubts election win possible 251
as environment minister 197
flogs environment message 255
Hawke refuses him his preferred ministry 259–260
in Keating camp 260
positive view of election prospects 257
suggests Hawke resign 271
supports Hawke 43, 46–47
Riley, Murray 133
Rockey, George 24
Rothwell's Bank, collapse of 204–205
Rowland, 'Tiny' 232
Ryan, Morgan 131–132
Ryan, Susan
activities of 127–129
advocates for women 127

dumped as education minister 197
made special minister of state 198
member of inner cabinet 97
only female delegate to NES 101
shift in education funding under 127

Saffron, Abe 131–132, 158–159
Sandringham home, let and later sold 95
SBS, politics of senior appointments 179
scare campaign by Liberals on capital gains tax 141
Schildberger, Michael 57
schism growing between Hawke and Keating 165
Schoenmaker, Mario 309
Scholes, Gordon, member of inner cabinet 97
*The Second Sex*, Simone de Beauvoir 129
secret ballot for leadership, Keating loses 283
secret succession meeting 223
security committee of cabinet 107
Senate 31, 148
*The 7.30 Report*, Pilger interviews Hawke 184–185
sex discrimination, bill outlawing 128, 129
Sex Discrimination Commissioner, Bryce appointed as 211
shadow ministries after 1980 32
shady characters, Hawke's relationships with 315
Shann, Mick 13
Shorten, Bill, Hawke and Keating support 323
Shulz, George 113, 149, 151
signing ceremony at Uluru 210
Sinclair, Ian 243
Sinclair, Jean 22, 34, 93, 285
Singleton, Jane 177
Singleton, John 189–190
*60 Minutes*
Hawke and d'Alpuget on 308, 310
Hawke's testy response to Carleton 240
Skase, Christopher 170, 232, 285
Snedden, Sir Billy 32–33
Socialist Left faction 17
soil salinity concerns 245
Sommervaille, Bob 200
Sorby, Bob 197
speculative activity creates great wealth for some 194–195
speculative bubbles popped 231–232
speeches by Hawke and Keating at business lunch 143
'spy' flight over Gordon River dam site 104
stagflation problem 88
State Savings Bank of Victoria, bought by Commonwealth Bank 264–265
Stephen, Sir Ninian, Fraser's race to 67–68
stock market collapse (1987) 203–204
stock market crash (1987), Reserve Bank misreads 230–231
Stone, John 89, 117–118
succession 220–221, 223–224, 224
Summers, Anne 46, 211, 1280129
superannuation lump-sum payments, pilots oppose plan to tax 235

Sydney underworld, Hawke fears disclosure of links to 158–159

tariff cuts by Whitlam 123
tax reduction policy, Howard's 189
tax reforms, Hawke claims agreement on 157
tax-avoidance schemes 135, 195
Teamsters Union, meeting with (1978) 110
Telecom, corporatising 197
telecommunications market, reshaping 264
television interviewer, as new career for Hawke 279
terms of trade, collapse in 192
Tham, Rudy 133–134
Thatcher, Margaret 88, 234
Tiananmen Square, student uprising crushed 248
*The Times on Sunday*
  damning feature on Hawke government 194
  Hawke's political obituary in 181
  Toohey appointed editor 203
TNT, massive program of expansion 201
Tonkin, David 57
Toohey, Brian 175, 194
trade deficits, widening 163–164
trade union movement, increasing irrelevance of 3 136
traditional Labor values being betrayed 185
Transport Workers' Union 239
treaty with original inhabitants 209
tree planting 245
Tuckey, Wilson, and US money 145
Turks, tribute to 262
TV debate, between Hawke and Peacock 143, 144
two-airline agreement 199, 233

UN Convention on the Elimination of All Forms of Discrimination Against Women ratified 211
uncompetitive industries to be abandoned 123
unemployment rate reduced 126
union movement accepts Prices and Incomes Accord 123–124
university students, Ryan fights against HECS fees 197–198
uranium mining 47–48, 286
Uren, Tom 48, 65, 153–154
US money in Hawke's possession 144–146
US naval ships, forbidden entry to NZ ports 151

Vietnamese refugees, arrival of 227

WA Inc 276
*Wall Street Journal* 176
Walsh, Eric 107–108
Walsh, Peter 97, 243–244, 259
Wannon electorate 108

Ward, Rogan 58, 59
Washington, Hawke and Keating visit 113
Wasowski, Vera, on Hazel and children 310
wealthy Australians get wealthier 203
wealthy patrons of Hawke 167, 192–193
wedding of Hawke and d'Alpuget (1995) 309
West, Stewart 97
White, Patrick 88
Whitehead, Geoffrey 178
Whitlam, Gough, achievements overshadow Hawke's 317
Whitton, Evan
  *Can of Worms* 201
  as editor of *National Times* (1978-1981) 175
Wilderness Society supports World Heritage listings 194
Wilkinson, Marian 175–176
Willis, Ralph 61, 97, 234–235, 290
Wills electorate 9, 29
*Winter in Jerusalem*, Blanche d'Alpuget 96
*Woman's Day*, Hawke and d'Alpuget spread in 310
*Woman's Day* feature on Hawke and d'Alpuget 308
women
  benefits for 211–212
  crucial to Hawke's success 127
  improvement in Hawke's attitude to debatable 212
Women's Budget Statement 128
Women's Electoral Lobby pressure group 211
women's equality, Liberal opposition to 212
World Heritage listing of four areas 194
Wran, Neville
  association with George Freeman 132
  blames media for allegations 133
  deals done to advantage Abeles 132–133
  election pitch dismissed by 71
  establishes royal commission on Murphy 132
  Hawke defends 178
  paid off by Abeles on retirement 201
  Phillip Adams' opinion of 132
  resigns as NSW premier 173, 174
  unsupportive of Hawke 46–47

Yaobang, Hu, visit of 152
Young, Alistair 18
Young, Major Peter 14
Young, Mick
  forced to resign Port Melbourne seat 214
  gives security commitee information to Eric Walsh 107–108
  and import duty scandal 131
  loses shadow ministry to Hawke 28
  member of inner cabinet 97
  plan to save 108

Ziyang, Zhao, visit by 115